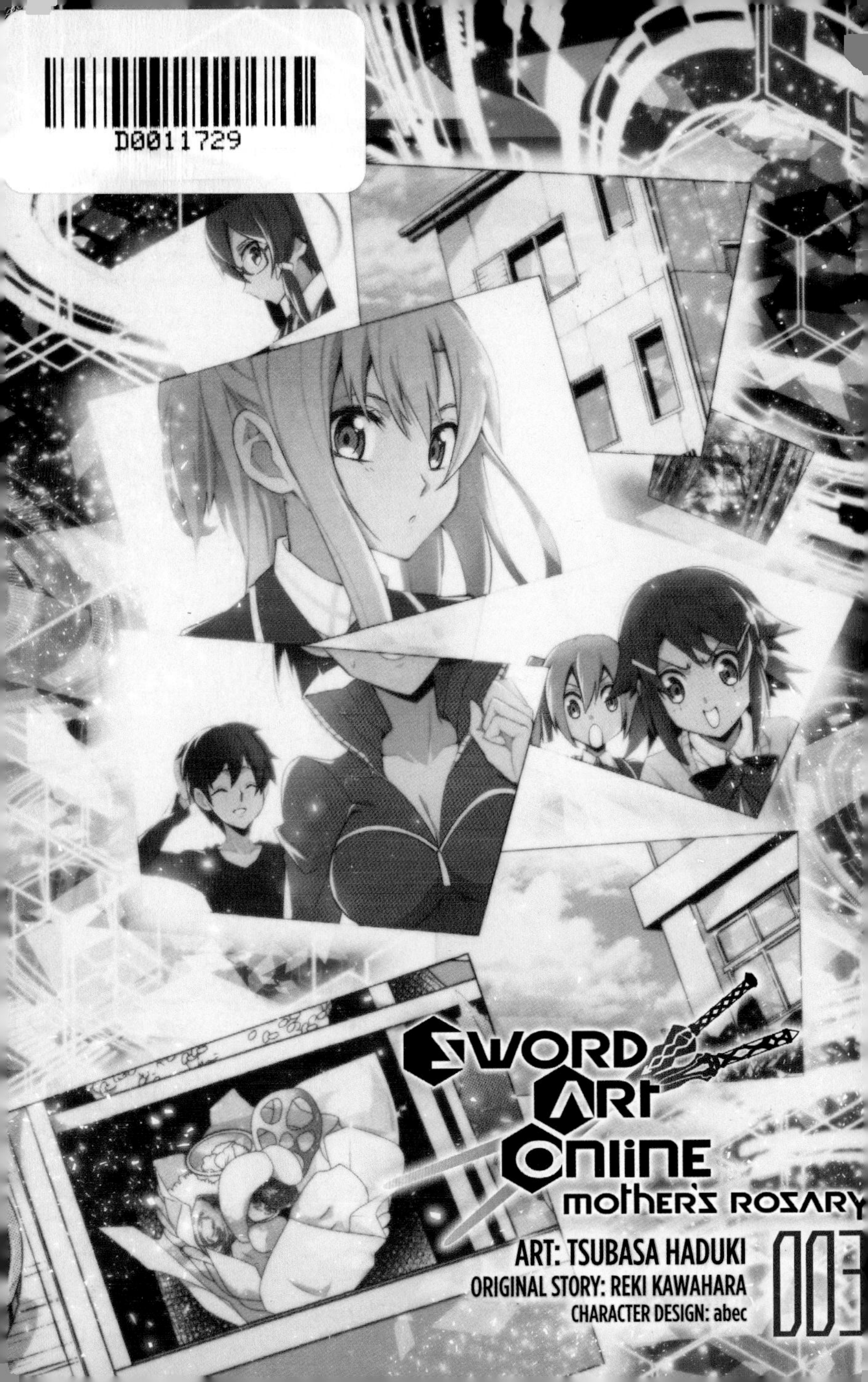
SWORD ART ONLINE
mother's ROSARY
003
ART: TSUBASA HADUKI
ORIGINAL STORY: REKI KAWAHARA
CHARACTER DESIGN: abec

SWORD ART ONLINE

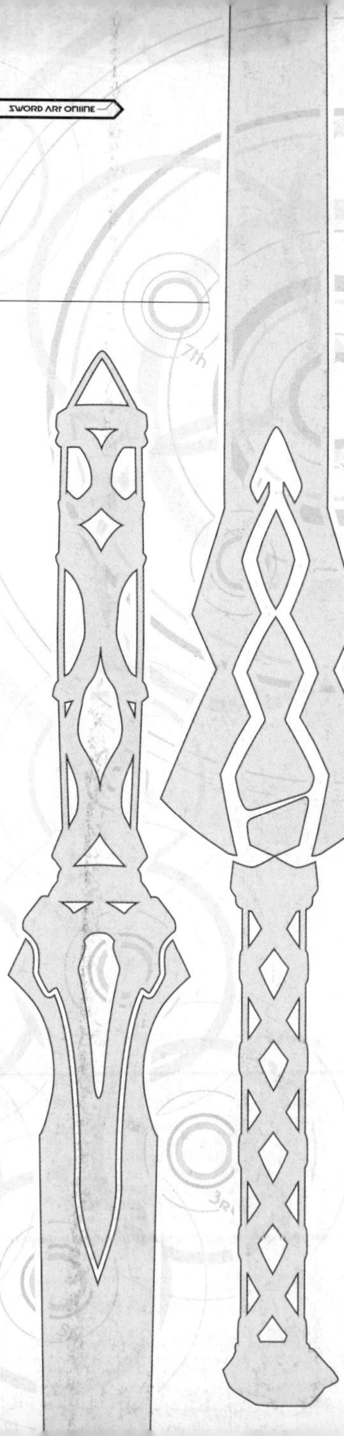

003

SWORD ART ONLINE mother's ROSARY

ART: tsubasa haduki
ORIGINAL STORY: REKI KAWAHARA
CHARACTER DESIGN: ABEC

contents

date: 29 mar 2026 sun 14:04

YMIR alfheim online

SWORD ART ONLINE
mother's rosary

003

SWORD ART ONLINE mother's rosary

art : tsubasa haduki
original story : reki kawahara
character design : abec

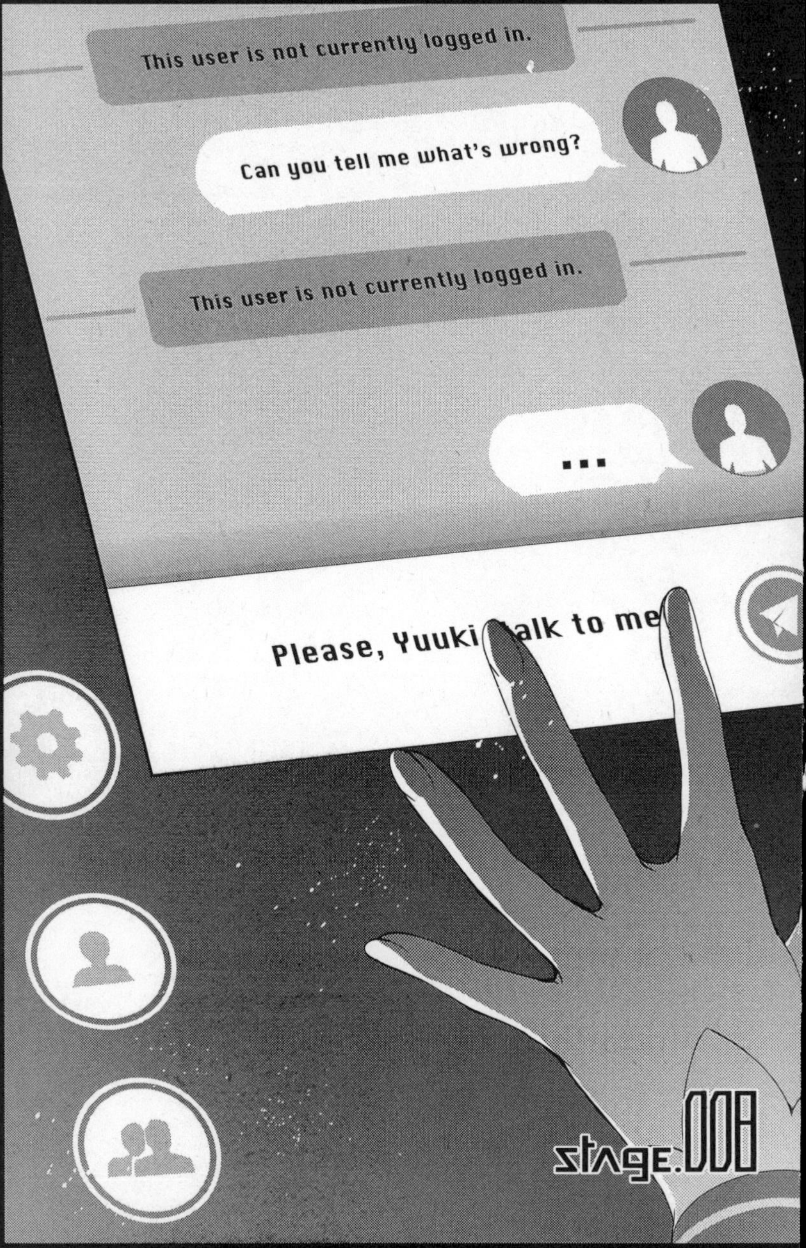
This user is not currently logged in.
Can you tell me what's wrong?
This user is not currently logged in.
...
Please, Yuuki alk to me
stage.008

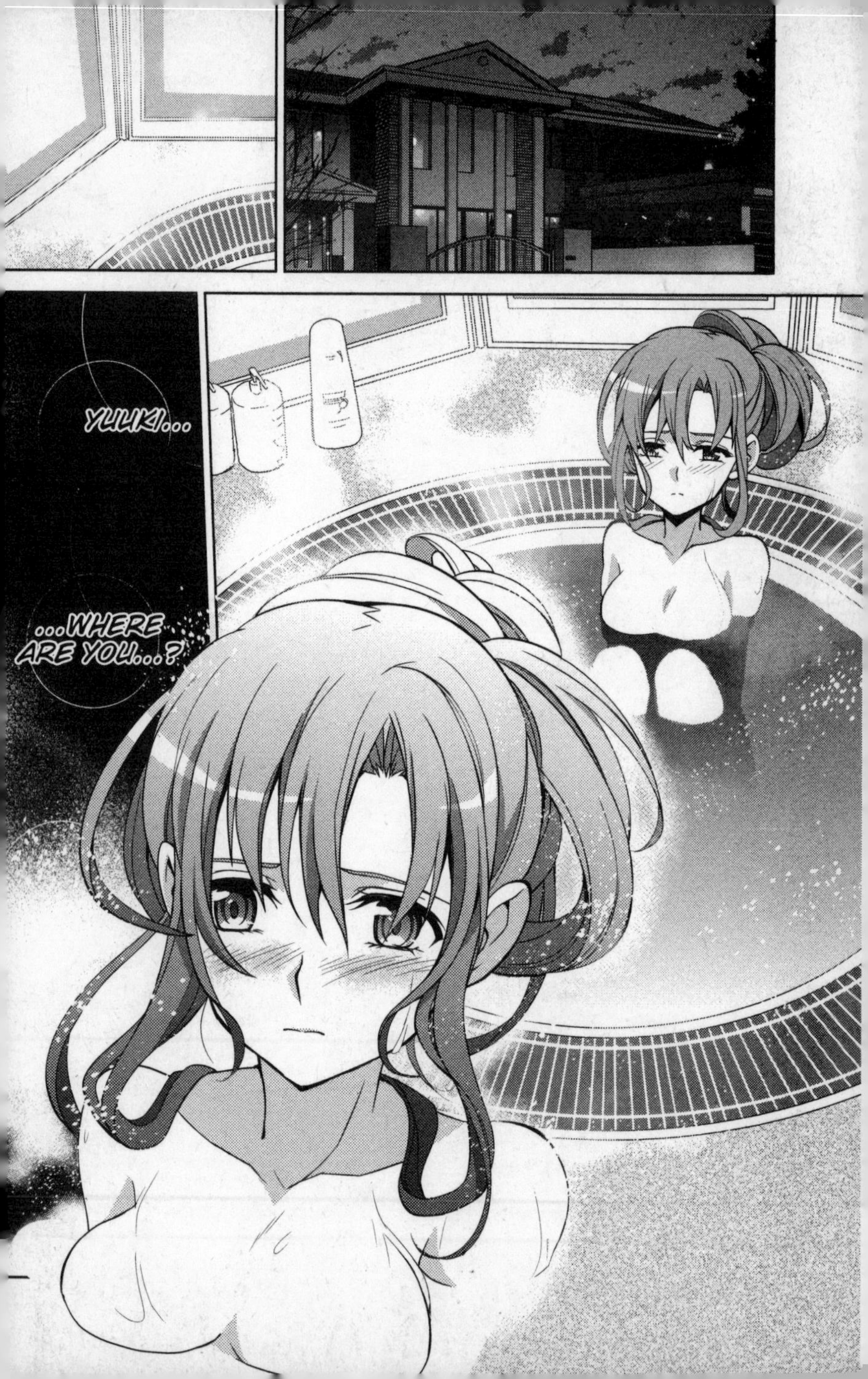
YUUKI...
...WHERE ARE YOU...?

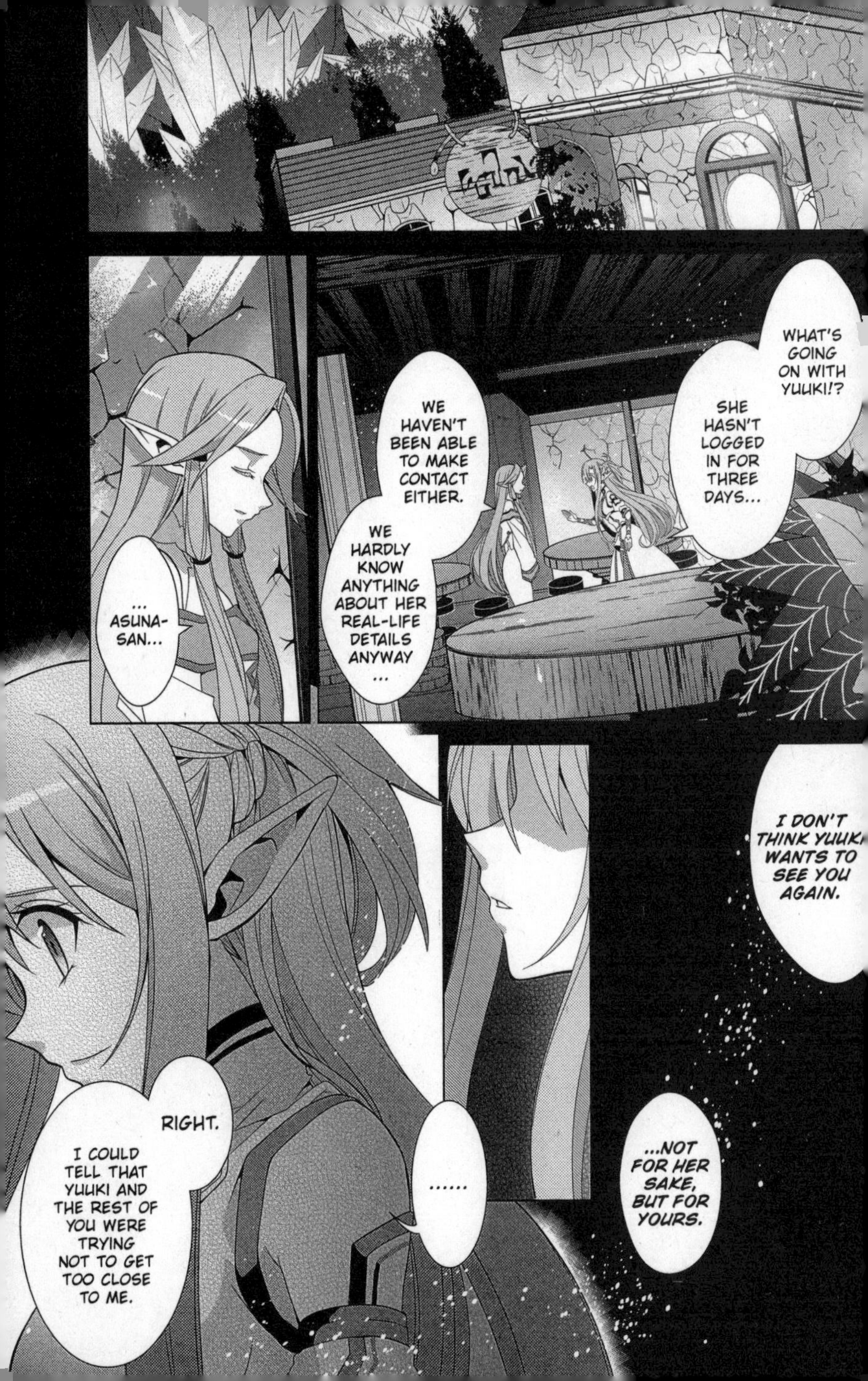
WHAT'S GOING ON WITH YUUKI!?
SHE HASN'T LOGGED IN FOR THREE DAYS...
WE HAVEN'T BEEN ABLE TO MAKE CONTACT EITHER.
WE HARDLY KNOW ANYTHING ABOUT HER REAL-LIFE DETAILS ANYWAY ...
... ASUNA-SAN...
I DON'T THINK YUUKI WANTS TO SEE YOU AGAIN.
...NOT FOR HER SAKE, BUT FOR YOURS.
......
RIGHT.
I COULD TELL THAT YUUKI AND THE REST OF YOU WERE TRYING NOT TO GET TOO CLOSE TO ME.

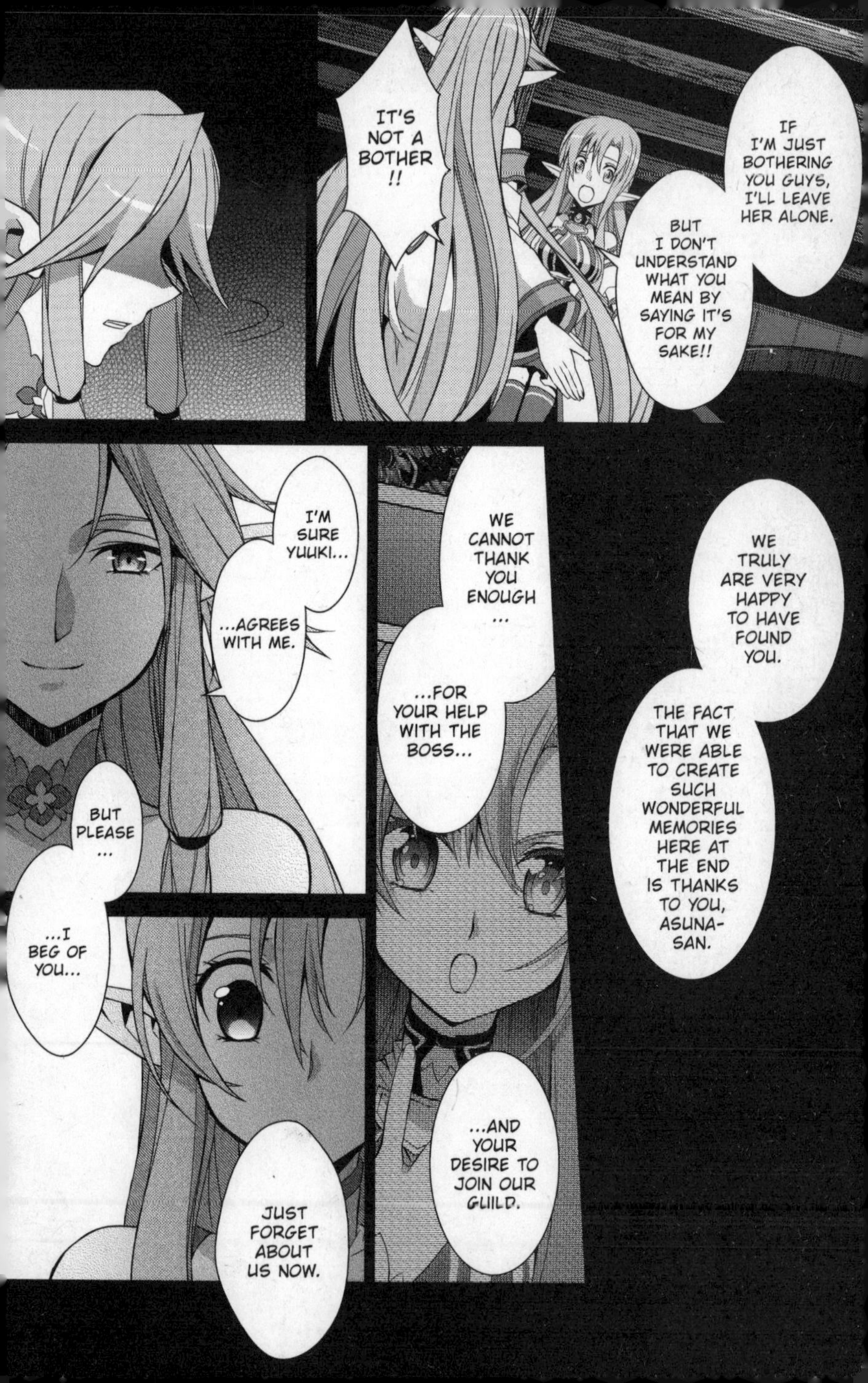
IF I'M JUST BOTHERING YOU GUYS, I'LL LEAVE HER ALONE.
BUT I DON'T UNDERSTAND WHAT YOU MEAN BY SAYING IT'S FOR MY SAKE!!
IT'S NOT A BOTHER !!
WE TRULY ARE VERY HAPPY TO HAVE FOUND YOU.
THE FACT THAT WE WERE ABLE TO CREATE SUCH WONDERFUL MEMORIES HERE AT THE END IS THANKS TO YOU, ASUNA-SAN.
WE CANNOT THANK YOU ENOUGH ...
...FOR YOUR HELP WITH THE BOSS...
...AND YOUR DESIRE TO JOIN OUR GUILD.
I'M SURE YUUKI...
...AGREES WITH ME.
BUT PLEASE ...
...I BEG OF YOU...
JUST FORGET ABOUT US NOW.

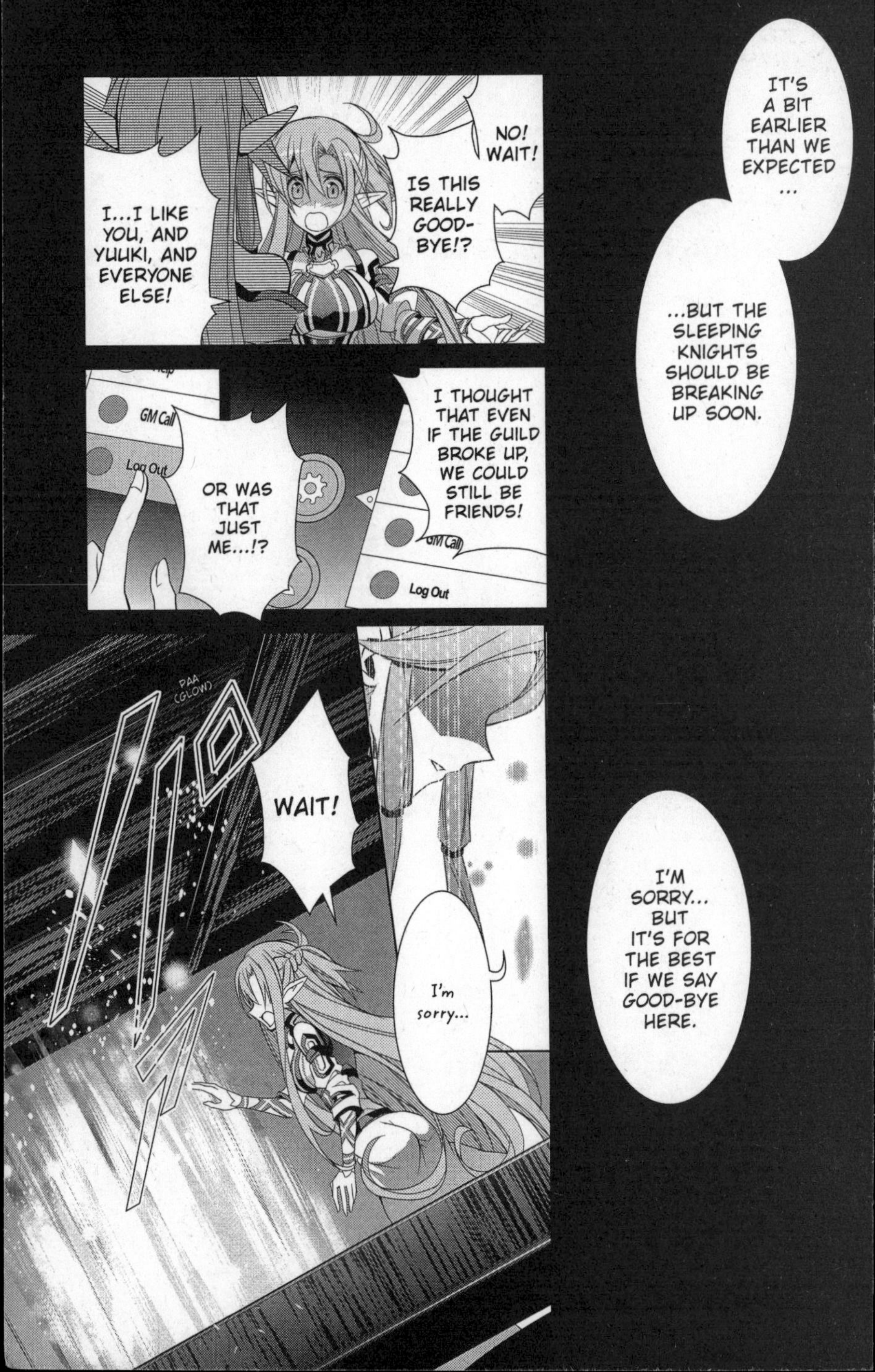
IT'S A BIT EARLIER THAN WE EXPECTED ...
...BUT THE SLEEPING KNIGHTS SHOULD BE BREAKING UP SOON.
I'M SORRY... BUT IT'S FOR THE BEST IF WE SAY GOOD-BYE HERE.
NO! WAIT!
IS THIS REALLY GOOD-BYE!?
I...I LIKE YOU, AND YUUKI, AND EVERYONE ELSE!
I THOUGHT THAT EVEN IF THE GUILD BROKE UP, WE COULD STILL BE FRIENDS!
GM Call
Log Out
GM Call
Log Out
OR WAS THAT JUST ME...!?
I'm sorry...
WAIT!
PAA (GLOW)

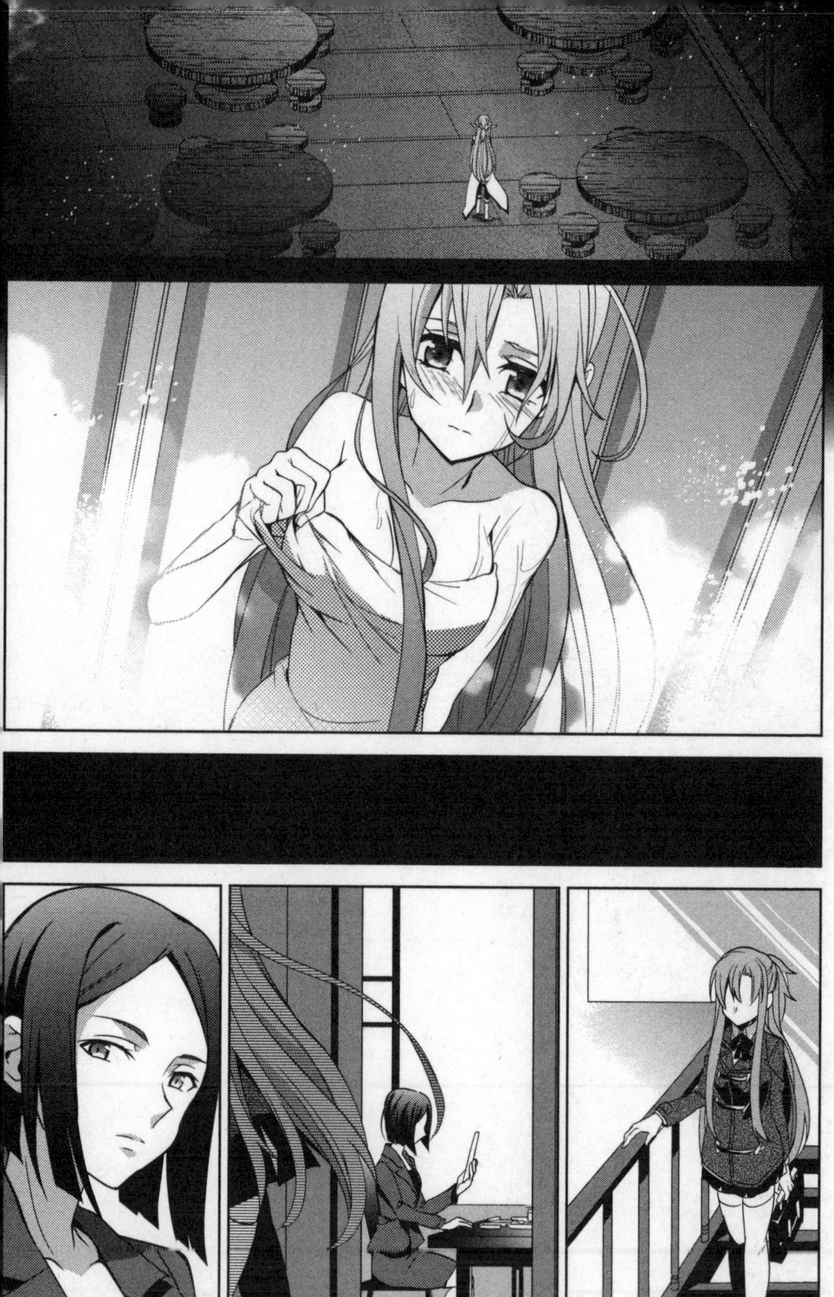

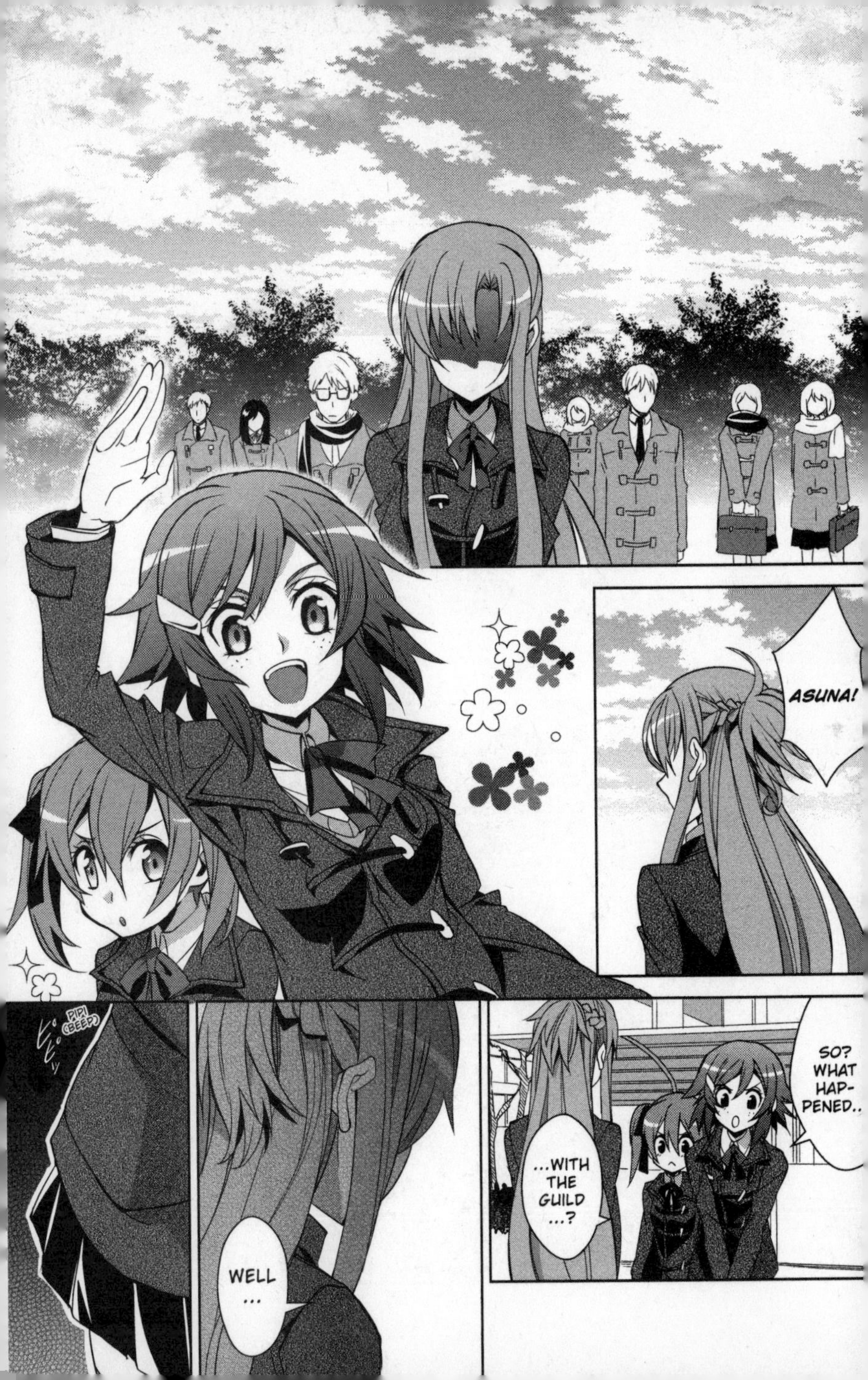
ASUNA!
SO? WHAT HAP-PENED..
...WITH THE GUILD ...?
WELL ...
PIPI (BEEP)

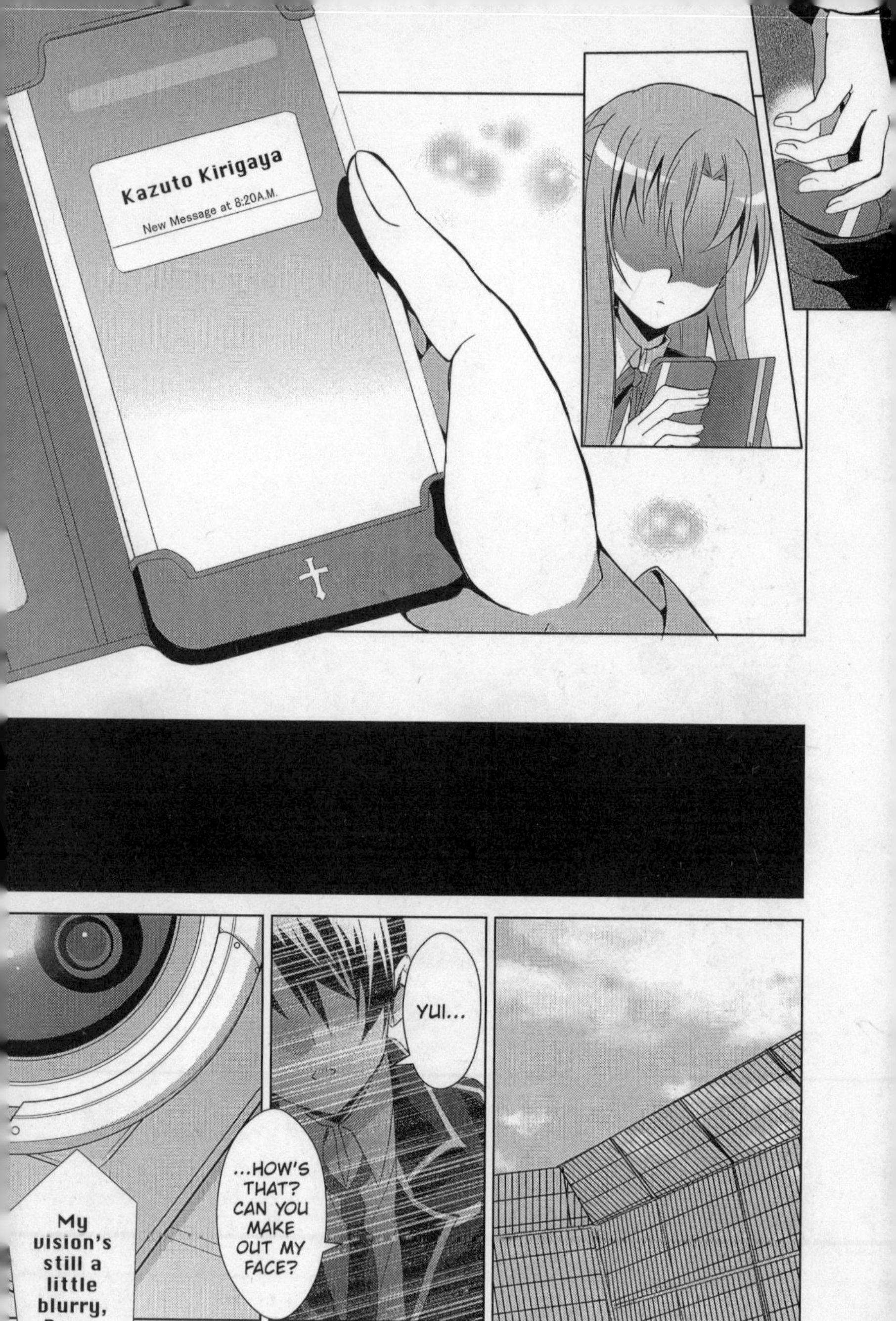
Kazuto Kirigaya
New Message at 8:20A.M.
YUI...
...HOW'S THAT? CAN YOU MAKE OUT MY FACE?
My vision's still a little blurry, Papa.

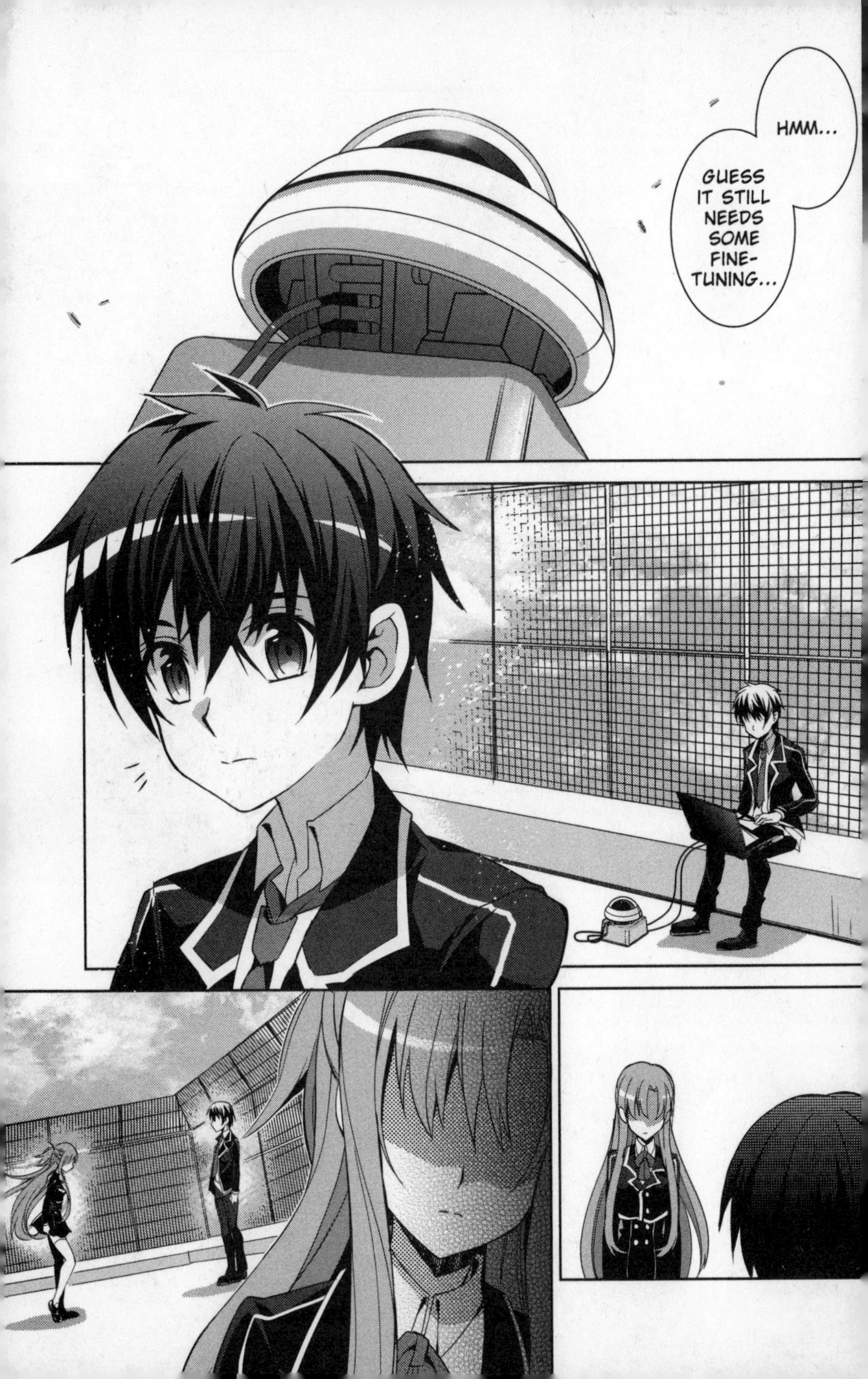
HMM... GUESS IT STILL NEEDS SOME FINE-TUNING...

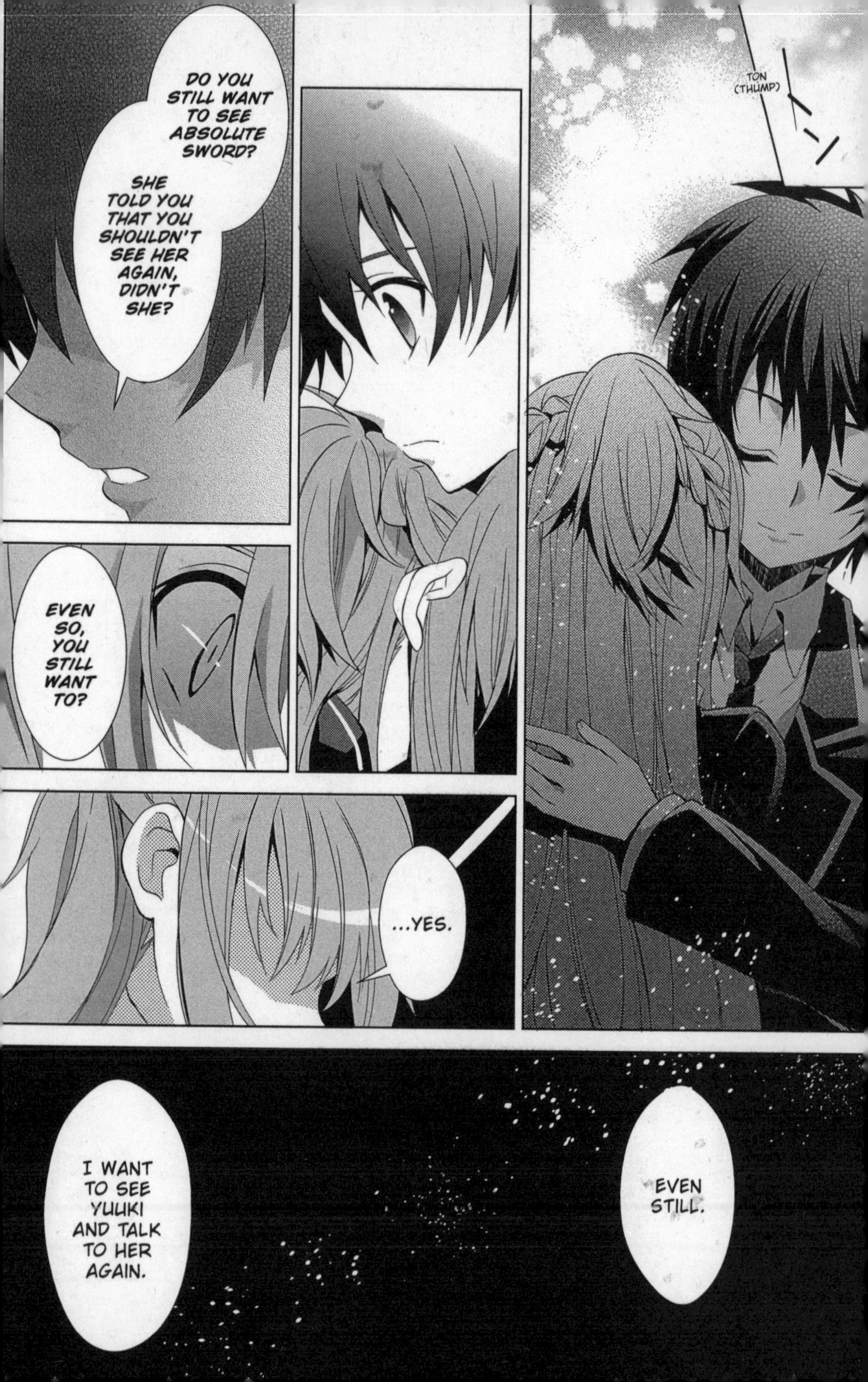
TON (THUMP)
DO YOU STILL WANT TO SEE ABSOLUTE SWORD?
SHE TOLD YOU THAT YOU SHOULDN'T SEE HER AGAIN, DIDN'T SHE?
EVEN SO, YOU STILL WANT TO?
...YES.
EVEN STILL.
I WANT TO SEE YUUKI AND TALK TO HER AGAIN.

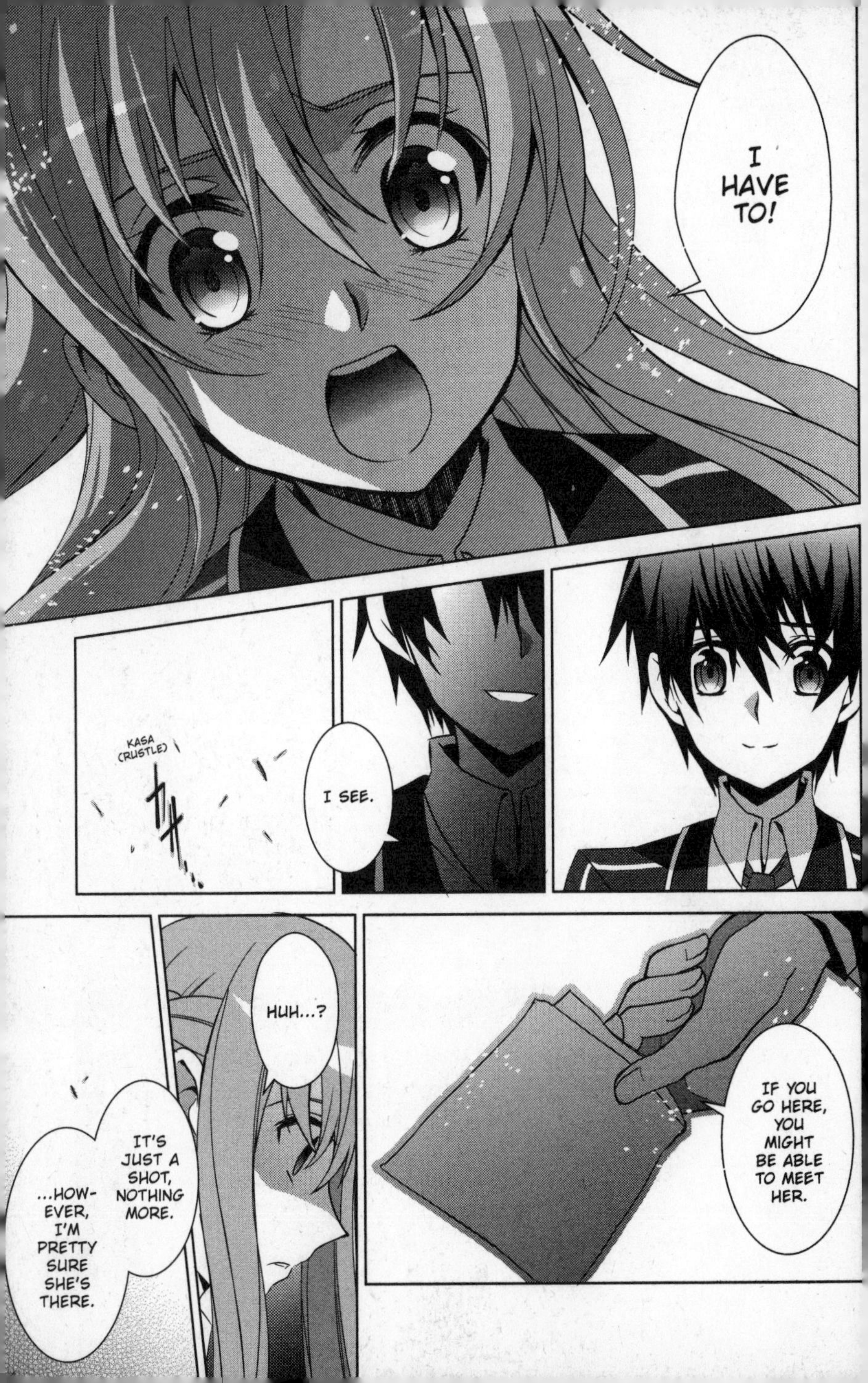
I HAVE TO!
I SEE.
KASA (RUSTLE)
IF YOU GO HERE, YOU MIGHT BE ABLE TO MEET HER.
HUH...?
IT'S JUST A SHOT, NOTHING MORE.
...HOW-EVER, I'M PRETTY SURE SHE'S THERE.

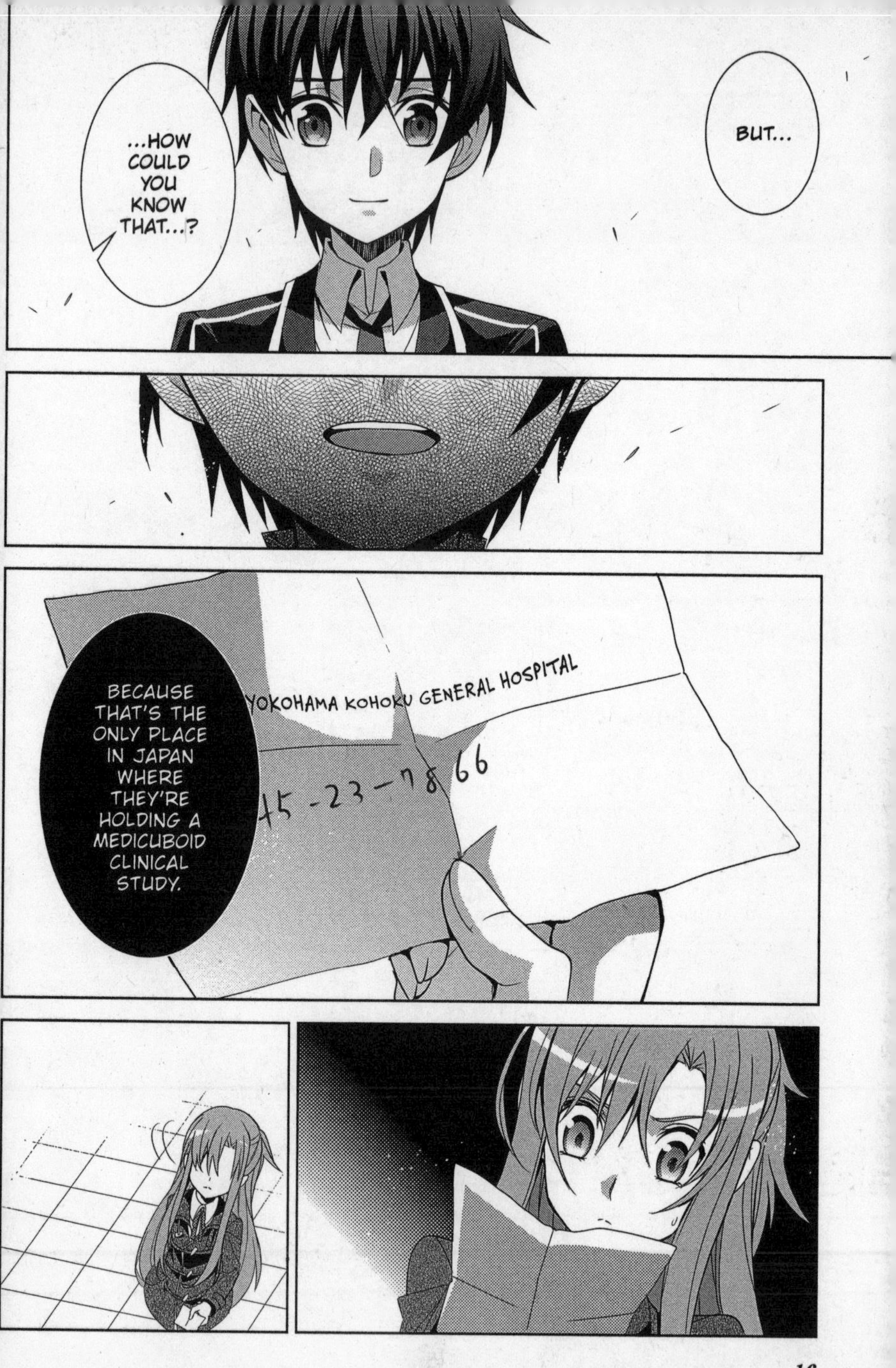
BUT...
...HOW COULD YOU KNOW THAT...?
YOKOHAMA KOHOKU GENERAL HOSPITAL
45-23-7866
BECAUSE THAT'S THE ONLY PLACE IN JAPAN WHERE THEY'RE HOLDING A MEDICUBOID CLINICAL STUDY.

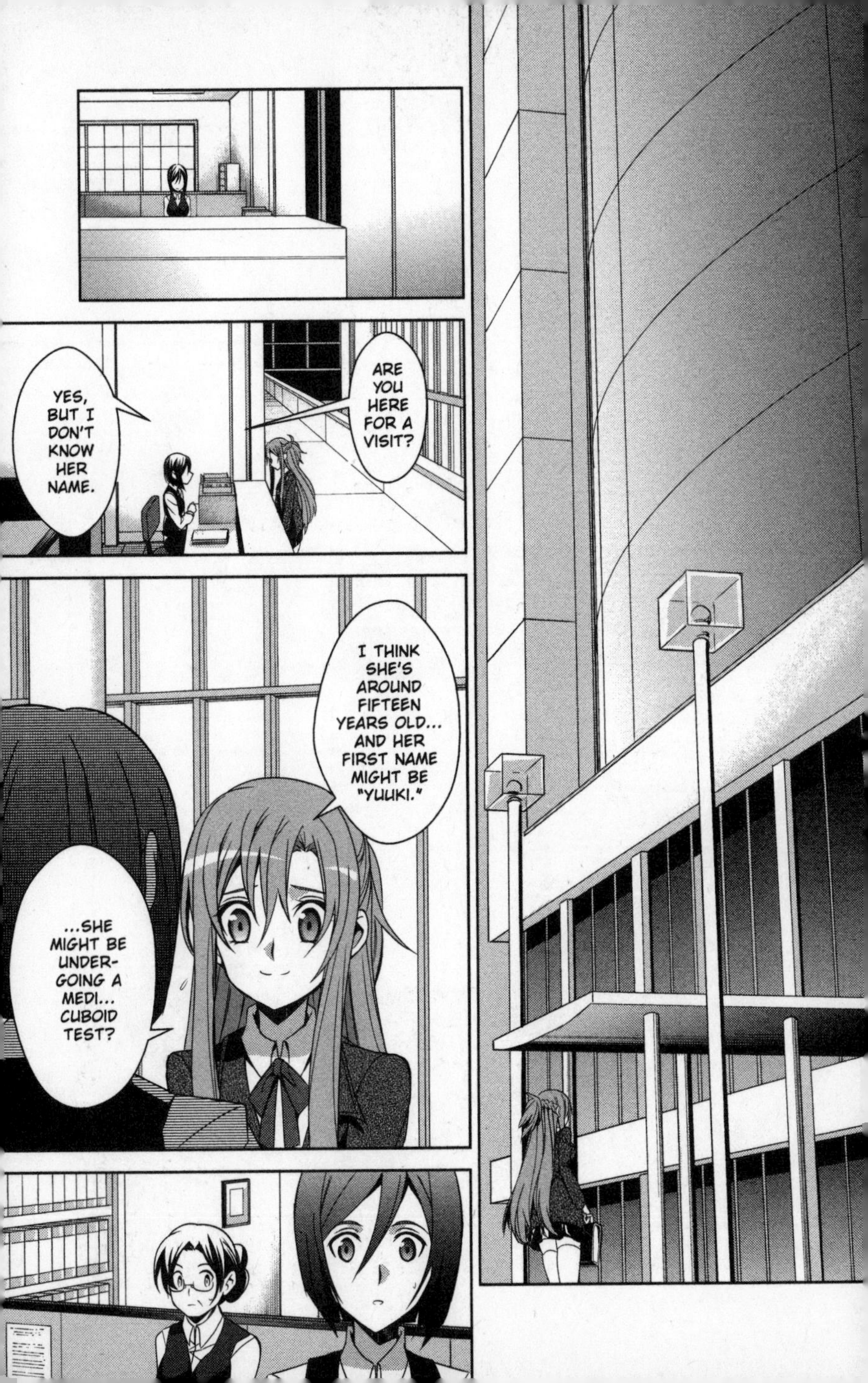
ARE YOU HERE FOR A VISIT?
YES, BUT I DON'T KNOW HER NAME.
I THINK SHE'S AROUND FIFTEEN YEARS OLD... AND HER FIRST NAME MIGHT BE "YUUKI."
...SHE MIGHT BE UNDERGOING A MEDI... CUBOID TEST?

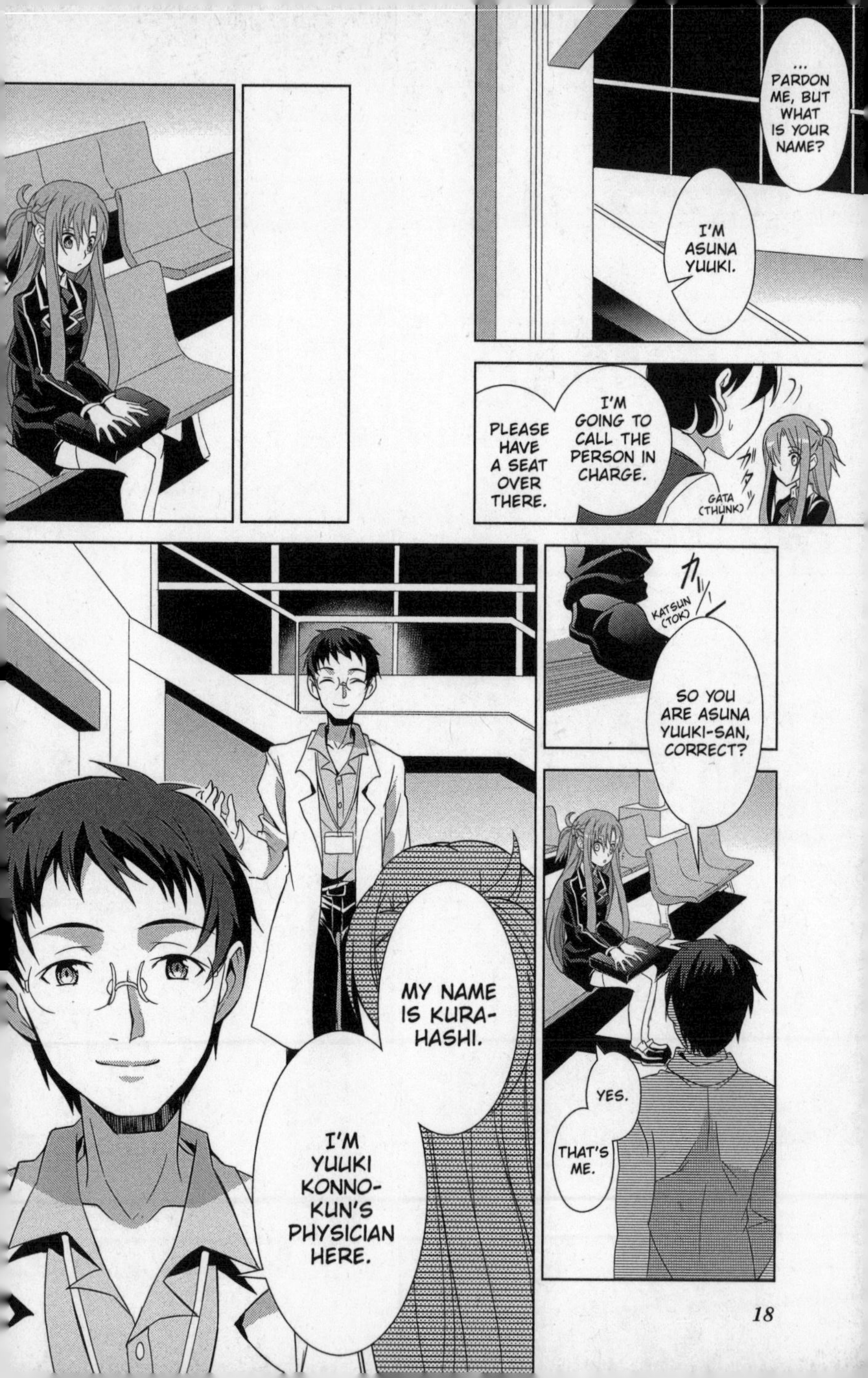
... PARDON ME, BUT WHAT IS YOUR NAME?
I'M ASUNA YUUKI.
GATA (THUNK)
I'M GOING TO CALL THE PERSON IN CHARGE.
PLEASE HAVE A SEAT OVER THERE.
KATSUN (TOK)
SO YOU ARE ASUNA YUUKI-SAN, CORRECT?
YES.
THAT'S ME.
MY NAME IS KURA-HASHI.
I'M YUUKI KONNO-KUN'S PHYSICIAN HERE.

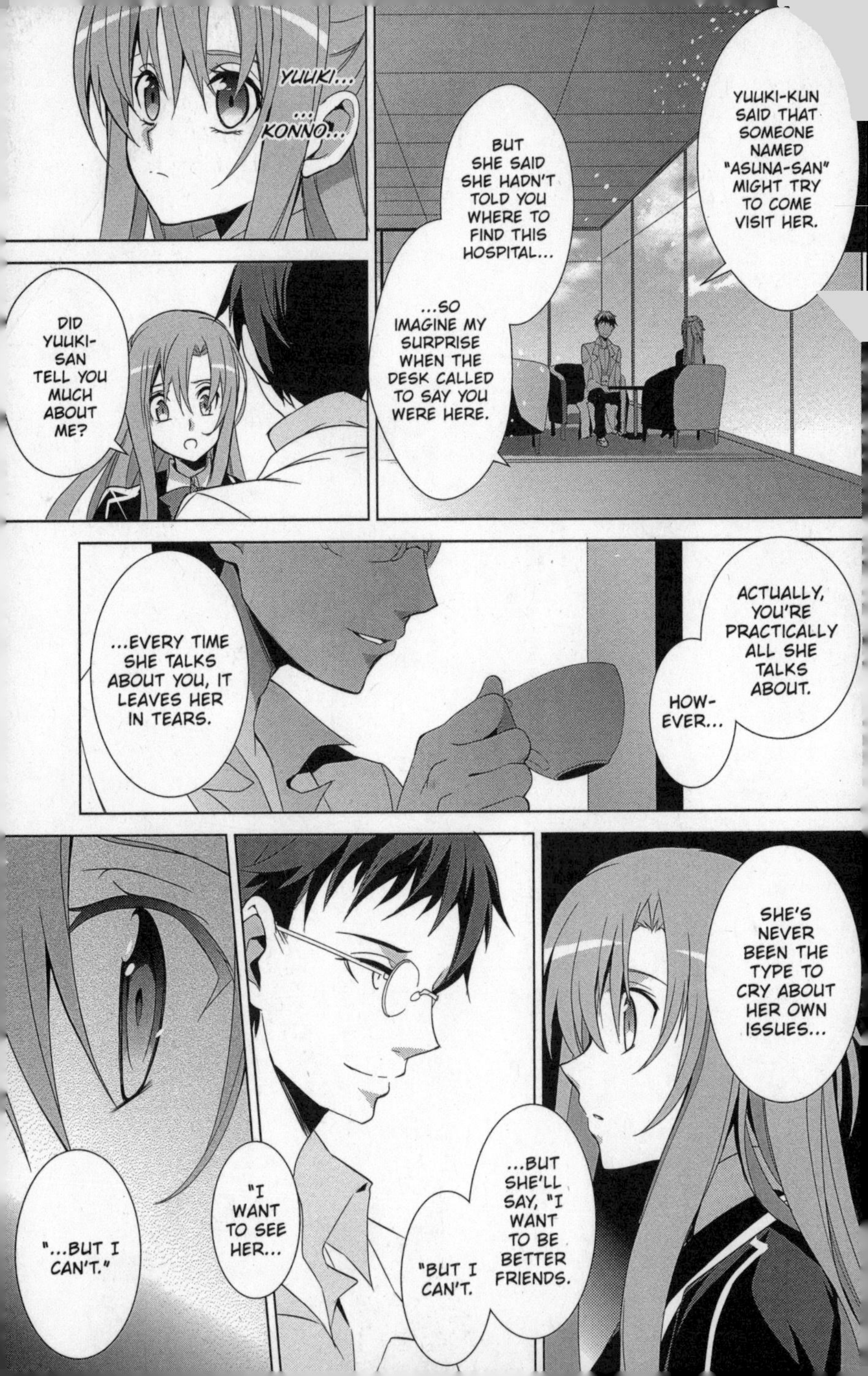
YUUKI-KUN SAID THAT SOMEONE NAMED "ASUNA-SAN" MIGHT TRY TO COME VISIT HER.
BUT SHE SAID SHE HADN'T TOLD YOU WHERE TO FIND THIS HOSPITAL...
...SO IMAGINE MY SURPRISE WHEN THE DESK CALLED TO SAY YOU WERE HERE.
YUUKI...
...KONNO...
DID YUUKI-SAN TELL YOU MUCH ABOUT ME?
ACTUALLY, YOU'RE PRACTICALLY ALL SHE TALKS ABOUT.
HOW-EVER...
...EVERY TIME SHE TALKS ABOUT YOU, IT LEAVES HER IN TEARS.
SHE'S NEVER BEEN THE TYPE TO CRY ABOUT HER OWN ISSUES...
...BUT SHE'LL SAY, "I WANT TO BE BETTER FRIENDS.
"BUT I CAN'T.
"I WANT TO SEE HER...
"...BUT I CAN'T."

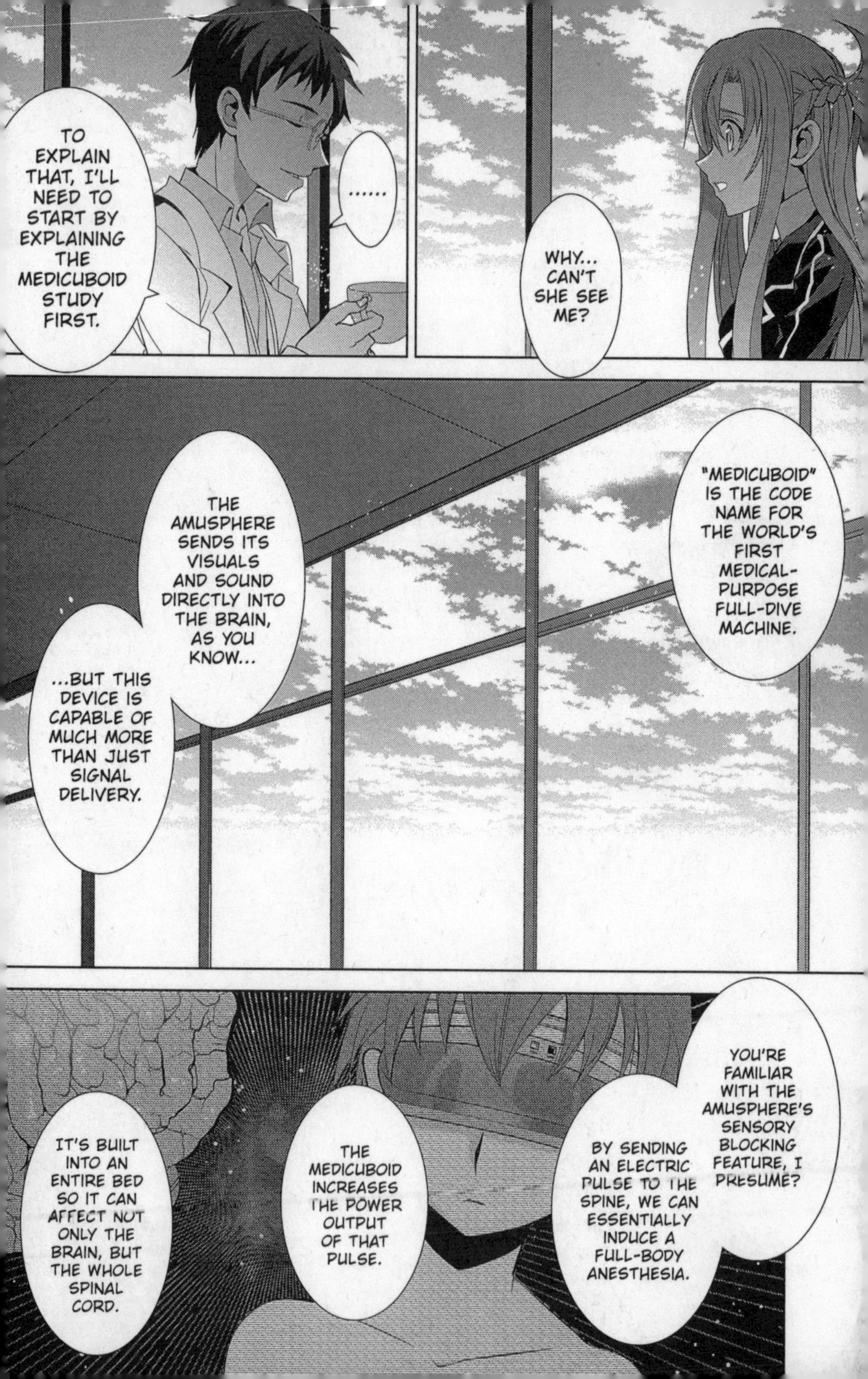
WHY... CAN'T SHE SEE ME?
......
TO EXPLAIN THAT, I'LL NEED TO START BY EXPLAINING THE MEDICUBOID STUDY FIRST.
"MEDICUBOID" IS THE CODE NAME FOR THE WORLD'S FIRST MEDICAL-PURPOSE FULL-DIVE MACHINE.
THE AMUSPHERE SENDS ITS VISUALS AND SOUND DIRECTLY INTO THE BRAIN, AS YOU KNOW...
...BUT THIS DEVICE IS CAPABLE OF MUCH MORE THAN JUST SIGNAL DELIVERY.
YOU'RE FAMILIAR WITH THE AMUSPHERE'S SENSORY BLOCKING FEATURE, I PRESUME?
BY SENDING AN ELECTRIC PULSE TO THE SPINE, WE CAN ESSENTIALLY INDUCE A FULL-BODY ANESTHESIA.
THE MEDICUBOID INCREASES THE POWER OUTPUT OF THAT PULSE.
IT'S BUILT INTO AN ENTIRE BED SO IT CAN AFFECT NOT ONLY THE BRAIN, BUT THE WHOLE SPINAL CORD.

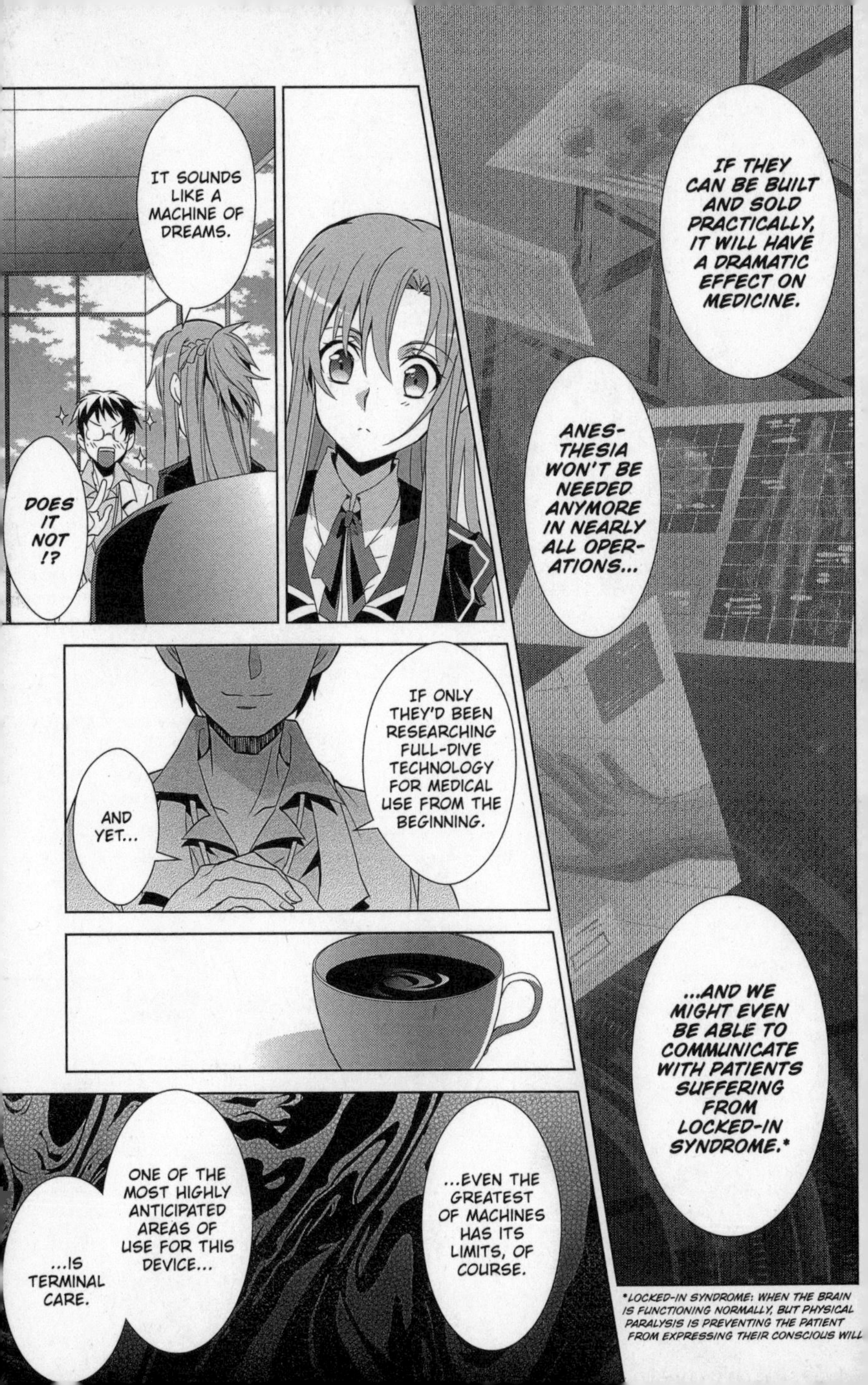
IF THEY CAN BE BUILT AND SOLD PRACTICALLY, IT WILL HAVE A DRAMATIC EFFECT ON MEDICINE.
ANES-THESIA WON'T BE NEEDED ANYMORE IN NEARLY ALL OPER-ATIONS...
...AND WE MIGHT EVEN BE ABLE TO COMMUNICATE WITH PATIENTS SUFFERING FROM LOCKED-IN SYNDROME.*
IT SOUNDS LIKE A MACHINE OF DREAMS.
DOES IT NOT !?
IF ONLY THEY'D BEEN RESEARCHING FULL-DIVE TECHNOLOGY FOR MEDICAL USE FROM THE BEGINNING.
AND YET...
...EVEN THE GREATEST OF MACHINES HAS ITS LIMITS, OF COURSE.
ONE OF THE MOST HIGHLY ANTICIPATED AREAS OF USE FOR THIS DEVICE...
...IS TERMINAL CARE.

*LOCKED-IN SYNDROME: WHEN THE BRAIN IS FUNCTIONING NORMALLY, BUT PHYSICAL PARALYSIS IS PREVENTING THE PATIENT FROM EXPRESSING THEIR CONSCIOUS WILL

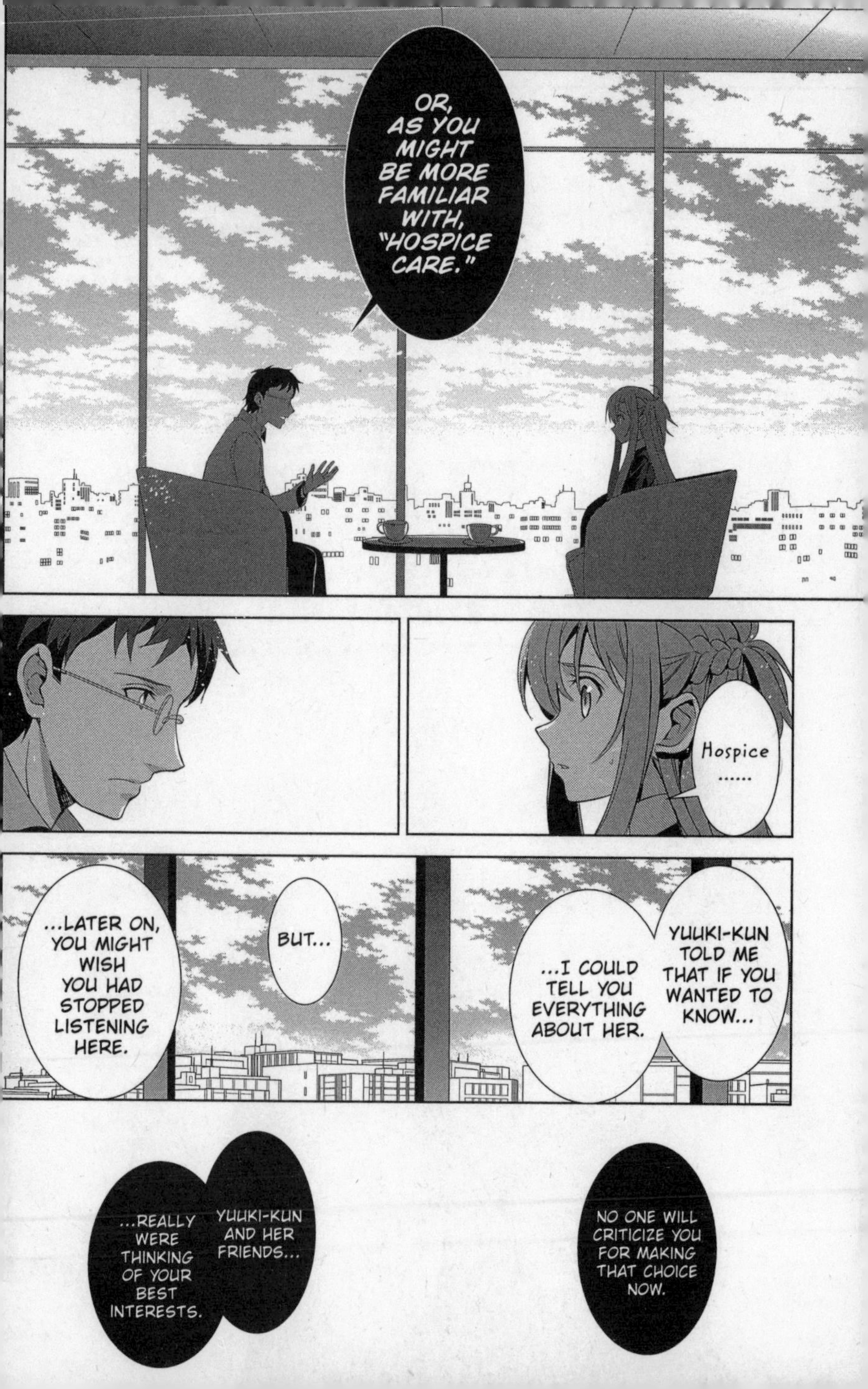
OR, AS YOU MIGHT BE MORE FAMILIAR WITH, "HOSPICE CARE."
Hospice ......
YUUKI-KUN TOLD ME THAT IF YOU WANTED TO KNOW...
...I COULD TELL YOU EVERYTHING ABOUT HER.
BUT...
...LATER ON, YOU MIGHT WISH YOU HAD STOPPED LISTENING HERE.
NO ONE WILL CRITICIZE YOU FOR MAKING THAT CHOICE NOW.
YUUKI-KUN AND HER FRIENDS...
...REALLY WERE THINKING OF YOUR BEST INTERESTS.

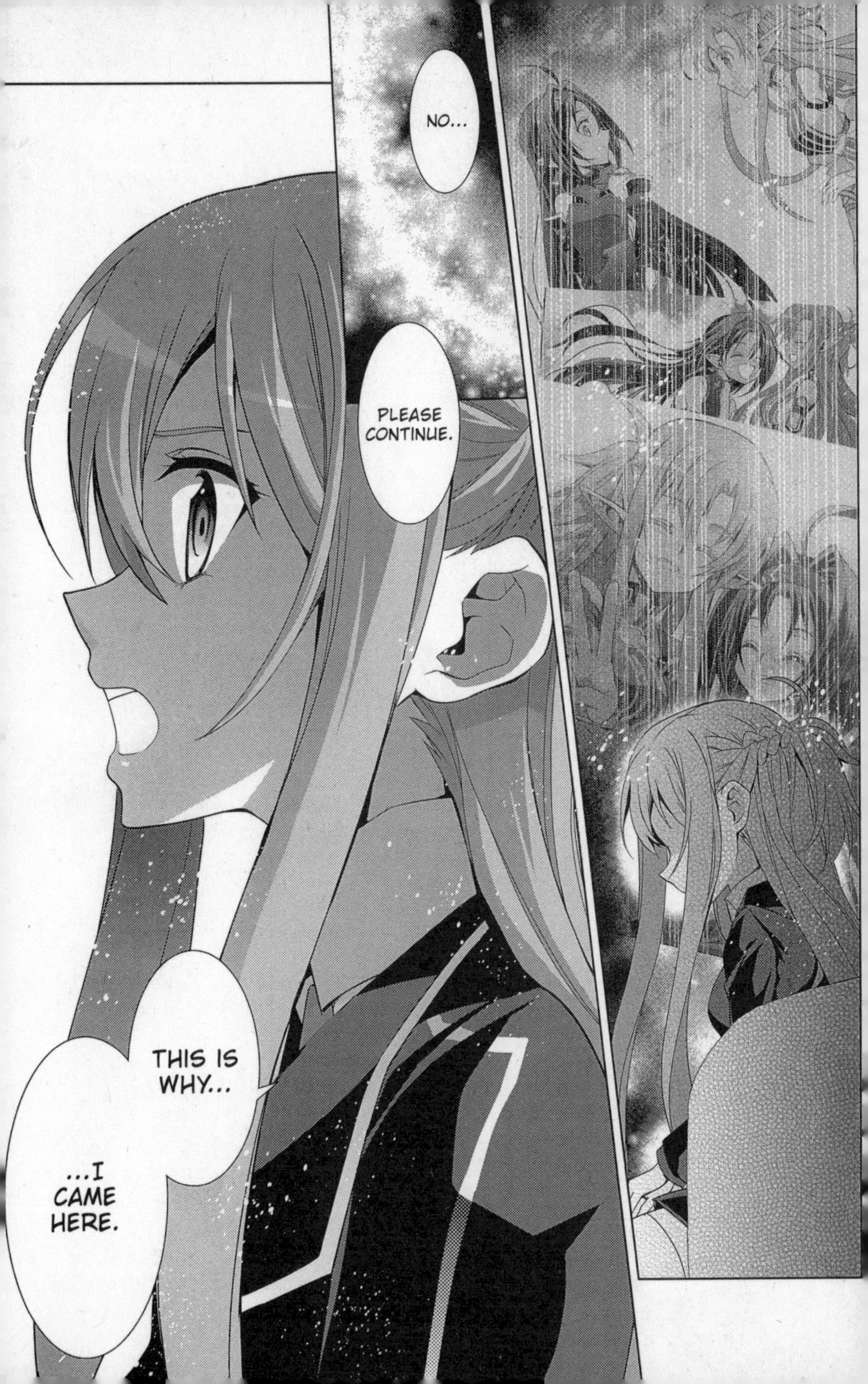
NO...
PLEASE CONTINUE.
THIS IS WHY...
...I CAME HERE.

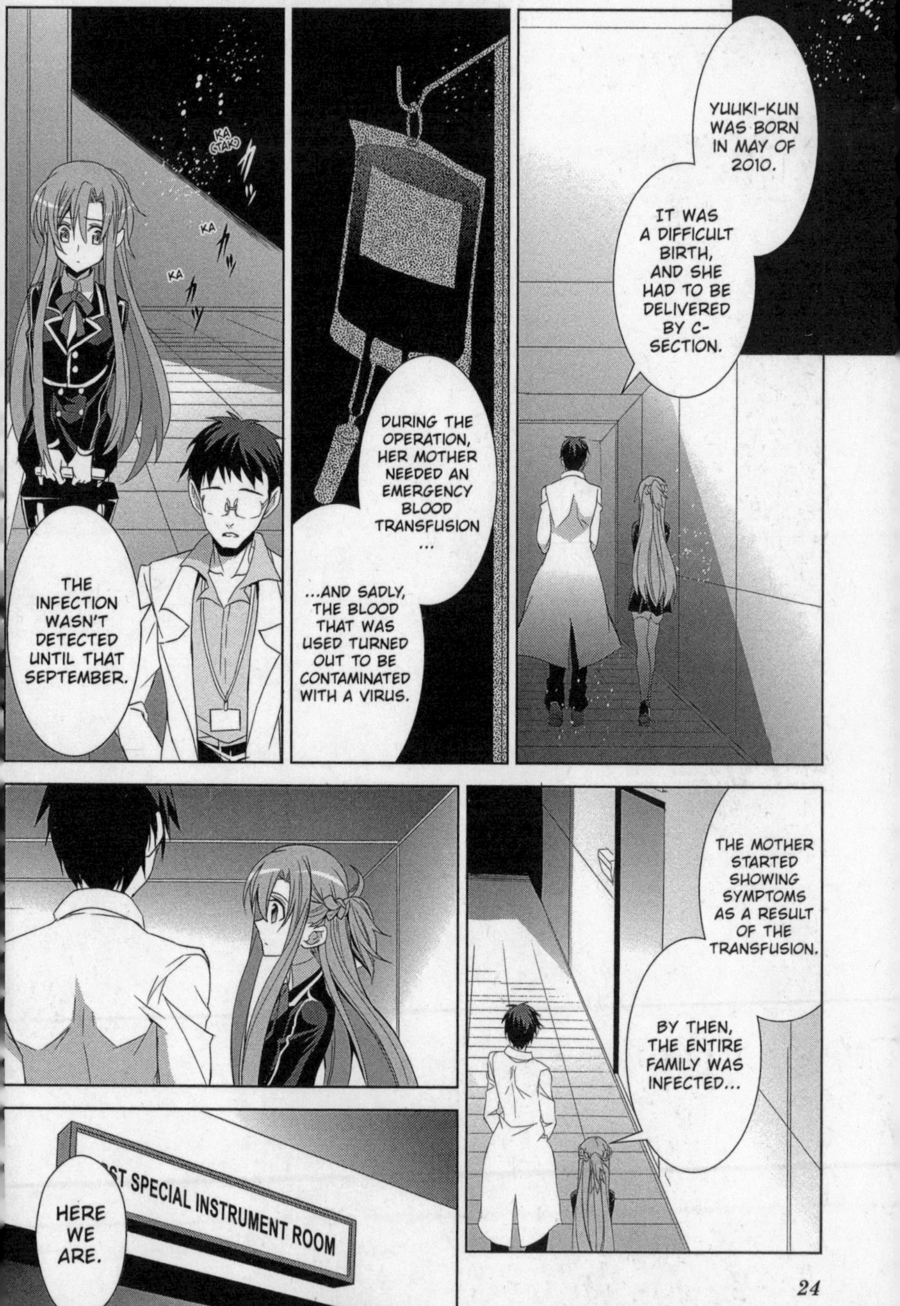
YUUKI-KUN WAS BORN IN MAY OF 2010.
IT WAS A DIFFICULT BIRTH, AND SHE HAD TO BE DELIVERED BY C-SECTION.
DURING THE OPERATION, HER MOTHER NEEDED AN EMERGENCY BLOOD TRANSFUSION ...
...AND SADLY, THE BLOOD THAT WAS USED TURNED OUT TO BE CONTAMINATED WITH A VIRUS.
KA (TAK)
KA
KA
THE INFECTION WASN'T DETECTED UNTIL THAT SEPTEMBER.
THE MOTHER STARTED SHOWING SYMPTOMS AS A RESULT OF THE TRANSFUSION.
BY THEN, THE ENTIRE FAMILY WAS INFECTED...
ST SPECIAL INSTRUMENT ROOM
HERE WE ARE.

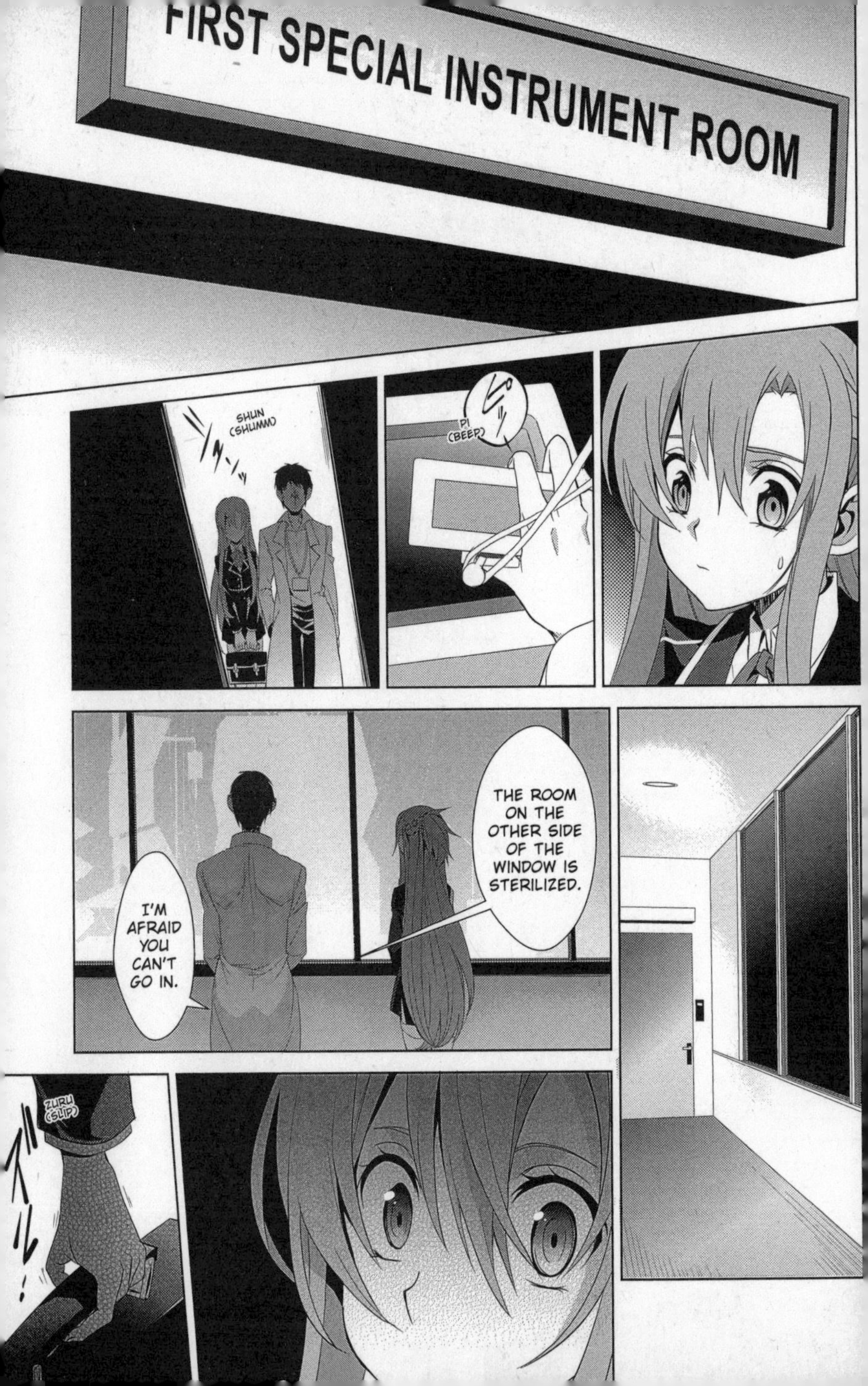
FIRST SPECIAL INSTRUMENT ROOM
PI (BEEP)
SHUN (SHUMM)
THE ROOM ON THE OTHER SIDE OF THE WINDOW IS STERILIZED.
I'M AFRAID YOU CAN'T GO IN.
ZURU (SLIP)

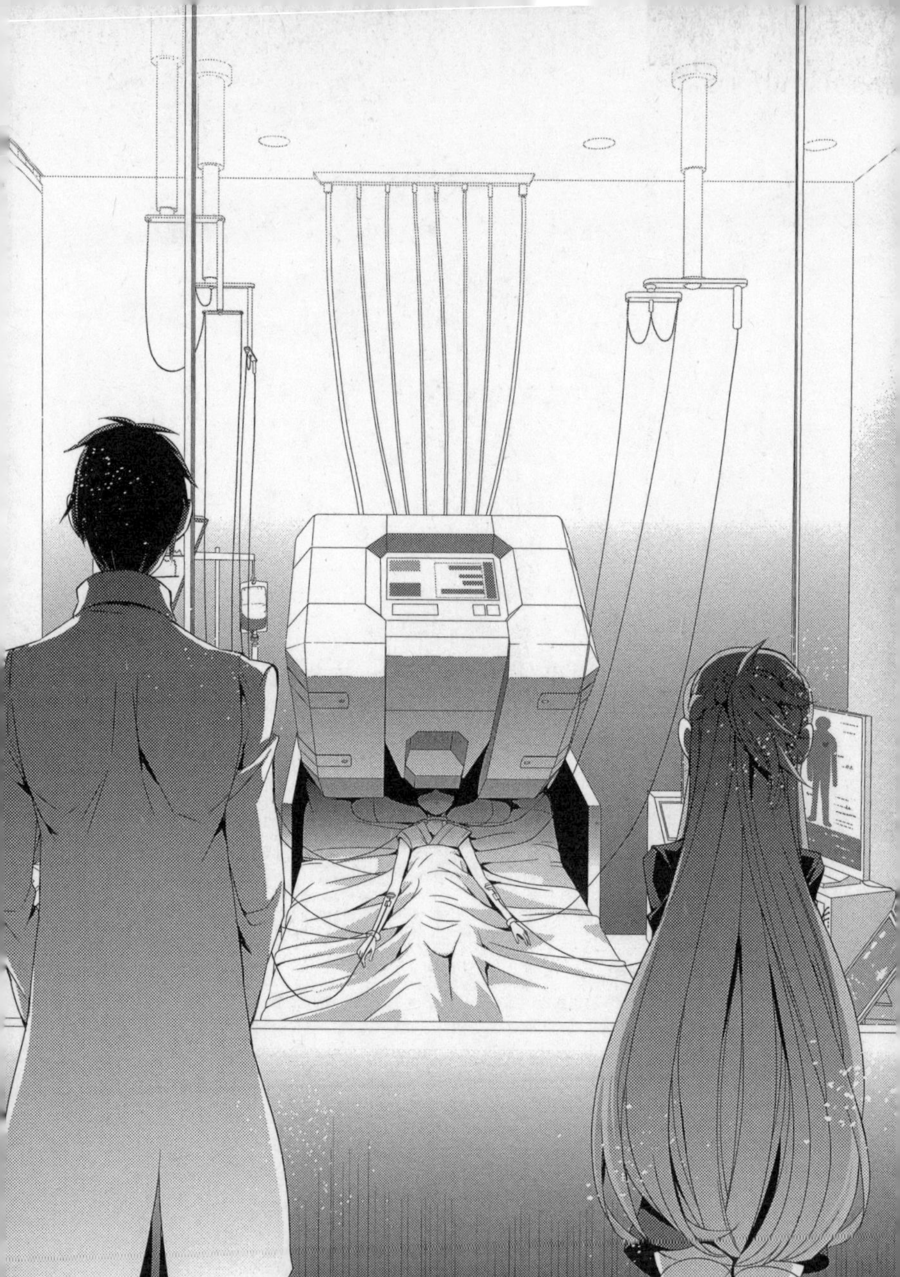

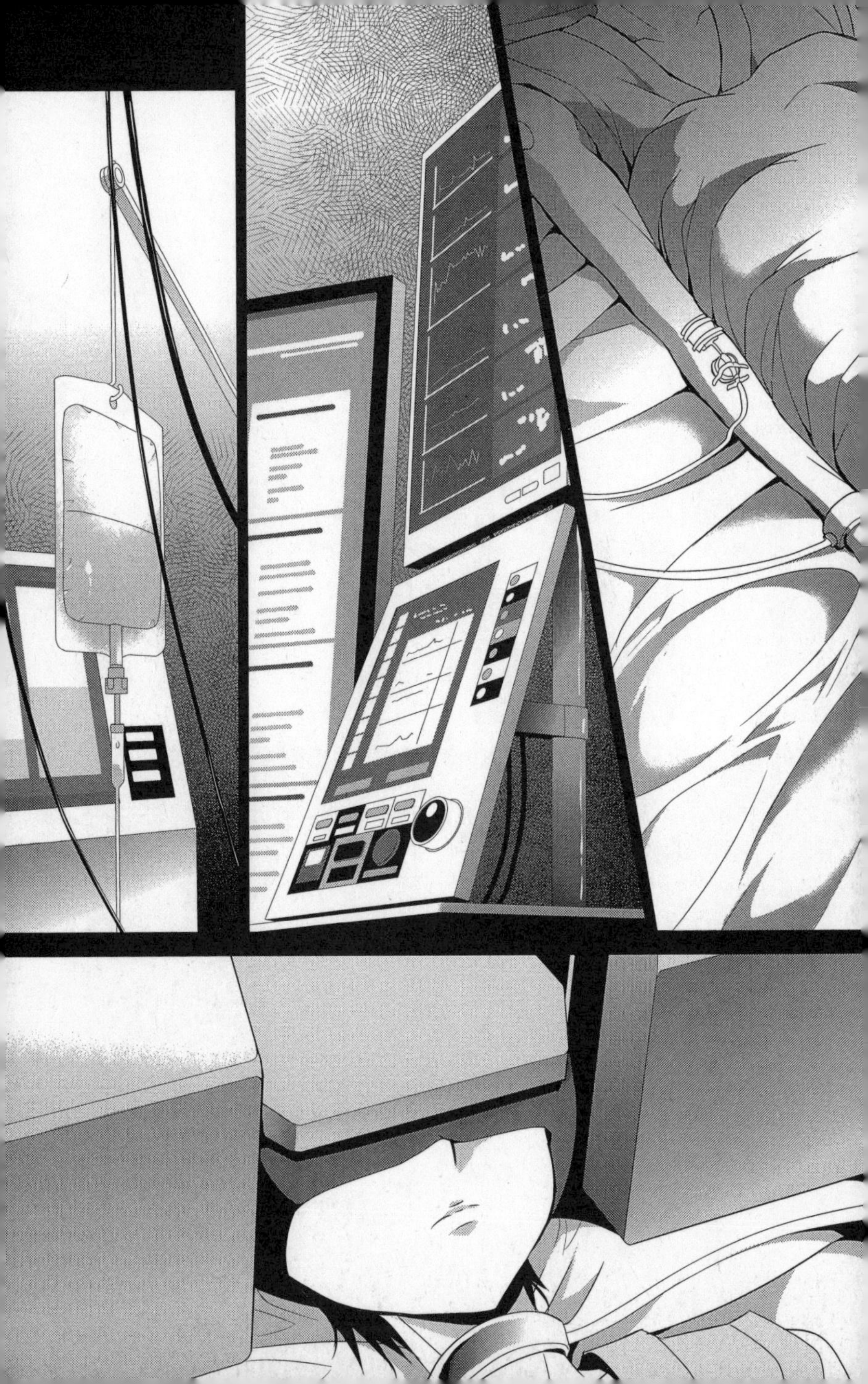

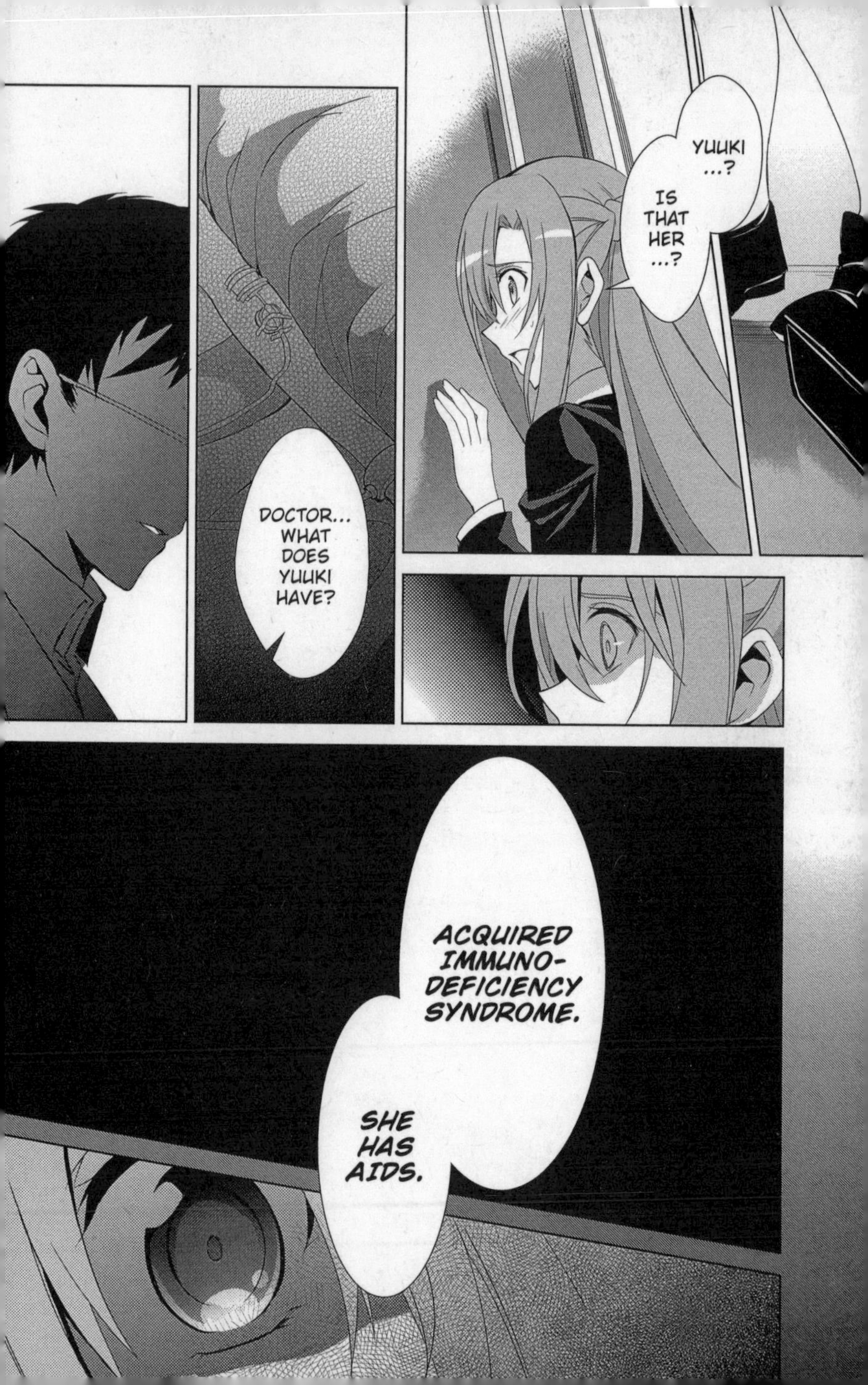
YUUKI ...?
IS THAT HER ...?
DOCTOR... WHAT DOES YUUKI HAVE?
ACQUIRED IMMUNO-DEFICIENCY SYNDROME.
SHE HAS AIDS.

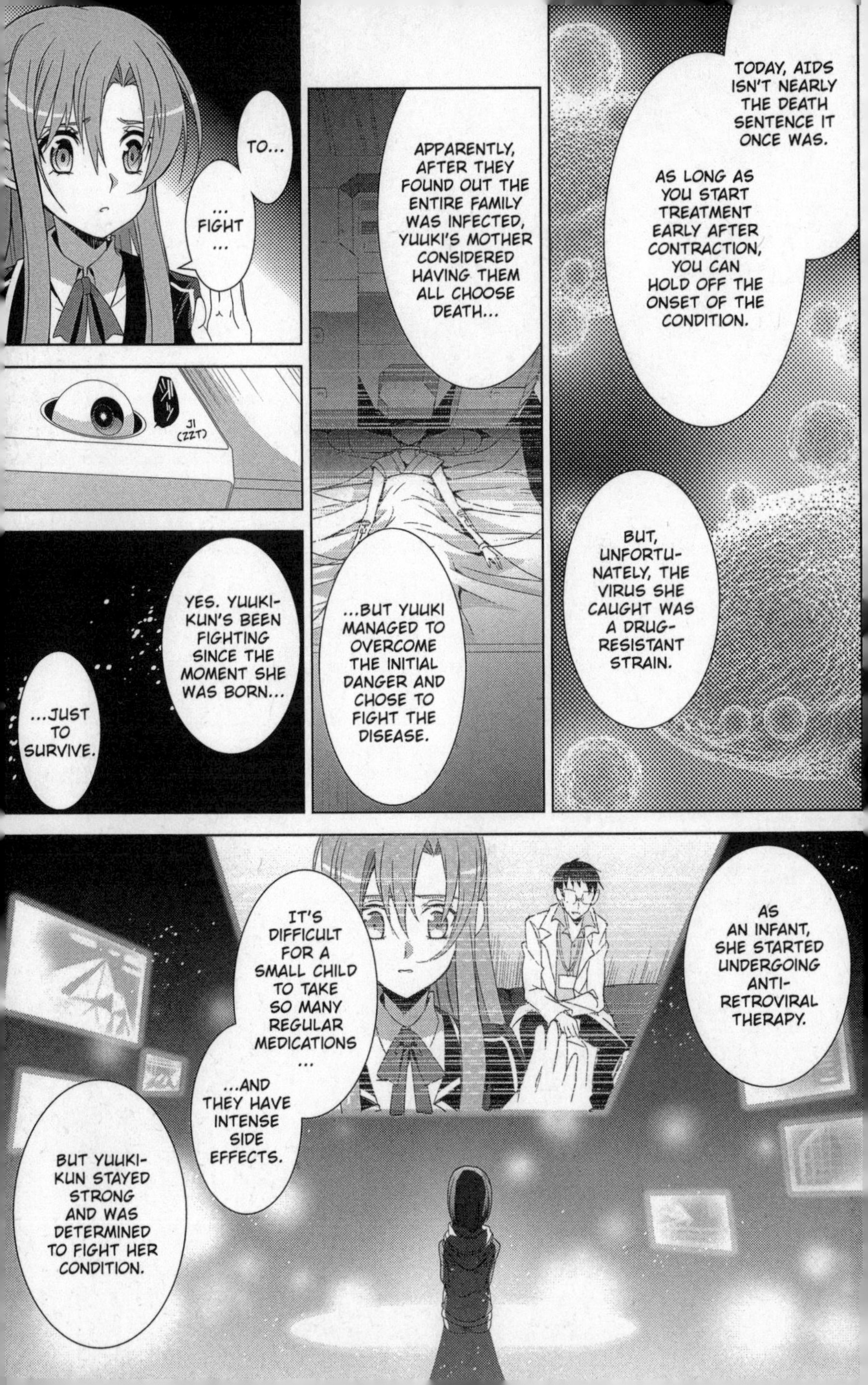
TODAY, AIDS ISN'T NEARLY THE DEATH SENTENCE IT ONCE WAS.
AS LONG AS YOU START TREATMENT EARLY AFTER CONTRACTION, YOU CAN HOLD OFF THE ONSET OF THE CONDITION.
BUT, UNFORTU-NATELY, THE VIRUS SHE CAUGHT WAS A DRUG-RESISTANT STRAIN.
APPARENTLY, AFTER THEY FOUND OUT THE ENTIRE FAMILY WAS INFECTED, YUUKI'S MOTHER CONSIDERED HAVING THEM ALL CHOOSE DEATH...
...BUT YUUKI MANAGED TO OVERCOME THE INITIAL DANGER AND CHOSE TO FIGHT THE DISEASE.
TO...
...FIGHT...
JI (ZZT)
YES. YUUKI-KUN'S BEEN FIGHTING SINCE THE MOMENT SHE WAS BORN...
...JUST TO SURVIVE.
AS AN INFANT, SHE STARTED UNDERGOING ANTI-RETROVIRAL THERAPY.
IT'S DIFFICULT FOR A SMALL CHILD TO TAKE SO MANY REGULAR MEDICATIONS...
...AND THEY HAVE INTENSE SIDE EFFECTS.
BUT YUUKI-KUN STAYED STRONG AND WAS DETERMINED TO FIGHT HER CONDITION.

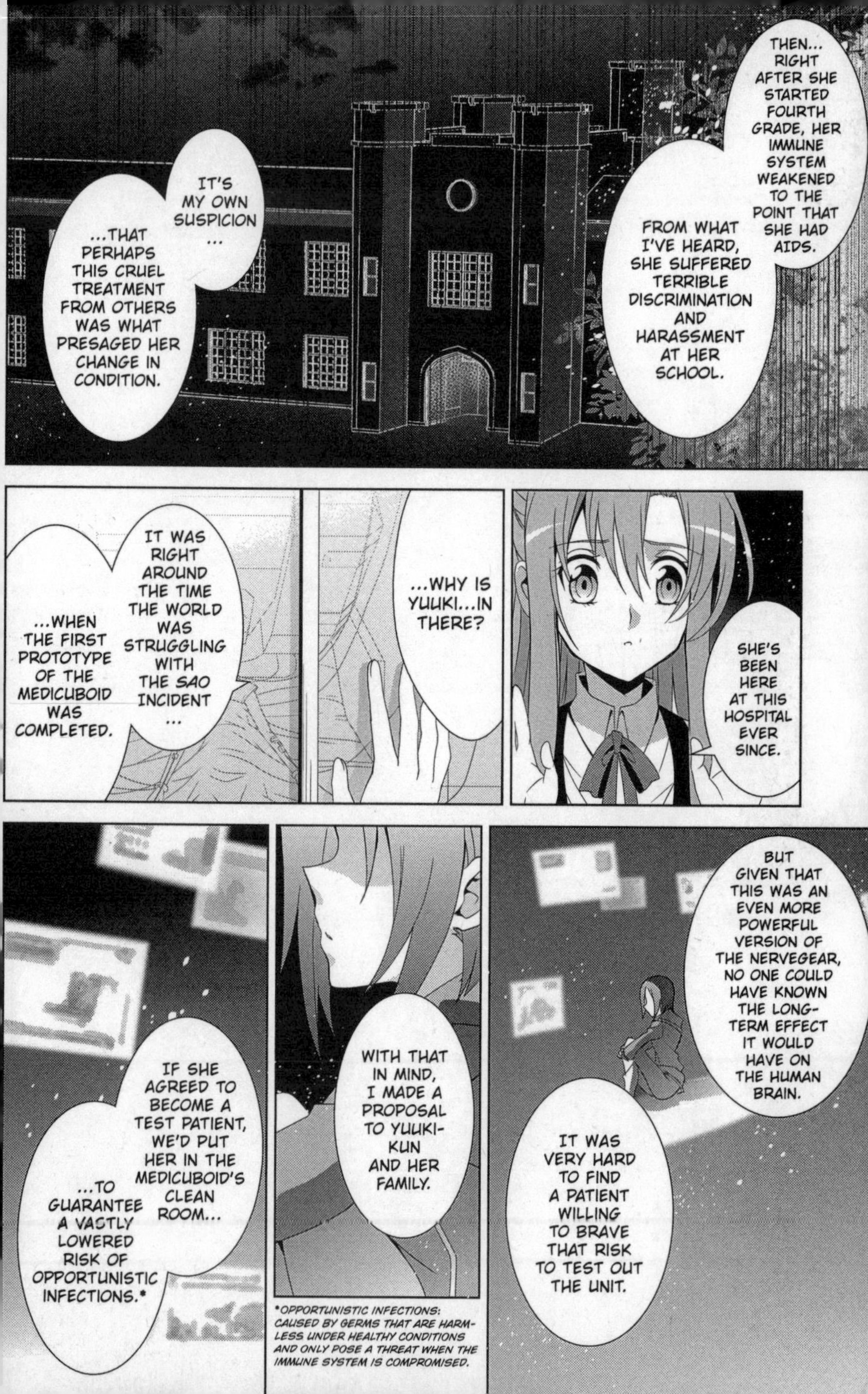
THEN... RIGHT AFTER SHE STARTED FOURTH GRADE, HER IMMUNE SYSTEM WEAKENED TO THE POINT THAT SHE HAD AIDS.
FROM WHAT I'VE HEARD, SHE SUFFERED TERRIBLE DISCRIMINATION AND HARASSMENT AT HER SCHOOL.
IT'S MY OWN SUSPICION...
...THAT PERHAPS THIS CRUEL TREATMENT FROM OTHERS WAS WHAT PRESAGED HER CHANGE IN CONDITION.
SHE'S BEEN HERE AT THIS HOSPITAL EVER SINCE.
...WHY IS YUUKI...IN THERE?
IT WAS RIGHT AROUND THE TIME THE WORLD WAS STRUGGLING WITH THE SAO INCIDENT...
...WHEN THE FIRST PROTOTYPE OF THE MEDICUBOID WAS COMPLETED.
BUT GIVEN THAT THIS WAS AN EVEN MORE POWERFUL VERSION OF THE NERVEGEAR, NO ONE COULD HAVE KNOWN THE LONG-TERM EFFECT IT WOULD HAVE ON THE HUMAN BRAIN.
IT WAS VERY HARD TO FIND A PATIENT WILLING TO BRAVE THAT RISK TO TEST OUT THE UNIT.
WITH THAT IN MIND, I MADE A PROPOSAL TO YUUKI-KUN AND HER FAMILY.
IF SHE AGREED TO BECOME A TEST PATIENT, WE'D PUT HER IN THE MEDICUBOID'S CLEAN ROOM...
...TO GUARANTEE A VASTLY LOWERED RISK OF OPPORTUNISTIC INFECTIONS.*

*OPPORTUNISTIC INFECTIONS: CAUSED BY GERMS THAT ARE HARMLESS UNDER HEALTHY CONDITIONS AND ONLY POSE A THREAT WHEN THE IMMUNE SYSTEM IS COMPROMISED.

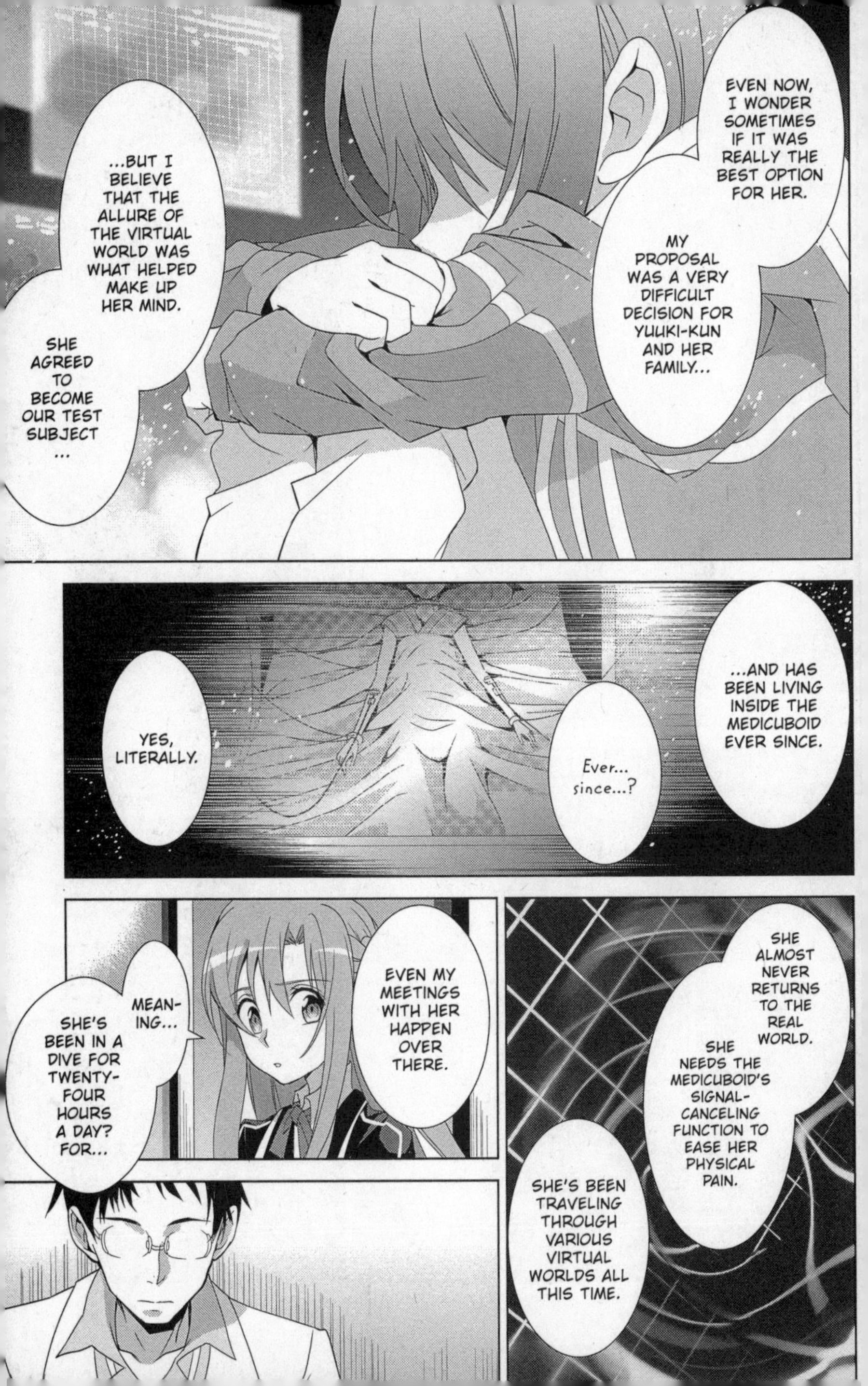
EVEN NOW, I WONDER SOMETIMES IF IT WAS REALLY THE BEST OPTION FOR HER.
MY PROPOSAL WAS A VERY DIFFICULT DECISION FOR YUUKI-KUN AND HER FAMILY...
...BUT I BELIEVE THAT THE ALLURE OF THE VIRTUAL WORLD WAS WHAT HELPED MAKE UP HER MIND.
SHE AGREED TO BECOME OUR TEST SUBJECT...
...AND HAS BEEN LIVING INSIDE THE MEDICUBOID EVER SINCE.
Ever... since...?
YES, LITERALLY.
SHE ALMOST NEVER RETURNS TO THE REAL WORLD.
SHE NEEDS THE MEDICUBOID'S SIGNAL-CANCELING FUNCTION TO EASE HER PHYSICAL PAIN.
SHE'S BEEN TRAVELING THROUGH VARIOUS VIRTUAL WORLDS ALL THIS TIME.
EVEN MY MEETINGS WITH HER HAPPEN OVER THERE.
MEAN-ING...
SHE'S BEEN IN A DIVE FOR TWENTY-FOUR HOURS A DAY? FOR...

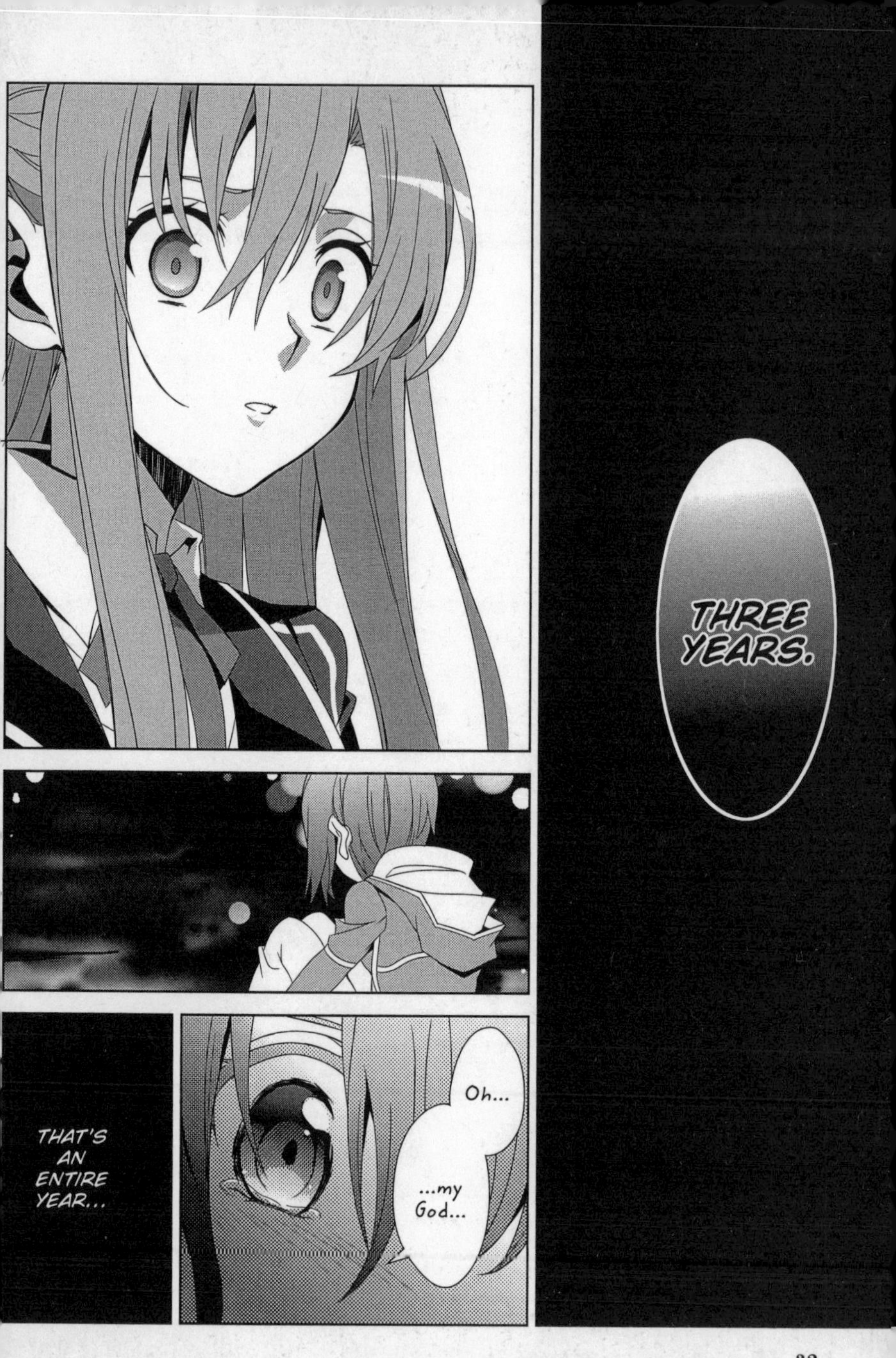
THREE YEARS.
Oh...
...my God...
THAT'S AN ENTIRE YEAR...

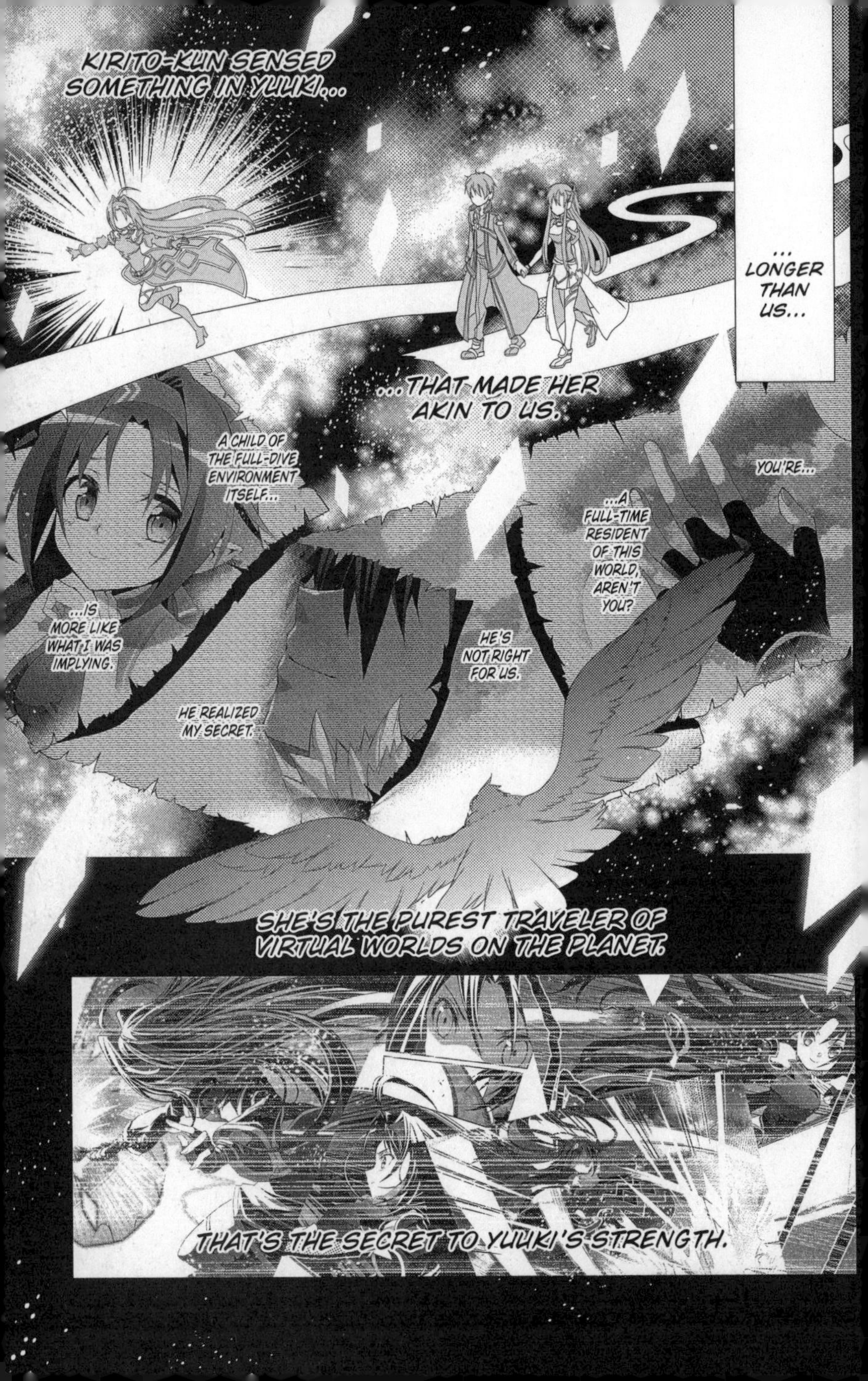

... LONGER THAN US...
KIRITO-KUN SENSED SOMETHING IN YUUKI...
...THAT MADE HER AKIN TO US.
YOU'RE...
...A FULL-TIME RESIDENT OF THIS WORLD, AREN'T YOU?
A CHILD OF THE FULL-DIVE ENVIRONMENT ITSELF...
...IS MORE LIKE WHAT I WAS IMPLYING.
HE'S NOT RIGHT FOR US.
HE REALIZED MY SECRET.
SHE'S THE PUREST TRAVELER OF VIRTUAL WORLDS ON THE PLANET.
THAT'S THE SECRET TO YUUKI'S STRENGTH.

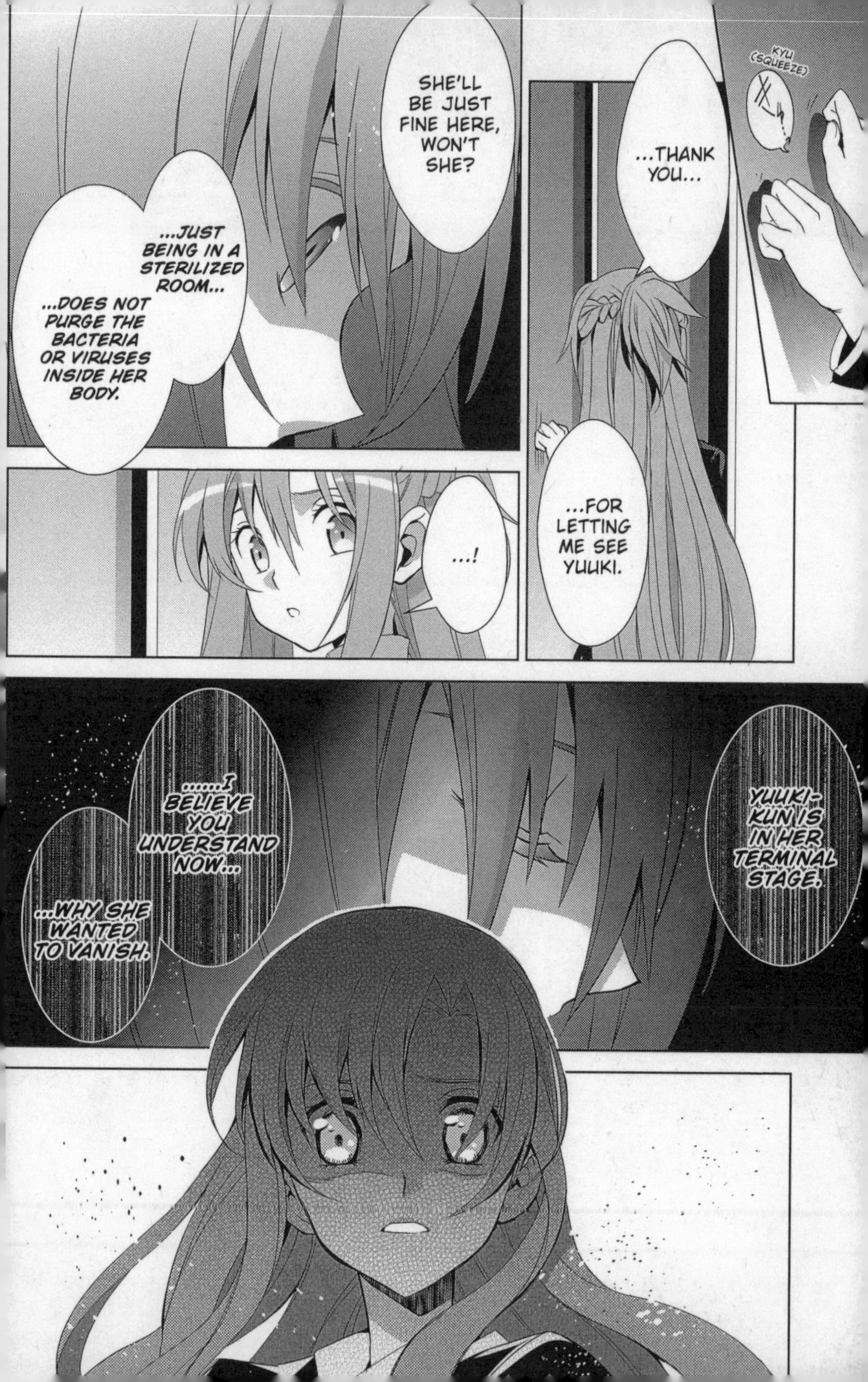
KYU (SQUEEZE)
...THANK YOU...
...FOR LETTING ME SEE YUUKI.
SHE'LL BE JUST FINE HERE, WON'T SHE?
...JUST BEING IN A STERILIZED ROOM...
...DOES NOT PURGE THE BACTERIA OR VIRUSES INSIDE HER BODY.
...!
YUUKI-KUN IS IN HER TERMINAL STAGE.
......I BELIEVE YOU UNDERSTAND NOW...
...WHY SHE WANTED TO VANISH.

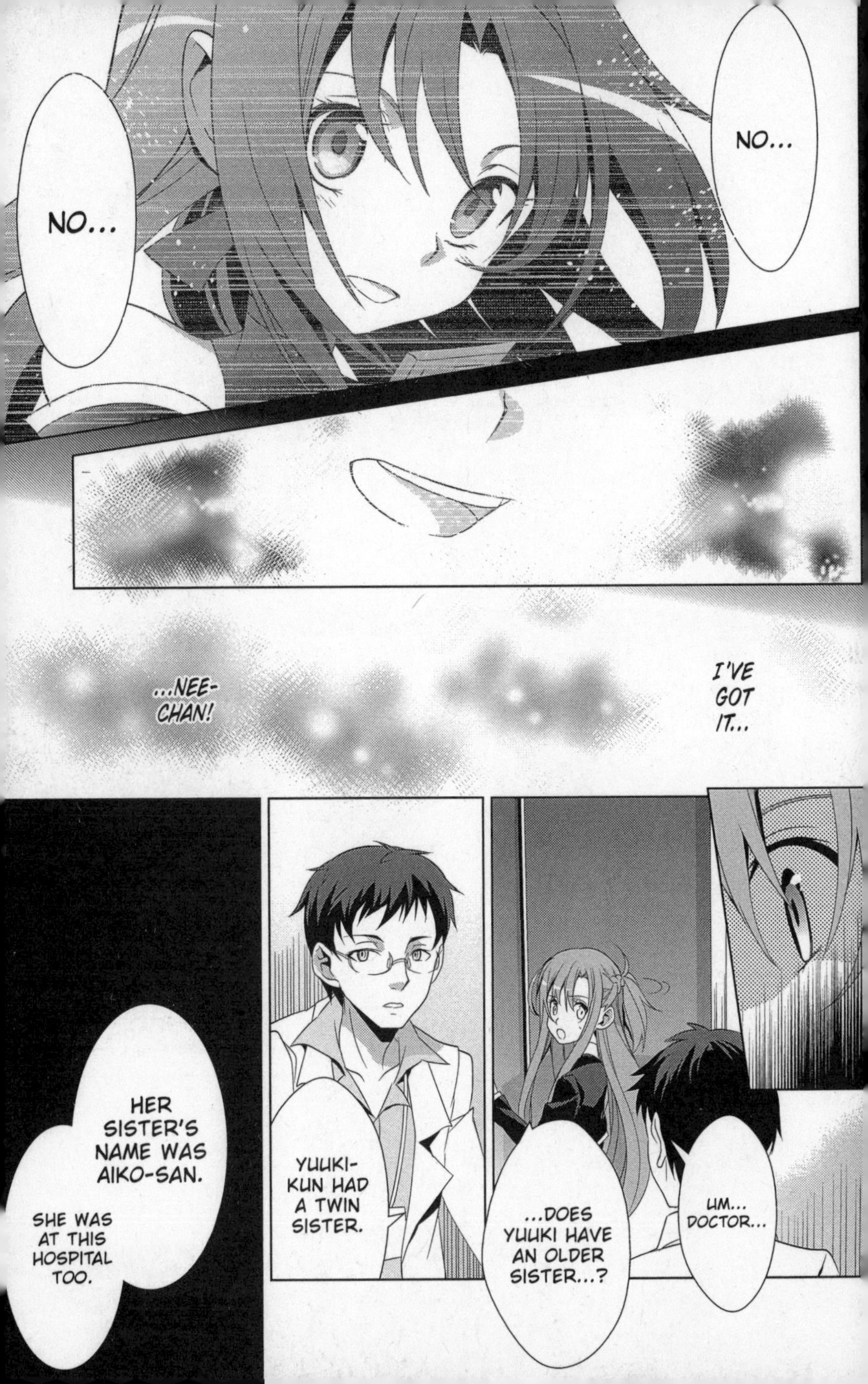
NO...
NO...
I'VE GOT IT...
...NEE-CHAN!
UM... DOCTOR...
...DOES YUUKI HAVE AN OLDER SISTER...?
YUUKI-KUN HAD A TWIN SISTER.
HER SISTER'S NAME WAS AIKO-SAN.
SHE WAS AT THIS HOSPITAL TOO.

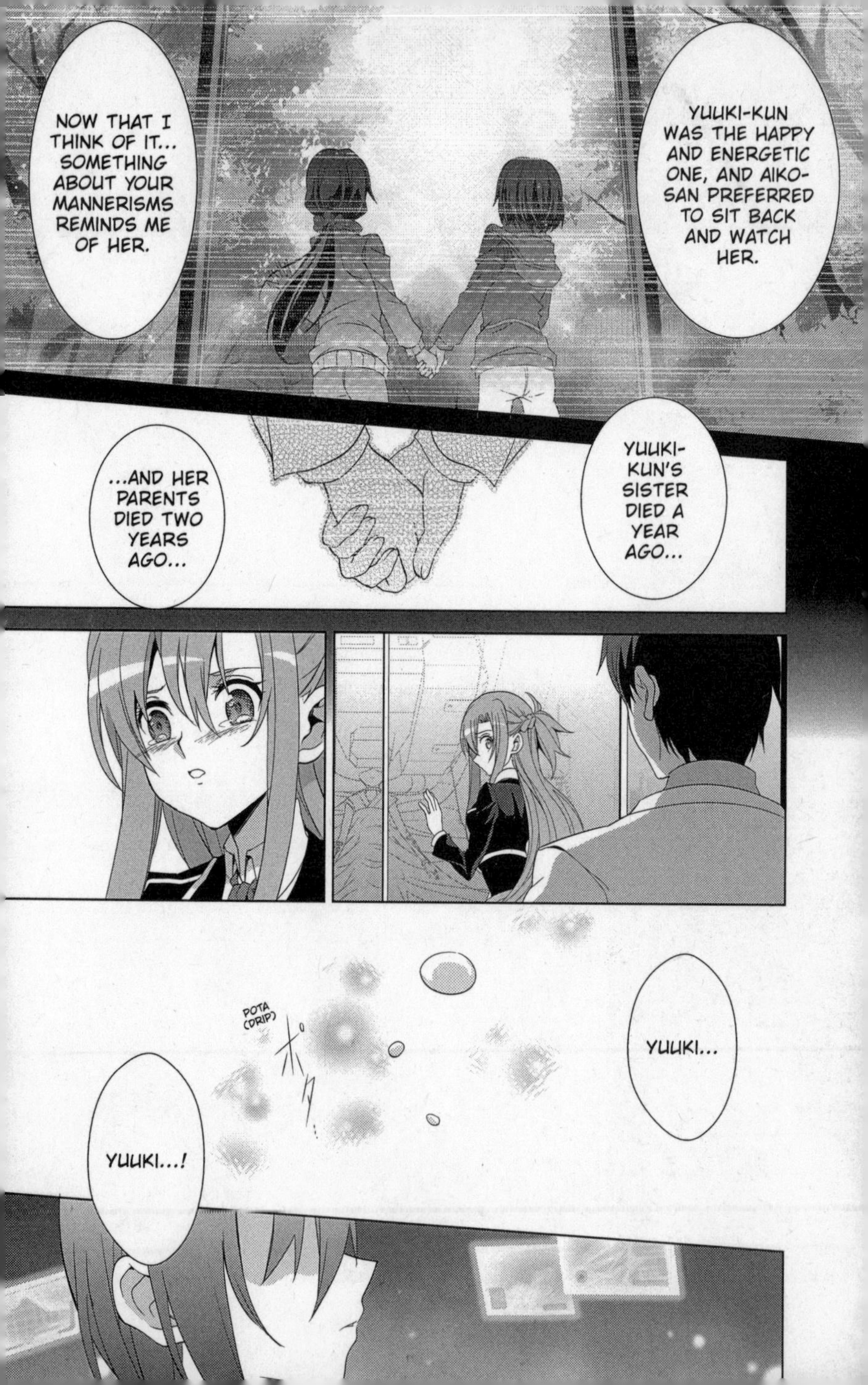
YUUKI-KUN WAS THE HAPPY AND ENERGETIC ONE, AND AIKO-SAN PREFERRED TO SIT BACK AND WATCH HER.
NOW THAT I THINK OF IT... SOMETHING ABOUT YOUR MANNERISMS REMINDS ME OF HER.
YUUKI-KUN'S SISTER DIED A YEAR AGO...
...AND HER PARENTS DIED TWO YEARS AGO...
YUUKI...
POTA (DRIP)
YUUKI...!

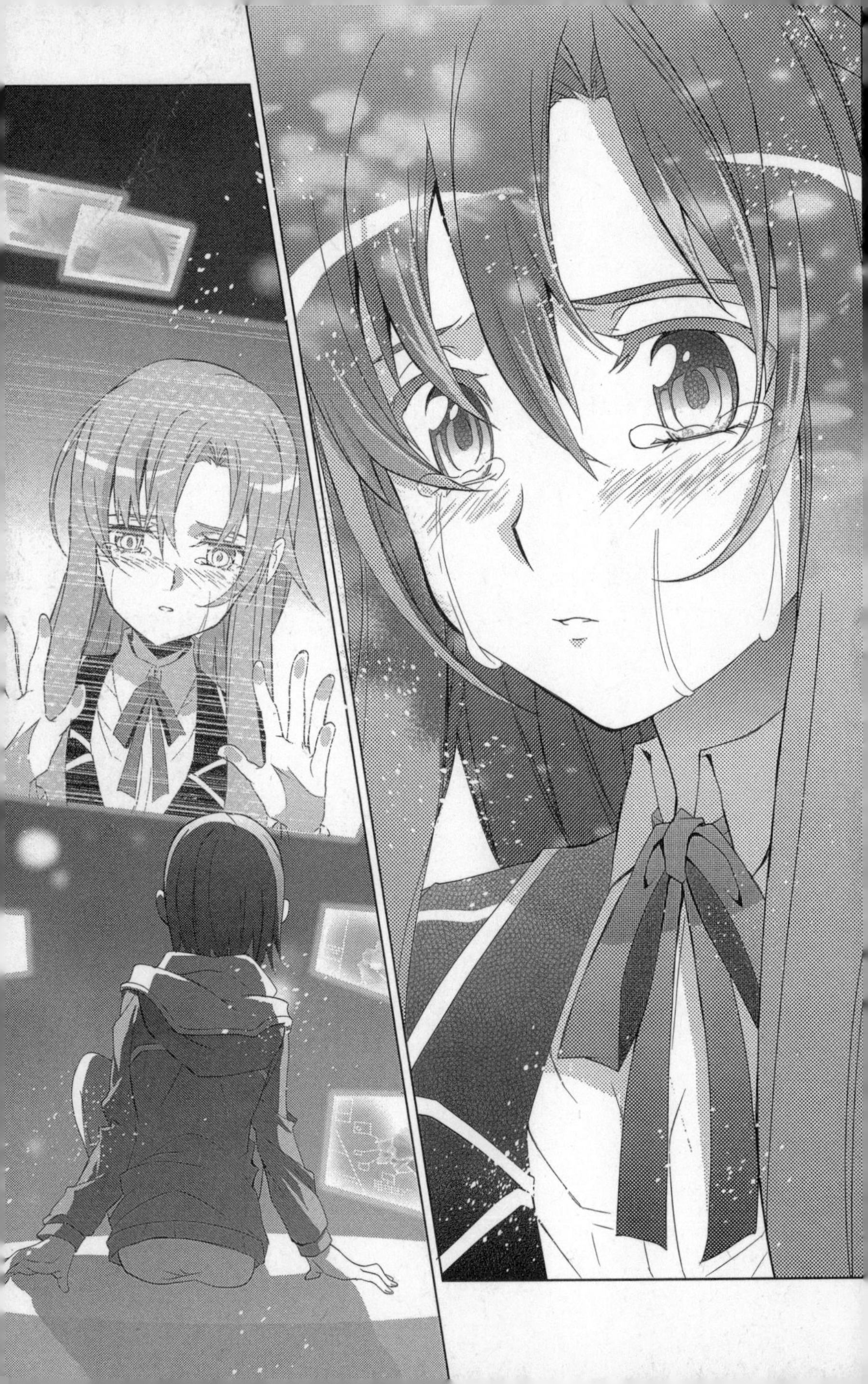

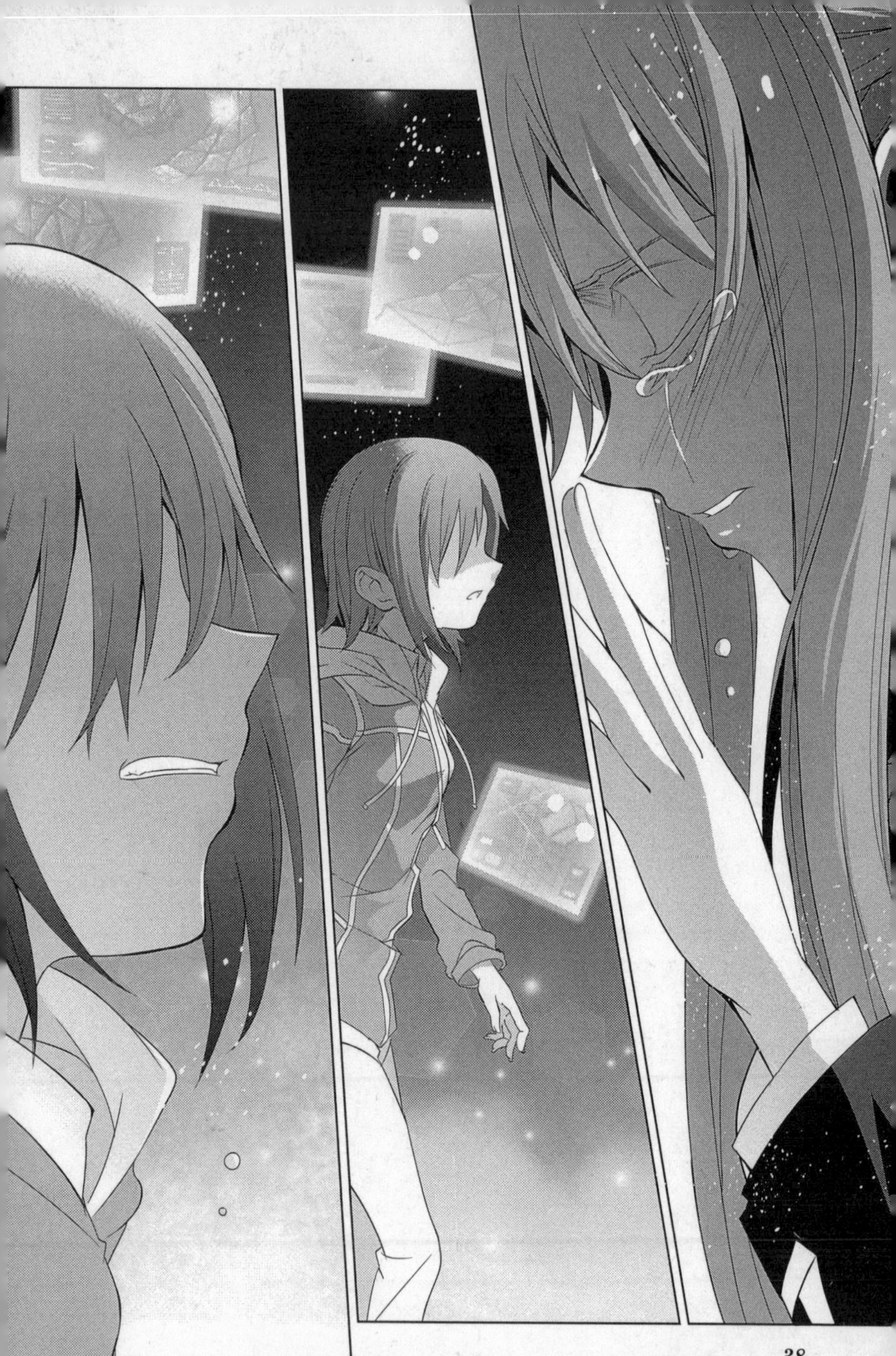

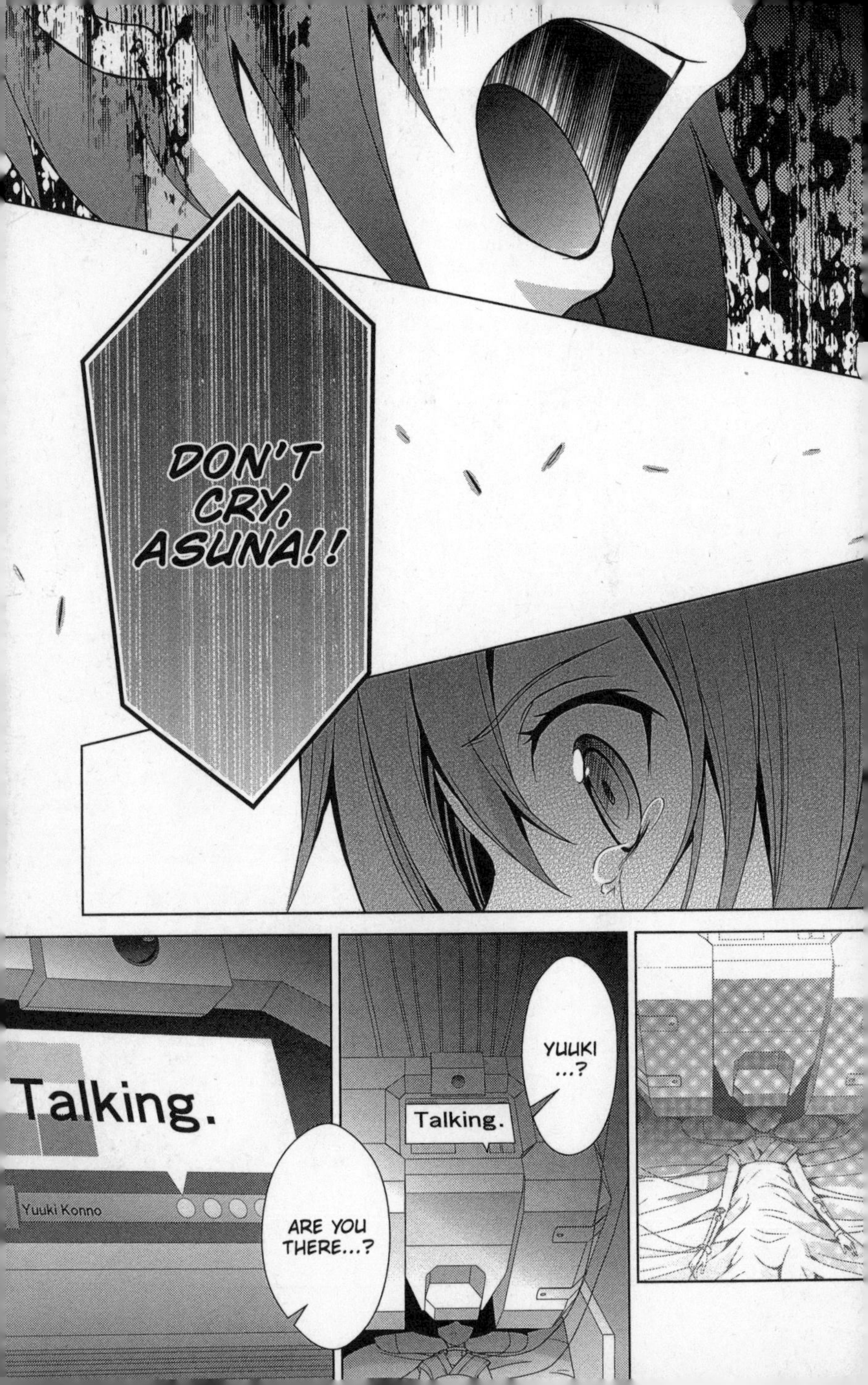
DON'T CRY, ASUNA!!
YUUKI ...?
Talking.
ARE YOU THERE...?
Talking.
Yuuki Konno

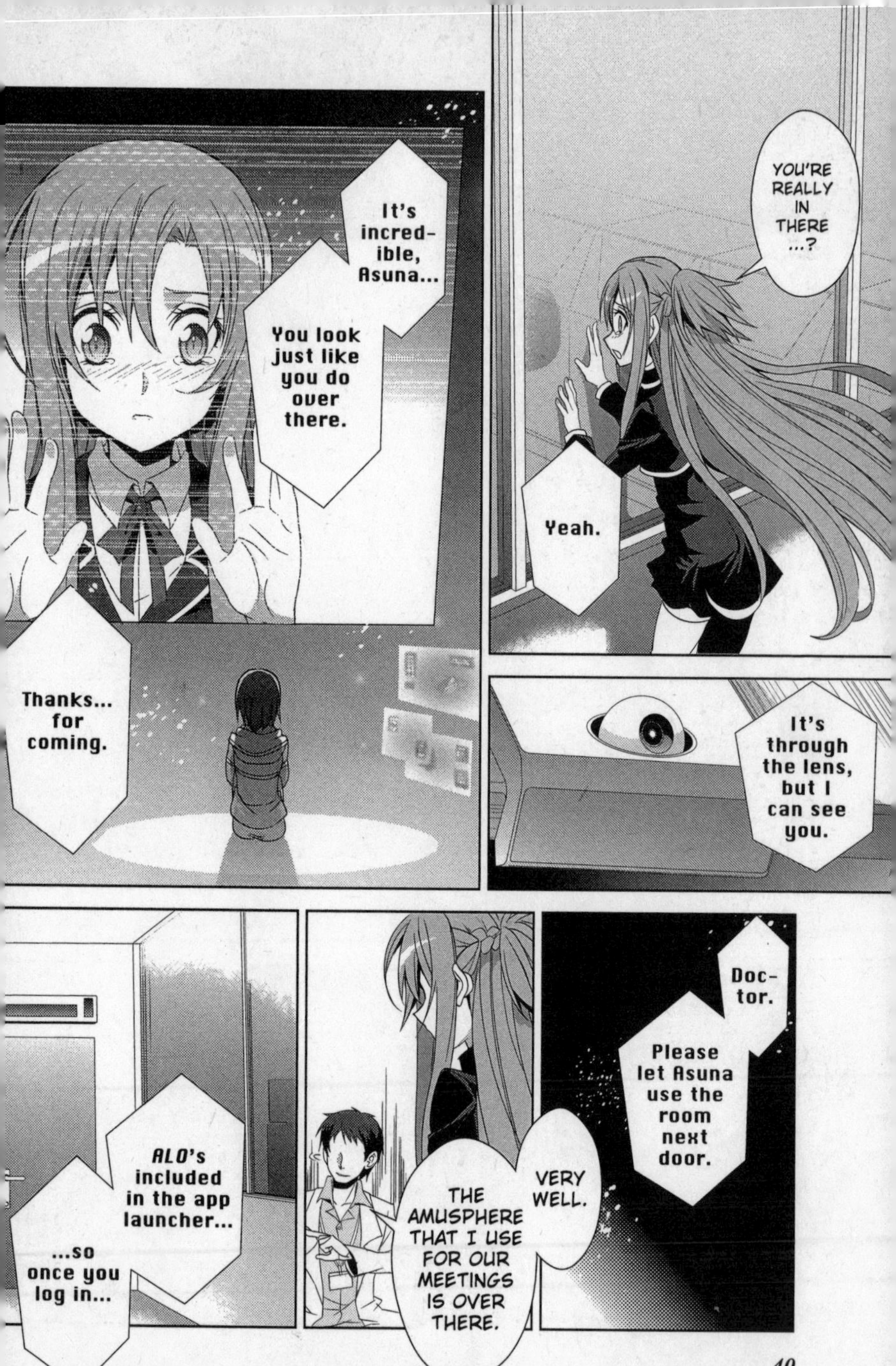
YOU'RE REALLY IN THERE ...?
Yeah.
It's incred-ible, Asuna...
You look just like you do over there.
It's through the lens, but I can see you.
Thanks... for coming.
Doc-tor.
Please let Asuna use the room next door.
VERY WELL.
THE AMUSPHERE THAT I USE FOR OUR MEETINGS IS OVER THERE.
ALO's included in the app launcher...
...so once you log in...

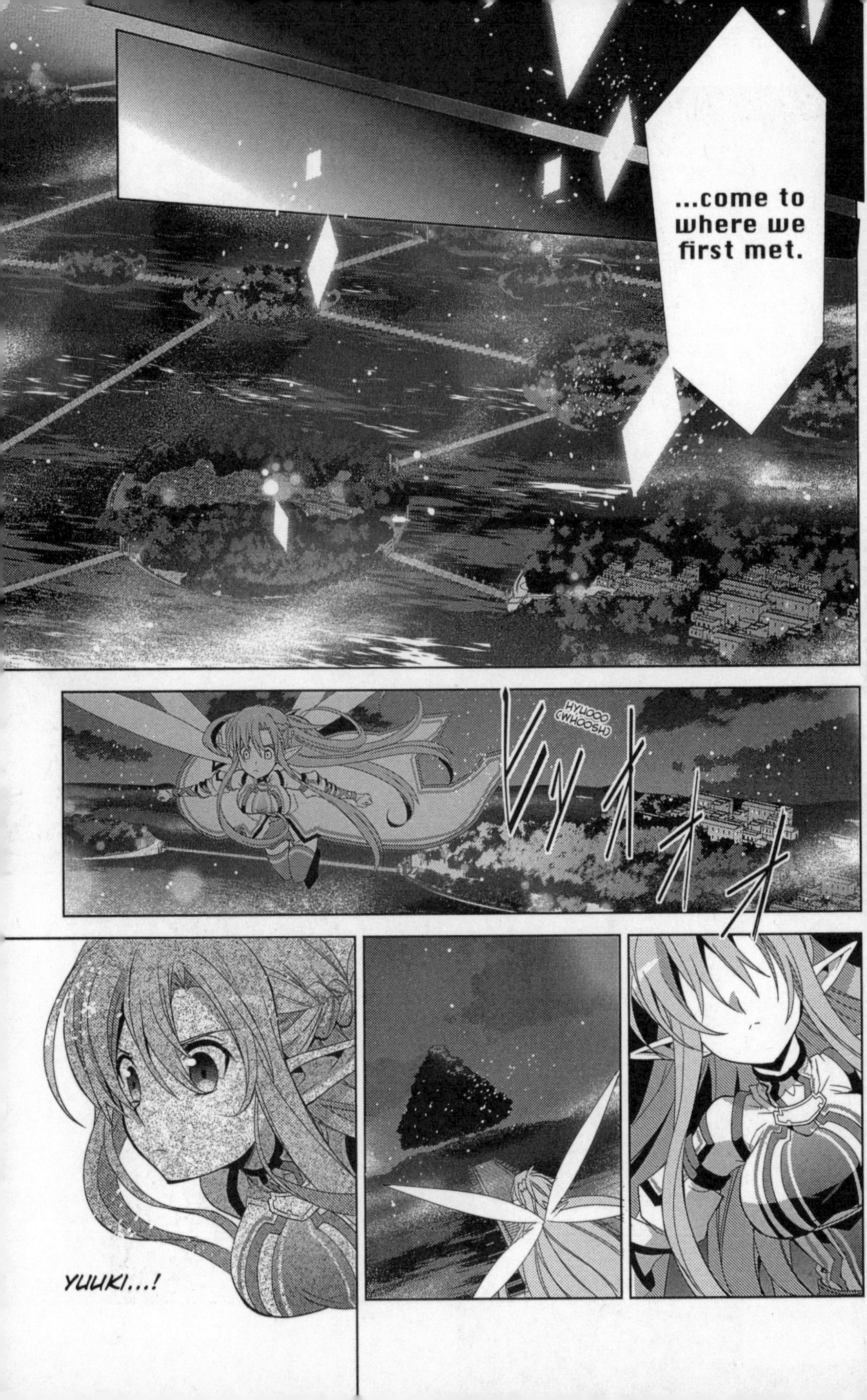
...come to where we first met.
HYUOOO (WHOOSH)
YUUKI...!

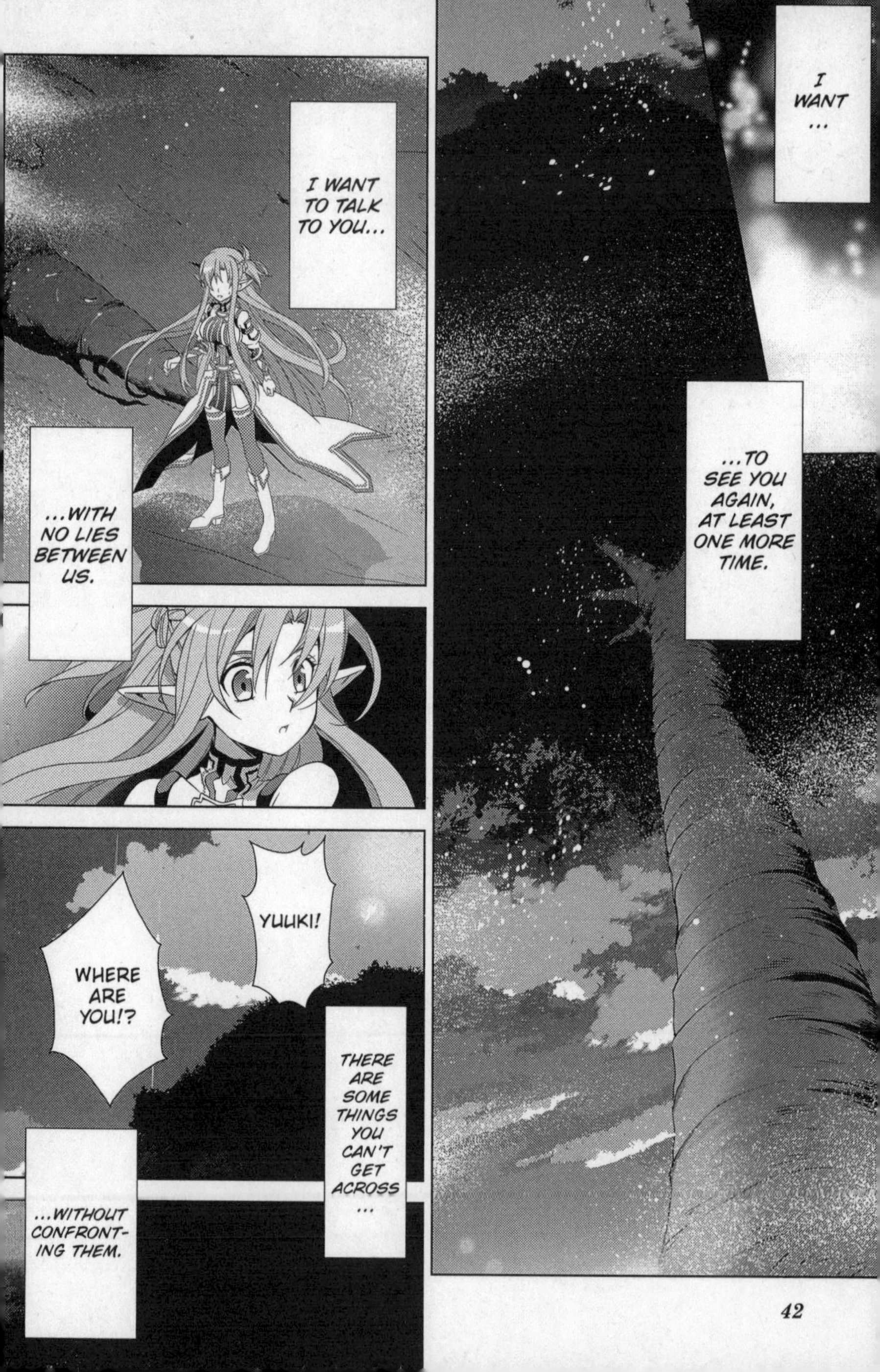

I WANT ...
...TO SEE YOU AGAIN, AT LEAST ONE MORE TIME.
I WANT TO TALK TO YOU...
...WITH NO LIES BETWEEN US.
YUUKI!
WHERE ARE YOU!?
THERE ARE SOME THINGS YOU CAN'T GET ACROSS ...
...WITHOUT CONFRONTING THEM.

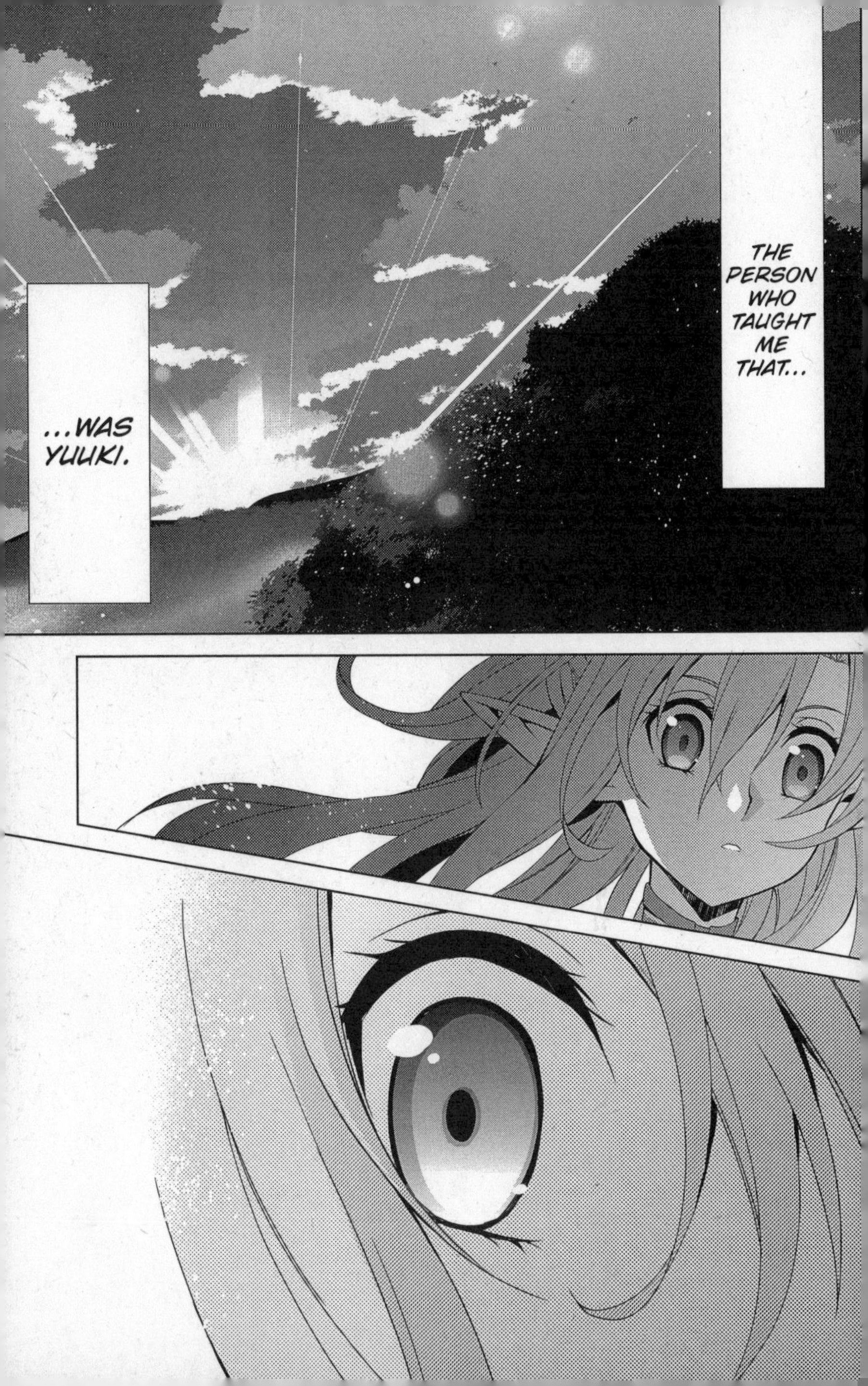
THE PERSON WHO TAUGHT ME THAT...
...WAS YUUKI.

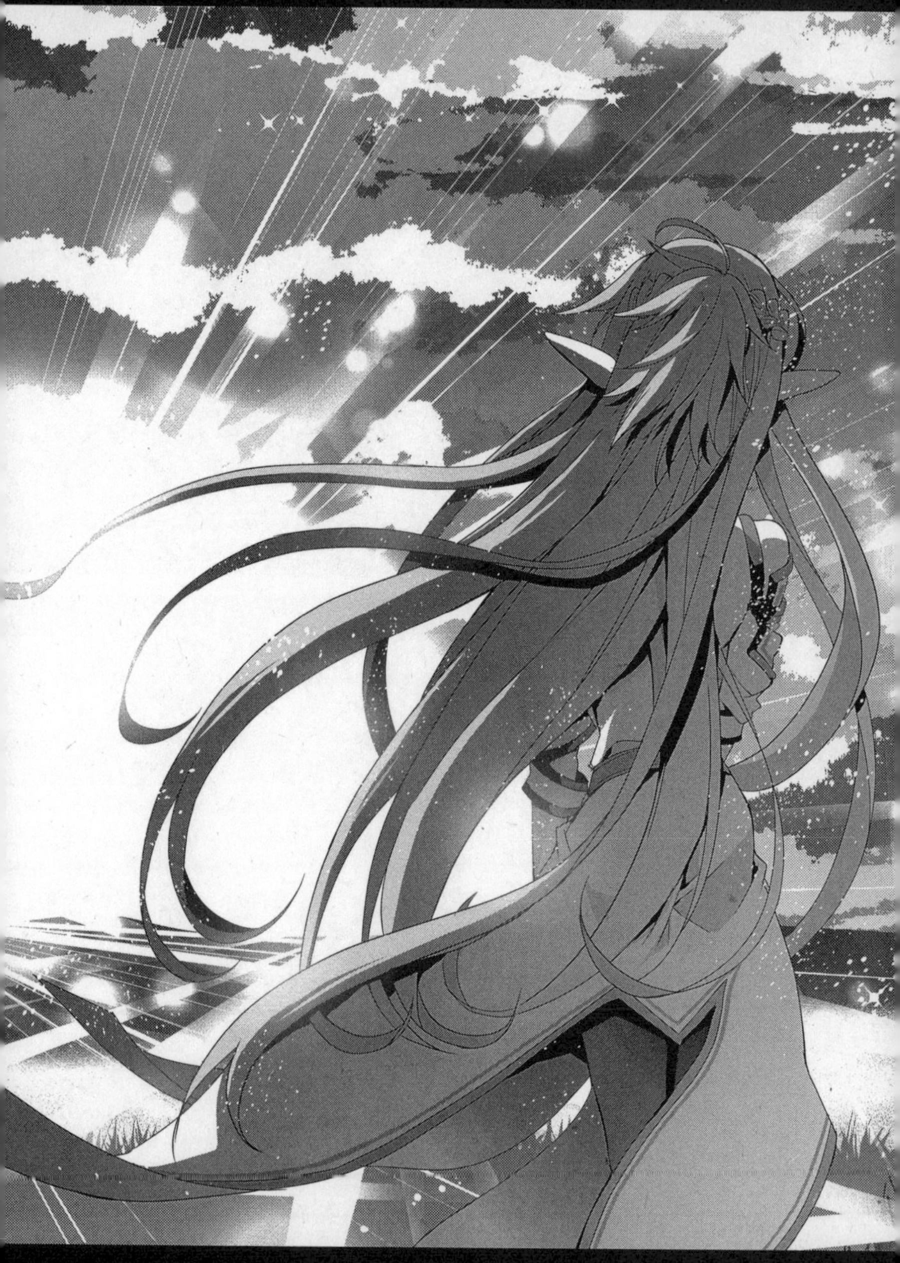

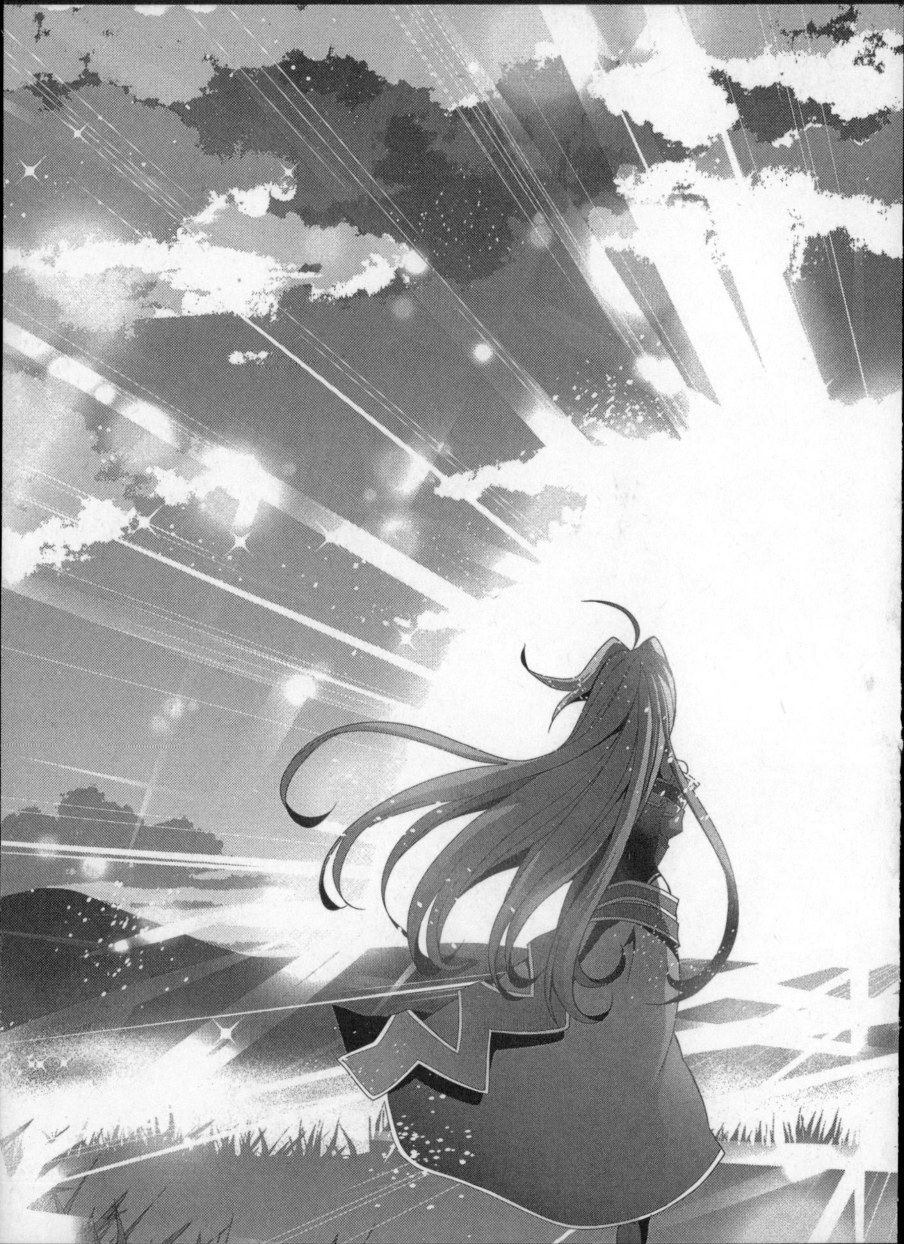

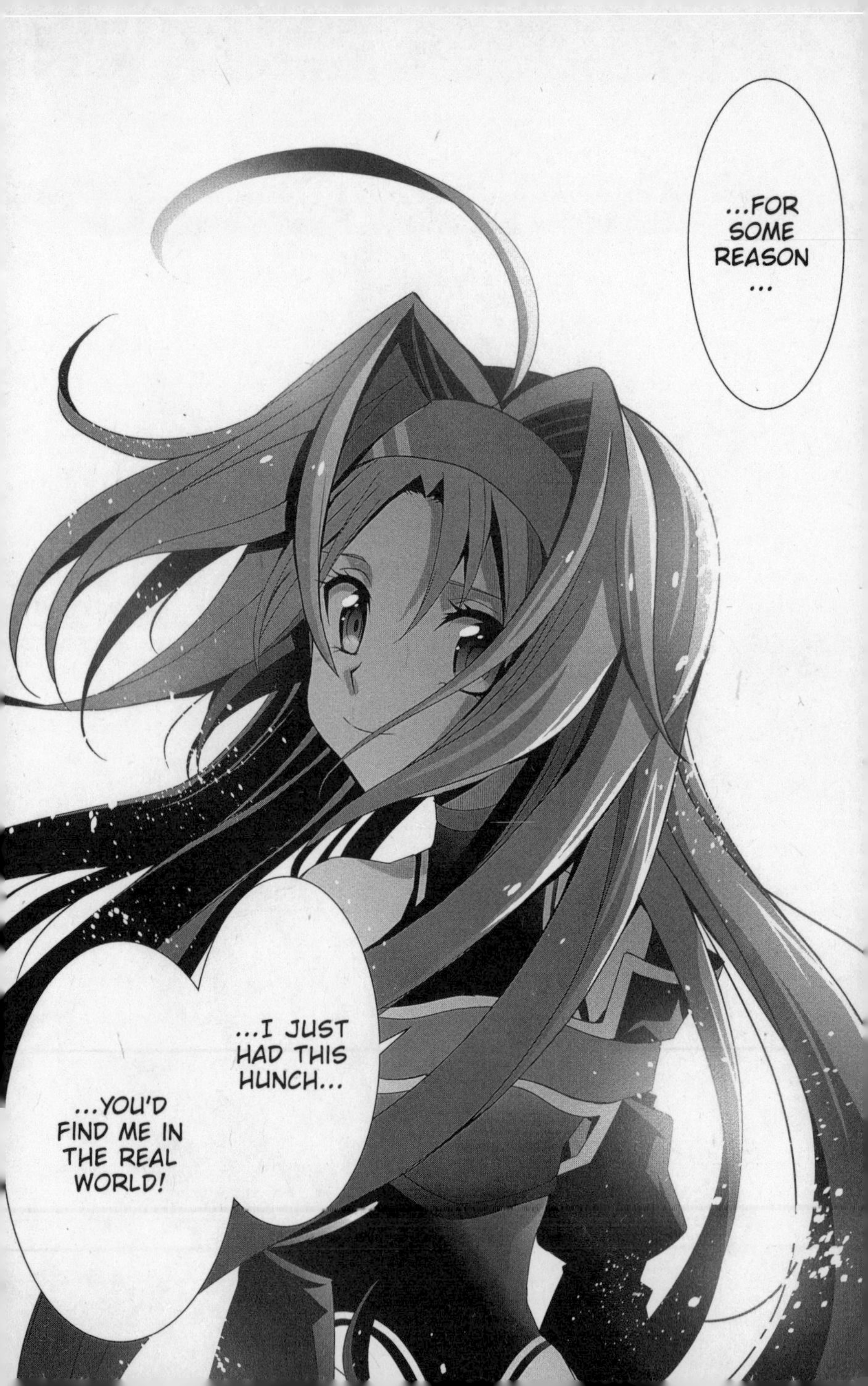
...FOR SOME REASON ...
...I JUST HAD THIS HUNCH...
...YOU'D FIND ME IN THE REAL WORLD!

SWORD ART ONLINE

mother's ROSARY

SWORD ART ONLINE **mother's rosary**
BACKGROUND GUIDE `01`

MEDICUBOID

A MEDICAL-USE FULL-DIVE MACHINE. IT FEATURES A STRONGER
VERSION OF THE AMUSPHERE'S SIGNAL-CANCELING FUNCTION
(WHICH DULLS REAL PHYSICAL SENSATIONS TO IMPROVE VIRTUAL
WORLD IMMERSION; WITHOUT IT, MOVING A VIRTUAL ARM MIGHT
ALSO MOVE ONE'S REAL ARM). THIS COMPLETELY REMOVES
ALL PAIN TO EASE THE SUFFERING OF PATIENTS WITH SERIOUS
CONDITIONS AND PROVIDES THEM WITH A VR ENVIRONMENT TO
SPEND THEIR TIME WITHOUT STRESS. IN THE ORIGINAL NOVEL,
DR. KURAHASHI EXPRESSES SOME RESERVATIONS ABOUT THE
QOL (QUALITY OF LIFE) OF PATIENTS STRAPPED DOWN PER-
MANENTLY INTO THE MEDICUBOID, BUT IF SUCH A TECHNOLOGY
WERE TO EXIST IN REAL LIFE, IT WOULD UNDOUBTEDLY BENEFIT
THOSE SUFFERING FROM SERIOUS ILLNESSES.

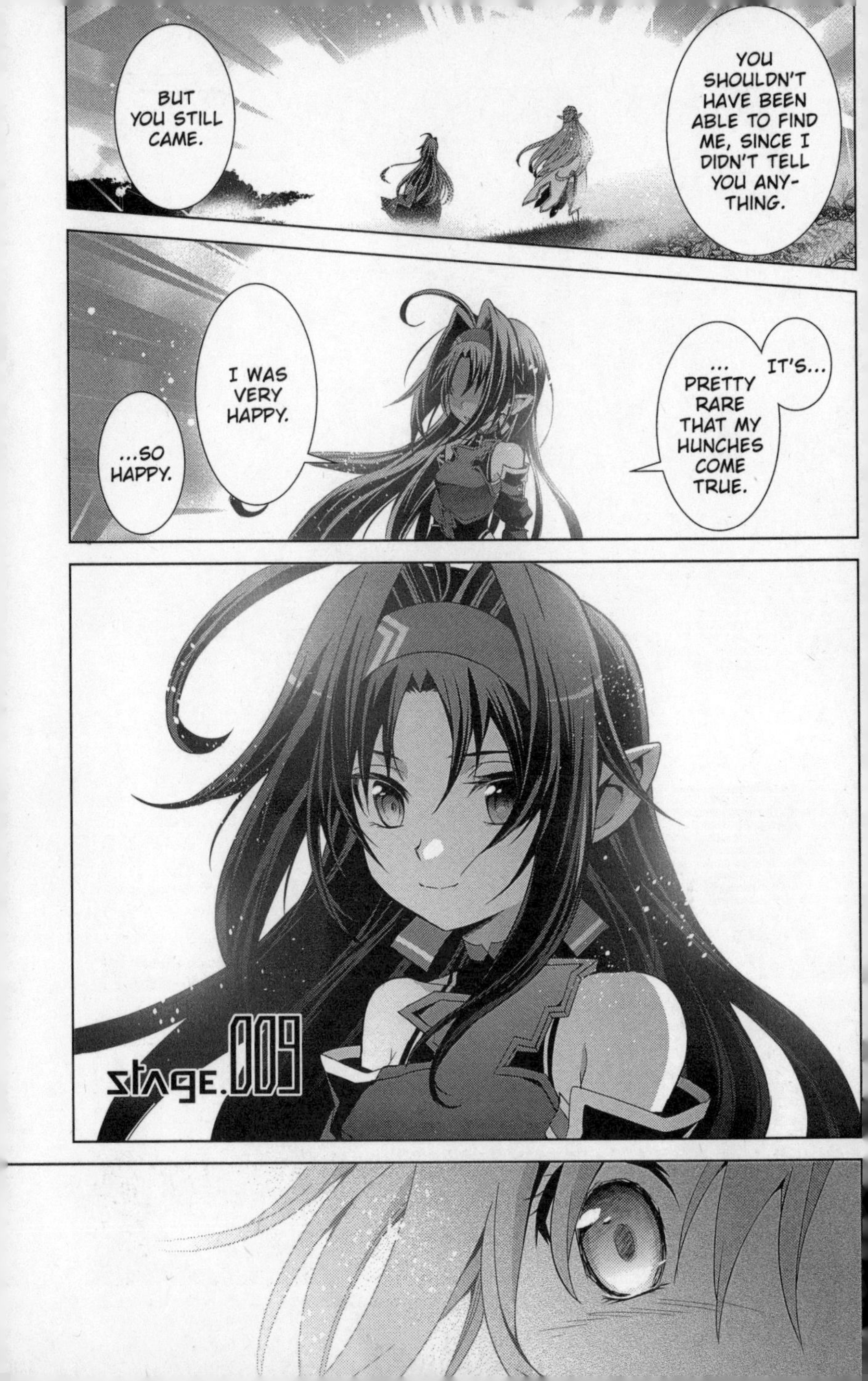
YOU SHOULDN'T HAVE BEEN ABLE TO FIND ME, SINCE I DIDN'T TELL YOU ANY-THING.
BUT YOU STILL CAME.
IT'S...
... PRETTY RARE THAT MY HUNCHES COME TRUE.
I WAS VERY HAPPY.
...SO HAPPY.
stage.009

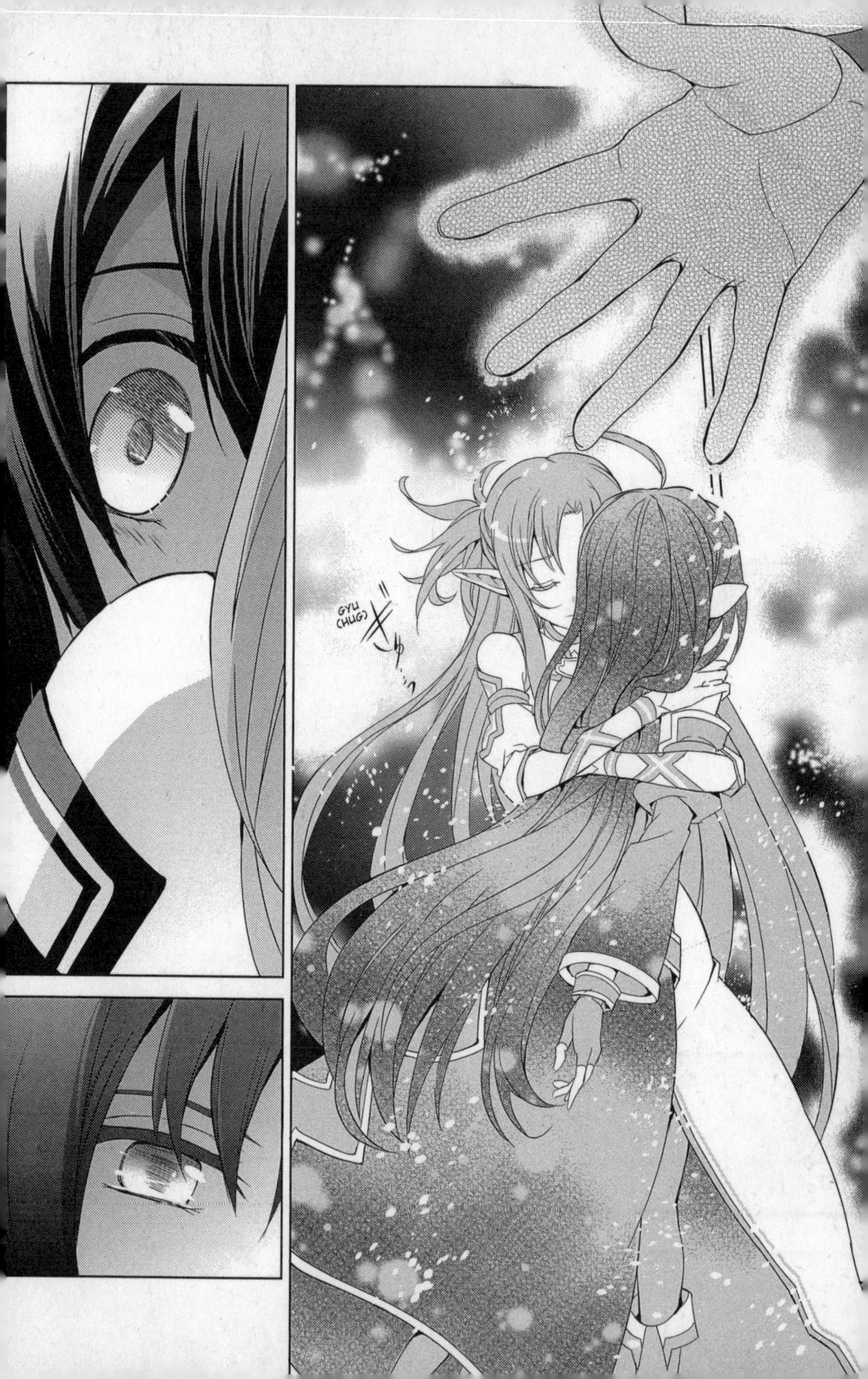
ぎゅ…っ
GYU (HUG)

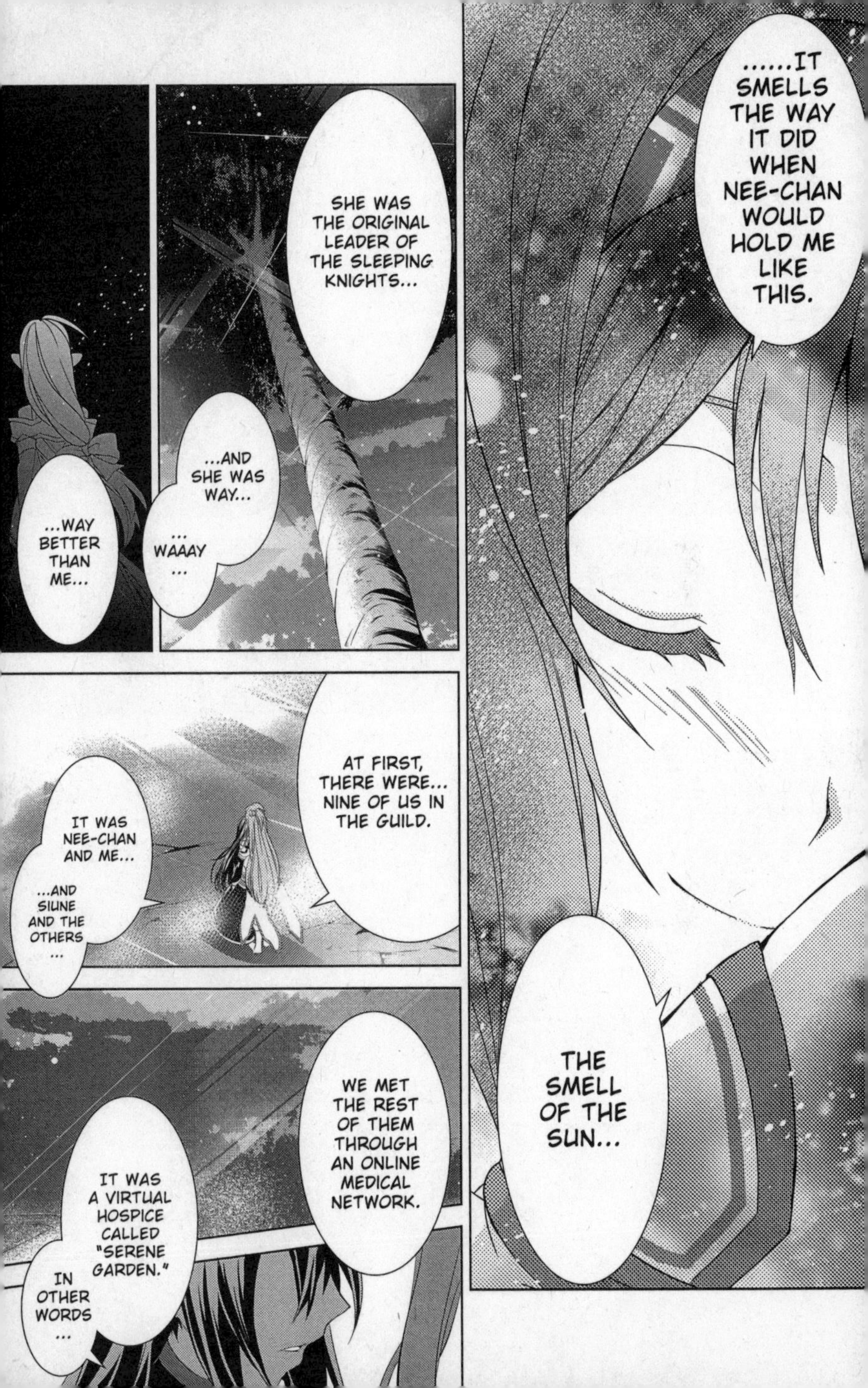
......IT SMELLS THE WAY IT DID WHEN NEE-CHAN WOULD HOLD ME LIKE THIS.
THE SMELL OF THE SUN...
SHE WAS THE ORIGINAL LEADER OF THE SLEEPING KNIGHTS...
...AND SHE WAS WAY...
... WAAAY ...
...WAY BETTER THAN ME...
AT FIRST, THERE WERE... NINE OF US IN THE GUILD.
IT WAS NEE-CHAN AND ME...
...AND SIUNE AND THE OTHERS ...
WE MET THE REST OF THEM THROUGH AN ONLINE MEDICAL NETWORK.
IT WAS A VIRTUAL HOSPICE CALLED "SERENE GARDEN."
IN OTHER WORDS ...

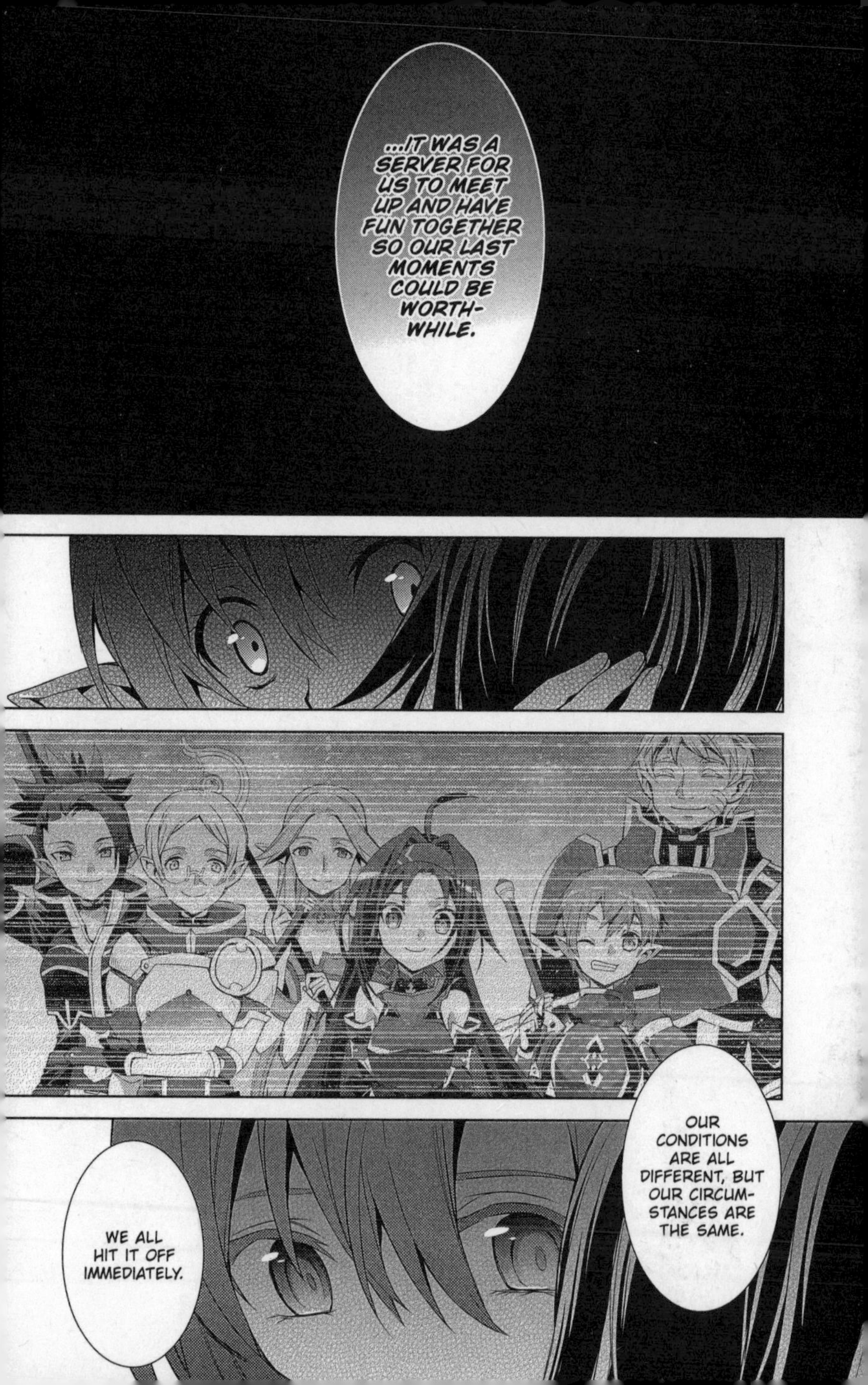
...IT WAS A SERVER FOR US TO MEET UP AND HAVE FUN TOGETHER SO OUR LAST MOMENTS COULD BE WORTH-WHILE.
OUR CONDITIONS ARE ALL DIFFERENT, BUT OUR CIRCUM-STANCES ARE THE SAME.
WE ALL HIT IT OFF IMMEDIATELY.

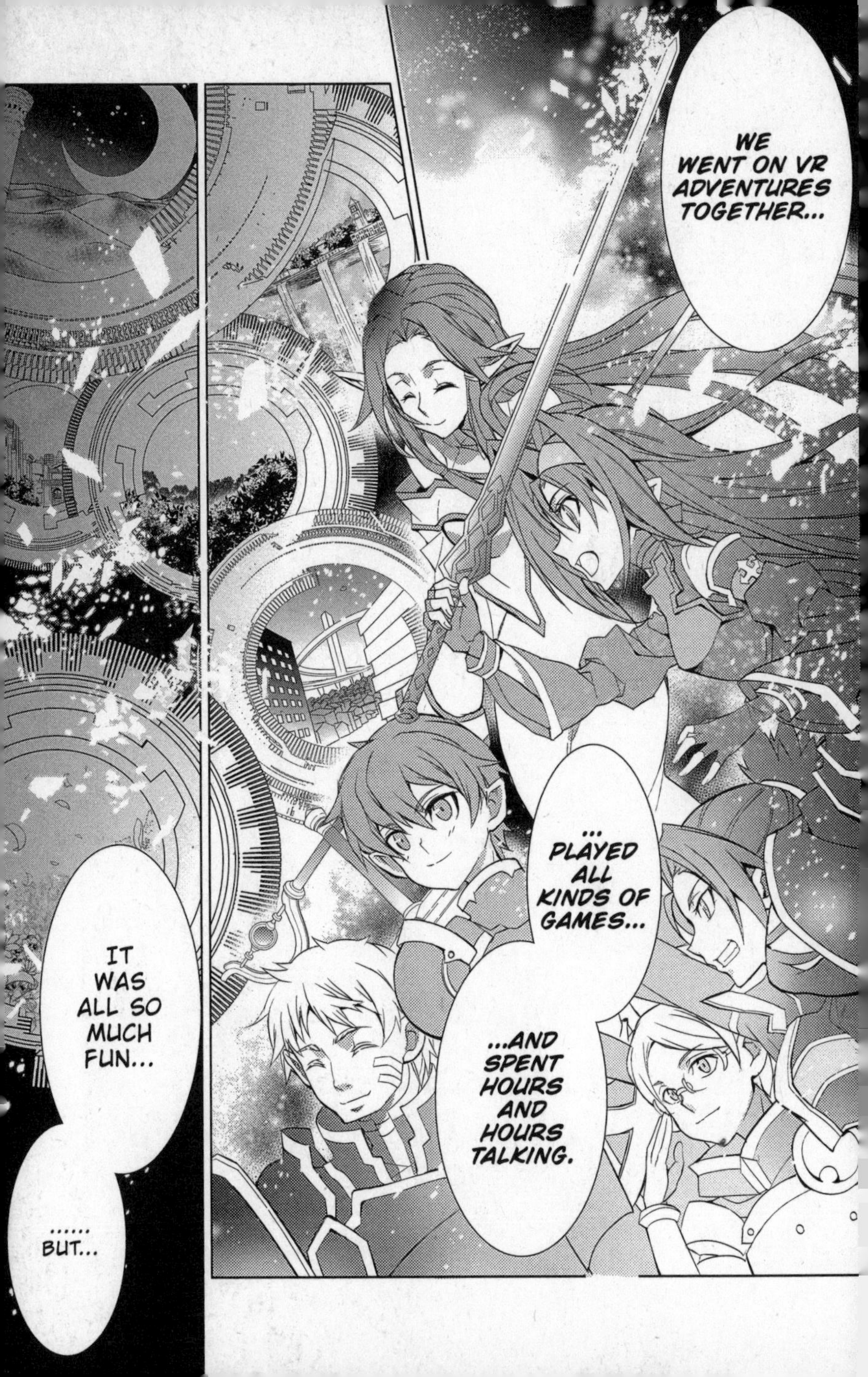
WE WENT ON VR ADVENTURES TOGETHER...
...PLAYED ALL KINDS OF GAMES...
...AND SPENT HOURS AND HOURS TALKING.
IT WAS ALL SO MUCH FUN...
...... BUT...

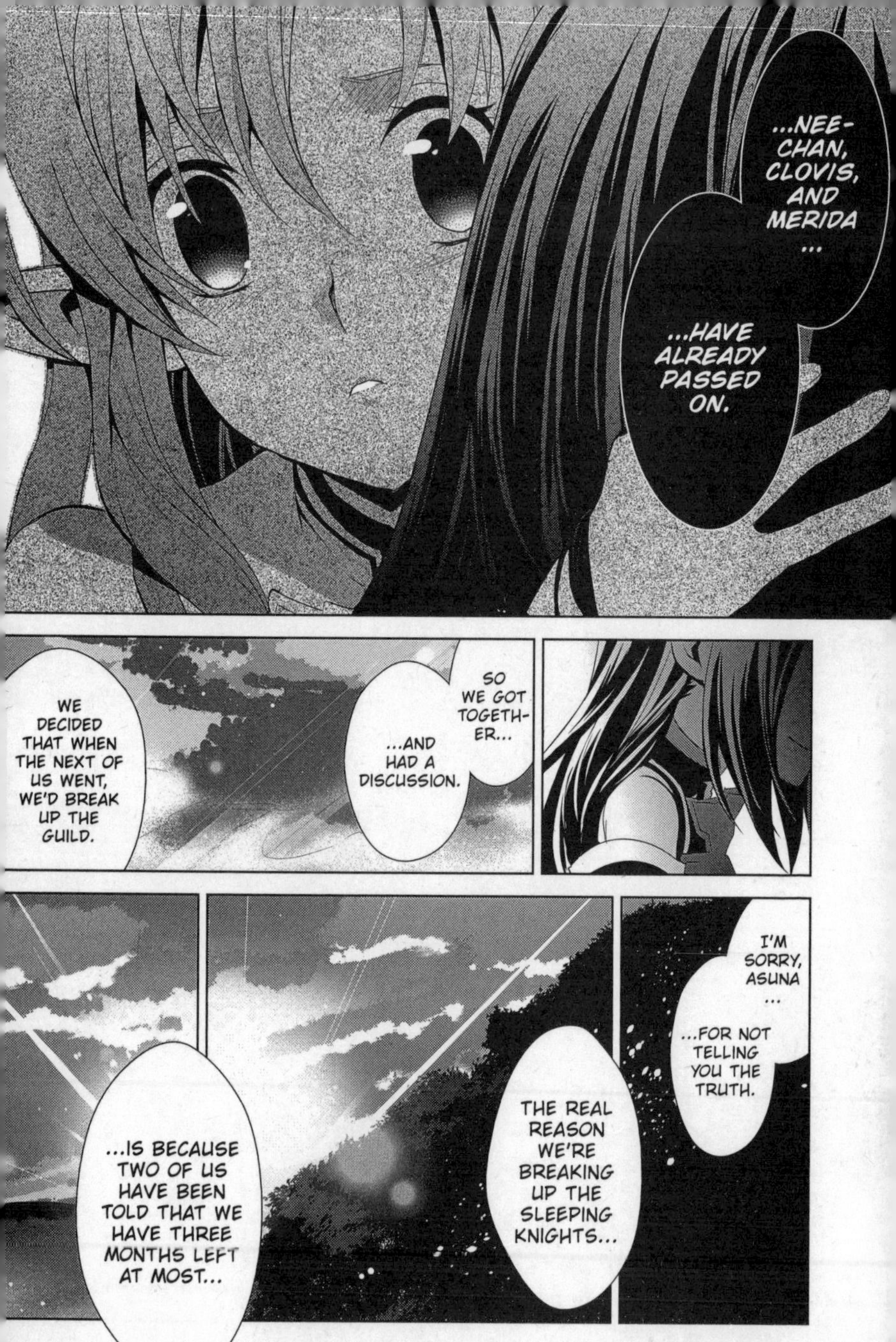
...NEE-CHAN, CLOVIS, AND MERIDA...
...HAVE ALREADY PASSED ON.
SO WE GOT TOGETHER...
...AND HAD A DISCUSSION.
WE DECIDED THAT WHEN THE NEXT OF US WENT, WE'D BREAK UP THE GUILD.
I'M SORRY, ASUNA...
...FOR NOT TELLING YOU THE TRUTH.
THE REAL REASON WE'RE BREAKING UP THE SLEEPING KNIGHTS...
...IS BECAUSE TWO OF US HAVE BEEN TOLD THAT WE HAVE THREE MONTHS LEFT AT MOST...

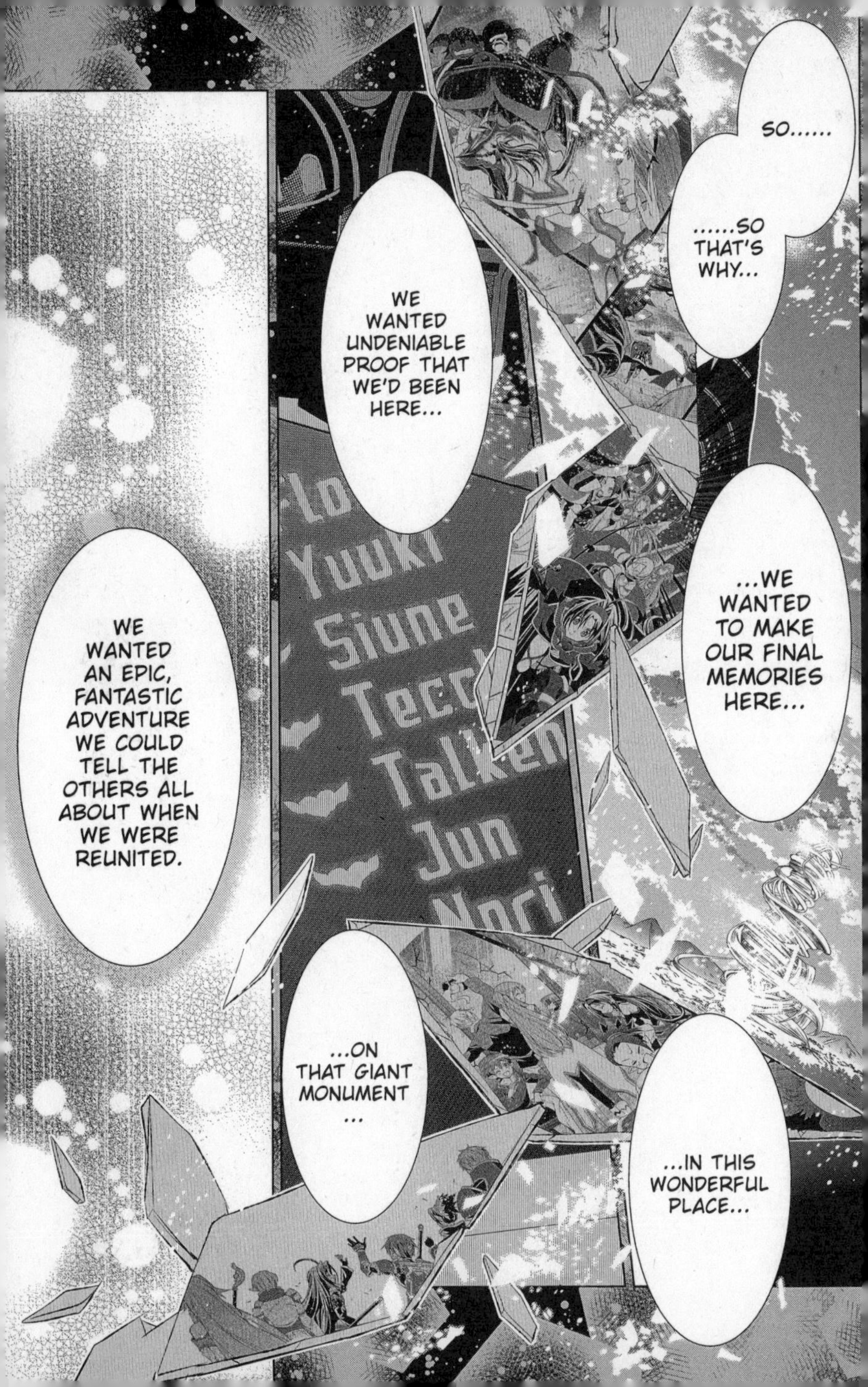
SO......
......SO THAT'S WHY...
WE WANTED UNDENIABLE PROOF THAT WE'D BEEN HERE...
...WE WANTED TO MAKE OUR FINAL MEMORIES HERE...
Yuuki
Siune
Talken
Jun
...ON THAT GIANT MONUMENT...
...IN THIS WONDERFUL PLACE...
WE WANTED AN EPIC, FANTASTIC ADVENTURE WE COULD TELL THE OTHERS ALL ABOUT WHEN WE WERE REUNITED.

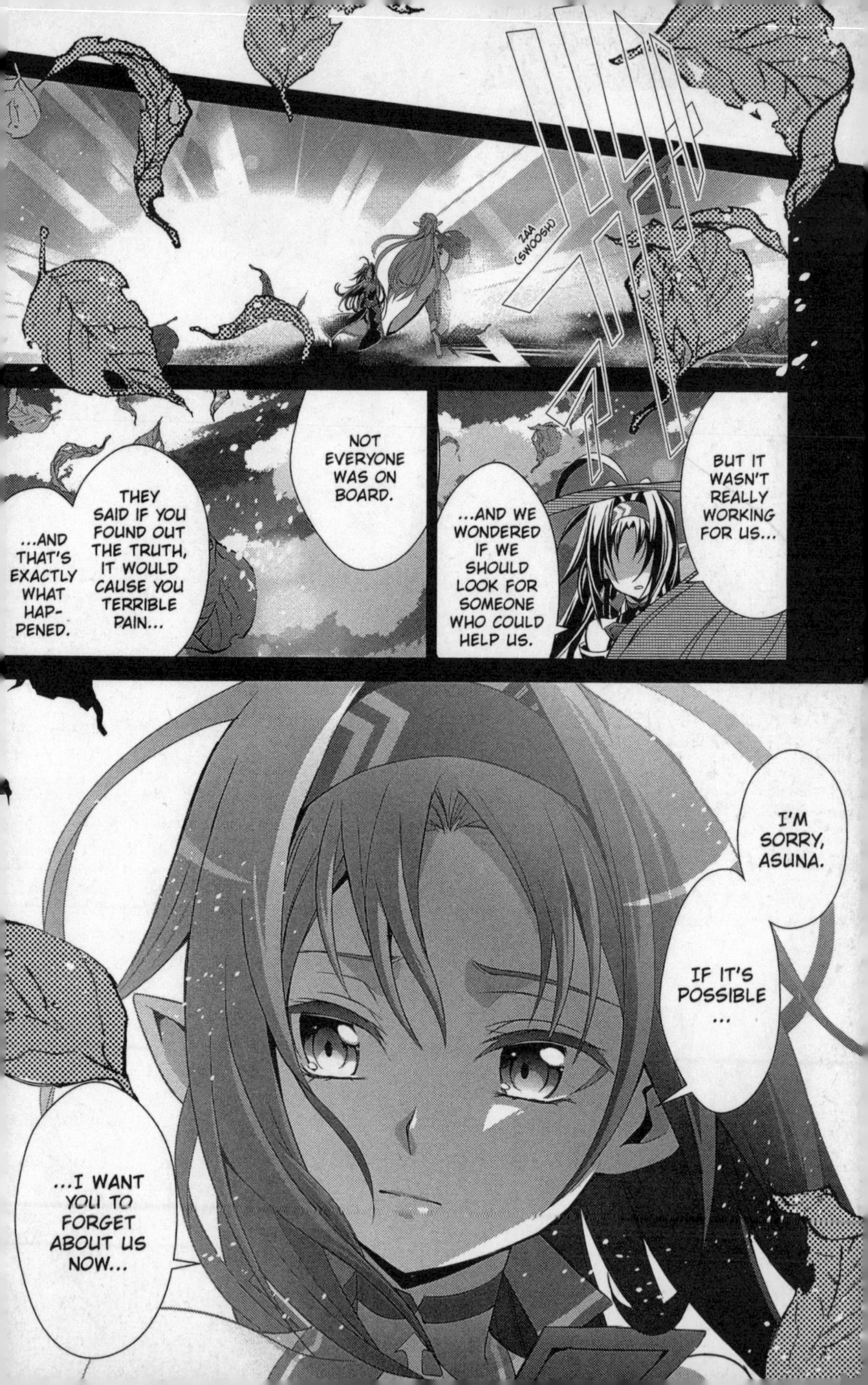
ZAA (SWOOSH)
BUT IT WASN'T REALLY WORKING FOR US...
...AND WE WONDERED IF WE SHOULD LOOK FOR SOMEONE WHO COULD HELP US.
NOT EVERYONE WAS ON BOARD.
THEY SAID IF YOU FOUND OUT THE TRUTH, IT WOULD CAUSE YOU TERRIBLE PAIN...
...AND THAT'S EXACTLY WHAT HAP-PENED.
I'M SORRY, ASUNA.
IF IT'S POSSIBLE...
...I WANT YOU TO FORGET ABOUT US NOW...

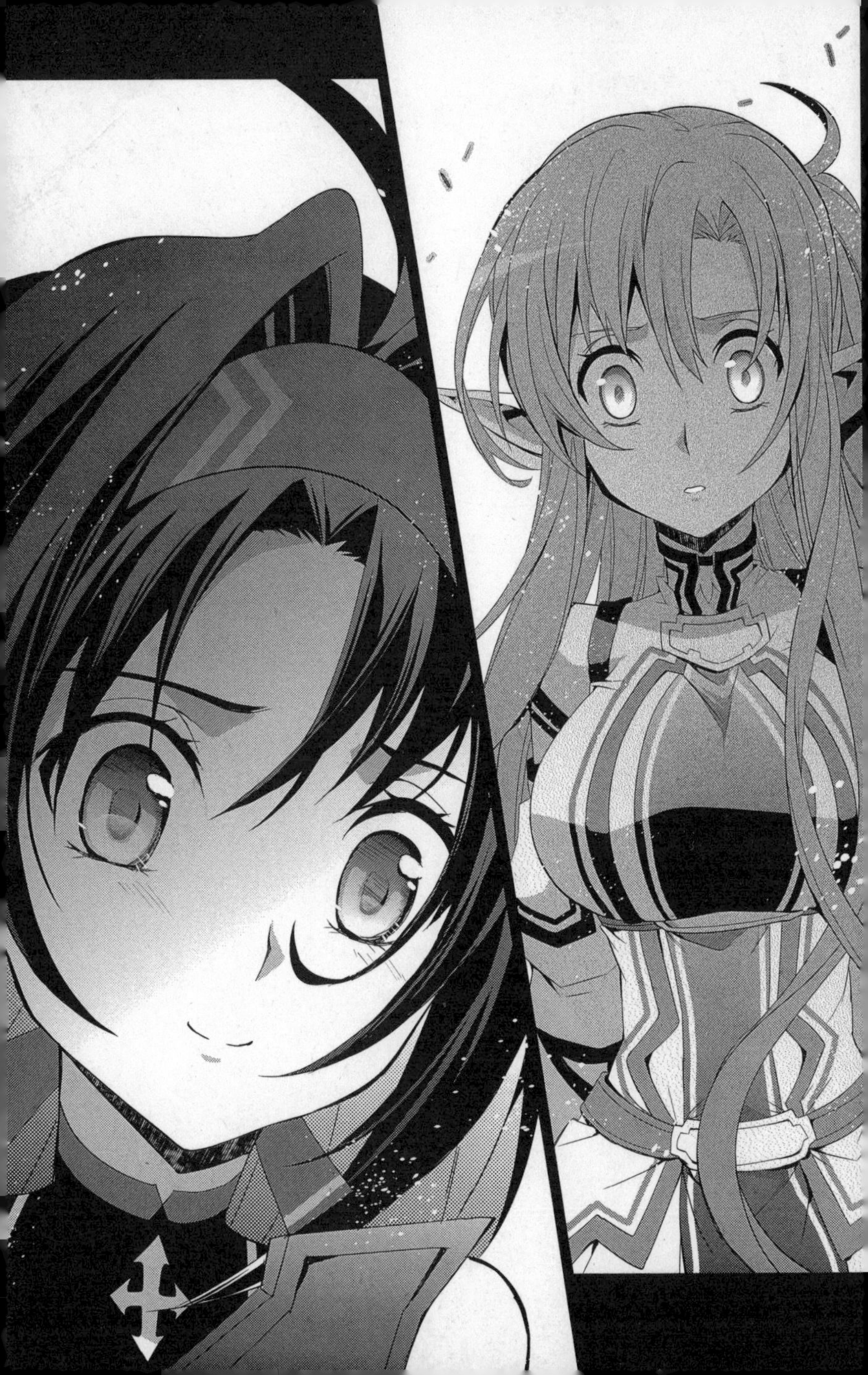

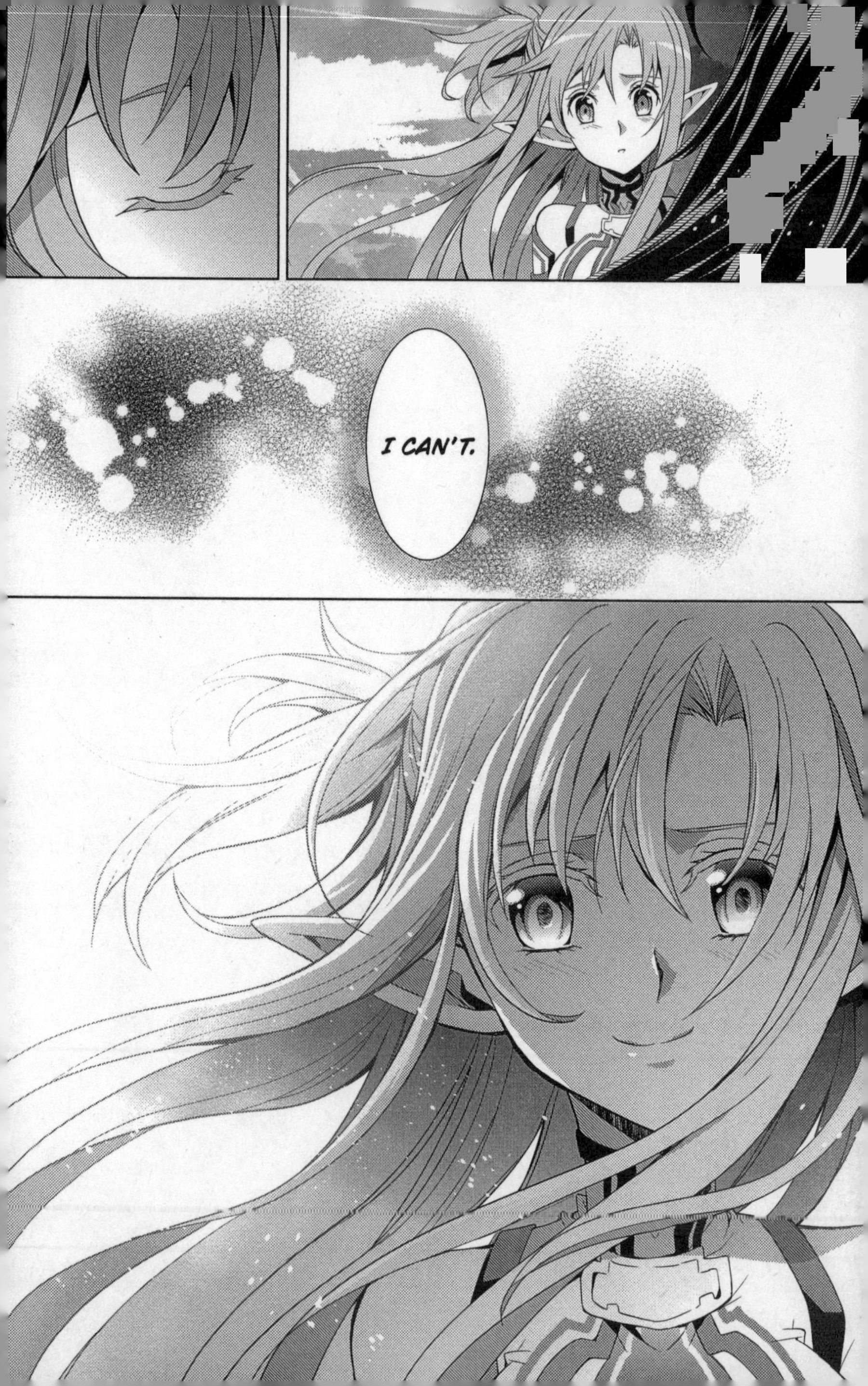
I CAN'T.

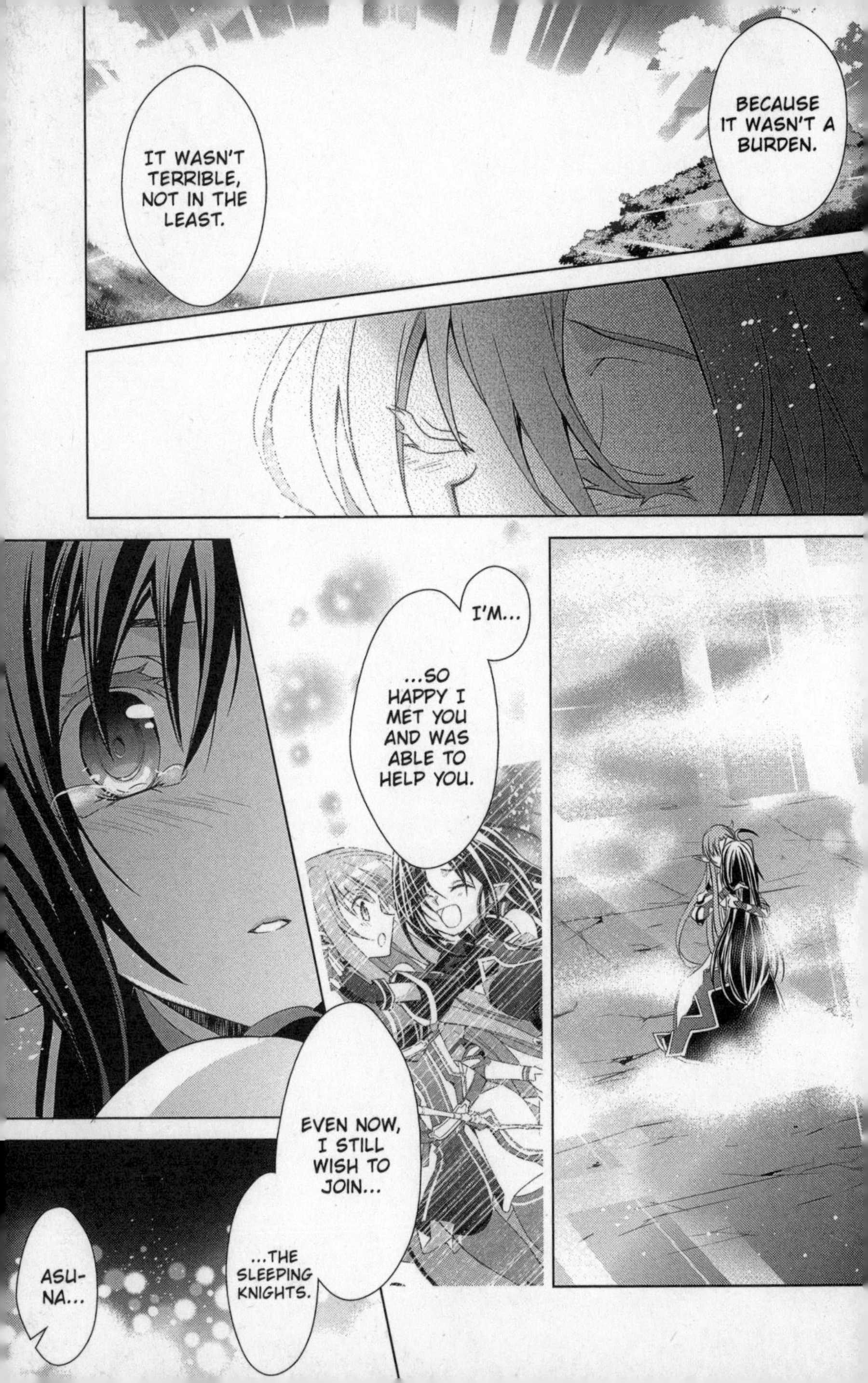
BECAUSE IT WASN'T A BURDEN.
IT WASN'T TERRIBLE, NOT IN THE LEAST.
I'M...
...SO HAPPY I MET YOU AND WAS ABLE TO HELP YOU.
EVEN NOW, I STILL WISH TO JOIN...
...THE SLEEPING KNIGHTS.
ASU-NA...

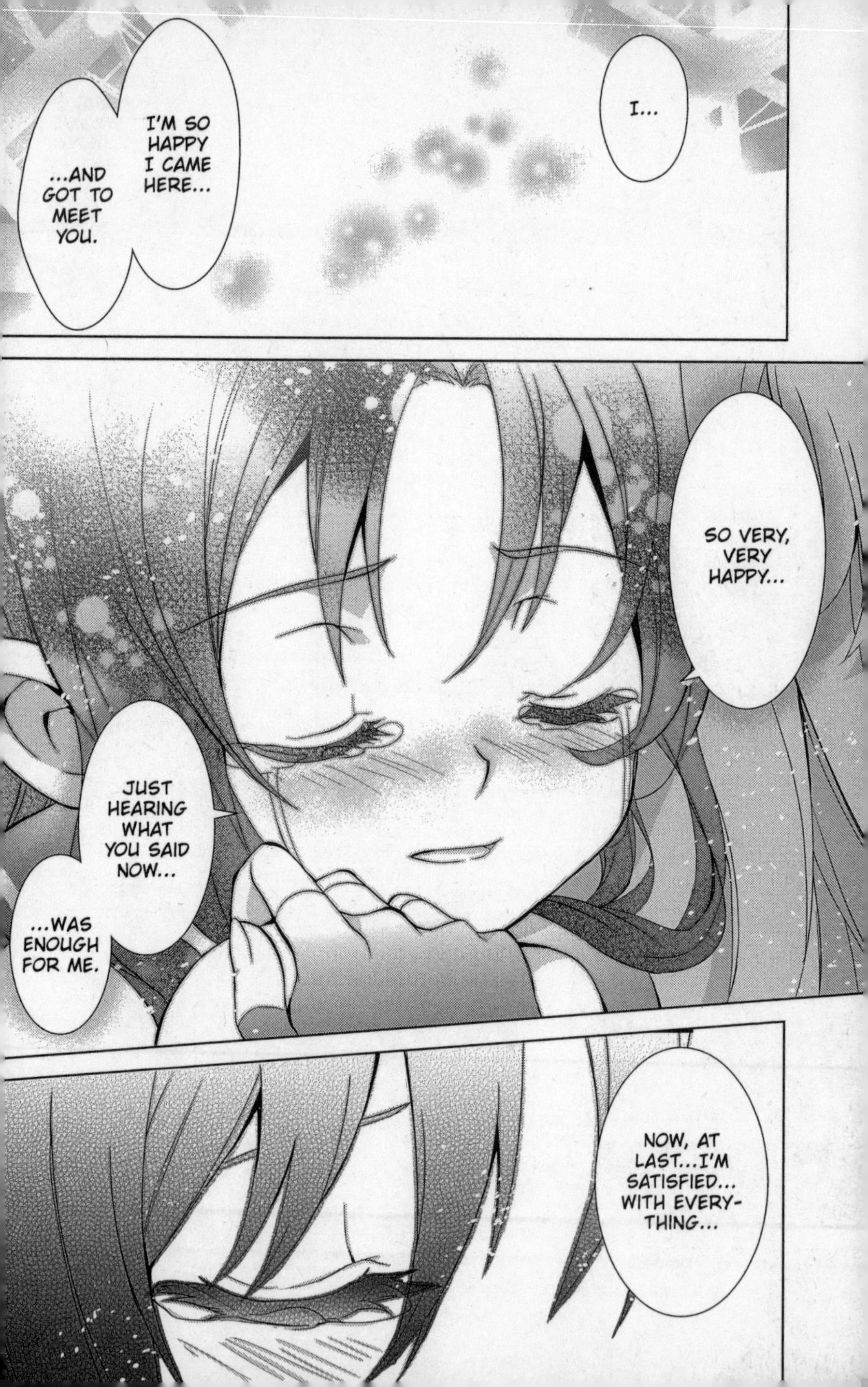
I...
I'M SO HAPPY I CAME HERE...
...AND GOT TO MEET YOU.
SO VERY, VERY HAPPY...
JUST HEARING WHAT YOU SAID NOW...
...WAS ENOUGH FOR ME.
NOW, AT LAST...I'M SATISFIED... WITH EVERY-THING...

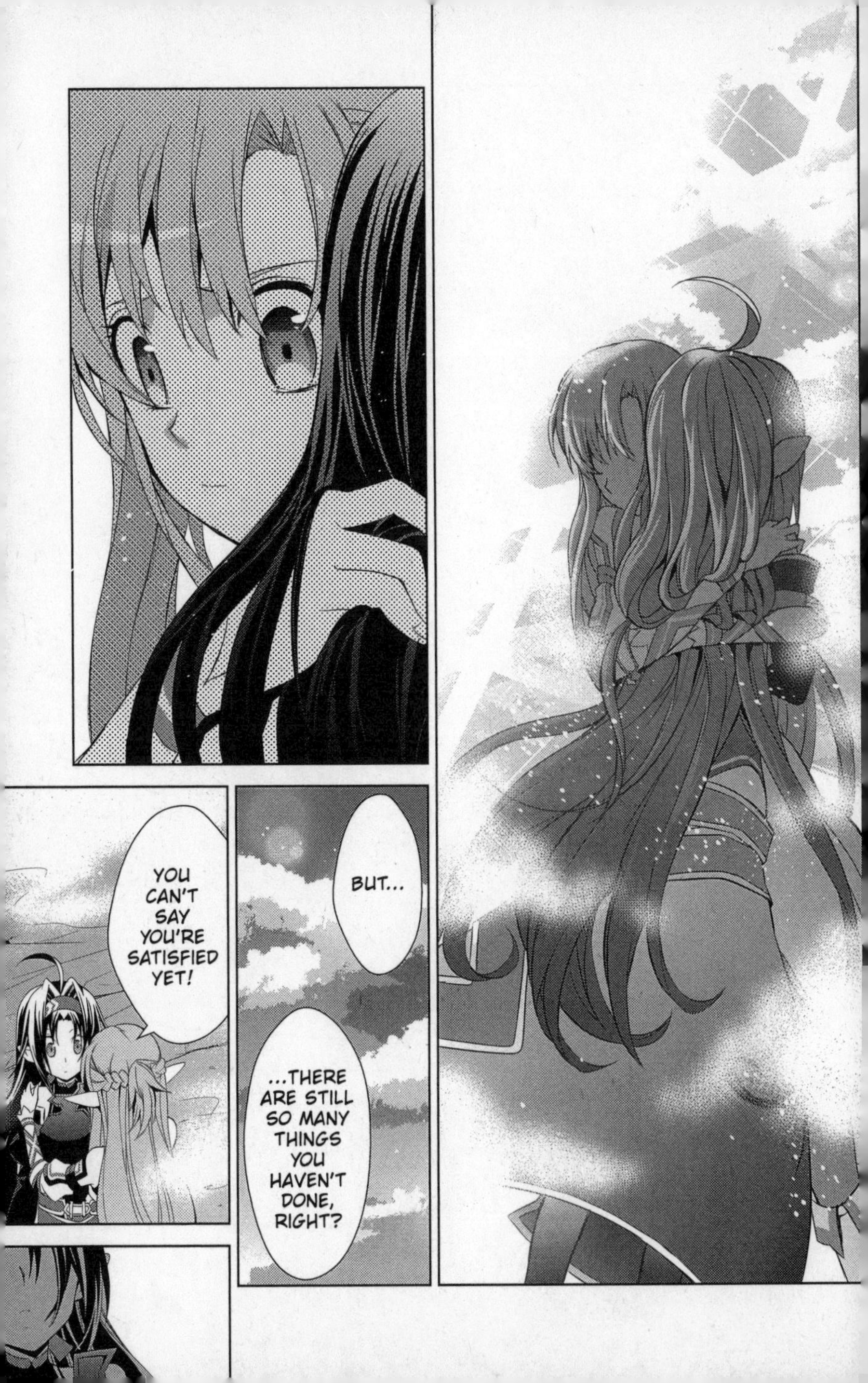
BUT...
...THERE ARE STILL SO MANY THINGS YOU HAVEN'T DONE, RIGHT?
YOU CAN'T SAY YOU'RE SATISFIED YET!

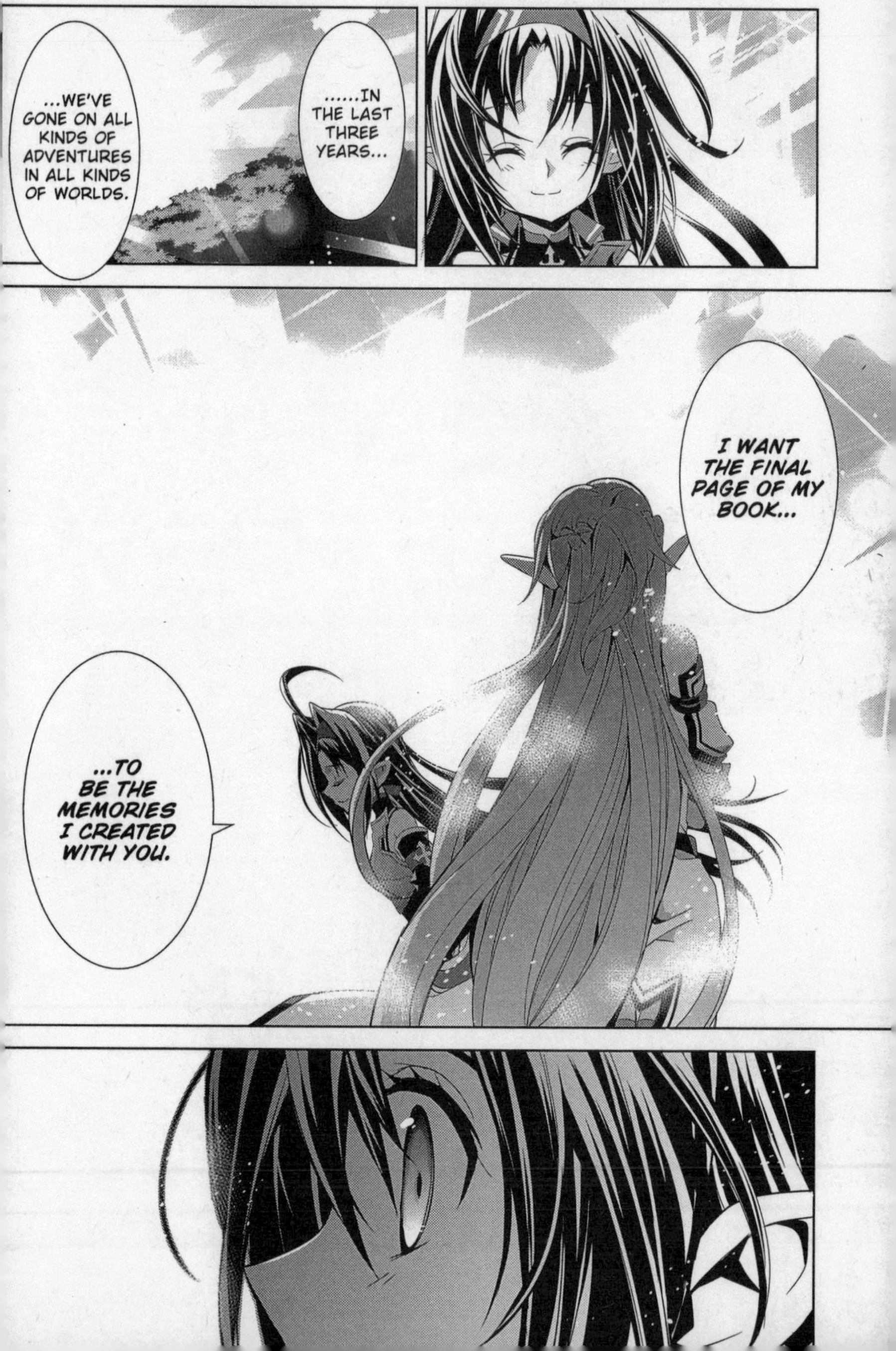
......IN THE LAST THREE YEARS...
...WE'VE GONE ON ALL KINDS OF ADVENTURES IN ALL KINDS OF WORLDS.
I WANT THE FINAL PAGE OF MY BOOK...
...TO BE THE MEMORIES I CREATED WITH YOU.

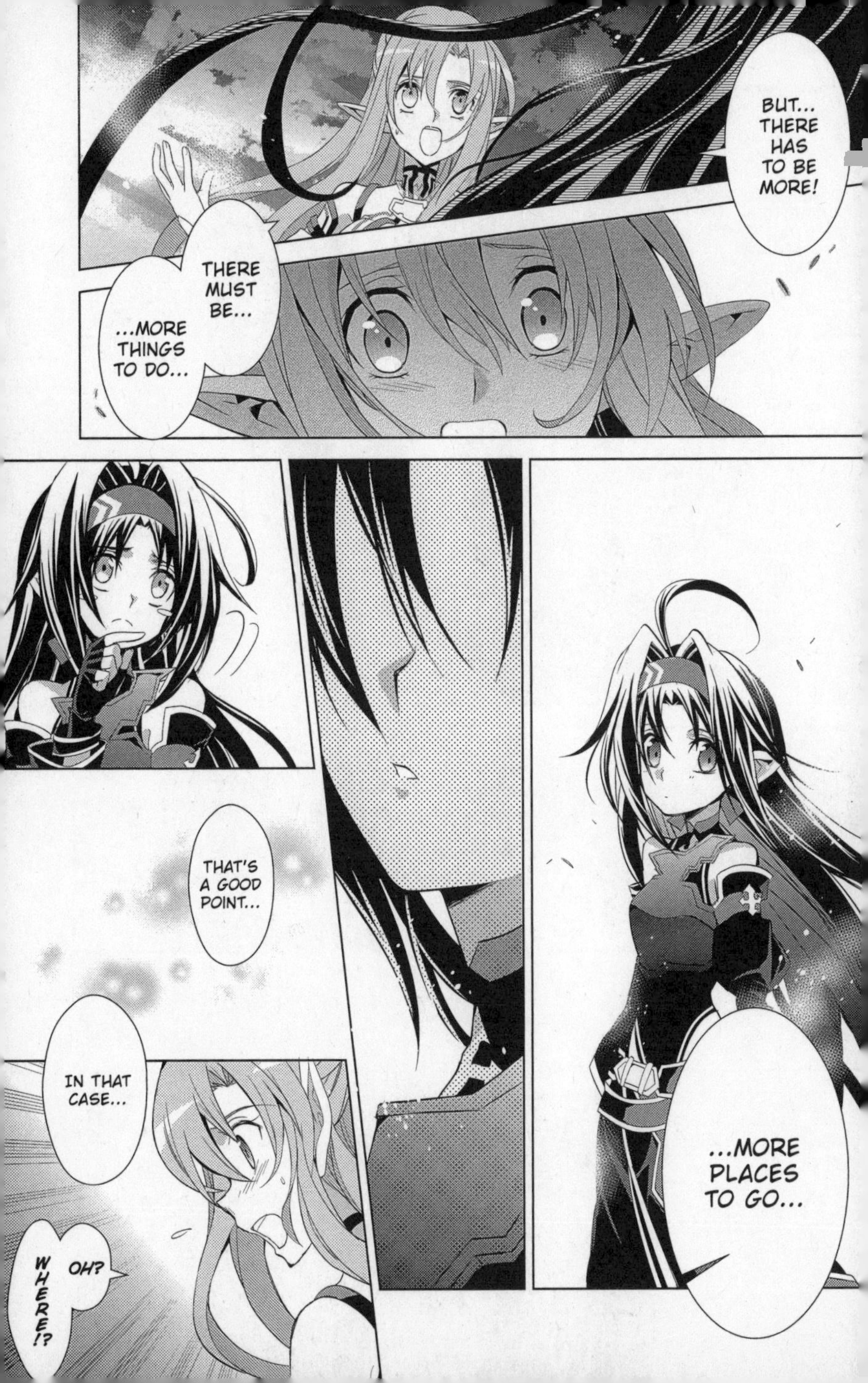
BUT... THERE HAS TO BE MORE!
THERE MUST BE...
...MORE THINGS TO DO...
...MORE PLACES TO GO...
THAT'S A GOOD POINT...
IN THAT CASE...
OH?
WHERE!?

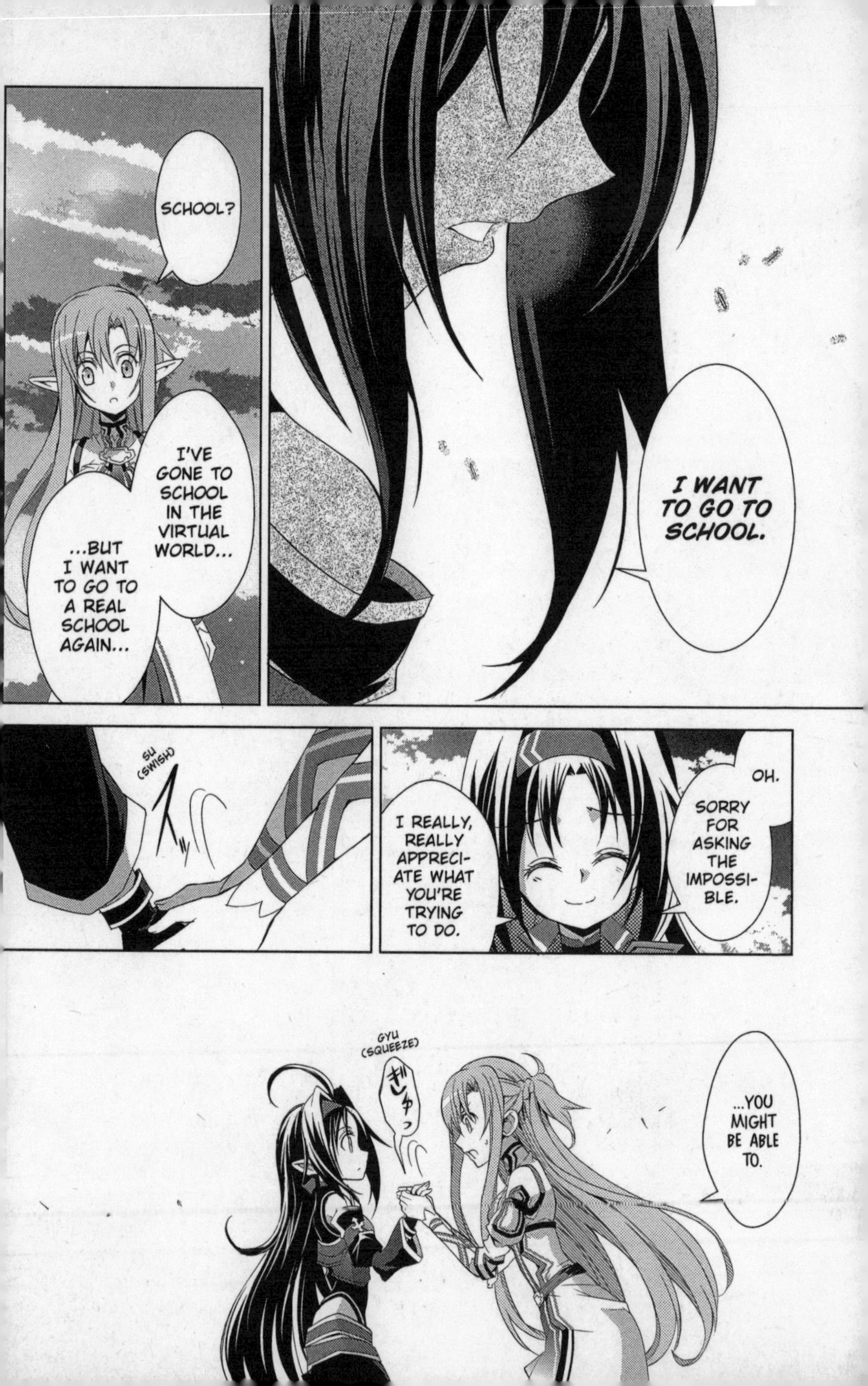
I WANT TO GO TO SCHOOL.
SCHOOL?
I'VE GONE TO SCHOOL IN THE VIRTUAL WORLD...
...BUT I WANT TO GO TO A REAL SCHOOL AGAIN...
OH.
SORRY FOR ASKING THE IMPOSSIBLE.
I REALLY, REALLY APPRECIATE WHAT YOU'RE TRYING TO DO.
SU (SWISH)
...YOU MIGHT BE ABLE TO.
GYU (SQUEEZE)
ぎゅっ

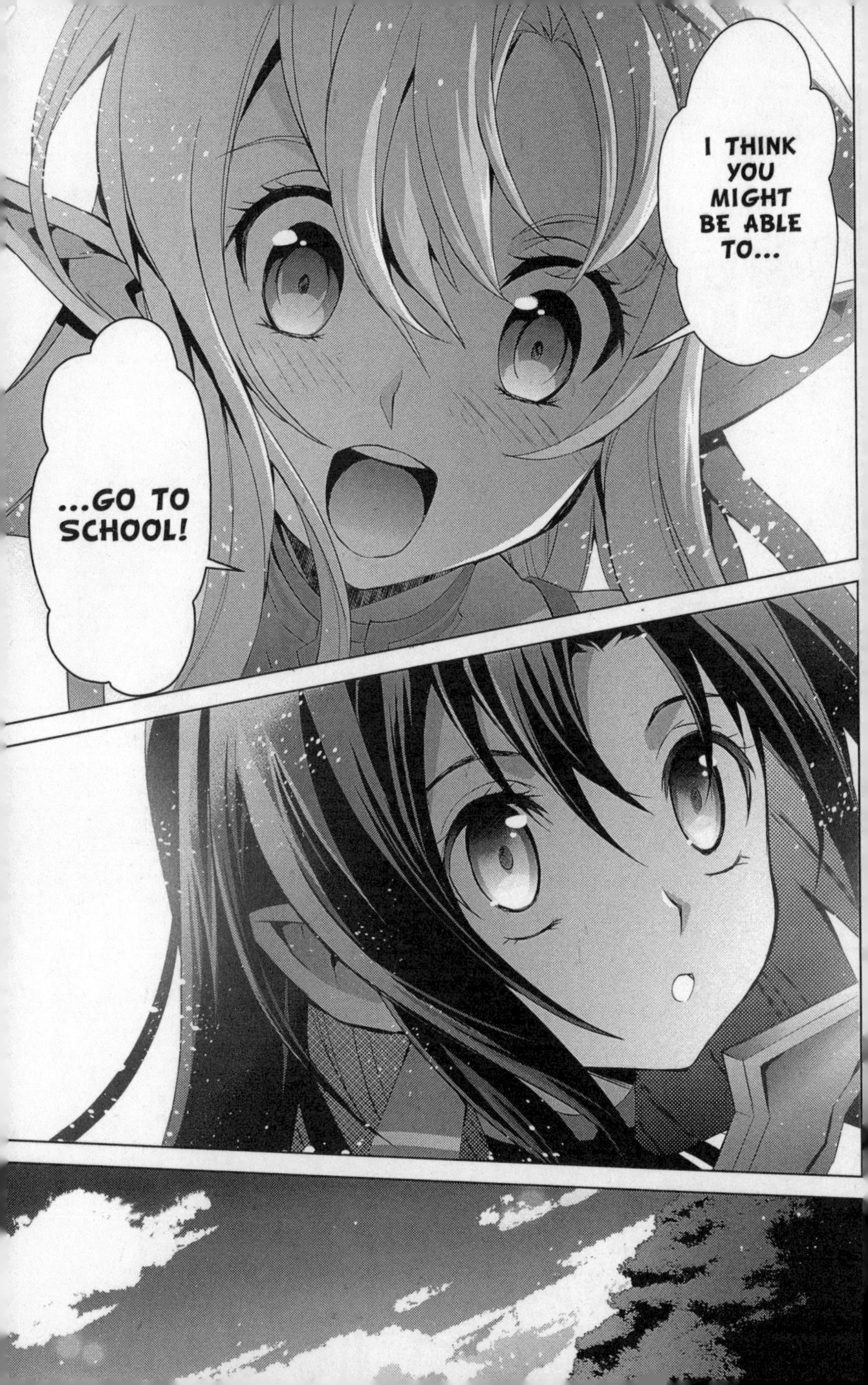
I THINK YOU MIGHT BE ABLE TO...
...GO TO SCHOOL!

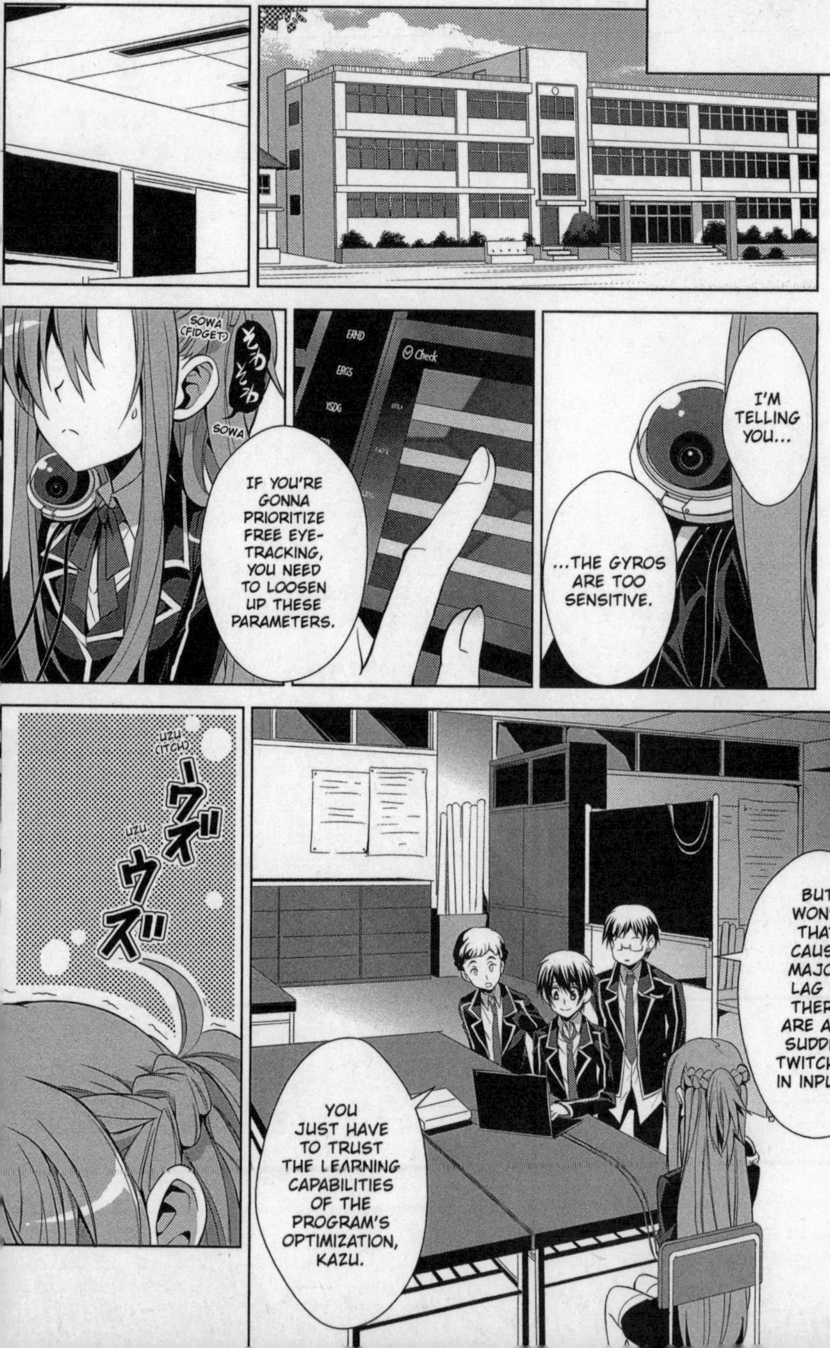
I'M TELLING YOU...
...THE GYROS ARE TOO SENSITIVE.
ERHD
ERGS
YSDG
Check
IF YOU'RE GONNA PRIORITIZE FREE EYE-TRACKING, YOU NEED TO LOOSEN UP THESE PARAMETERS.
SOWA (FIDGET)
そわそわ
SOWA
BUT WON'T THAT CAUSE MAJOR LAG IF THERE ARE ANY SUDDEN TWITCHES IN INPUT?
YOU JUST HAVE TO TRUST THE LEARNING CAPABILITIES OF THE PROGRAM'S OPTIMIZATION, KAZU.
UZU (ITCH)
ウズ
UZU
ウズ

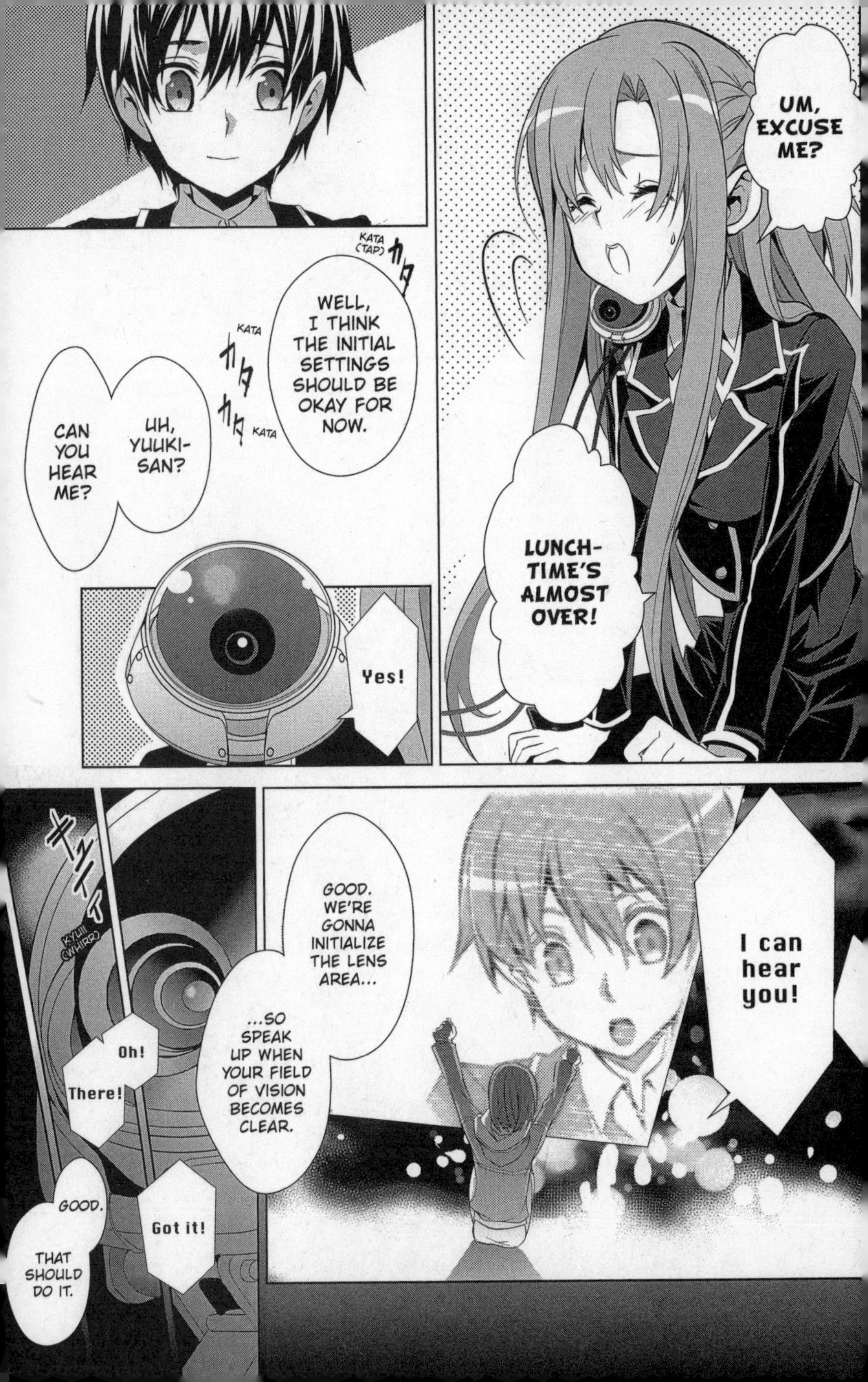
UM, EXCUSE ME?
LUNCH-TIME'S ALMOST OVER!
KATA (TAP) カタ
WELL, I THINK THE INITIAL SETTINGS SHOULD BE OKAY FOR NOW.
KATA カタ
カタ KATA
UH, YUUKI-SAN?
CAN YOU HEAR ME?
Yes!
I can hear you!
GOOD. WE'RE GONNA INITIALIZE THE LENS AREA...
...SO SPEAK UP WHEN YOUR FIELD OF VISION BECOMES CLEAR.
KYUII (WHIRR)
Oh!
There!
Got it!
GOOD.
THAT SHOULD DO IT.

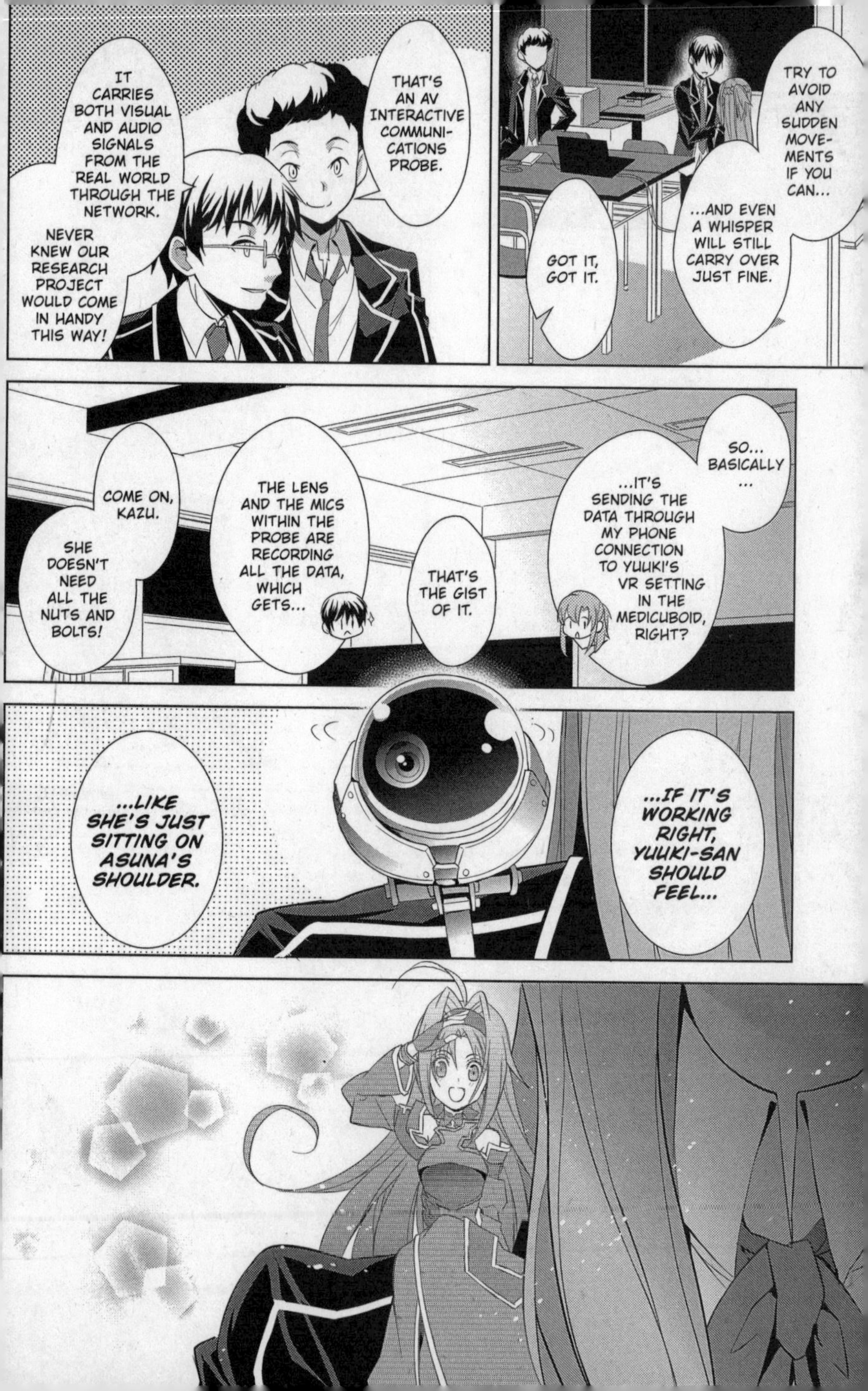
TRY TO AVOID ANY SUDDEN MOVEMENTS IF YOU CAN...
...AND EVEN A WHISPER WILL STILL CARRY OVER JUST FINE.
GOT IT, GOT IT.
THAT'S AN AV INTERACTIVE COMMUNICATIONS PROBE.
IT CARRIES BOTH VISUAL AND AUDIO SIGNALS FROM THE REAL WORLD THROUGH THE NETWORK.
NEVER KNEW OUR RESEARCH PROJECT WOULD COME IN HANDY THIS WAY!
SO... BASICALLY...
...IT'S SENDING THE DATA THROUGH MY PHONE CONNECTION TO YUUKI'S VR SETTING IN THE MEDICUBOID, RIGHT?
THAT'S THE GIST OF IT.
THE LENS AND THE MICS WITHIN THE PROBE ARE RECORDING ALL THE DATA, WHICH GETS...
COME ON, KAZU.
SHE DOESN'T NEED ALL THE NUTS AND BOLTS!
...IF IT'S WORKING RIGHT, YUUKI-SAN SHOULD FEEL...
...LIKE SHE'S JUST SITTING ON ASUNA'S SHOULDER.

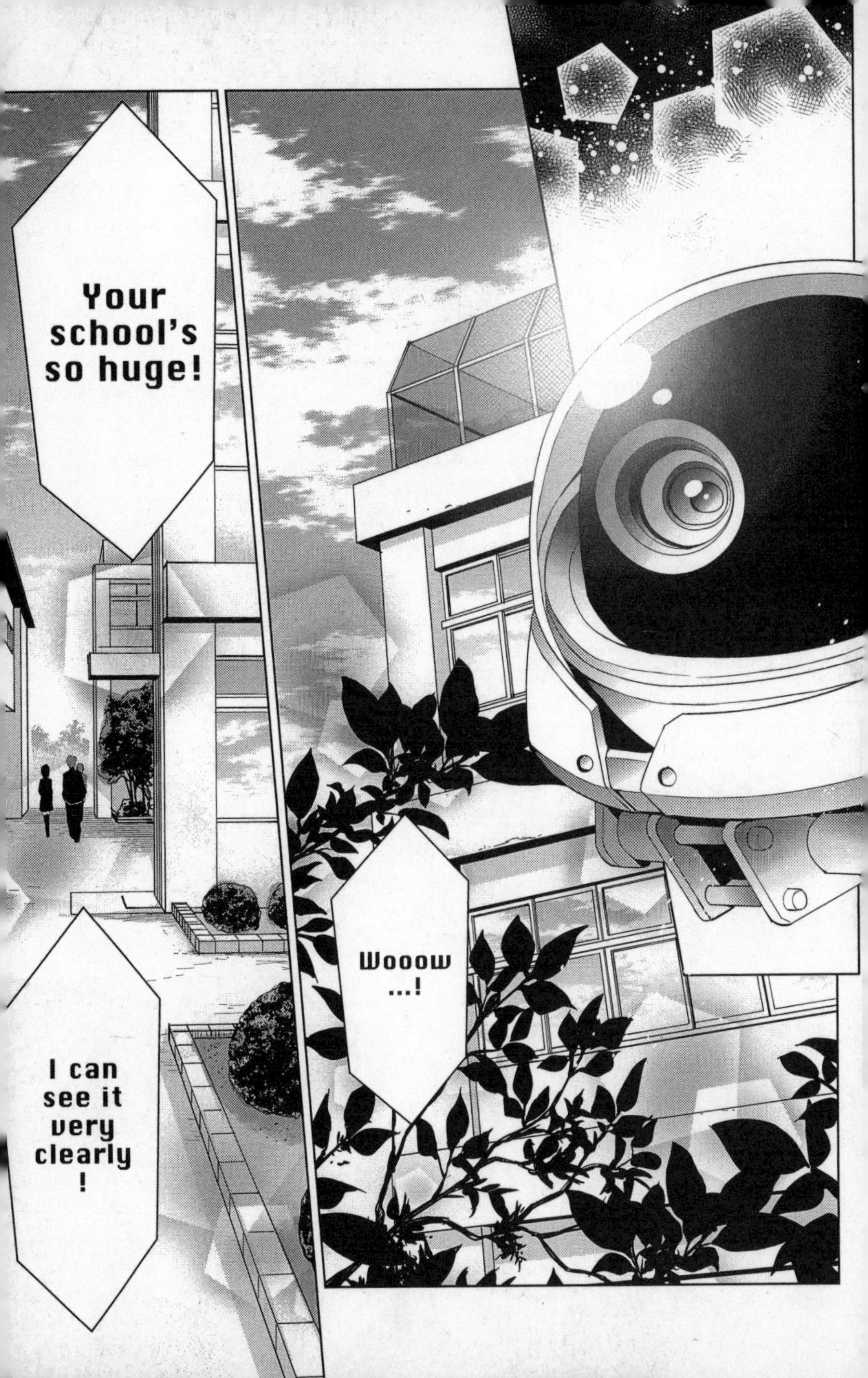
Wooow ...!
Your school's so huge!
I can see it very clearly!

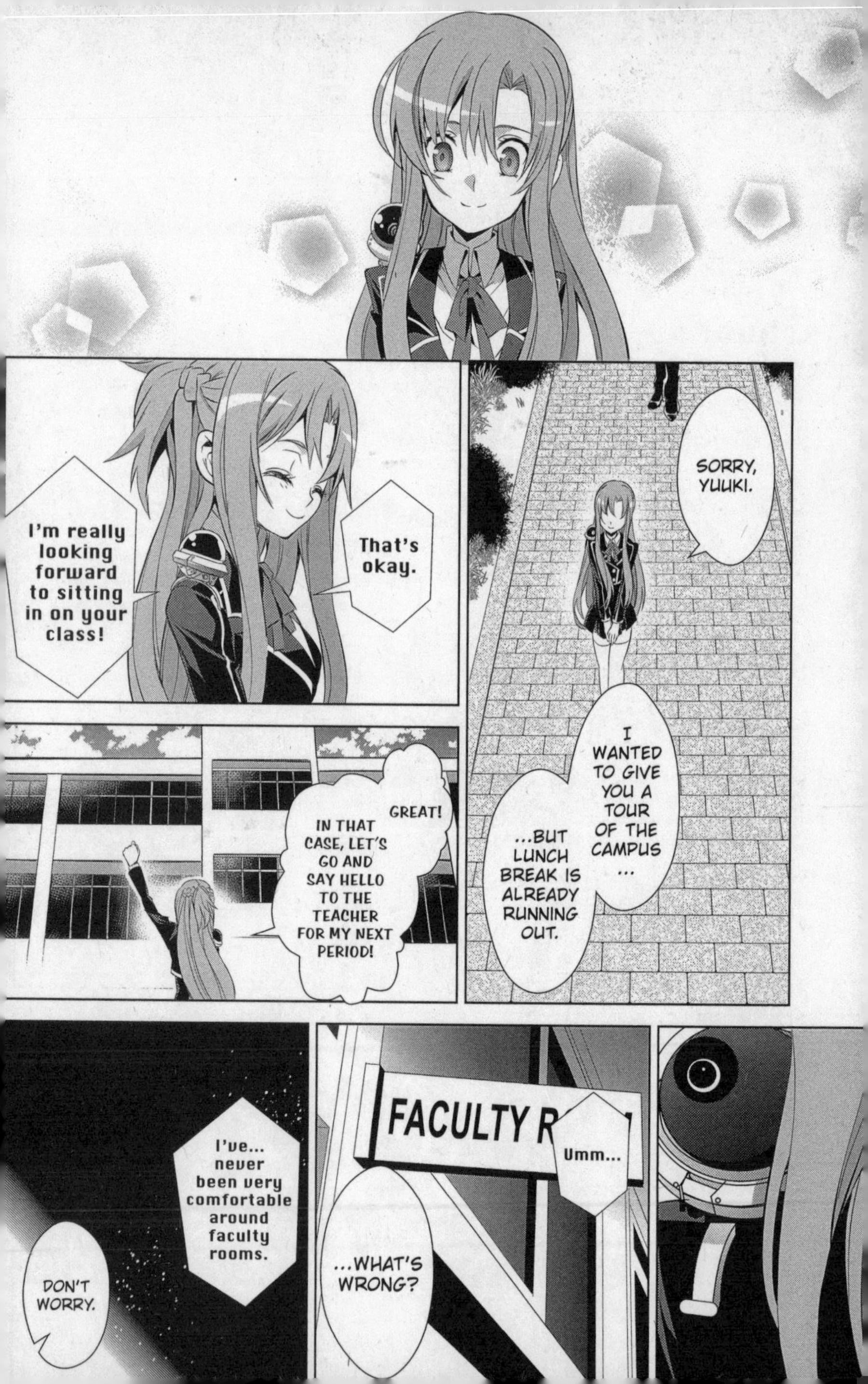
SORRY, YUUKI.
I WANTED TO GIVE YOU A TOUR OF THE CAMPUS...
...BUT LUNCH BREAK IS ALREADY RUNNING OUT.
That's okay.
I'm really looking forward to sitting in on your class!
GREAT!
IN THAT CASE, LET'S GO AND SAY HELLO TO THE TEACHER FOR MY NEXT PERIOD!
FACULTY R
Umm...
...WHAT'S WRONG?
I've... never been very comfortable around faculty rooms.
DON'T WORRY.

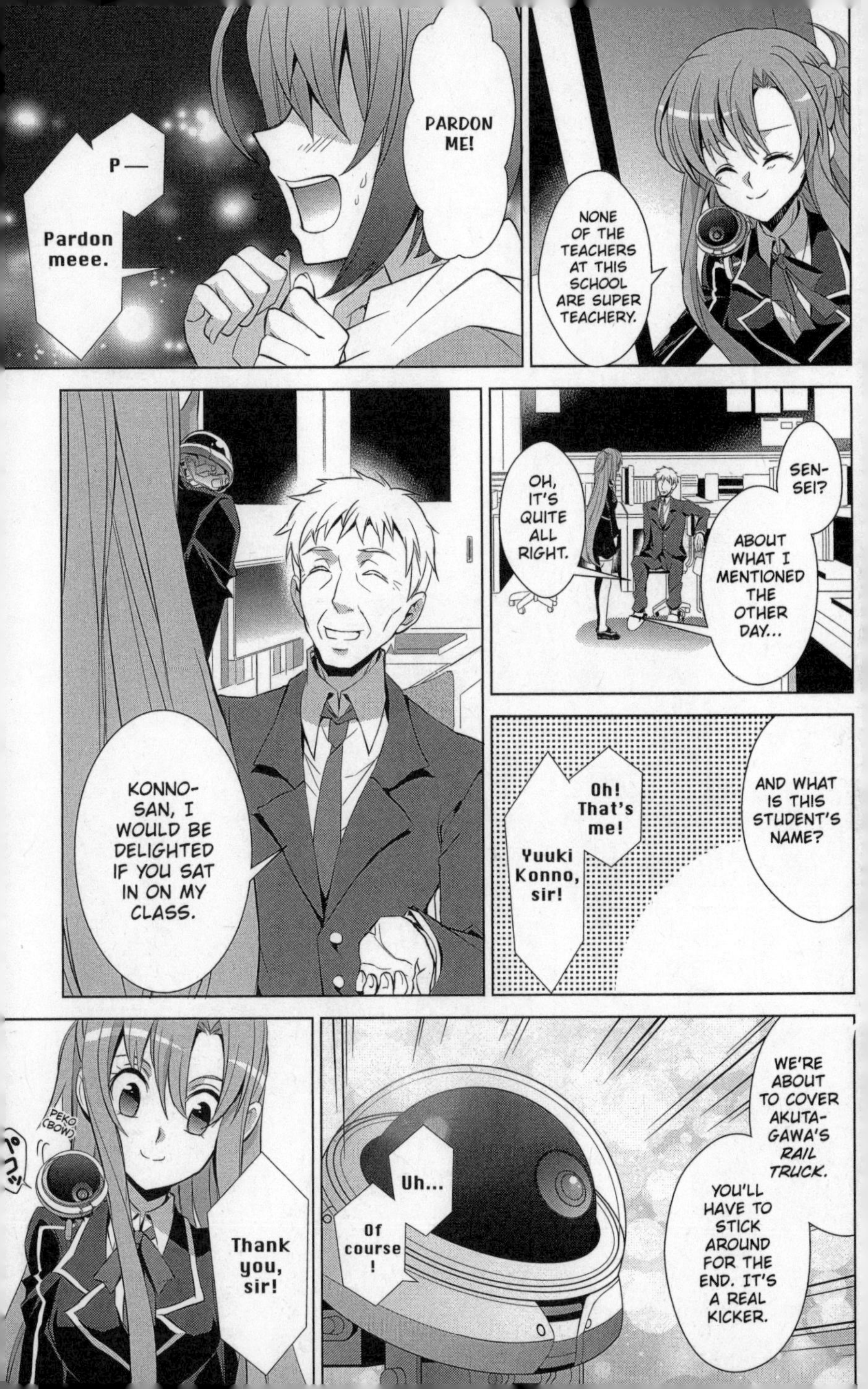
NONE OF THE TEACHERS AT THIS SCHOOL ARE SUPER TEACHERY.
PARDON ME!
P—
Pardon meee.
SEN-SEI?
ABOUT WHAT I MENTIONED THE OTHER DAY...
OH, IT'S QUITE ALL RIGHT.
AND WHAT IS THIS STUDENT'S NAME?
Oh! That's me!
Yuuki Konno, sir!
KONNO-SAN, I WOULD BE DELIGHTED IF YOU SAT IN ON MY CLASS.
WE'RE ABOUT TO COVER AKUTAGAWA'S *RAIL TRUCK*.
YOU'LL HAVE TO STICK AROUND FOR THE END. IT'S A REAL KICKER.
Uh...
Of course!
Thank you, sir!
PEKO (BOW)

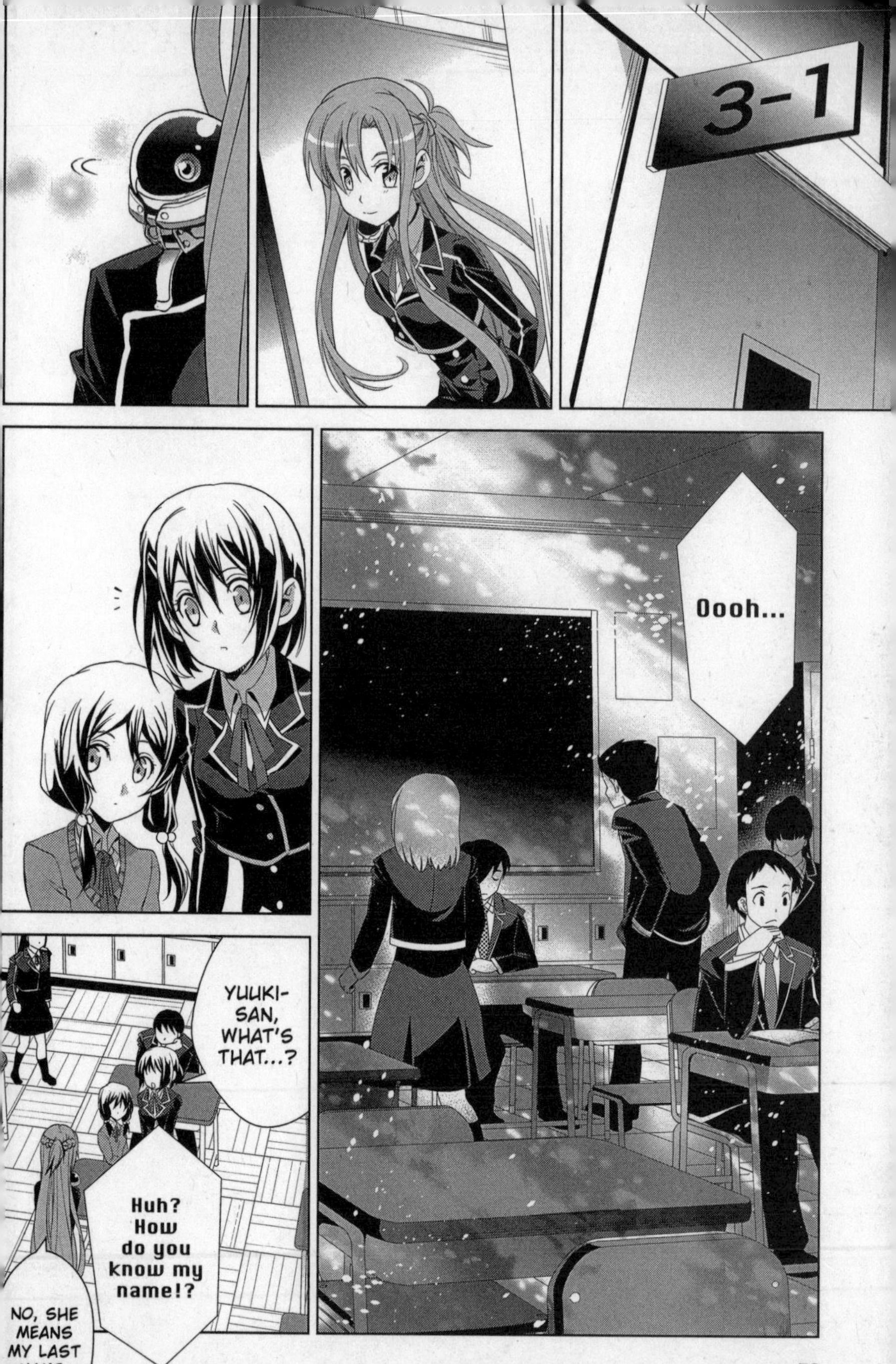
3-1
Oooh...
YUUKI-SAN, WHAT'S THAT...?
Huh? How do you know my name!?
NO, SHE MEANS MY LAST NAME.

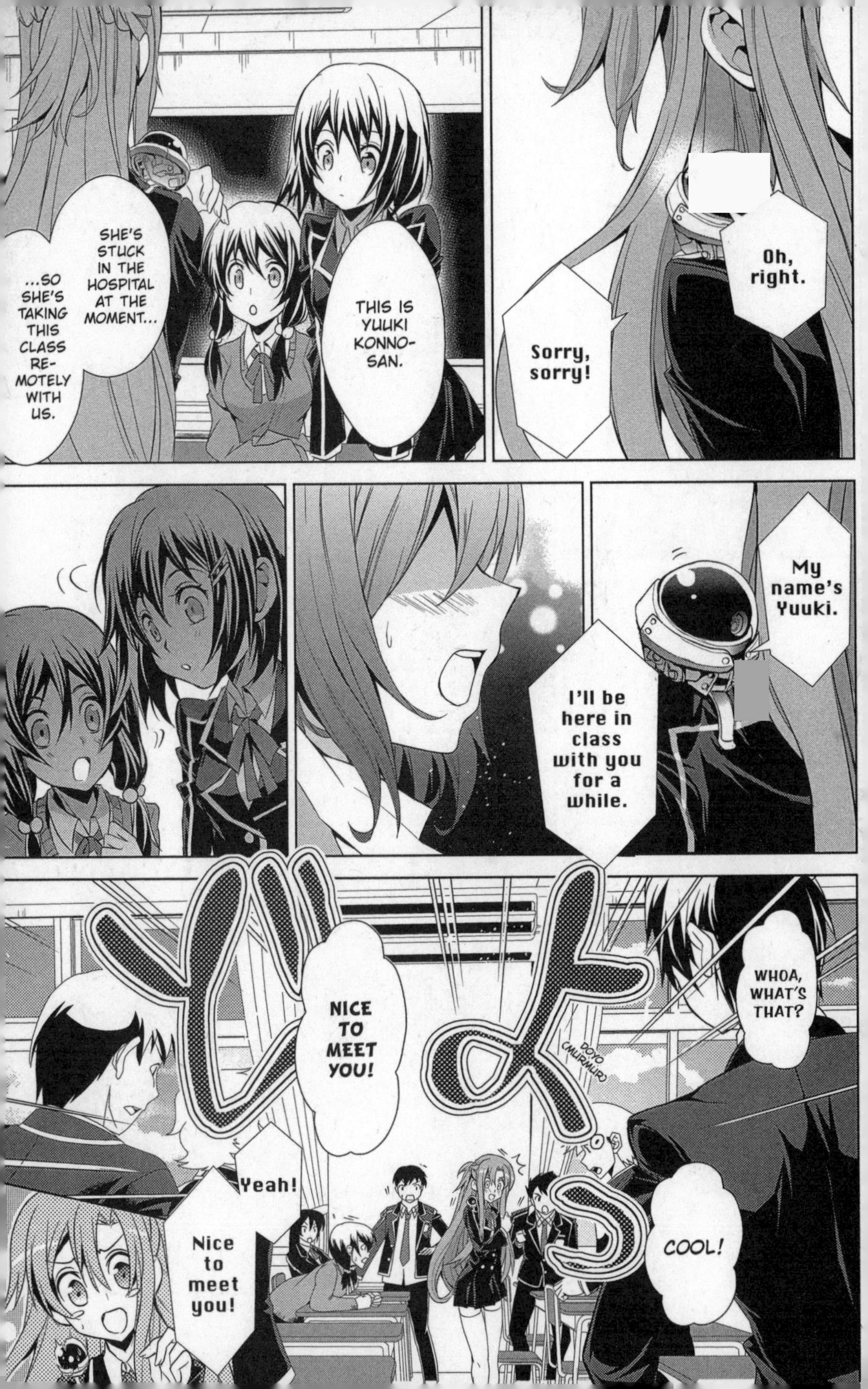
Oh, right.
Sorry, sorry!
THIS IS YUUKI KONNO-SAN.
SHE'S STUCK IN THE HOSPITAL AT THE MOMENT...
...SO SHE'S TAKING THIS CLASS REMOTELY WITH US.
My name's Yuuki.
I'll be here in class with you for a while.
WHOA, WHAT'S THAT?
DOYO (MURMUR)
COOL!
NICE TO MEET YOU!
Yeah!
Nice to meet you!

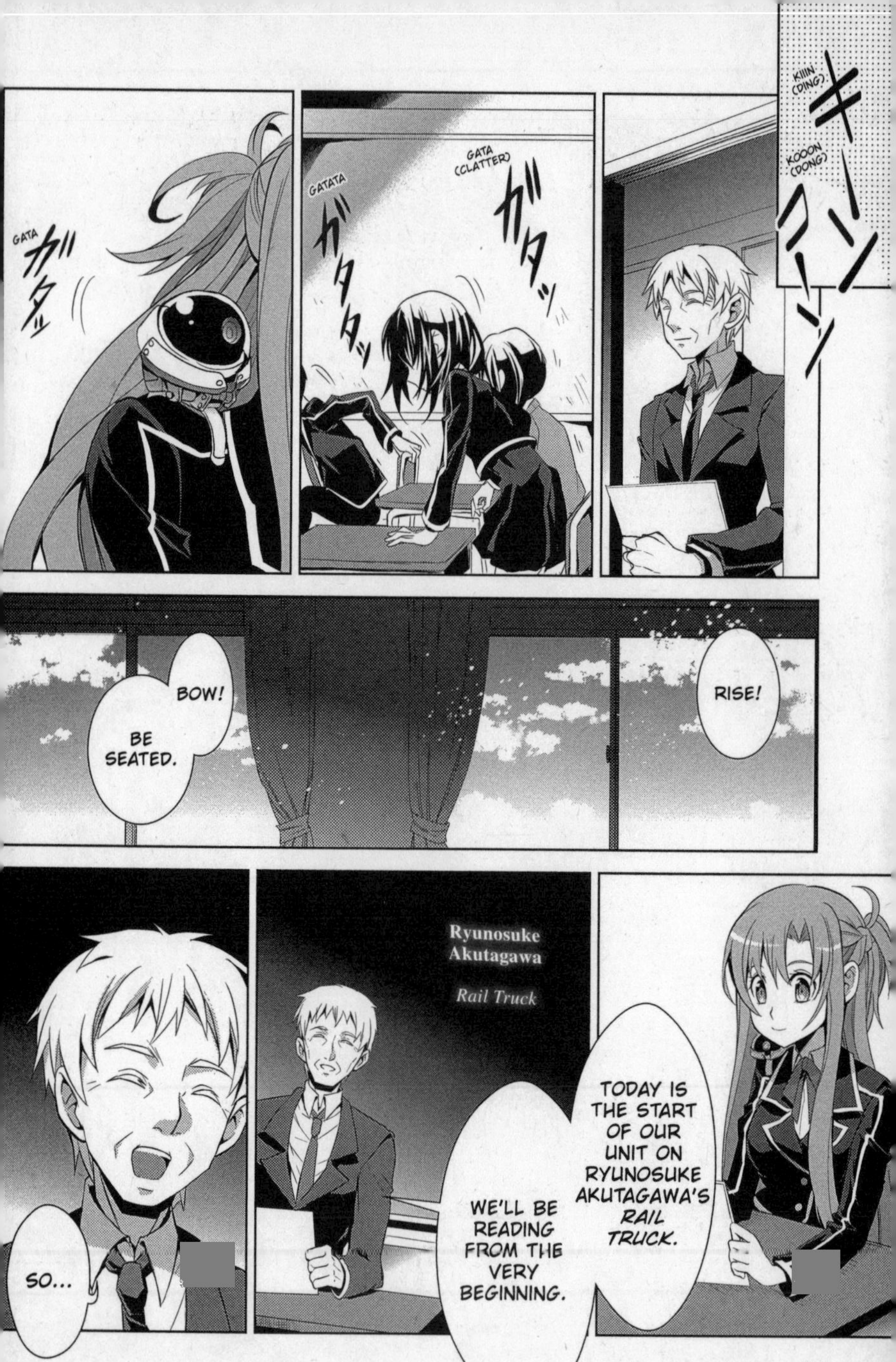
KIIIN (DING)
KOOON (DONG)
GATA (CLATTER)
GATATA
GATA
RISE!
BOW!
BE SEATED.
TODAY IS THE START OF OUR UNIT ON RYUNOSUKE AKUTAGAWA'S *RAIL TRUCK*.
WE'LL BE READING FROM THE VERY BEGINNING.
Ryunosuke Akutagawa
Rail Truck
SO...

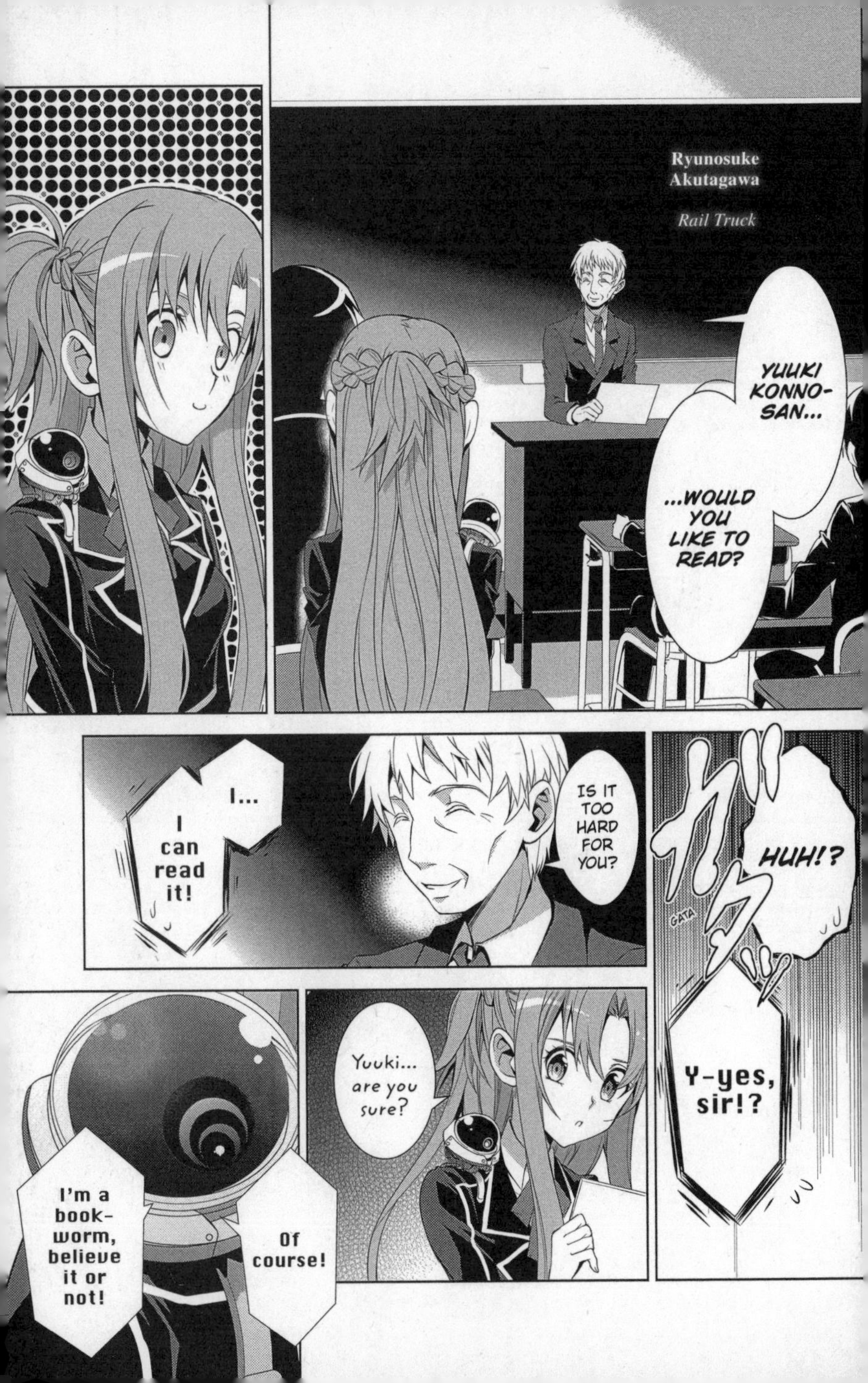
Ryunosuke Akutagawa
Rail Truck
YUUKI KONNO-SAN...
...WOULD YOU LIKE TO READ?
GATA
HUH!?
Y-yes, sir!?
IS IT TOO HARD FOR YOU?
I... I can read it!
Yuuki... are you sure?
Of course!
I'm a bookworm, believe it or not!

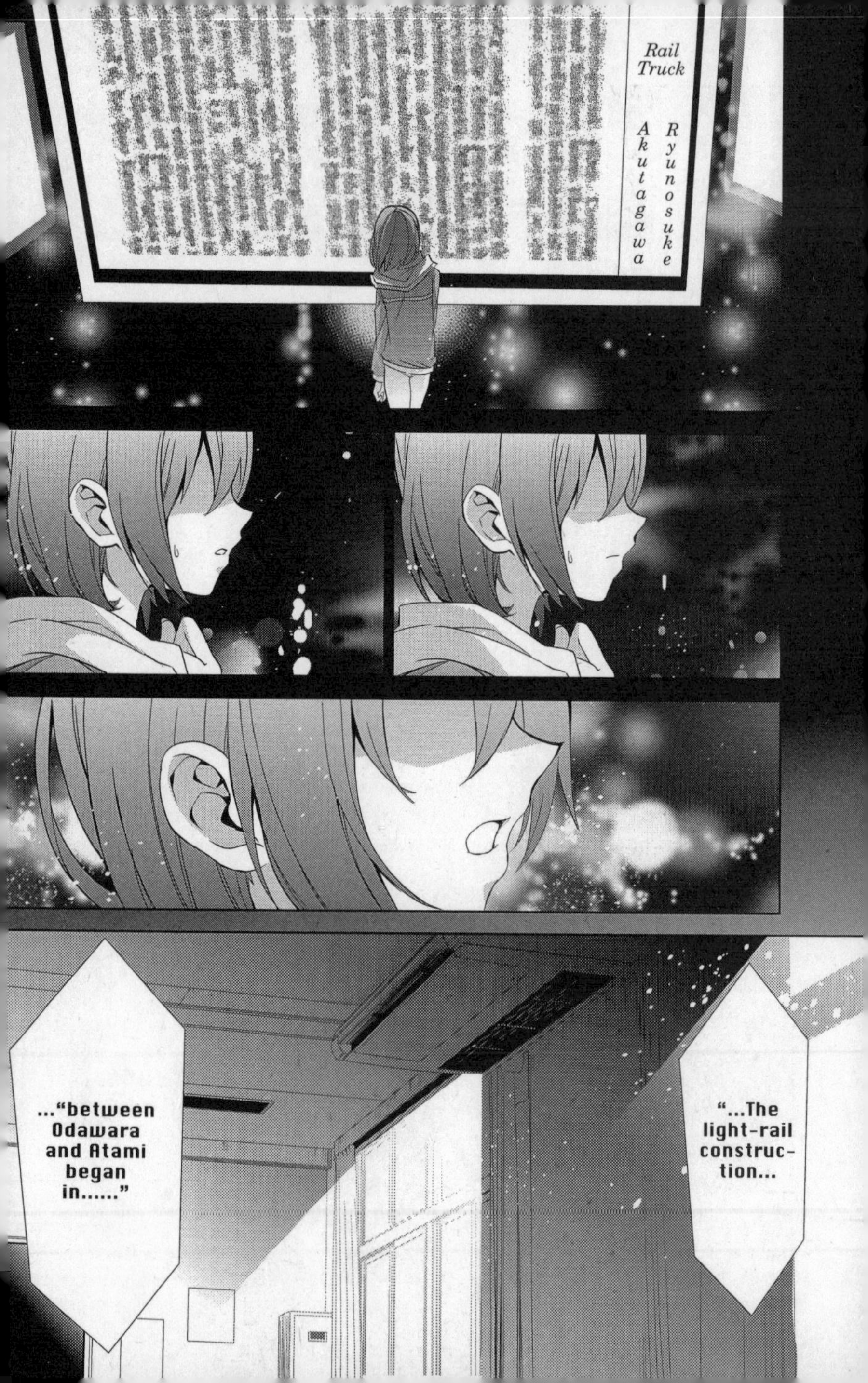
Rail Truck
Ryunosuke Akutagawa
"...The light-rail construction...
..."between Odawara and Atami began in......"

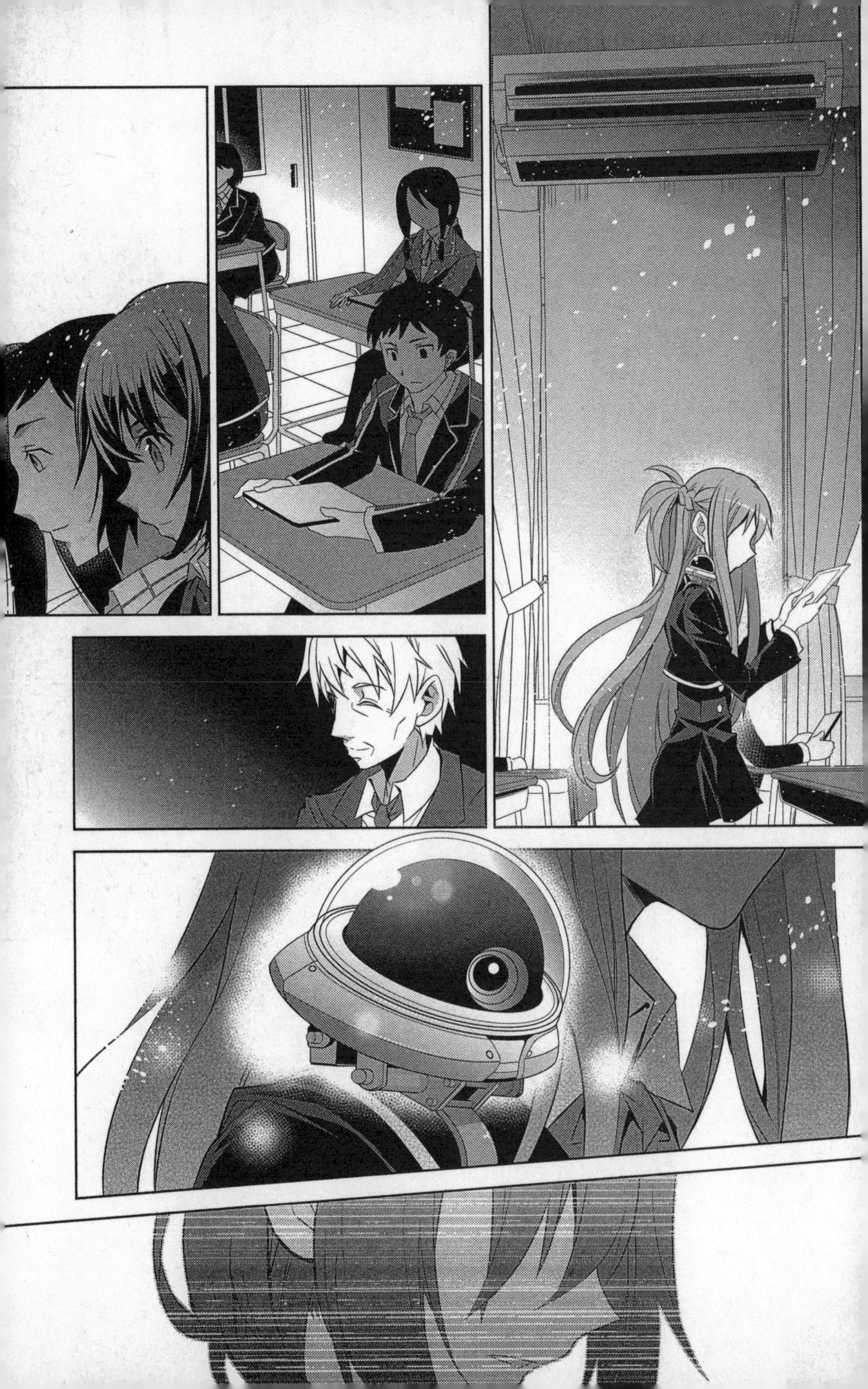

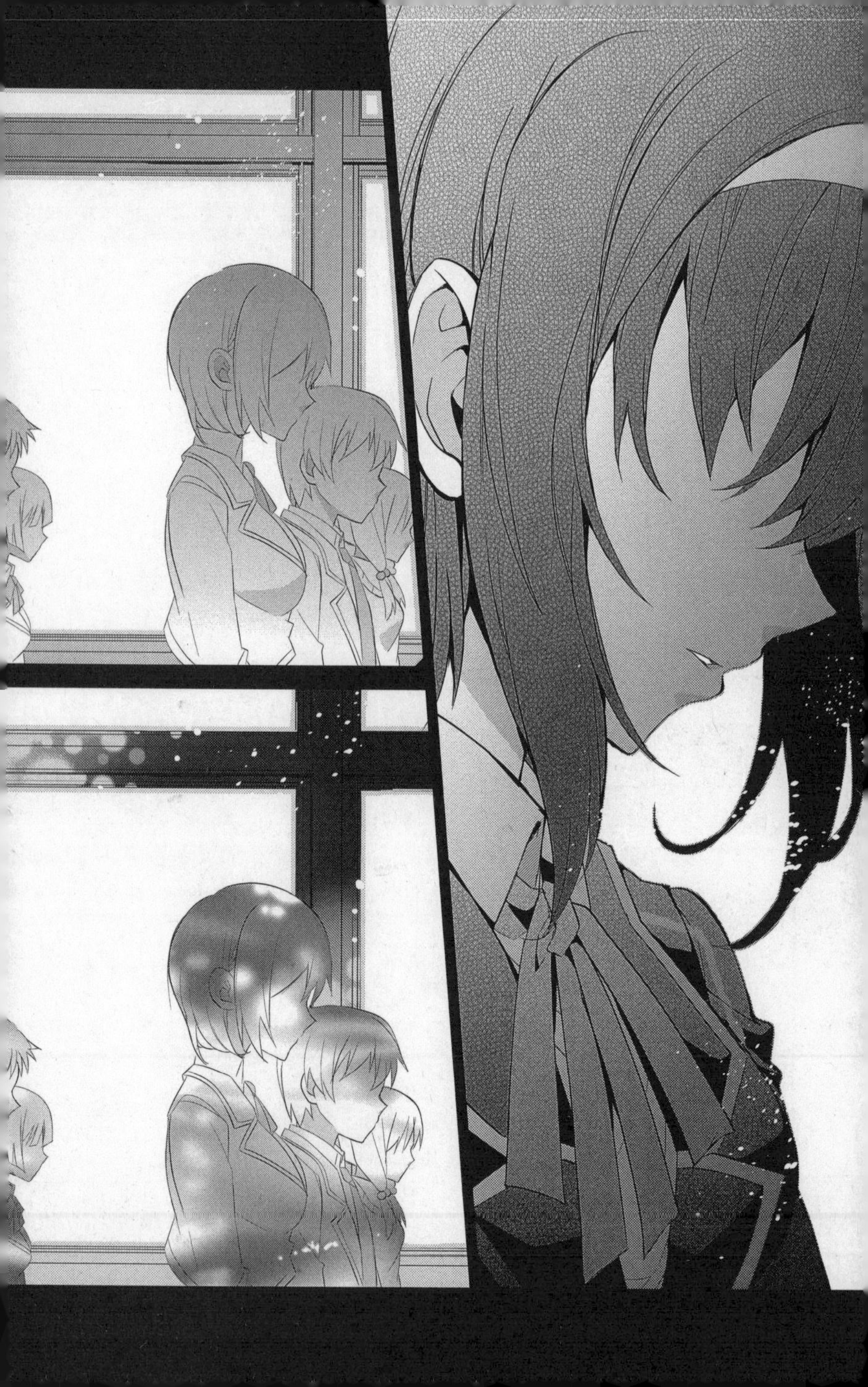

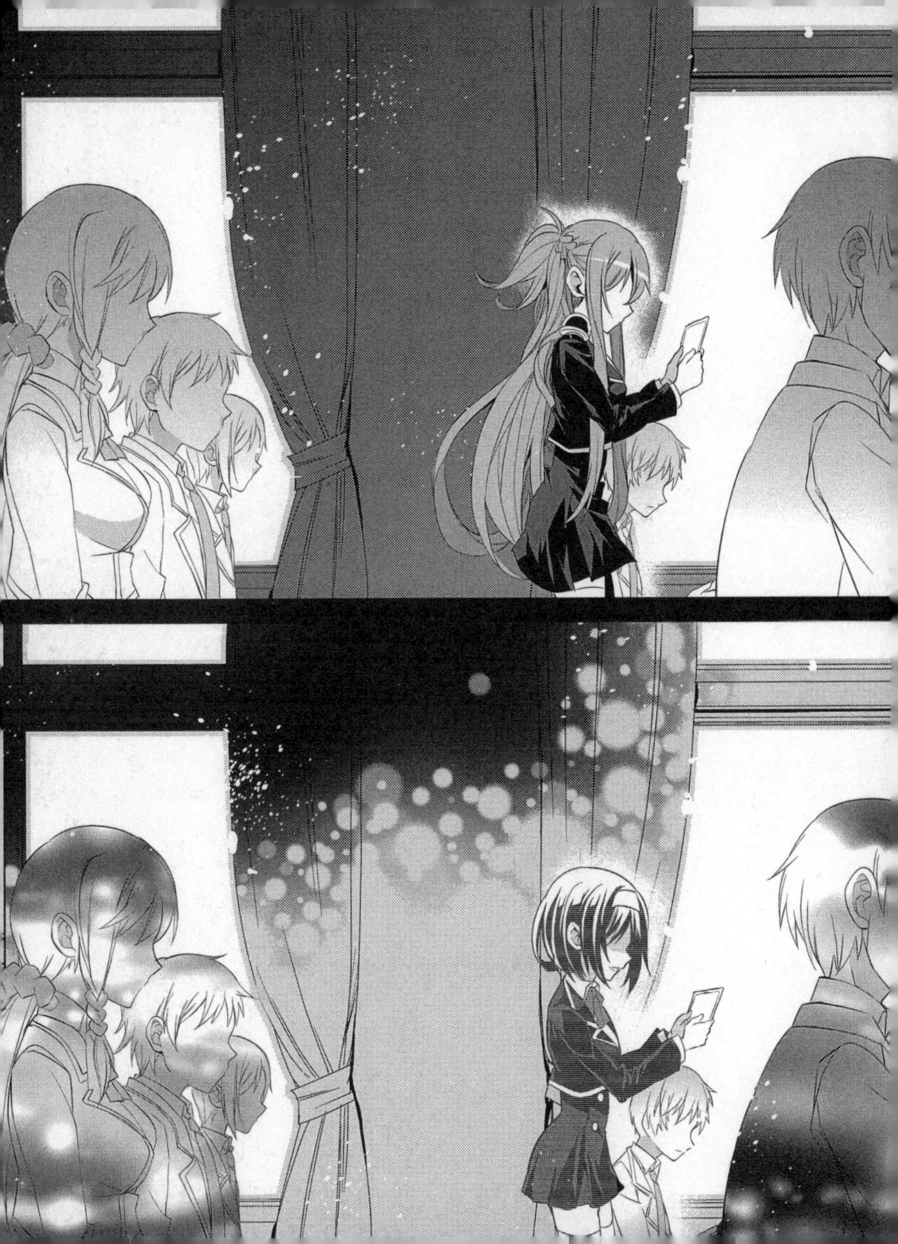

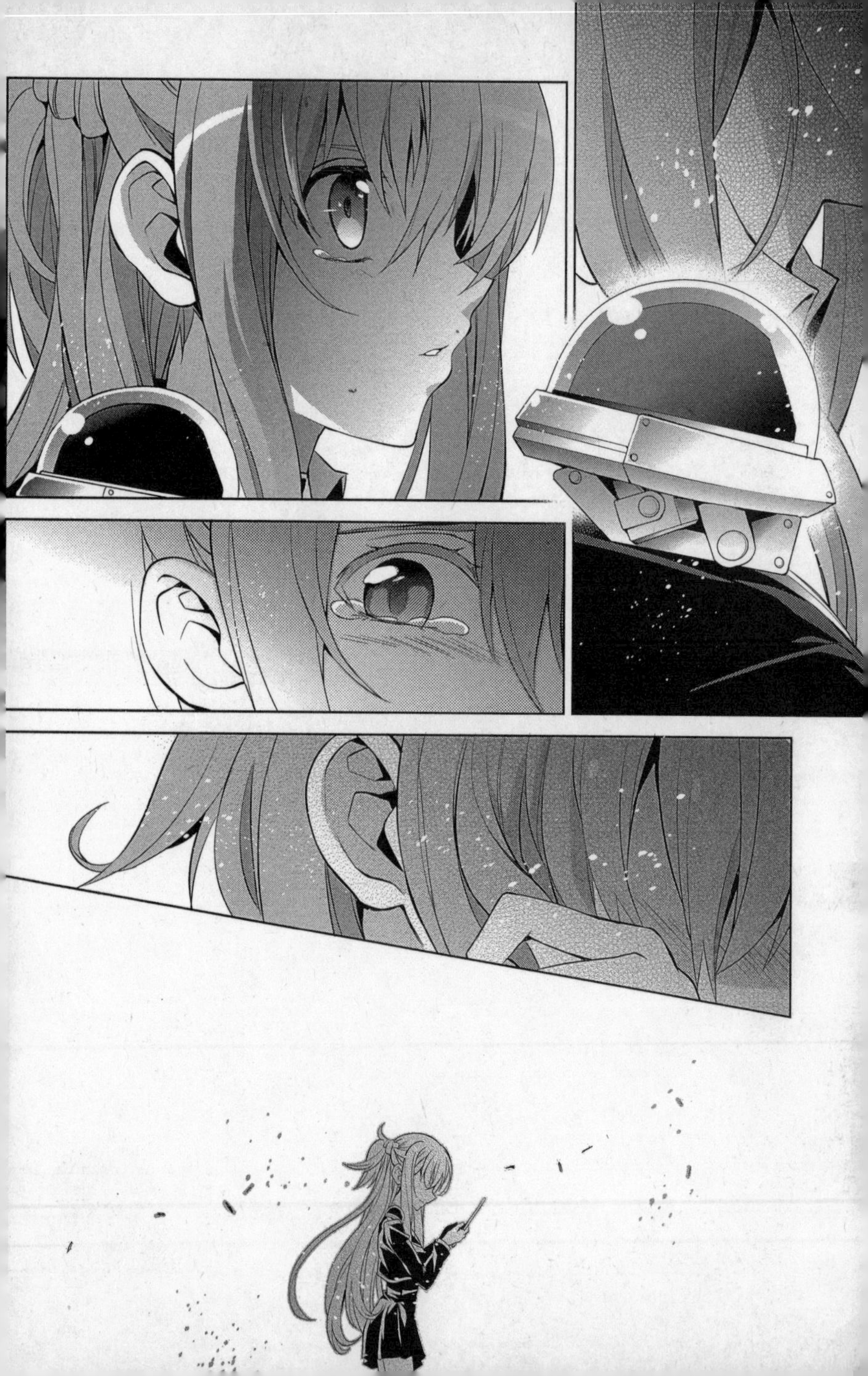

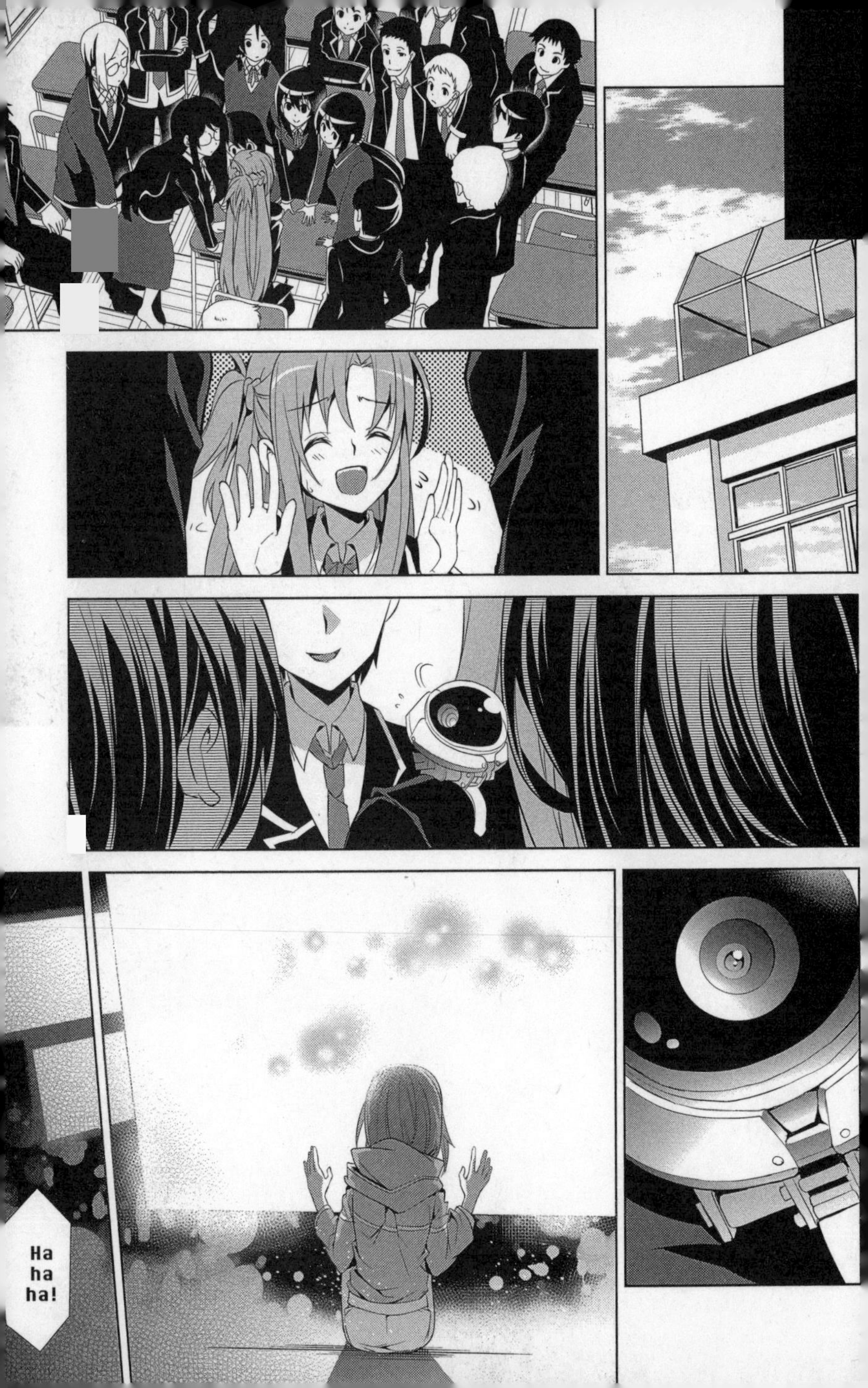
Ha ha ha!

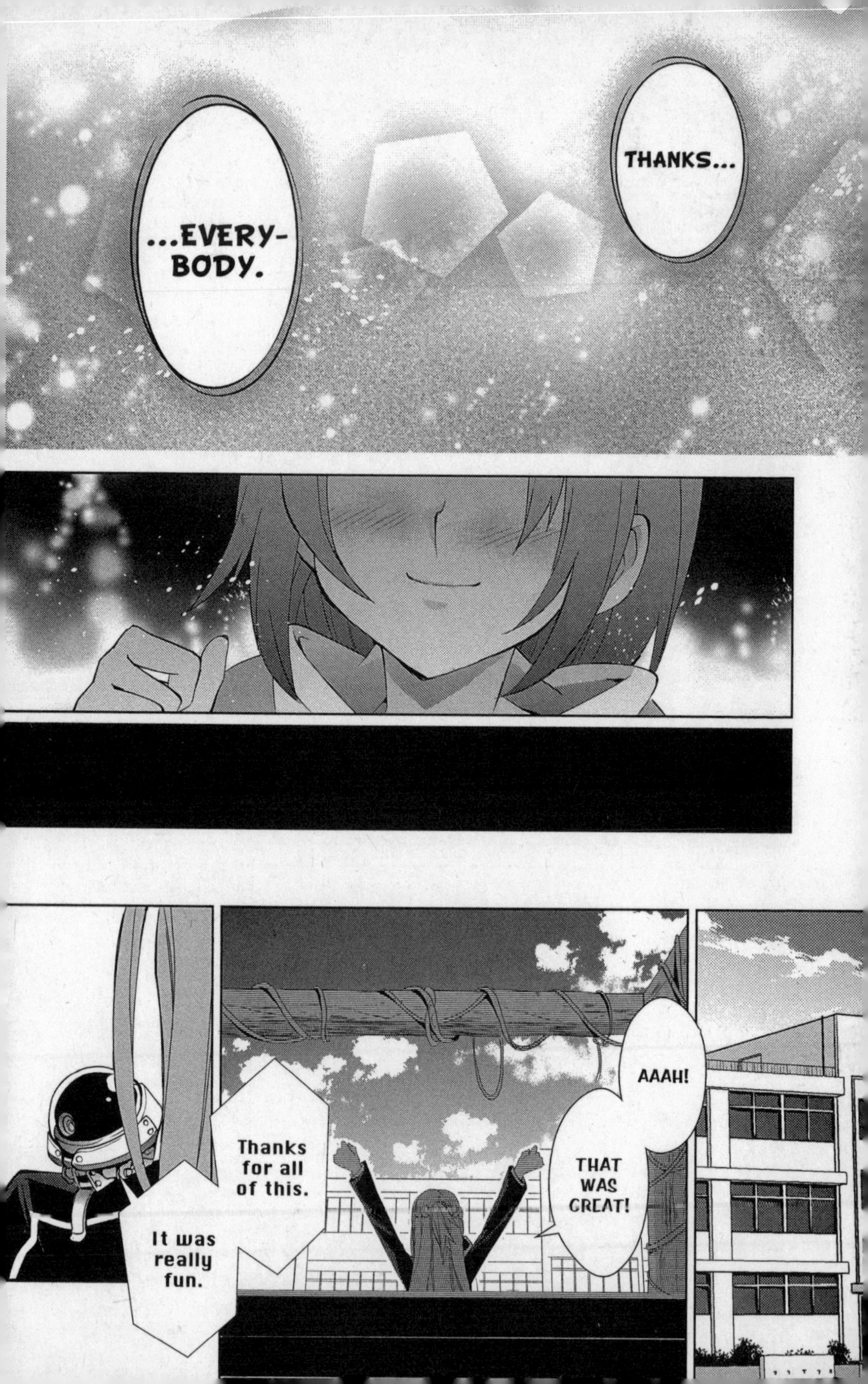
THANKS...
...EVERY-BODY.
AAAH!
THAT WAS GREAT!
Thanks for all of this.
It was really fun.

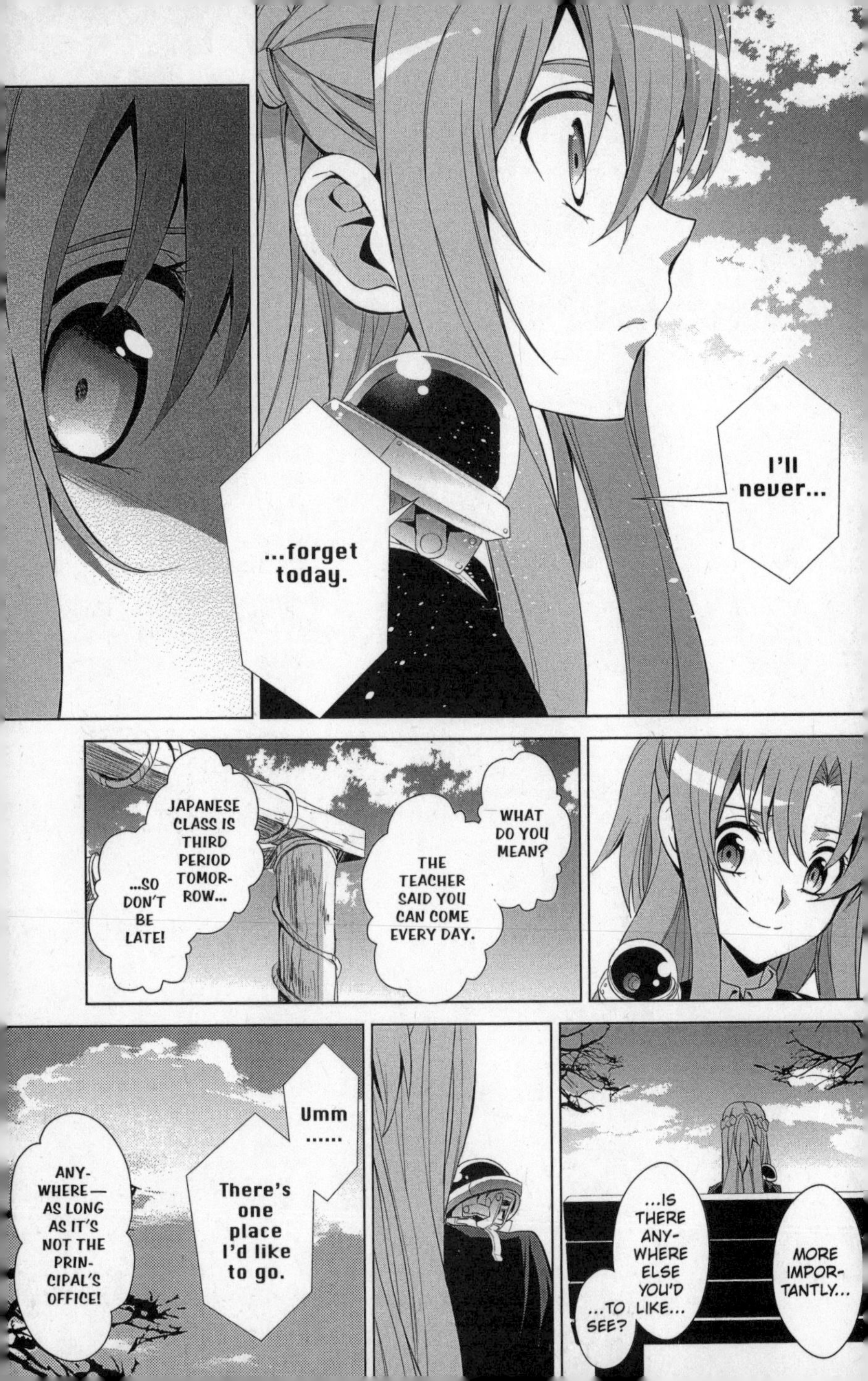
I'll never...
...forget today.
WHAT DO YOU MEAN?
THE TEACHER SAID YOU CAN COME EVERY DAY.
JAPANESE CLASS IS THIRD PERIOD TOMORROW...
...SO DON'T BE LATE!
MORE IMPORTANTLY...
...IS THERE ANYWHERE ELSE YOU'D LIKE...
...TO SEE?
Umm ......
There's one place I'd like to go.
ANYWHERE— AS LONG AS IT'S NOT THE PRINCIPAL'S OFFICE!

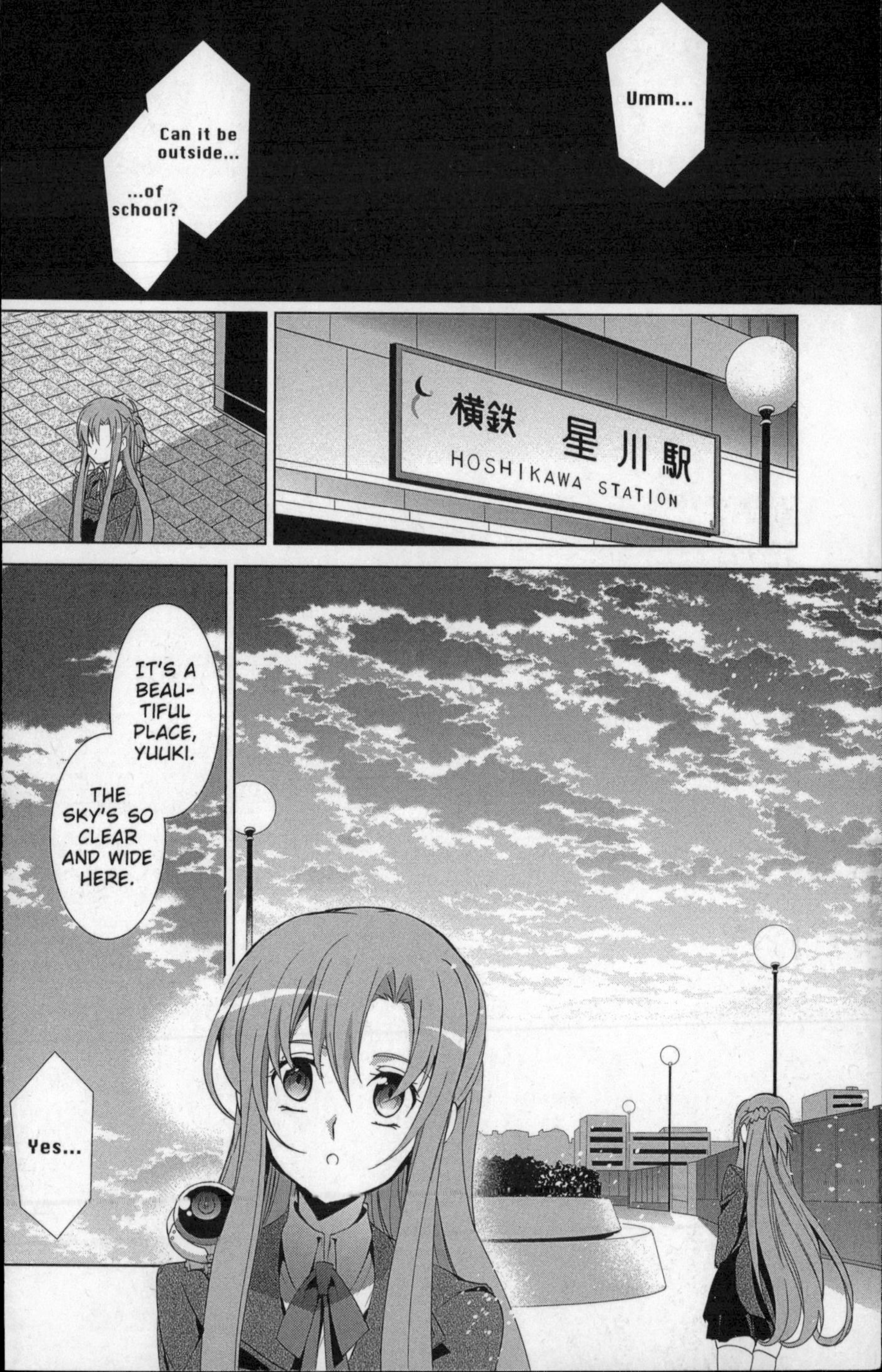
Umm...
Can it be outside...
...of school?
横鉄 星川駅
HOSHIKAWA STATION
IT'S A BEAUTIFUL PLACE, YUUKI.
THE SKY'S SO CLEAR AND WIDE HERE.
Yes...

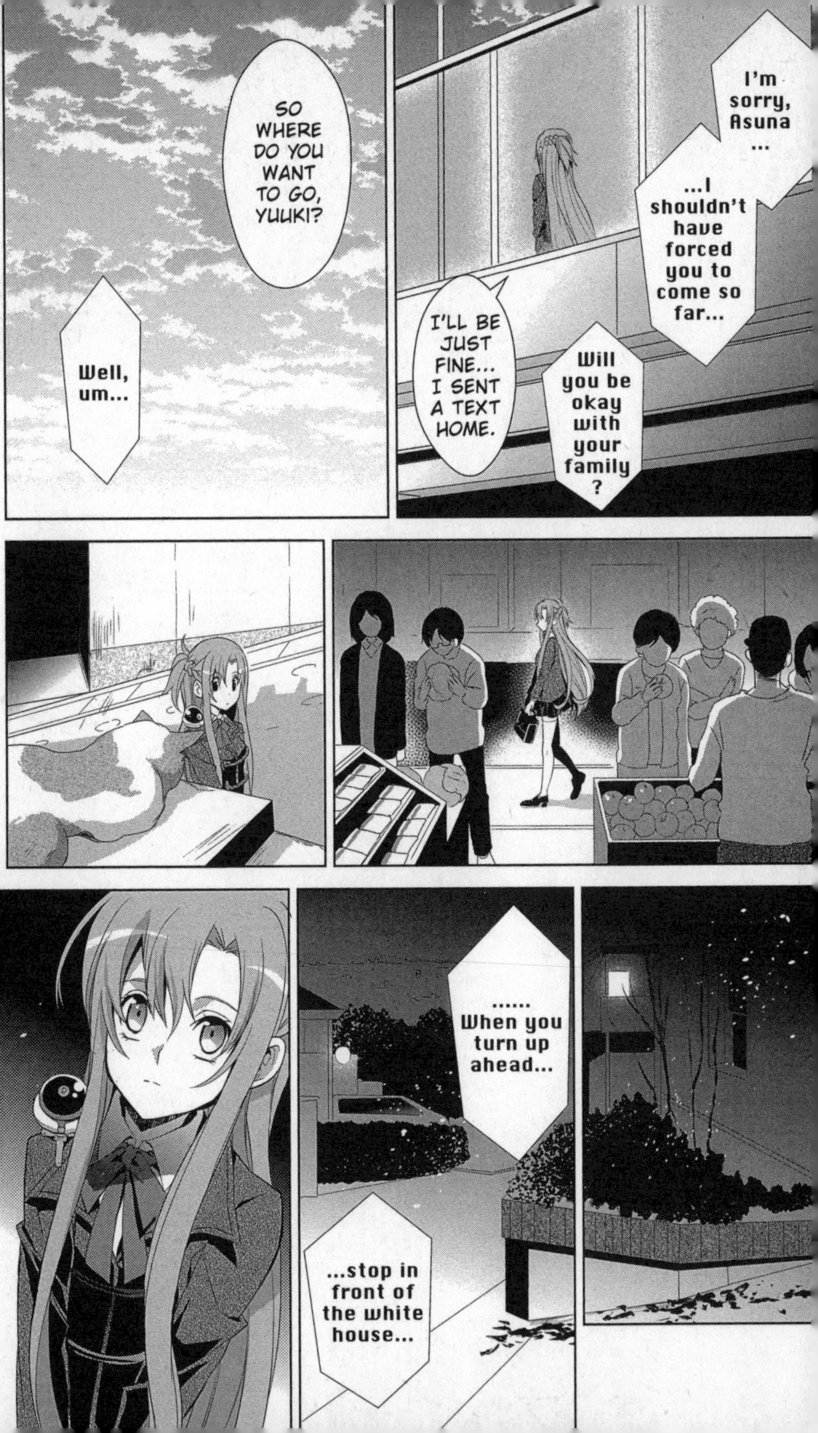
I'm sorry, Asuna...
...I shouldn't have forced you to come so far...
Will you be okay with your family?
I'LL BE JUST FINE... I SENT A TEXT HOME.
SO WHERE DO YOU WANT TO GO, YUUKI?
Well, um...
...... When you turn up ahead...
...stop in front of the white house...

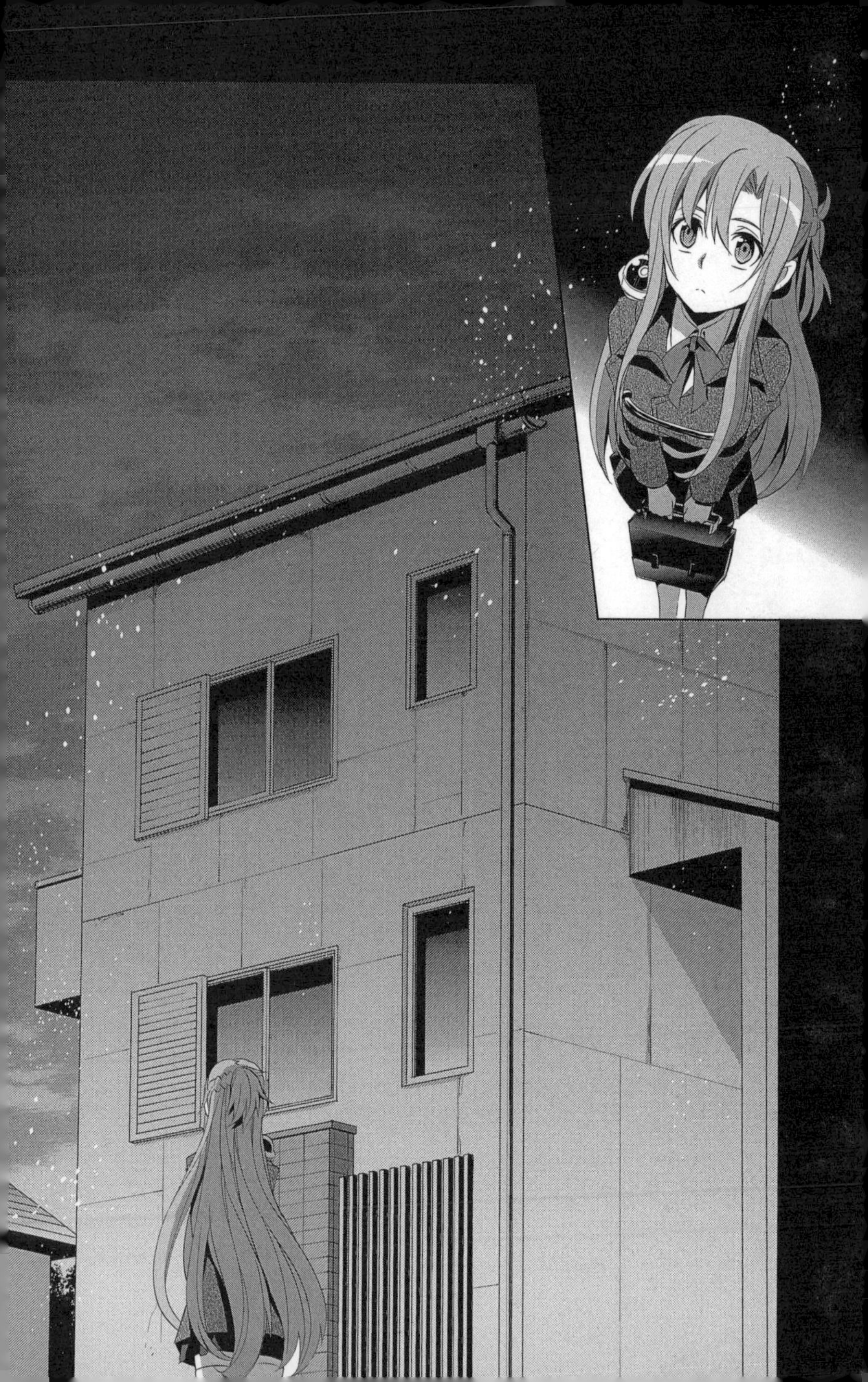

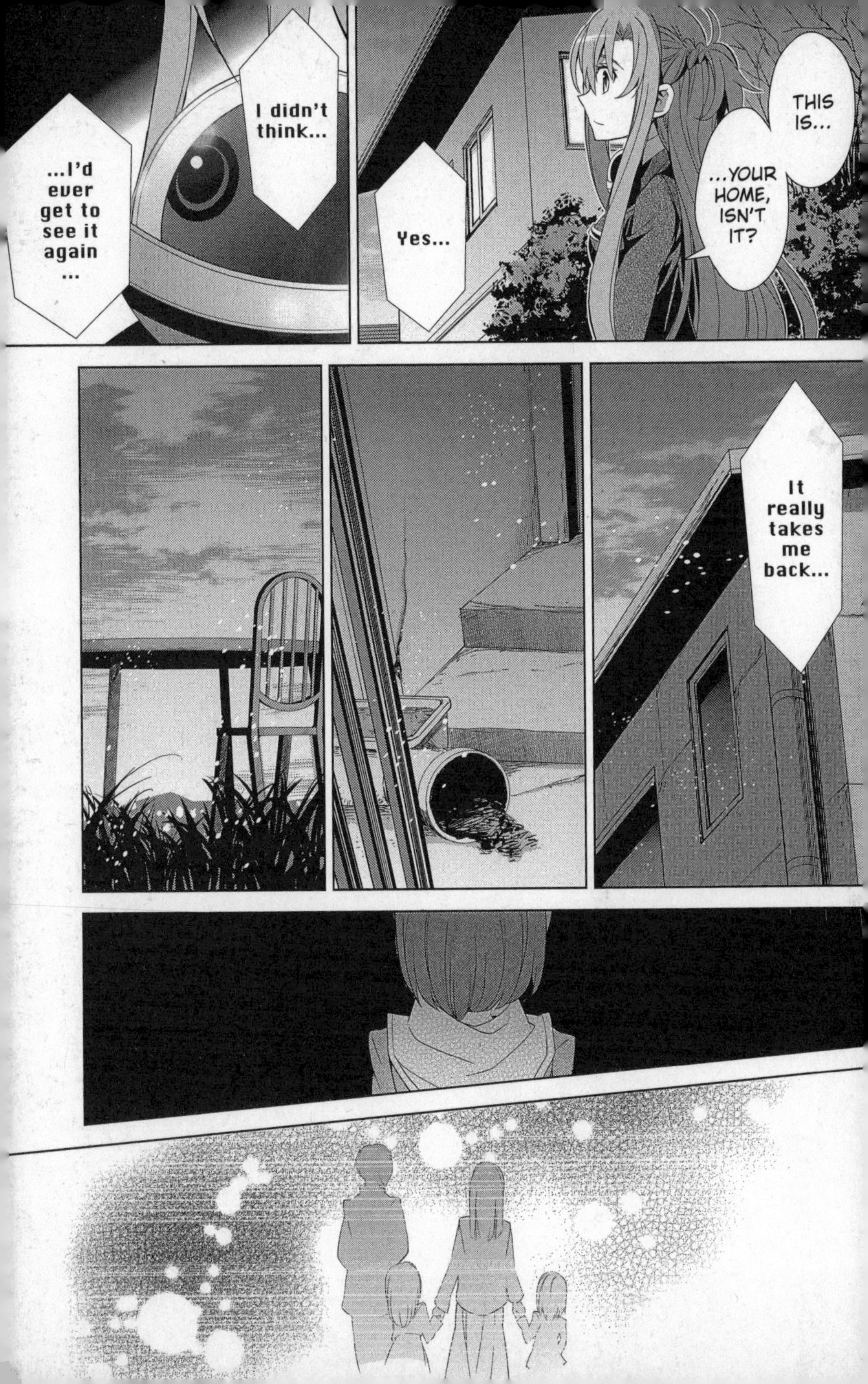
THIS IS...
...YOUR HOME, ISN'T IT?
Yes...
I didn't think...
...I'd ever get to see it again...
It really takes me back...

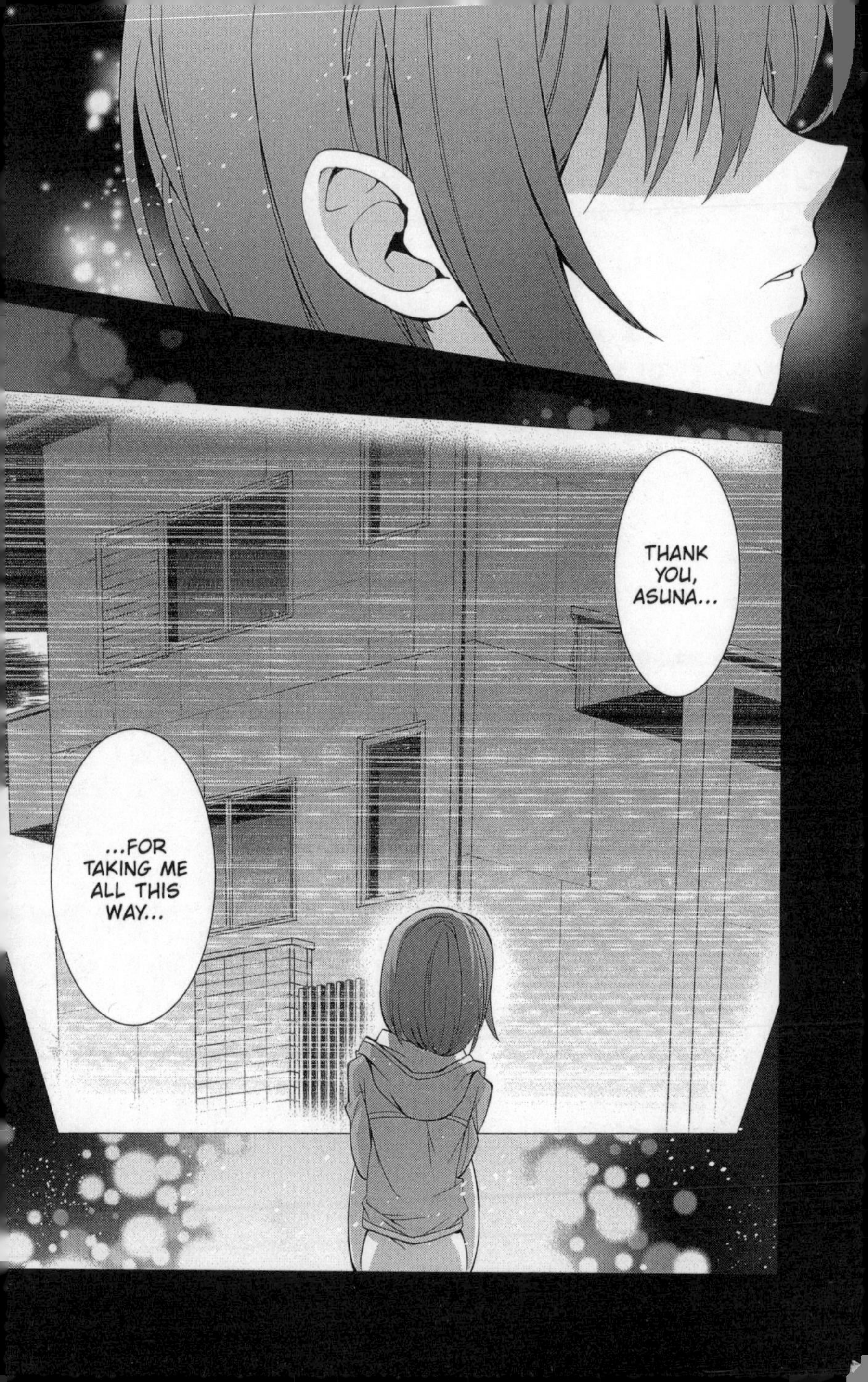
THANK YOU, ASUNA...
...FOR TAKING ME ALL THIS WAY...

SWORD ART ONLINE
mother's ROSARY

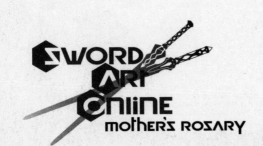

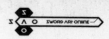

SWORD ART ONLINE mother's rosary
BACKGROUND GUIDE 02

KIRITO'S HOMEMADE PROBE

ALSO KNOWN AS THE "AV INTERACTIVE COMMUNICATIONS PROBE." AS SHOWN IN THE MANGA, IT SENDS VISUAL AND AUDIO DATA TO A REMOTE LOCATION, ALLOWING THE DISTANT USER TO FEEL AS THOUGH THEY ARE RIGHT THERE WITH YOU. THE PROBE CONTAINS A CAMERA AND SENSORS FOR RECORDING AUDIOVISUAL DATA, AS WELL AS A NEAR-FIELD WIRELESS COMMUNICATIONS DEVICE (WHAT WE'D CALL BLUETOOTH TODAY) WHICH ENABLES IT TO SEND DATA TO ASUNA'S SMARTPHONE AND THROUGH THE NETWORK TO YUUKI'S MEDICUBOID.

IT'LL PROBABLY TAKE SOME TIME UNTIL THE REMOTE USER WILL REALLY "FEEL LIKE SHE'S THERE" AS DEPICTED IN THE STORY HERE, BUT IT'S A TYPE OF TECHNOLOGY THAT SEEMS VERY LIKELY TO BE DEVELOPED IN THE NEAR FUTURE.

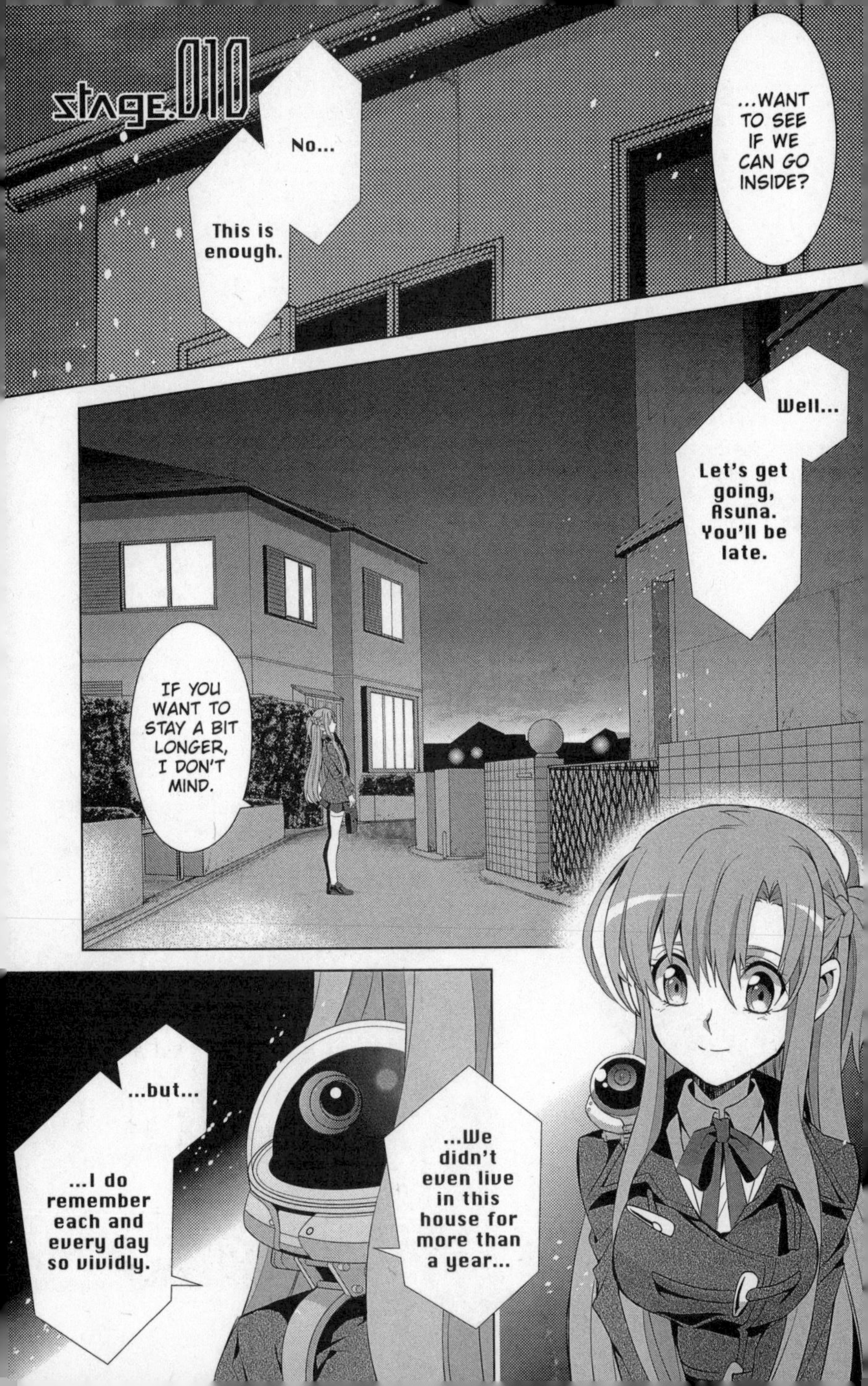
stage.010
...WANT TO SEE IF WE CAN GO INSIDE?
No...
This is enough.
IF YOU WANT TO STAY A BIT LONGER, I DON'T MIND.
Well...
Let's get going, Asuna. You'll be late.
...We didn't even live in this house for more than a year...
...but...
...I do remember each and every day so vividly.

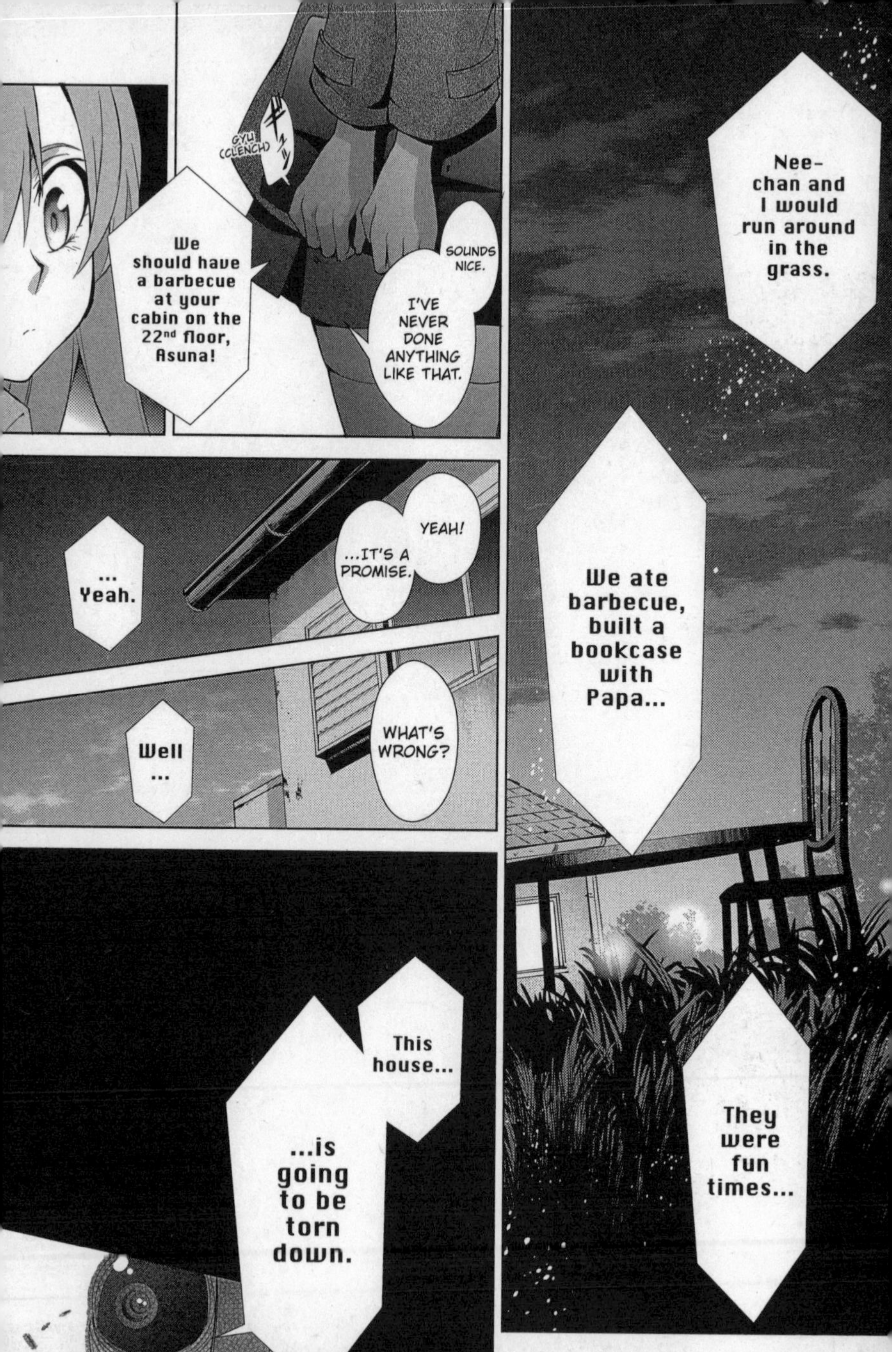
Nee-chan and I would run around in the grass.
We ate barbecue, built a bookcase with Papa...
They were fun times...
GYU (CLENCH)
SOUNDS NICE.
I'VE NEVER DONE ANYTHING LIKE THAT.
We should have a barbecue at your cabin on the 22nd floor, Asuna!
YEAH!
...IT'S A PROMISE.
... Yeah.
WHAT'S WRONG?
Well ...
This house...
...is going to be torn down.

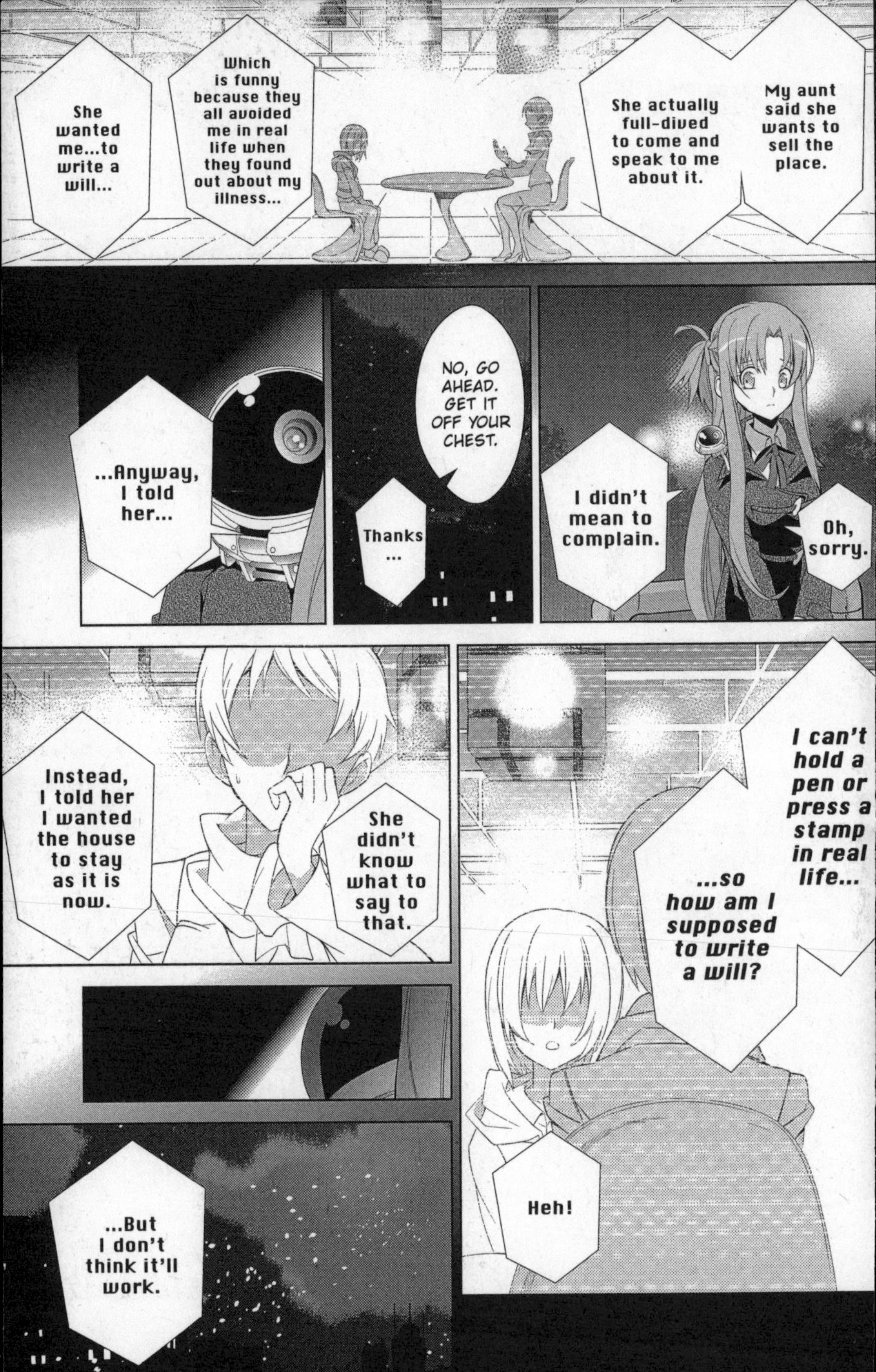
My aunt said she wants to sell the place.
She actually full-dived to come and speak to me about it.
Which is funny because they all avoided me in real life when they found out about my illness...
She wanted me...to write a will...
Oh, sorry.
I didn't mean to complain.
NO, GO AHEAD. GET IT OFF YOUR CHEST.
Thanks...
...Anyway, I told her...
I can't hold a pen or press a stamp in real life...
...so how am I supposed to write a will?
Heh!
Instead, I told her I wanted the house to stay as it is now.
She didn't know what to say to that.
...But I don't think it'll work.

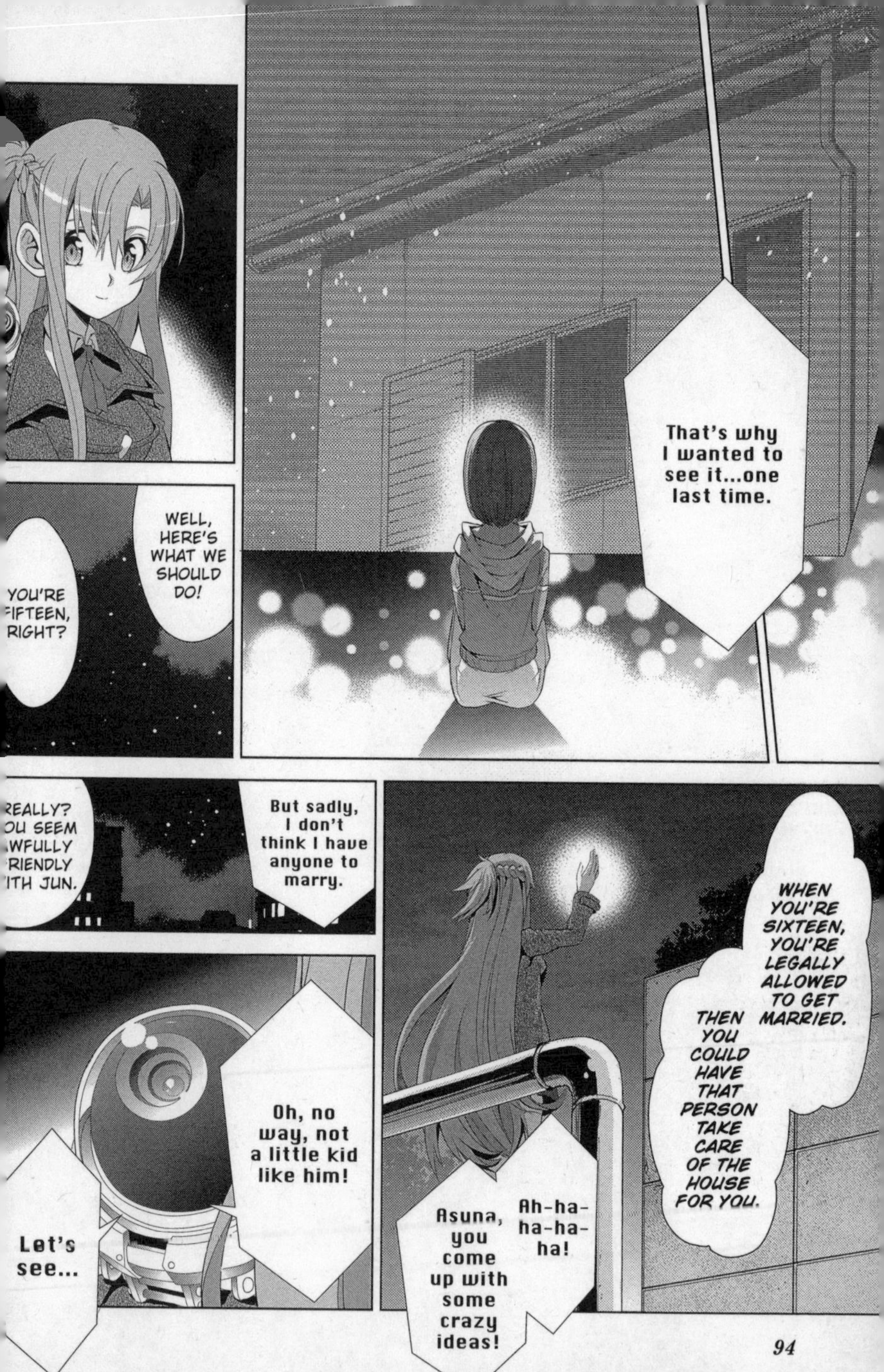
That's why I wanted to see it...one last time.
WELL, HERE'S WHAT WE SHOULD DO!
YOU'RE FIFTEEN, RIGHT?
WHEN YOU'RE SIXTEEN, YOU'RE LEGALLY ALLOWED TO GET MARRIED.
THEN YOU COULD HAVE THAT PERSON TAKE CARE OF THE HOUSE FOR YOU.
Ah-ha-ha-ha-ha!
Asuna, you come up with some crazy ideas!
But sadly, I don't think I have anyone to marry.
REALLY? OU SEEM WFULLY FRIENDLY ITH JUN.
Oh, no way, not a little kid like him!
Let's see...

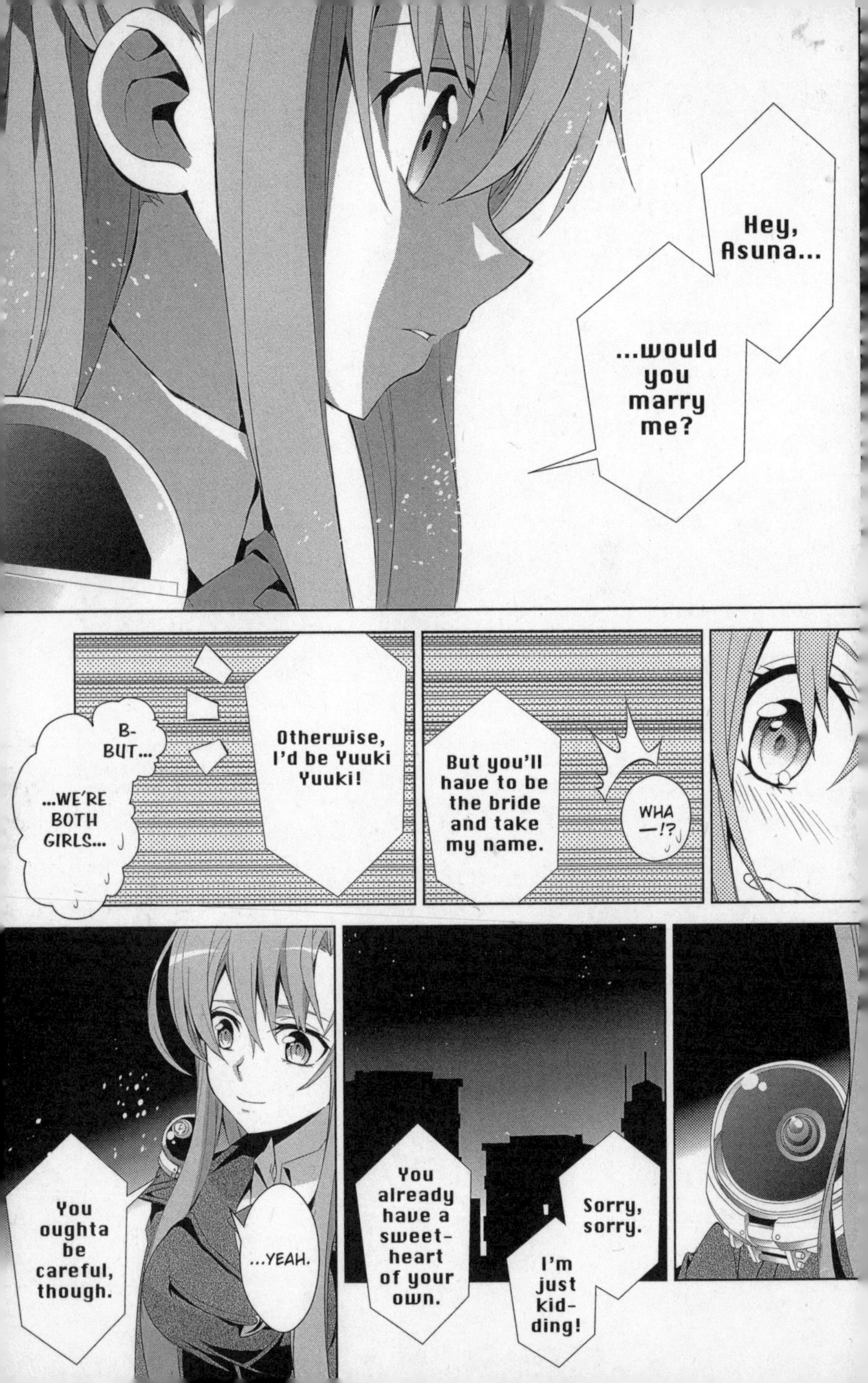
Hey, Asuna...
...would you marry me?
WHA—!?
But you'll have to be the bride and take my name.
Otherwise, I'd be Yuuki Yuuki!
B-BUT...
...WE'RE BOTH GIRLS...
Sorry, sorry.
I'm just kid-ding!
You already have a sweet-heart of your own.
...YEAH.
You oughta be careful, though.

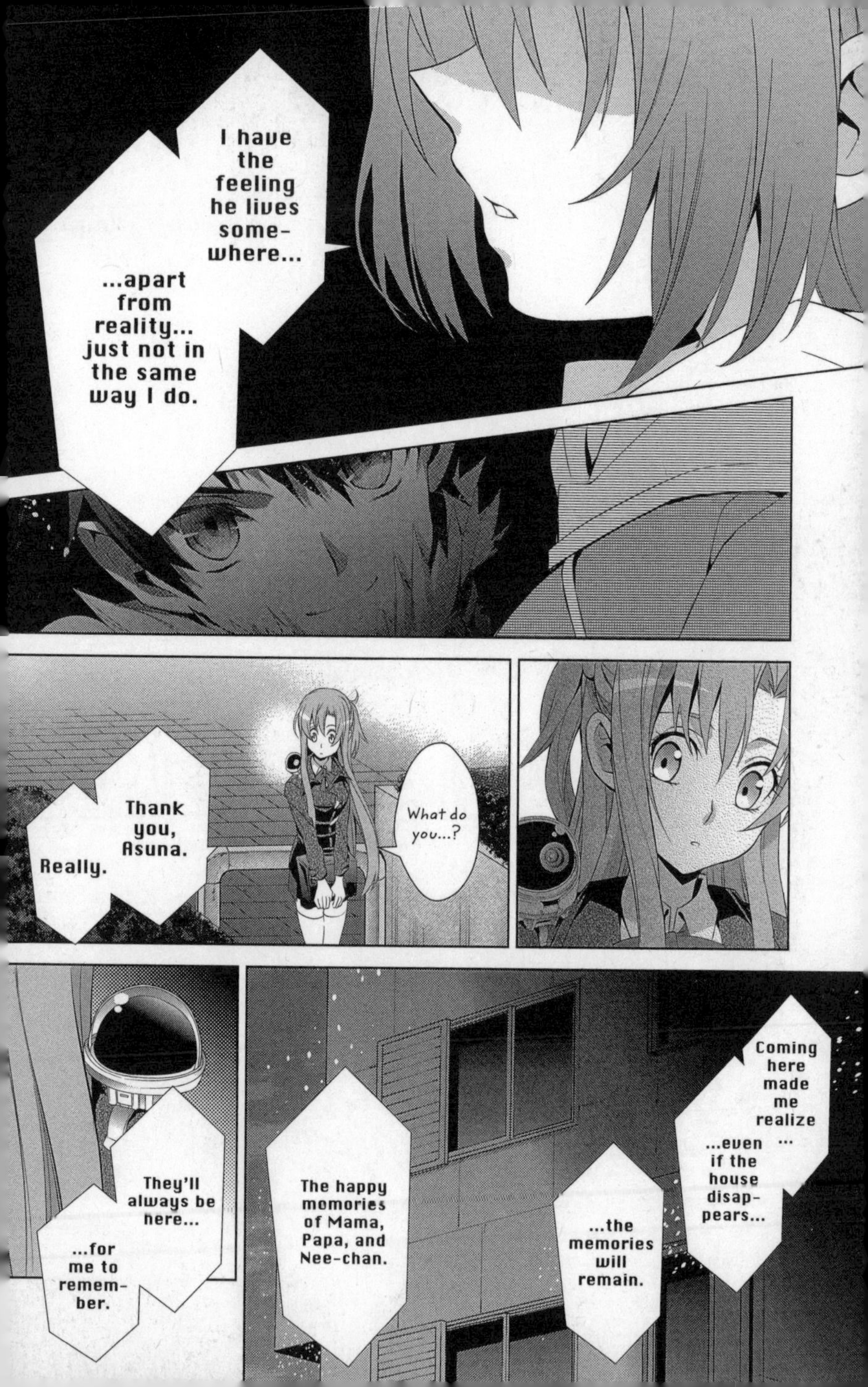
I have the feeling he lives somewhere...
...apart from reality... just not in the same way I do.
Thank you, Asuna. Really.
What do you...?
Coming here made me realize...
...even if the house disappears...
...the memories will remain.
The happy memories of Mama, Papa, and Nee-chan.
They'll always be here...
...for me to remember.

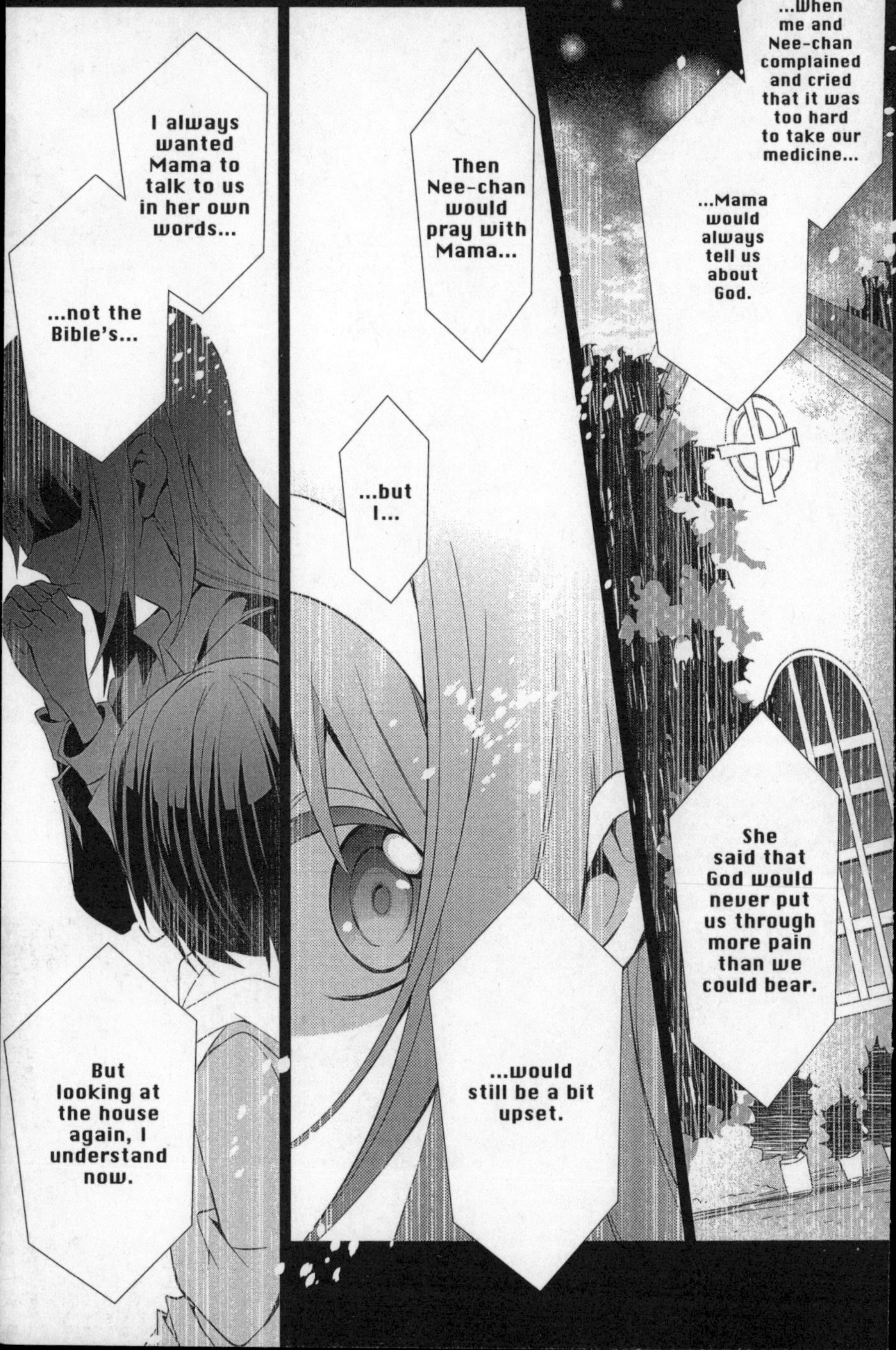
...When me and Nee-chan complained and cried that it was too hard to take our medicine...
...Mama would always tell us about God.
She said that God would never put us through more pain than we could bear.
Then Nee-chan would pray with Mama...
...but I...
...would still be a bit upset.
I always wanted Mama to talk to us in her own words...
...not the Bible's...
But looking at the house again, I understand now.

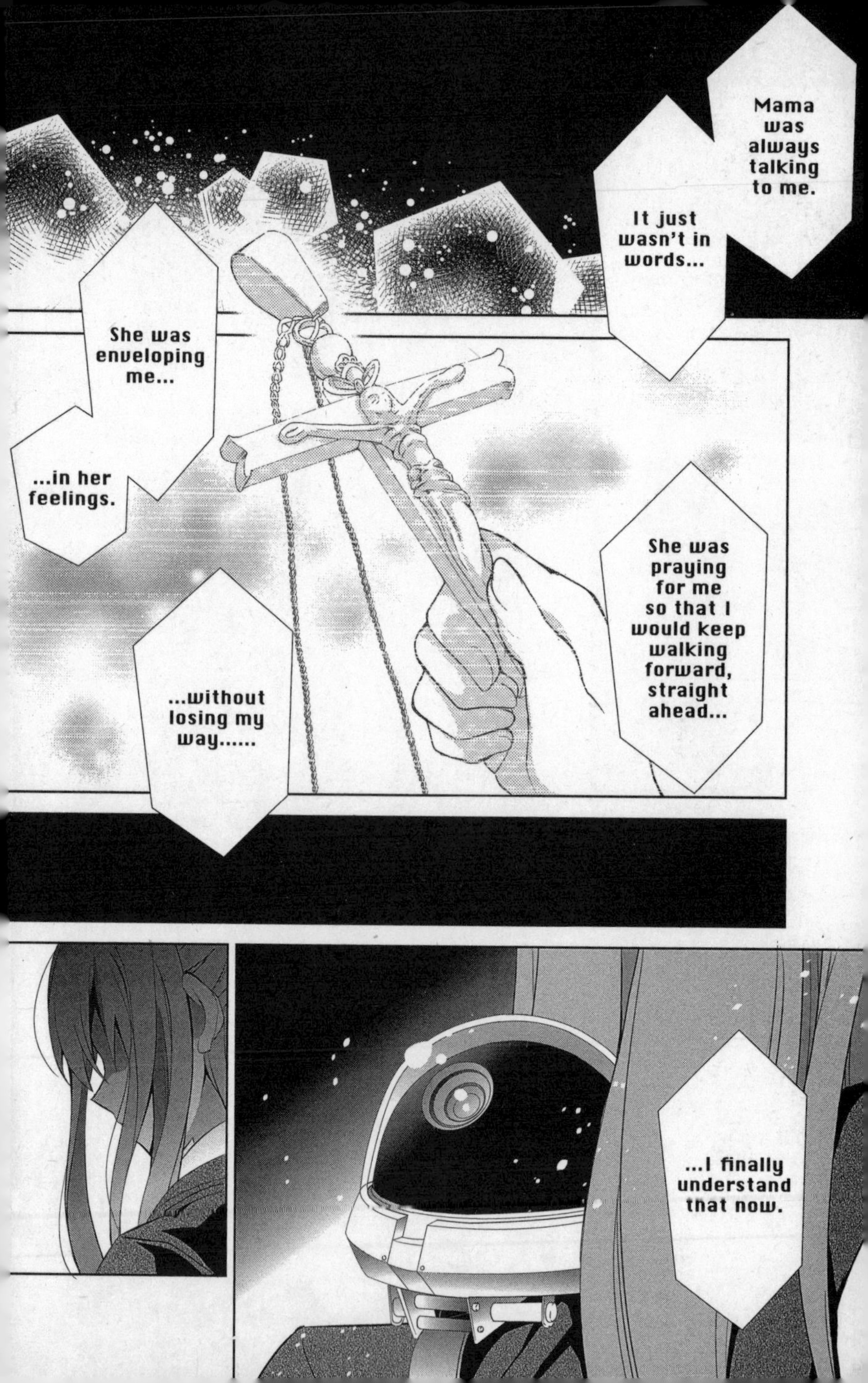
Mama was always talking to me.
It just wasn't in words...
She was enveloping me...
...in her feelings.
She was praying for me so that I would keep walking forward, straight ahead...
...without losing my way......
...I finally understand that now.

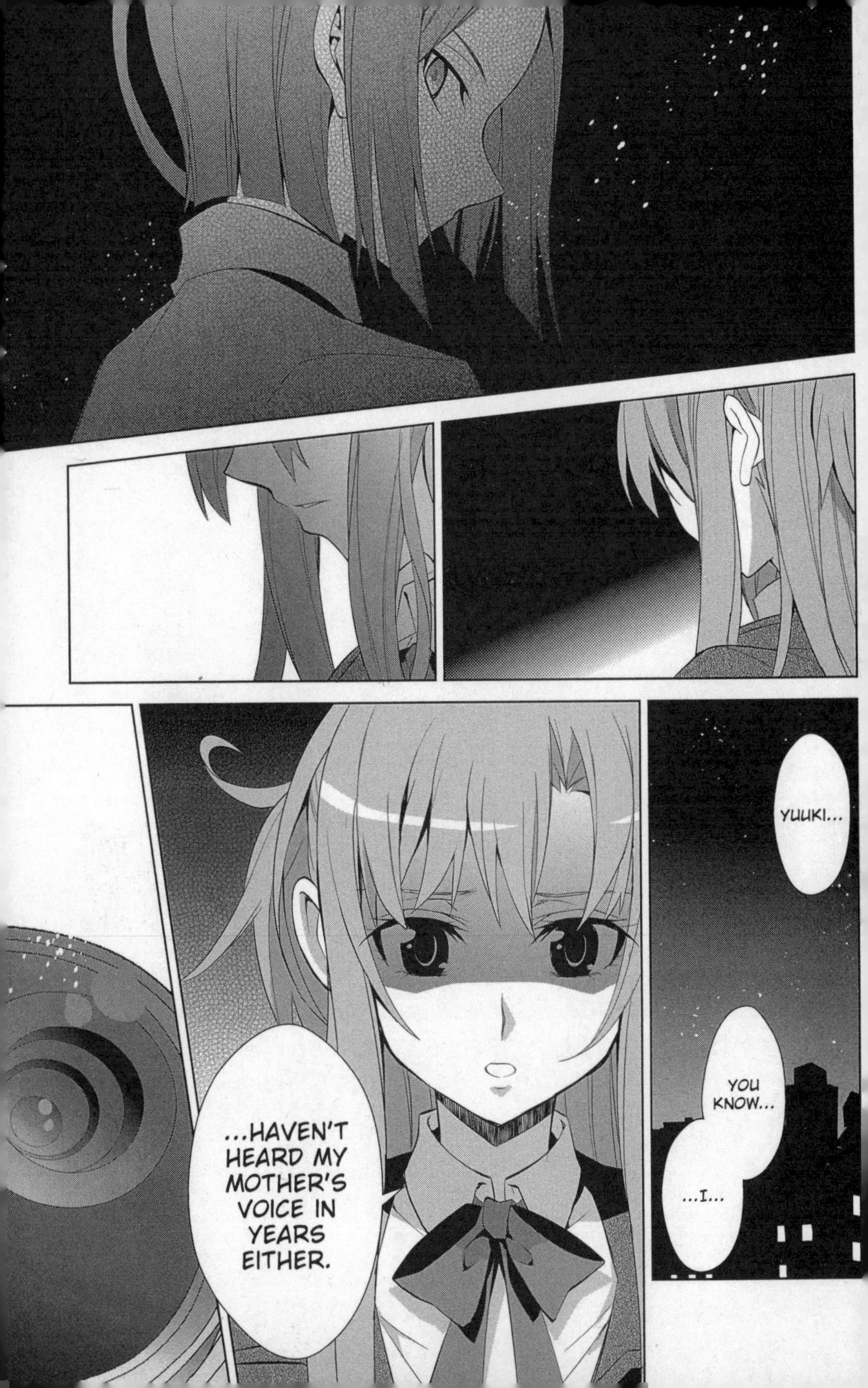
YUUKI...
YOU KNOW...
...I...
...HAVEN'T HEARD MY MOTHER'S VOICE IN YEARS EITHER.

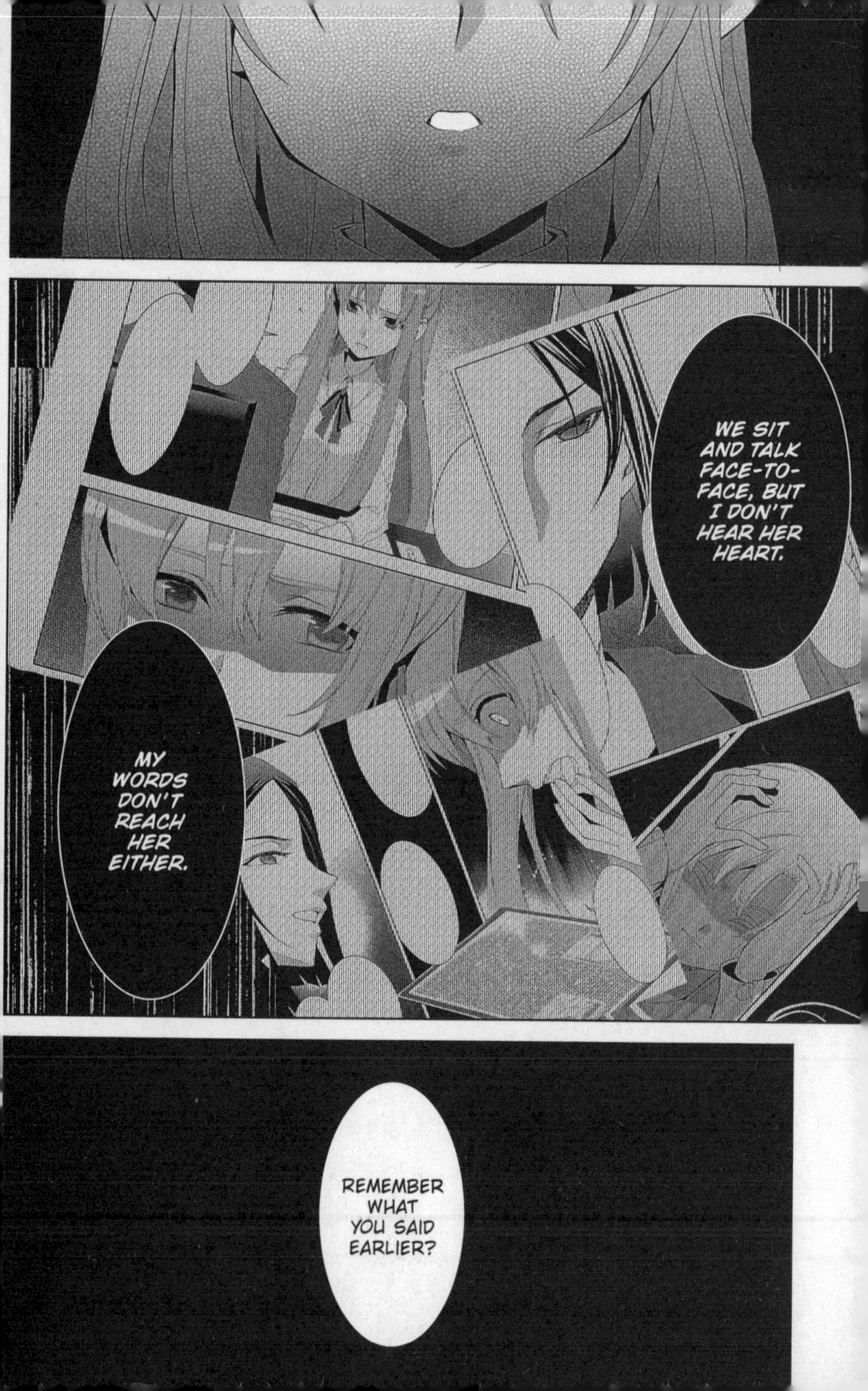
WE SIT AND TALK FACE-TO-FACE, BUT I DON'T HEAR HER HEART.
MY WORDS DON'T REACH HER EITHER.
REMEMBER WHAT YOU SAID EARLIER?

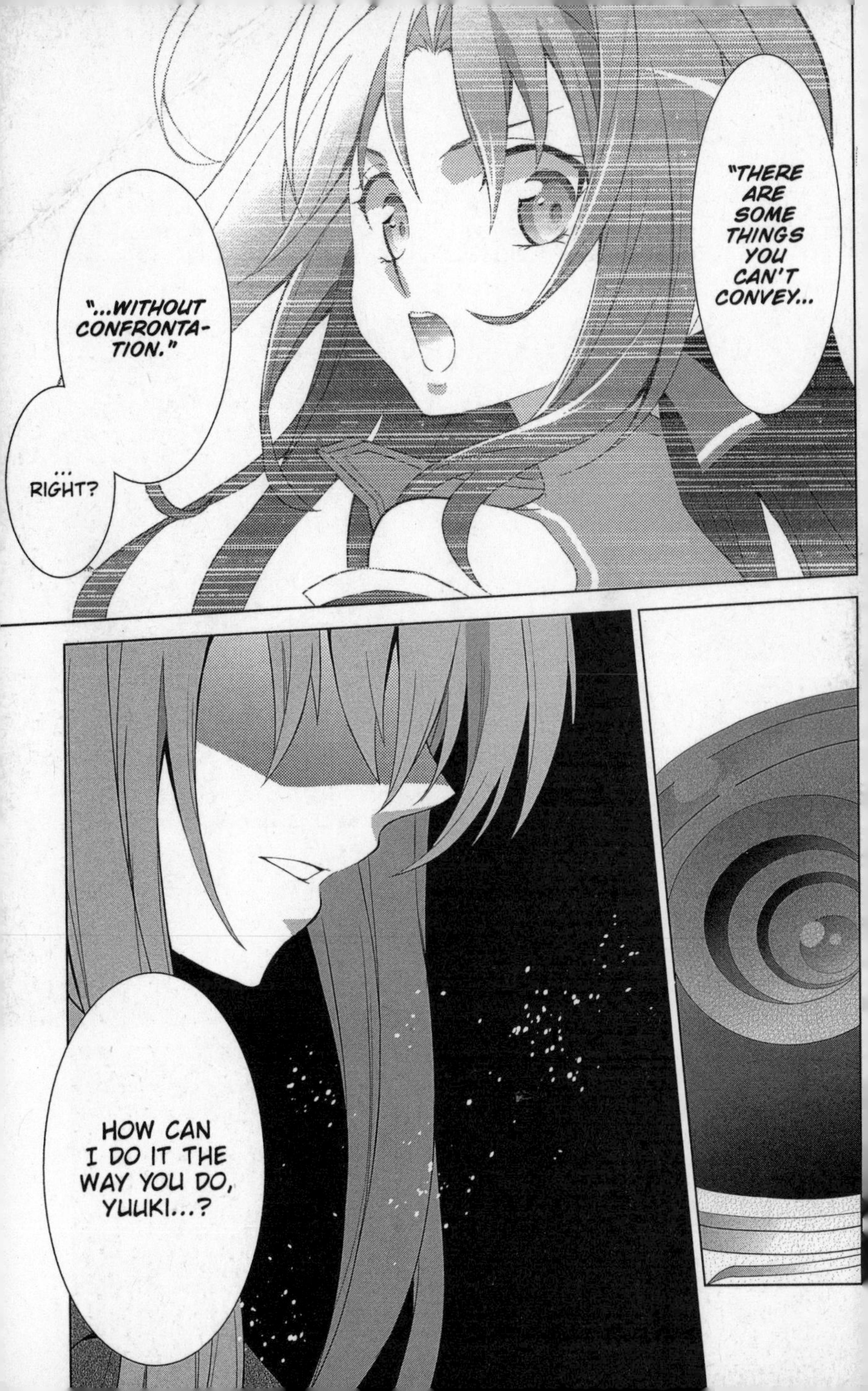
"THERE ARE SOME THINGS YOU CAN'T CONVEY...
"...WITHOUT CONFRONTATION."
... RIGHT?
HOW CAN I DO IT THE WAY YOU DO, YUUKI...?

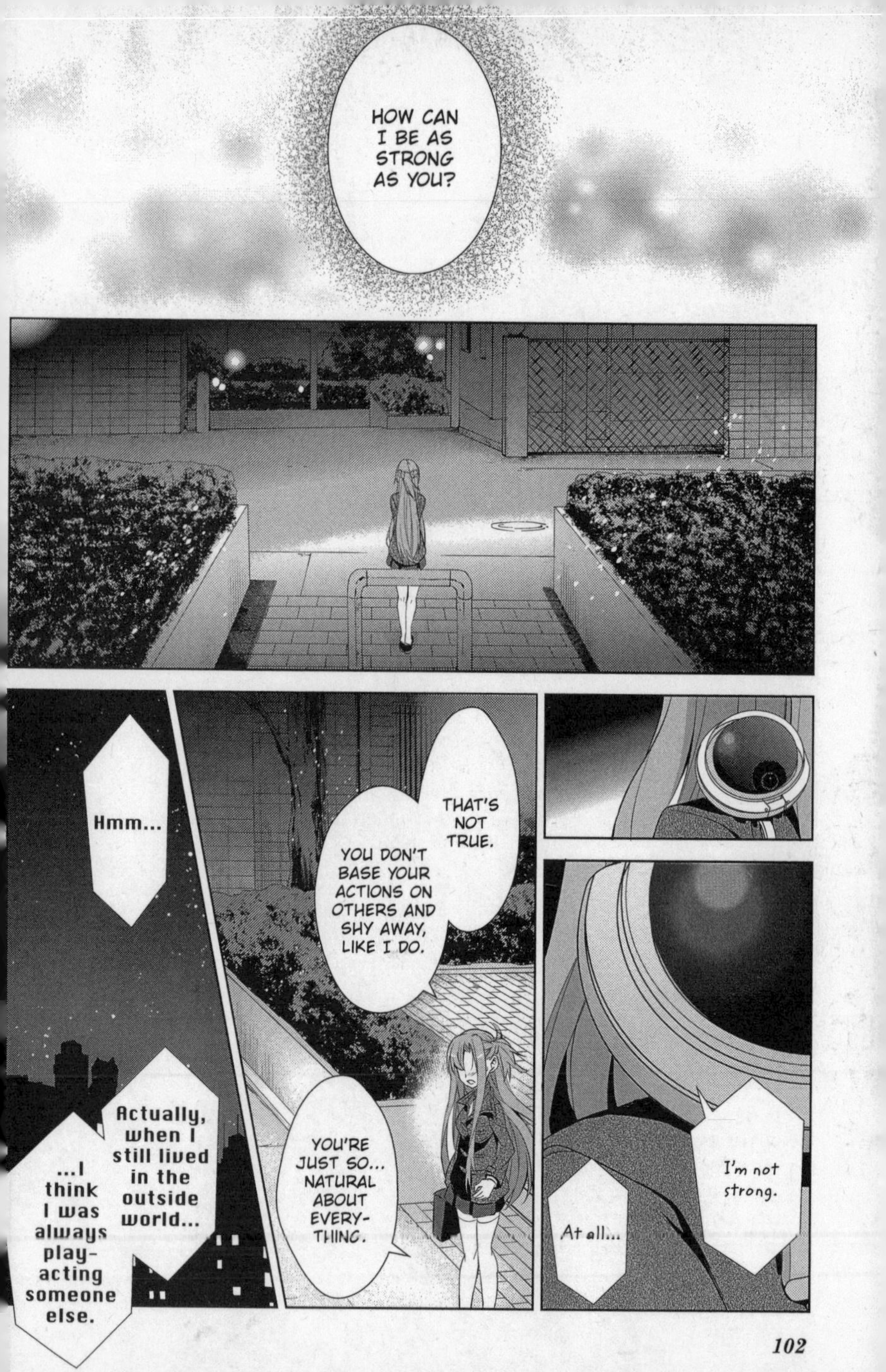
HOW CAN I BE AS STRONG AS YOU?
I'm not strong.
At all...
THAT'S NOT TRUE.
YOU DON'T BASE YOUR ACTIONS ON OTHERS AND SHY AWAY, LIKE I DO.
YOU'RE JUST SO... NATURAL ABOUT EVERY-THING.
Hmm...
Actually, when I still lived in the outside world...
...I think I was always play-acting someone else.

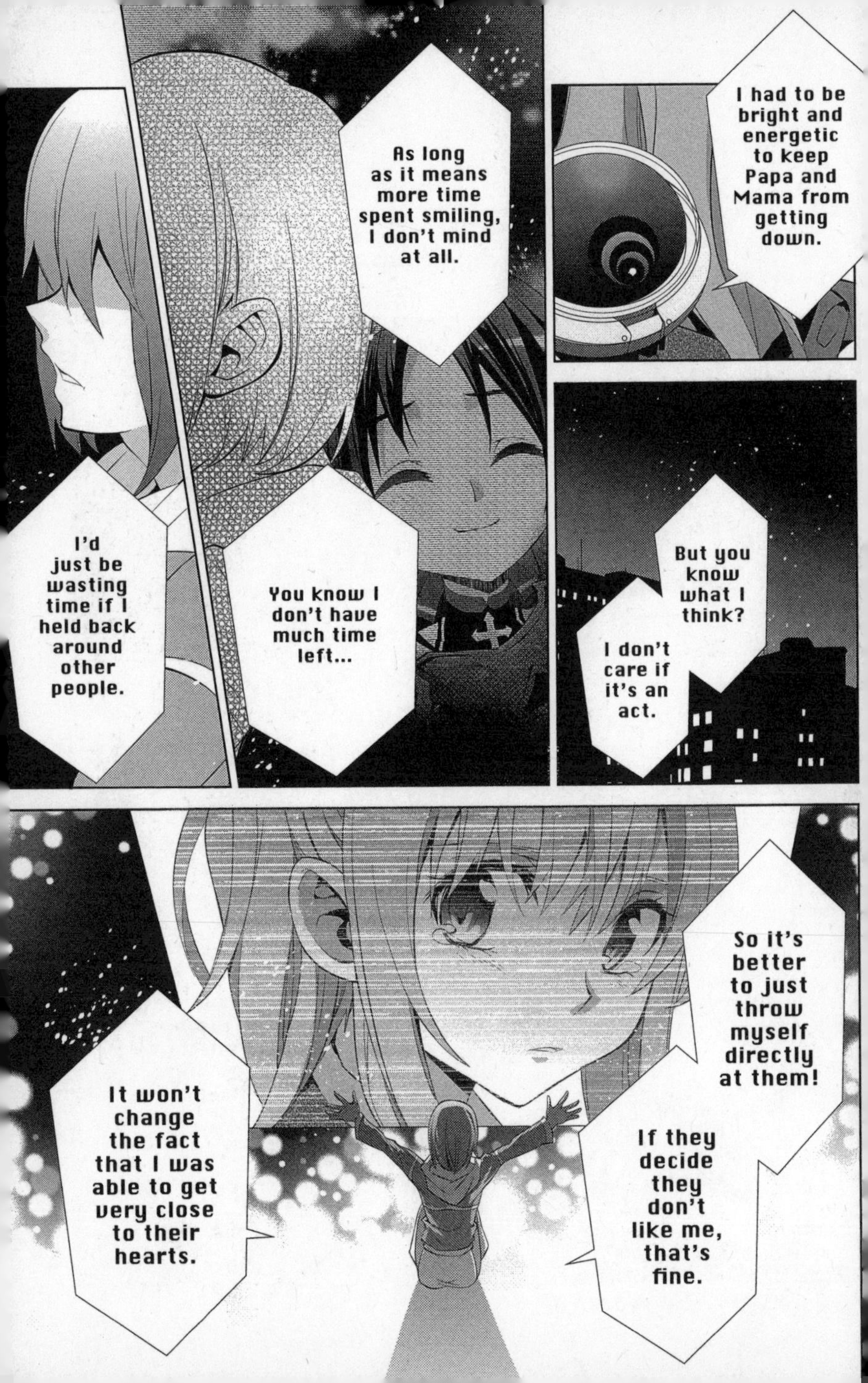
I had to be bright and energetic to keep Papa and Mama from getting down.
But you know what I think?
I don't care if it's an act.
As long as it means more time spent smiling, I don't mind at all.
You know I don't have much time left...
I'd just be wasting time if I held back around other people.
So it's better to just throw myself directly at them!
If they decide they don't like me, that's fine.
It won't change the fact that I was able to get very close to their hearts.

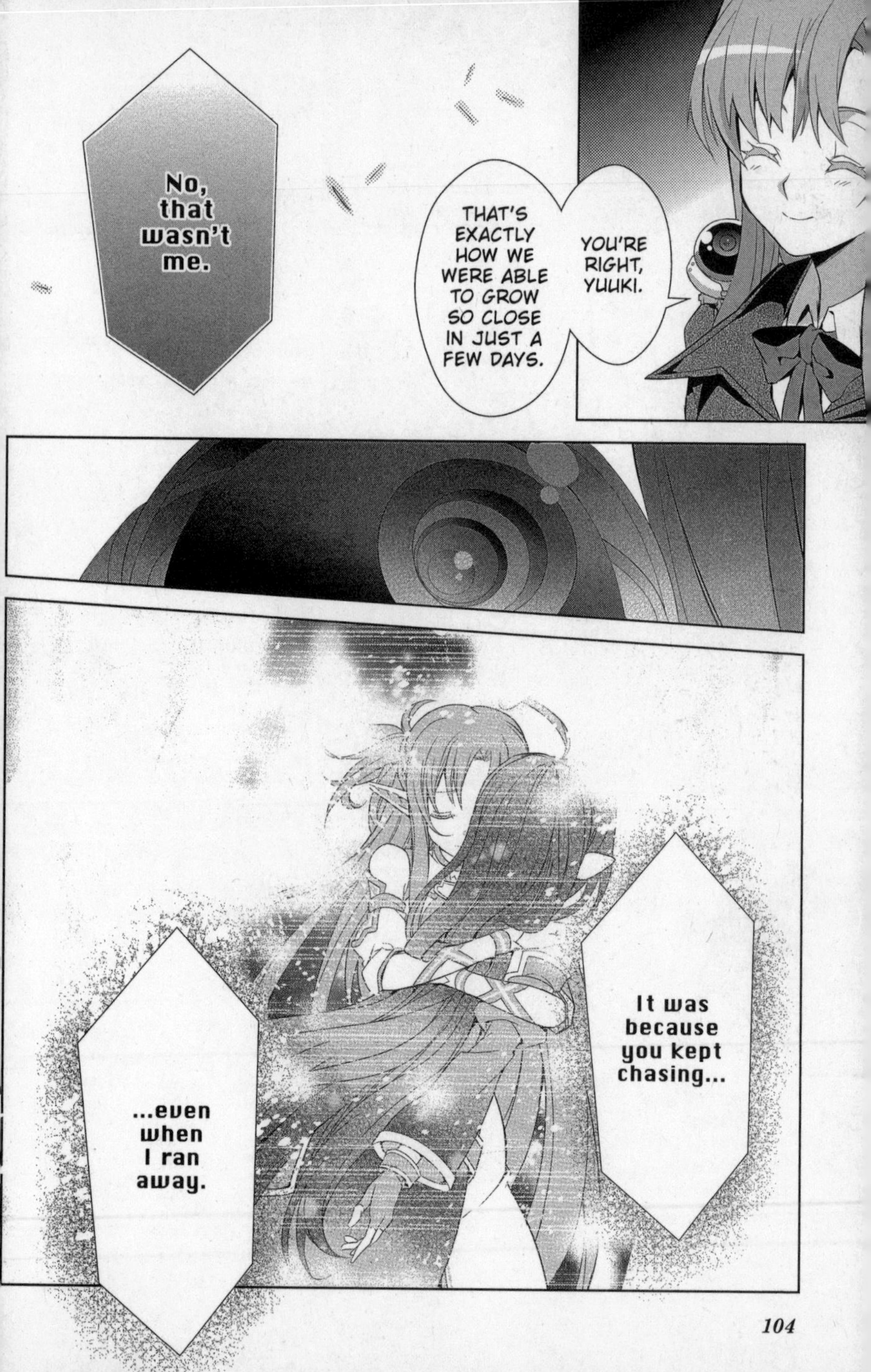
YOU'RE RIGHT, YUUKI.
THAT'S EXACTLY HOW WE WERE ABLE TO GROW SO CLOSE IN JUST A FEW DAYS.
No, that wasn't me.
It was because you kept chasing...
...even when I ran away.

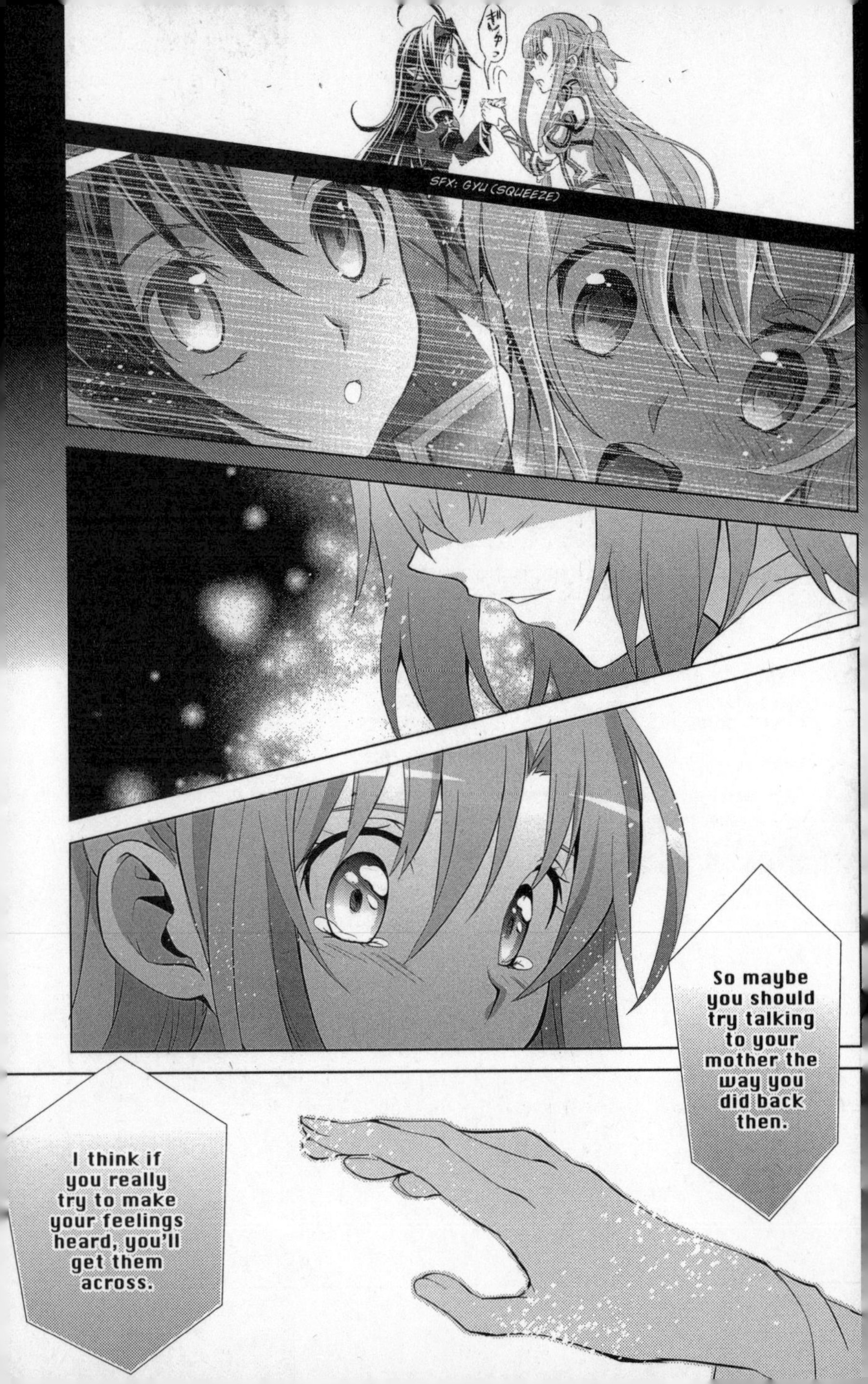
SFX: GYU (SQUEEZE)
So maybe you should try talking to your mother the way you did back then.
I think if you really try to make your feelings heard, you'll get them across.

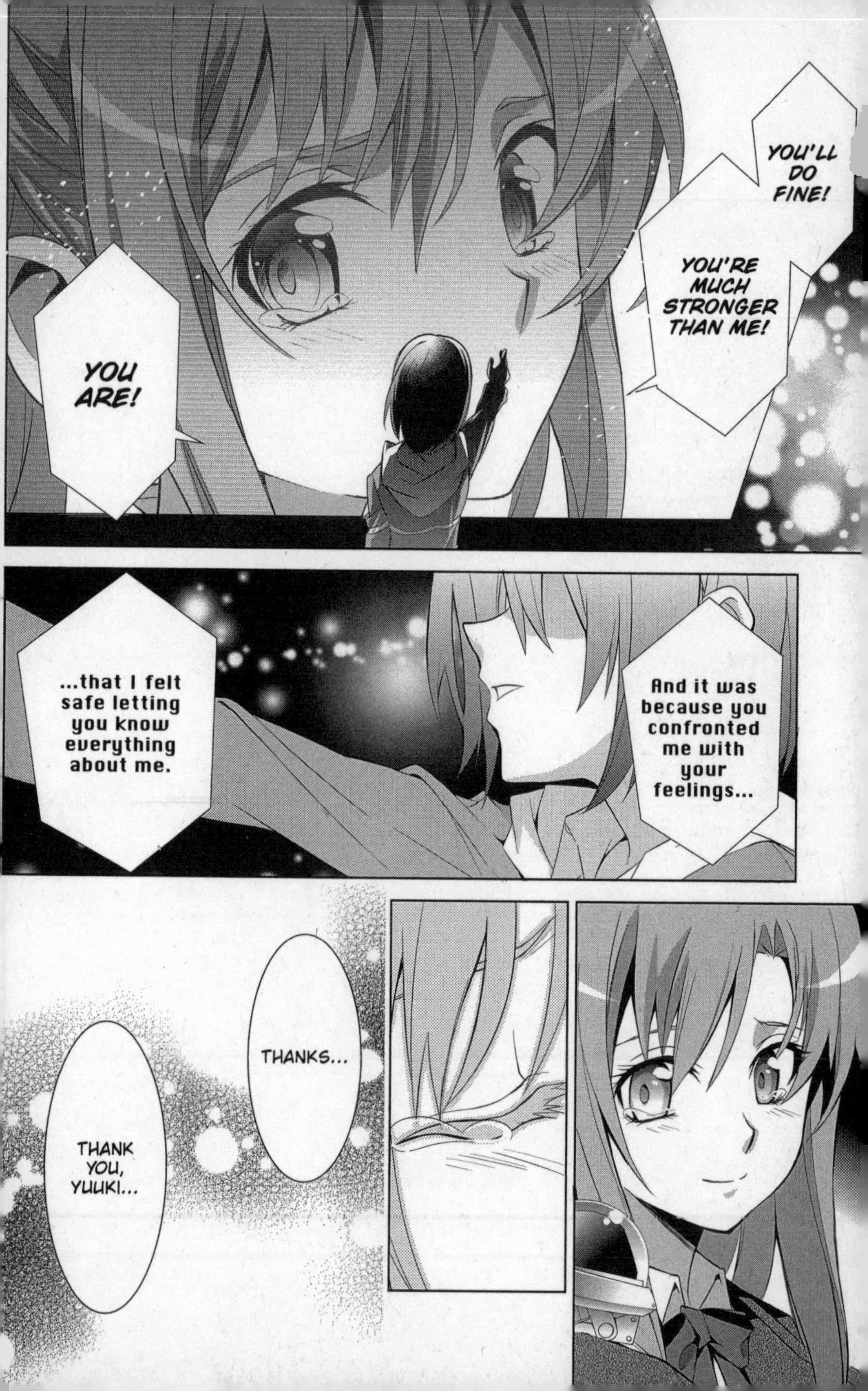
YOU'LL DO FINE!
YOU'RE MUCH STRONGER THAN ME!
YOU ARE!
And it was because you confronted me with your feelings...
...that I felt safe letting you know everything about me.
THANKS...
THANK YOU, YUUKI...

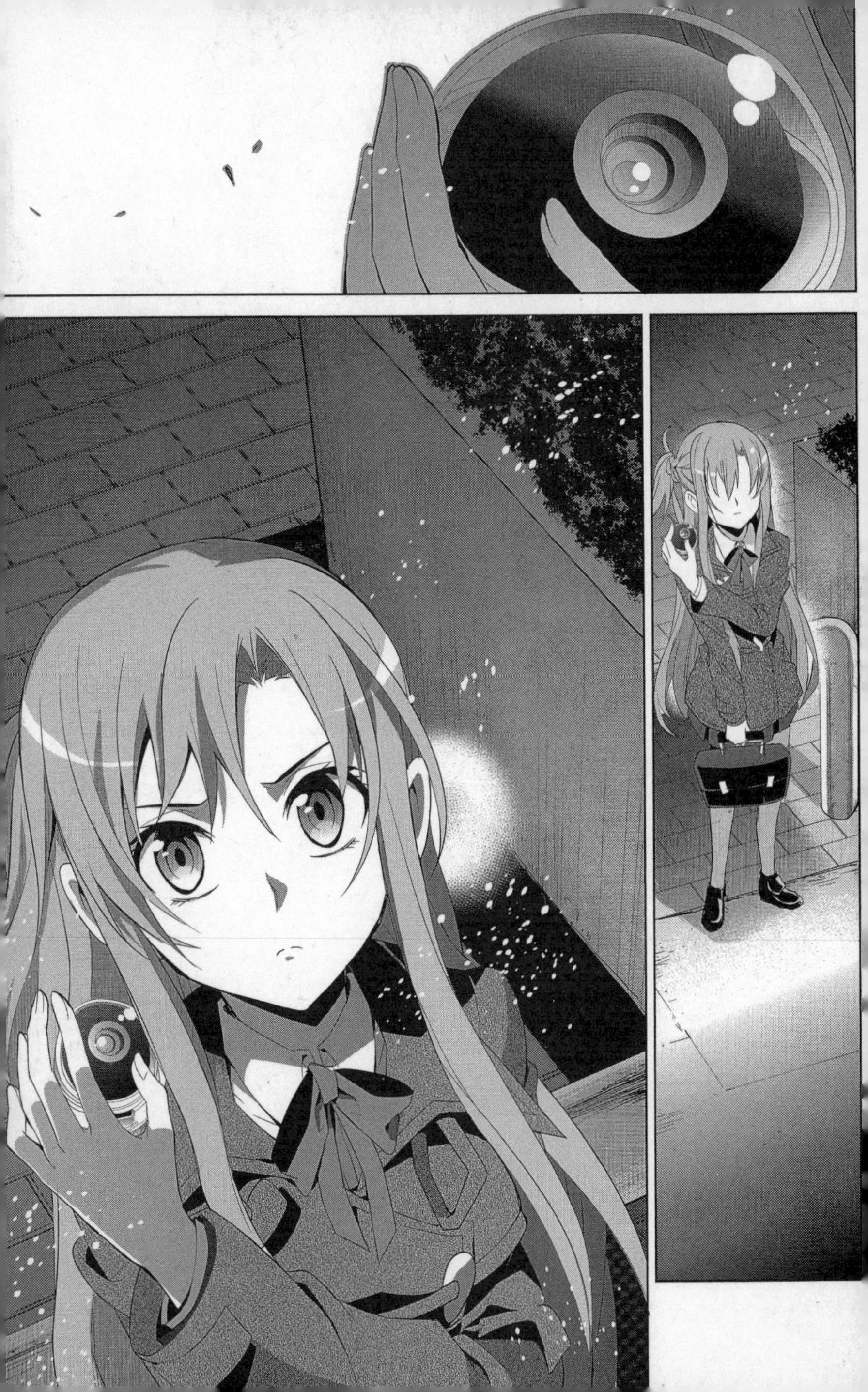

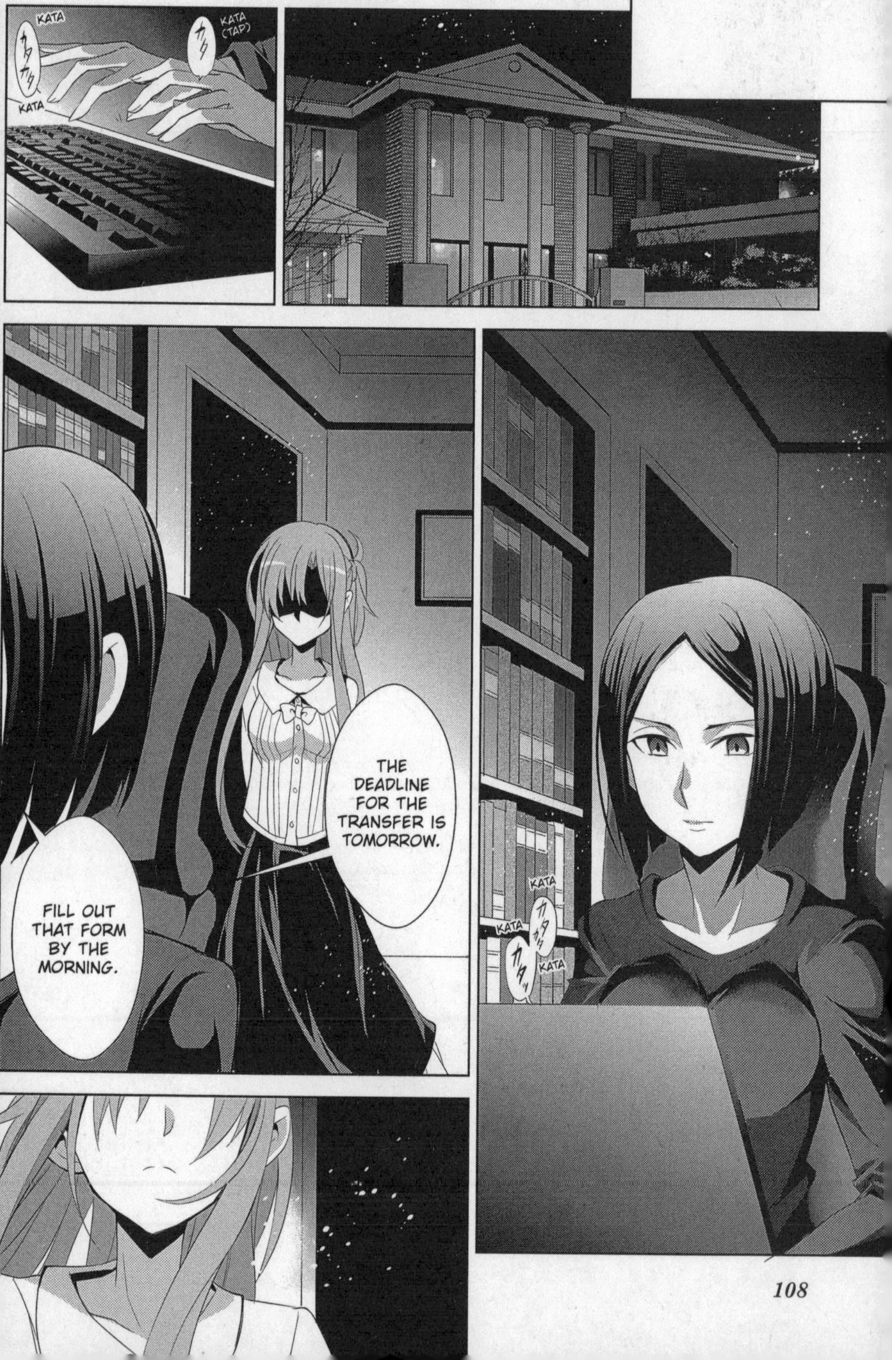
KATA
KATA (TAP)
KATA
KATA
KATA
KATA
THE DEADLINE FOR THE TRANSFER IS TOMORROW.
FILL OUT THAT FORM BY THE MORNING.

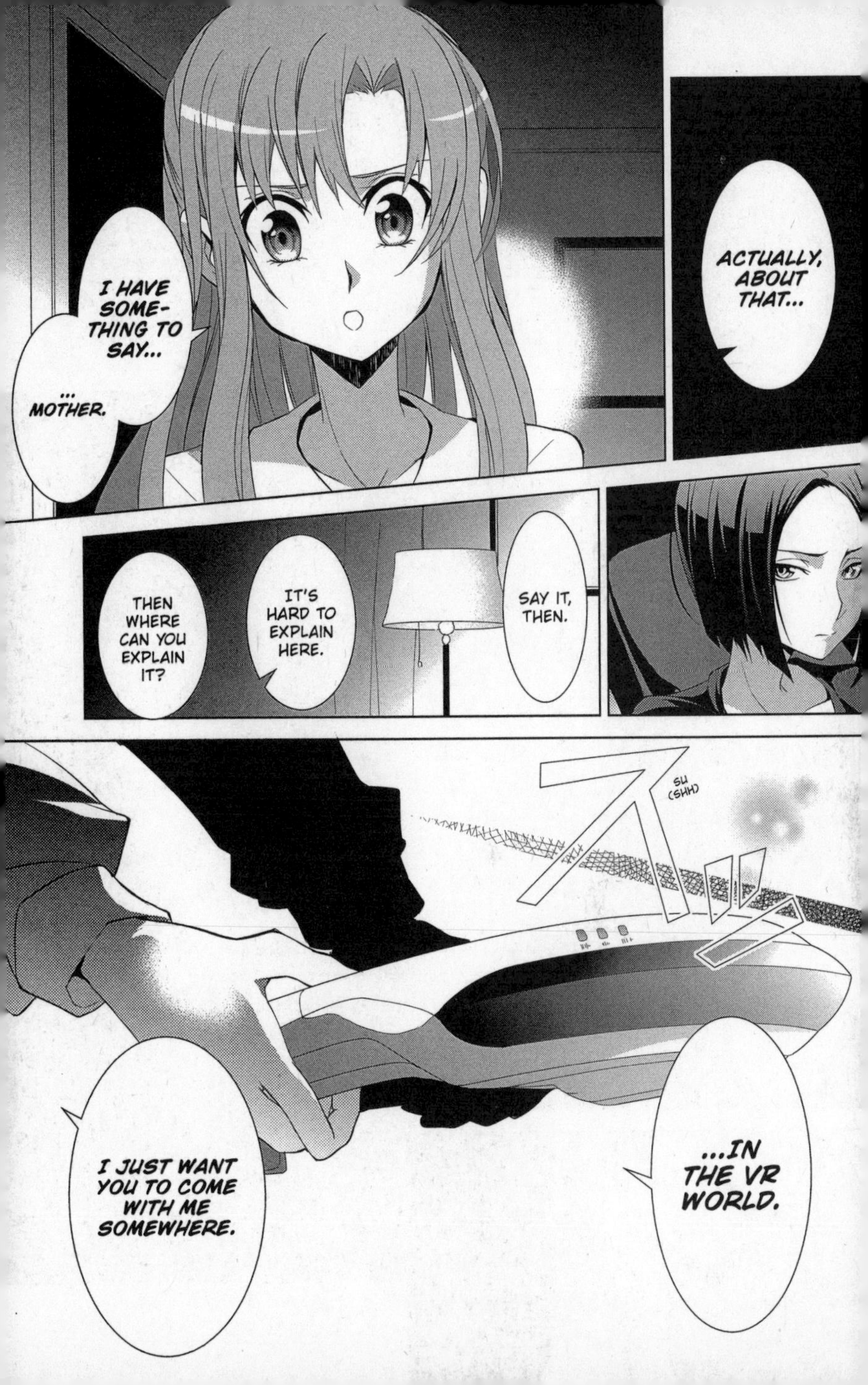
ACTUALLY, ABOUT THAT...
I HAVE SOME-THING TO SAY...
...MOTHER.
SAY IT, THEN.
IT'S HARD TO EXPLAIN HERE.
THEN WHERE CAN YOU EXPLAIN IT?
SU (SHH)
...IN THE VR WORLD.
I JUST WANT YOU TO COME WITH ME SOMEWHERE.

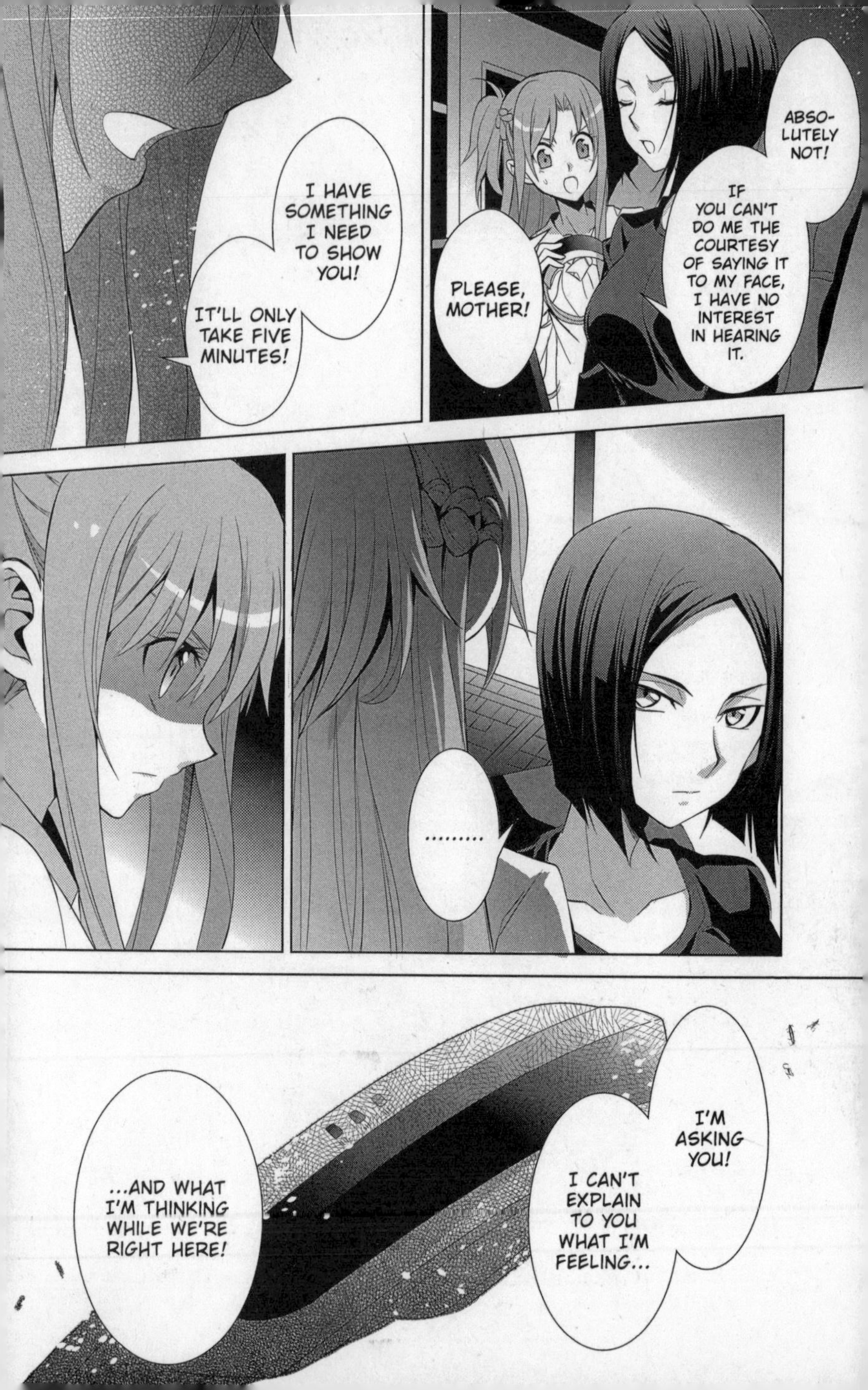
ABSO-LUTELY NOT!
IF YOU CAN'T DO ME THE COURTESY OF SAYING IT TO MY FACE, I HAVE NO INTEREST IN HEARING IT.
PLEASE, MOTHER!
I HAVE SOMETHING I NEED TO SHOW YOU!
IT'LL ONLY TAKE FIVE MINUTES!
....
I'M ASKING YOU!
I CAN'T EXPLAIN TO YOU WHAT I'M FEELING...
...AND WHAT I'M THINKING WHILE WE'RE RIGHT HERE!

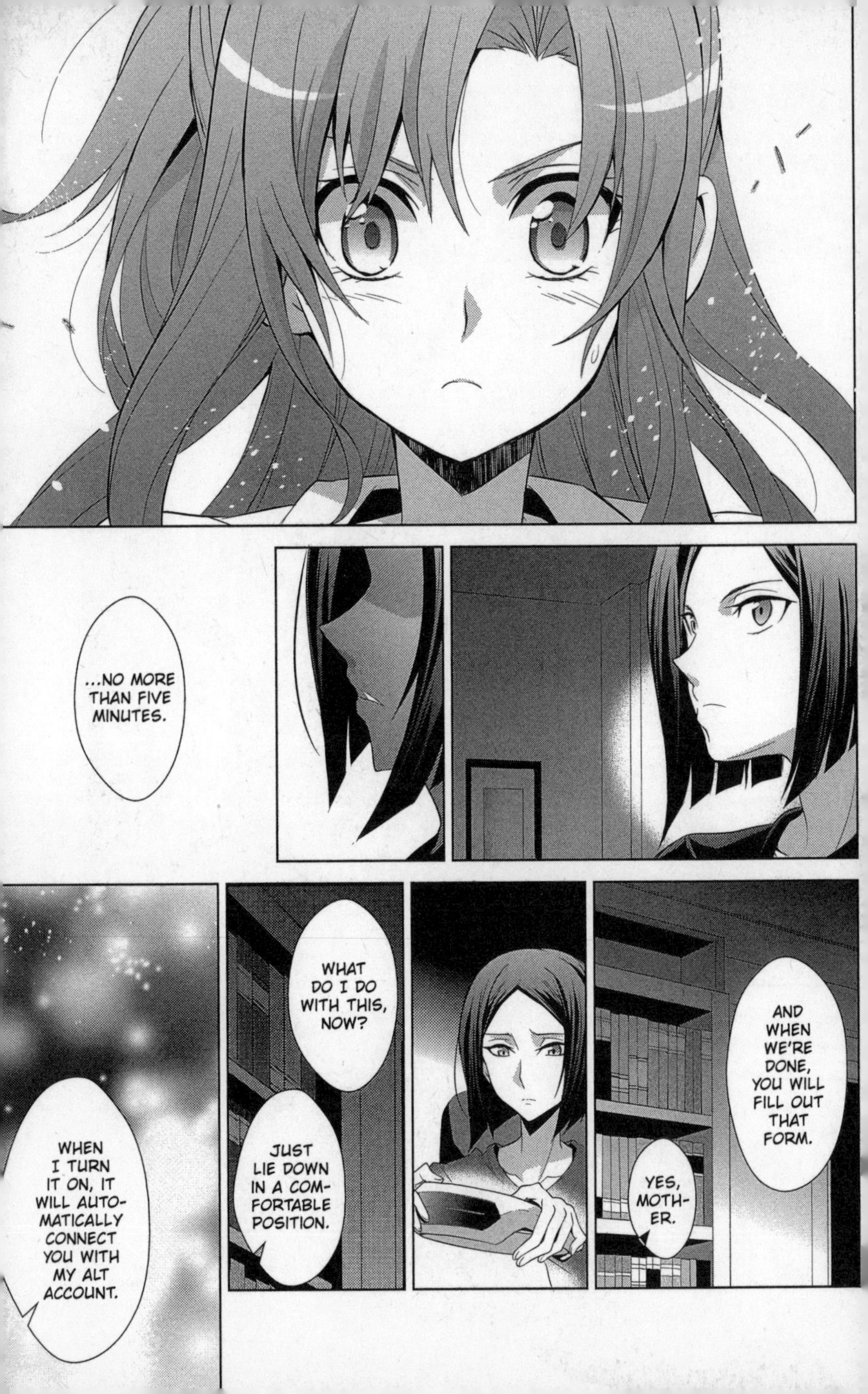
...NO MORE THAN FIVE MINUTES.
AND WHEN WE'RE DONE, YOU WILL FILL OUT THAT FORM.
YES, MOTHER.
WHAT DO I DO WITH THIS, NOW?
JUST LIE DOWN IN A COM-FORTABLE POSITION.
WHEN I TURN IT ON, IT WILL AUTO-MATICALLY CONNECT YOU WITH MY ALT ACCOUNT.

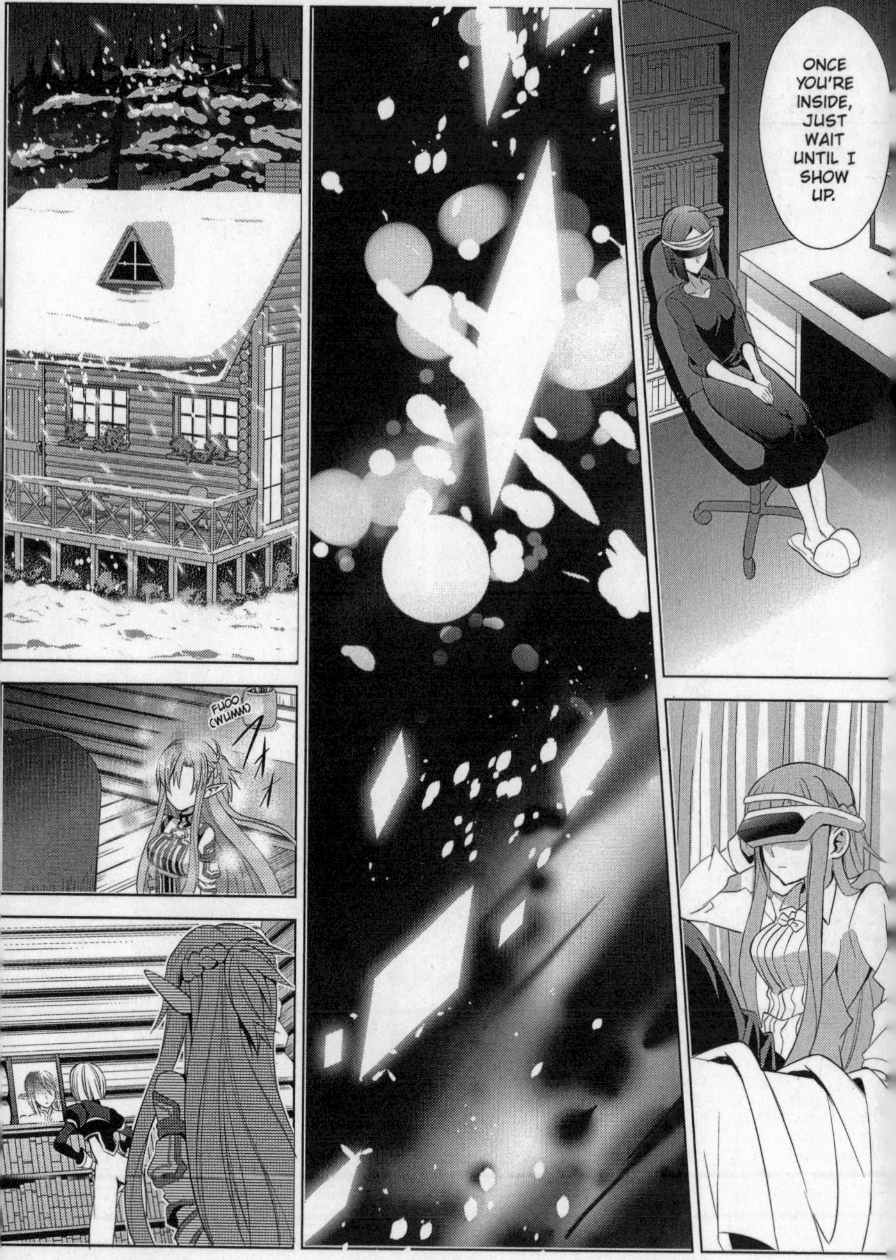
ONCE YOU'RE INSIDE, JUST WAIT UNTIL I SHOW UP.
FUOO (WLMM)

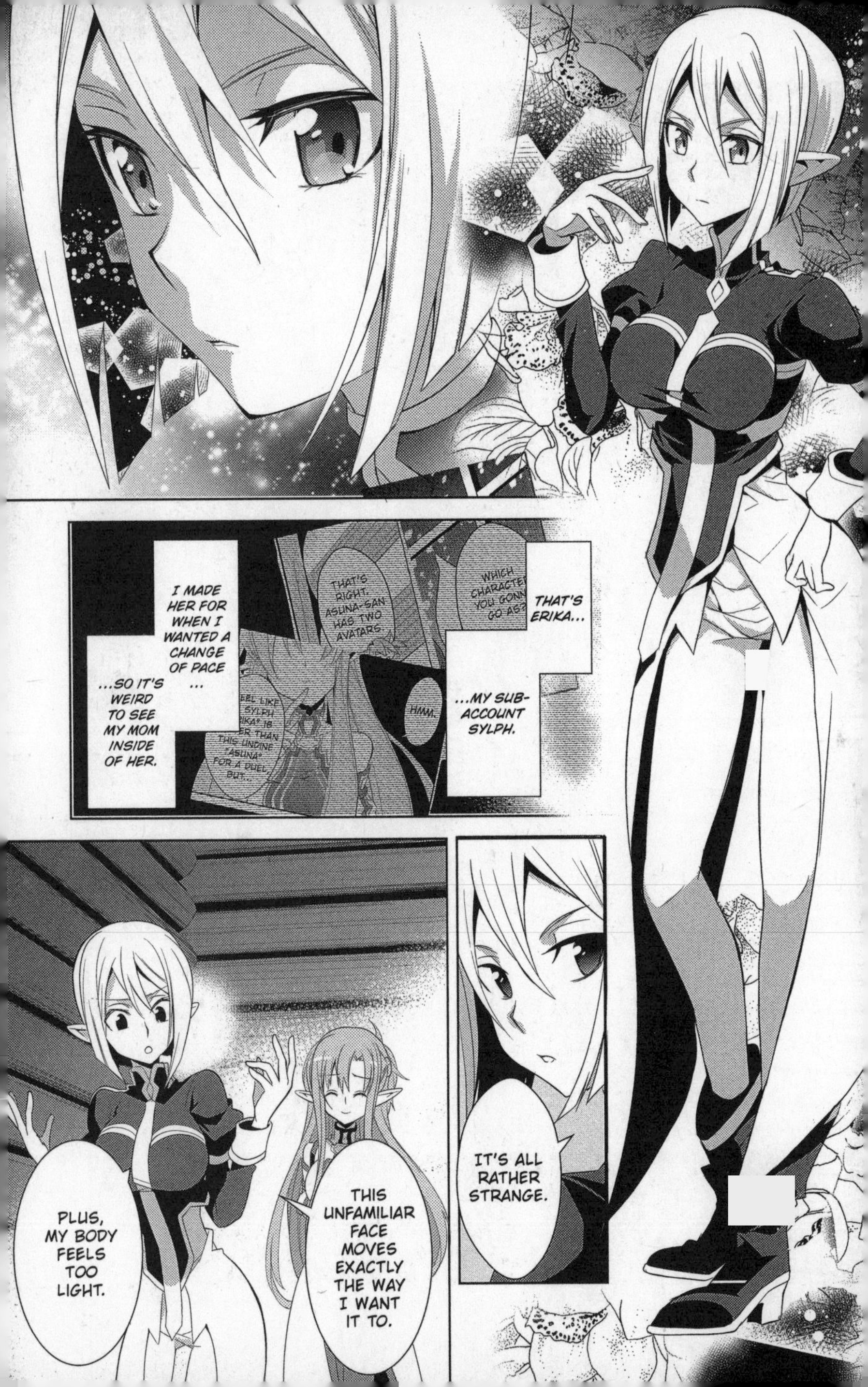
THAT'S ERIKA...
THAT'S RIGHT. ASUNA-SAN HAS TWO AVATARS.
HMM...
...MY SUB-ACCOUNT SYLPH.
I MADE HER FOR WHEN I WANTED A CHANGE OF PACE...
...SO IT'S WEIRD TO SEE MY MOM INSIDE OF HER.
IT'S ALL RATHER STRANGE.
THIS UNFAMILIAR FACE MOVES EXACTLY THE WAY I WANT IT TO.
PLUS, MY BODY FEELS TOO LIGHT.

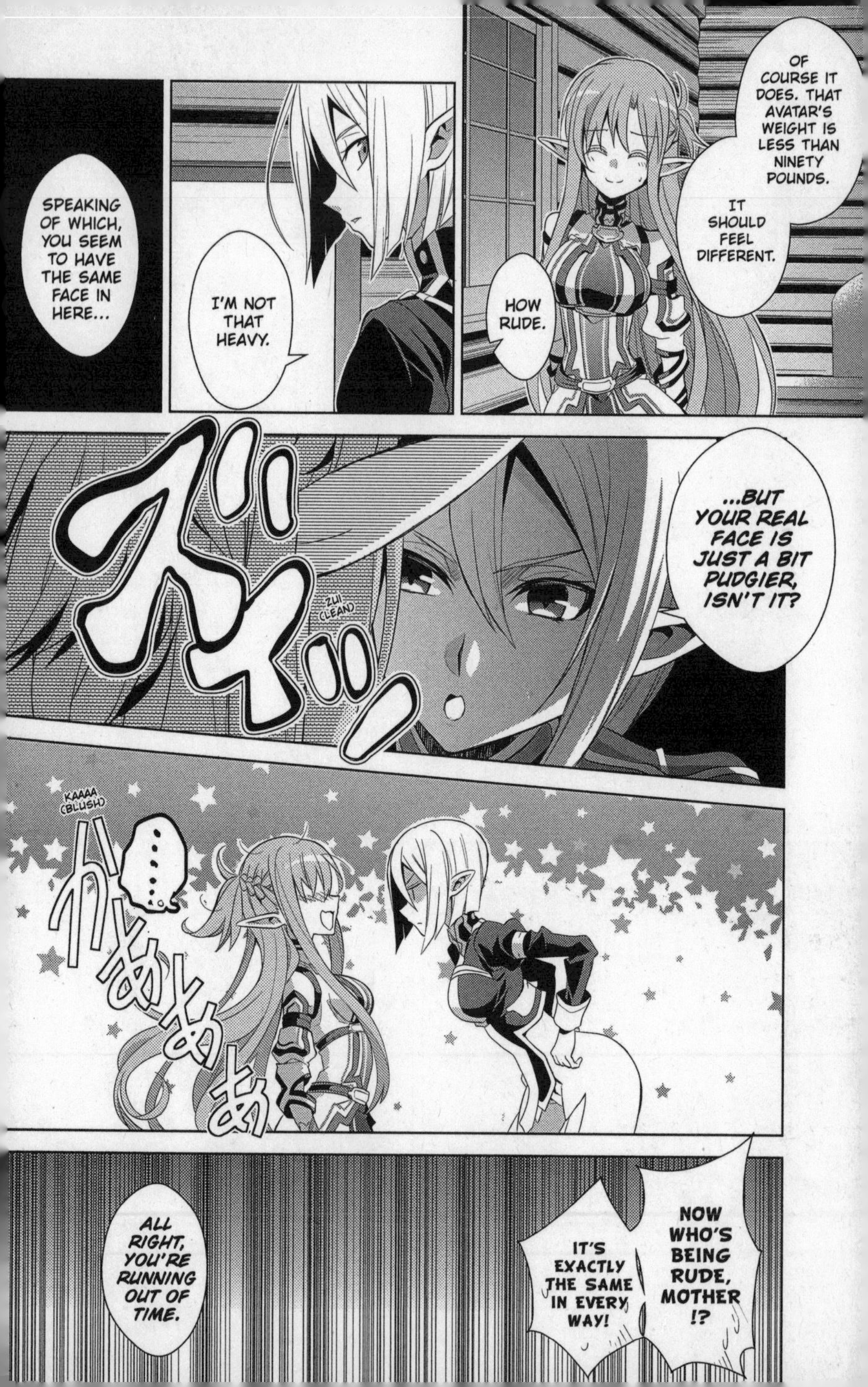

OF COURSE IT DOES. THAT AVATAR'S WEIGHT IS LESS THAN NINETY POUNDS.
IT SHOULD FEEL DIFFERENT.
HOW RUDE.
I'M NOT THAT HEAVY.
SPEAKING OF WHICH, YOU SEEM TO HAVE THE SAME FACE IN HERE...
...BUT YOUR REAL FACE IS JUST A BIT PUDGIER, ISN'T IT?
ZUI (LEAN)
KAAAA (BLUSH)
......
NOW WHO'S BEING RUDE, MOTHER!?
IT'S EXACTLY THE SAME IN EVERY WAY!
ALL RIGHT, YOU'RE RUNNING OUT OF TIME.

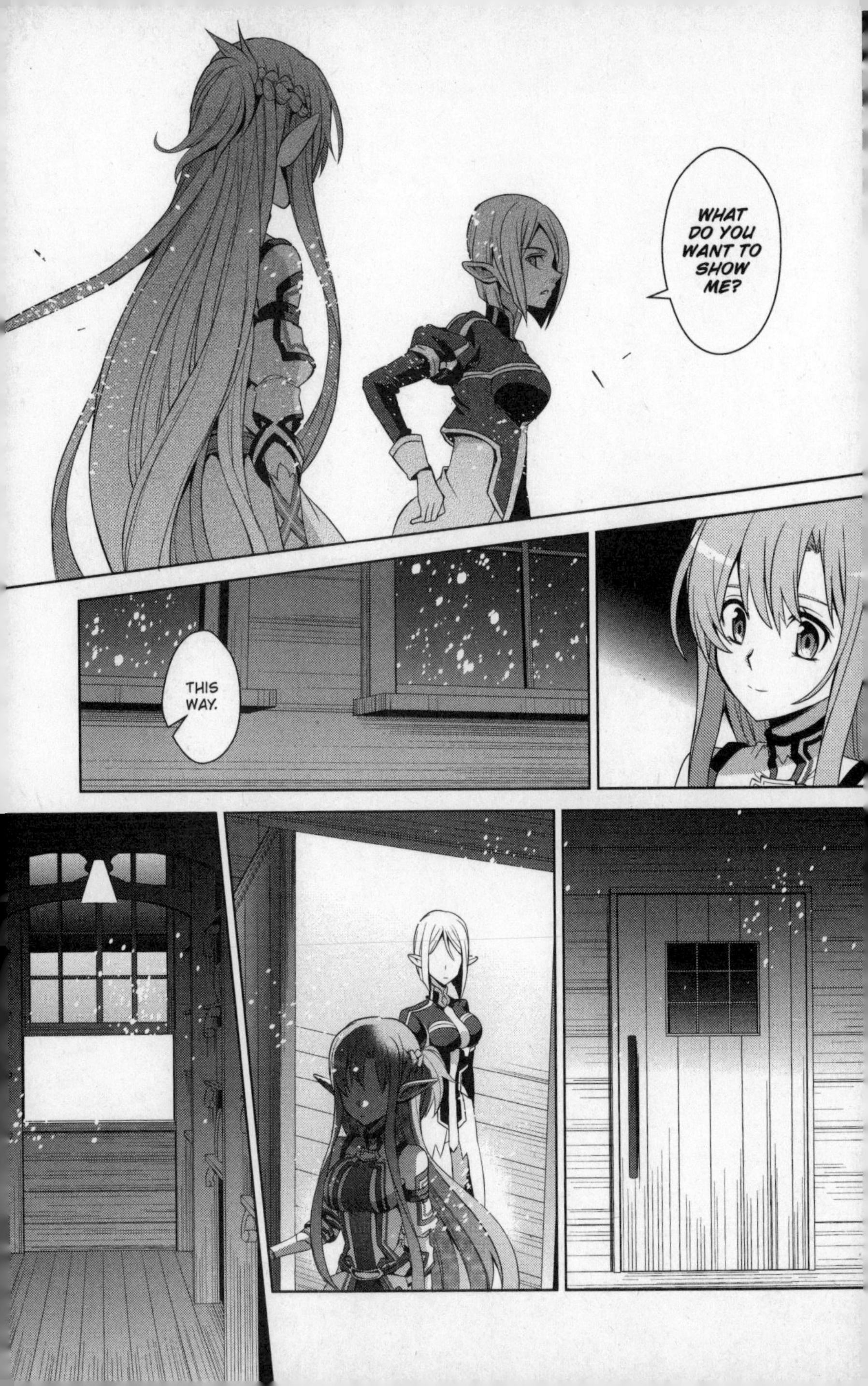
WHAT DO YOU WANT TO SHOW ME?
THIS WAY.

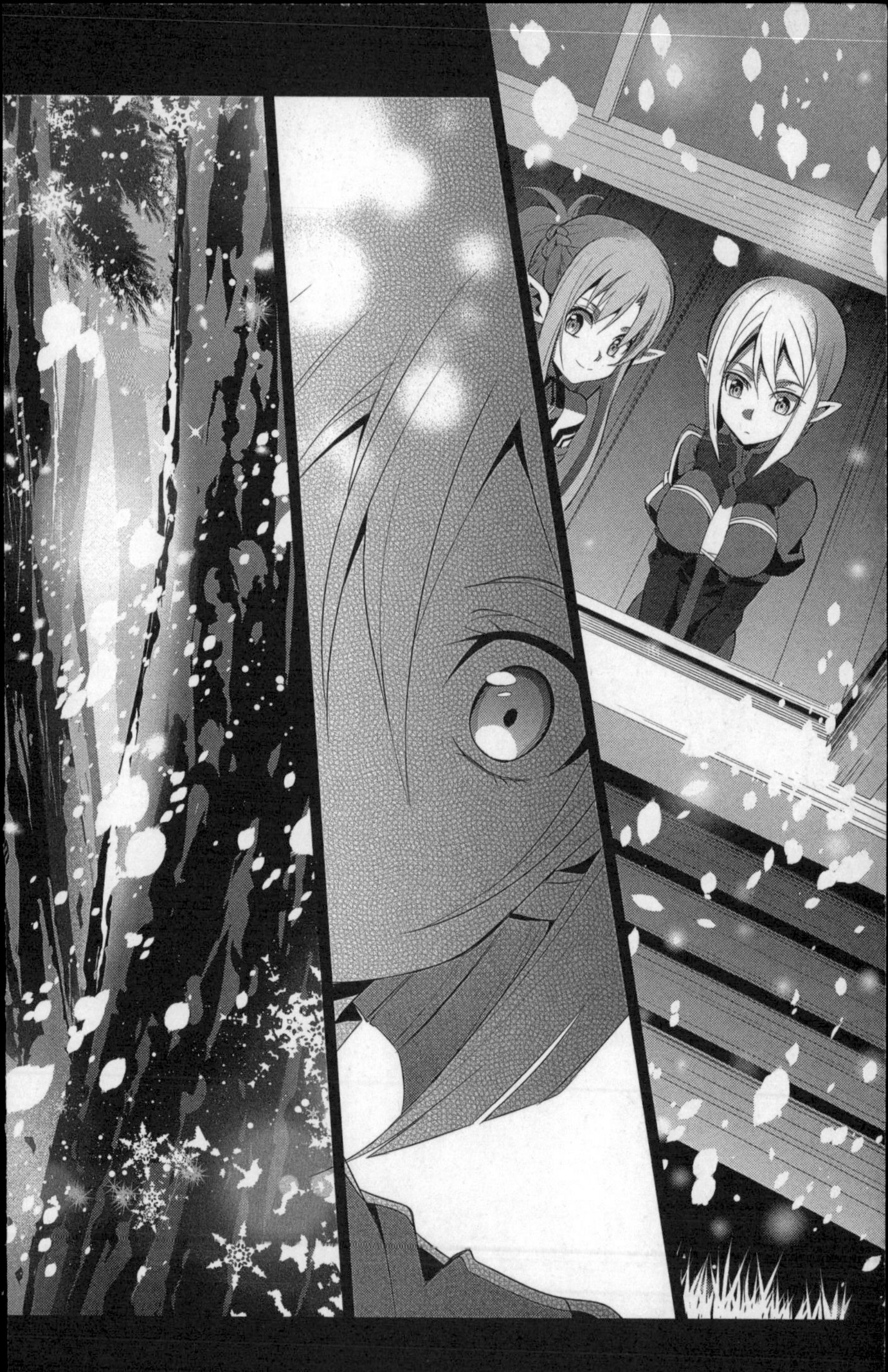

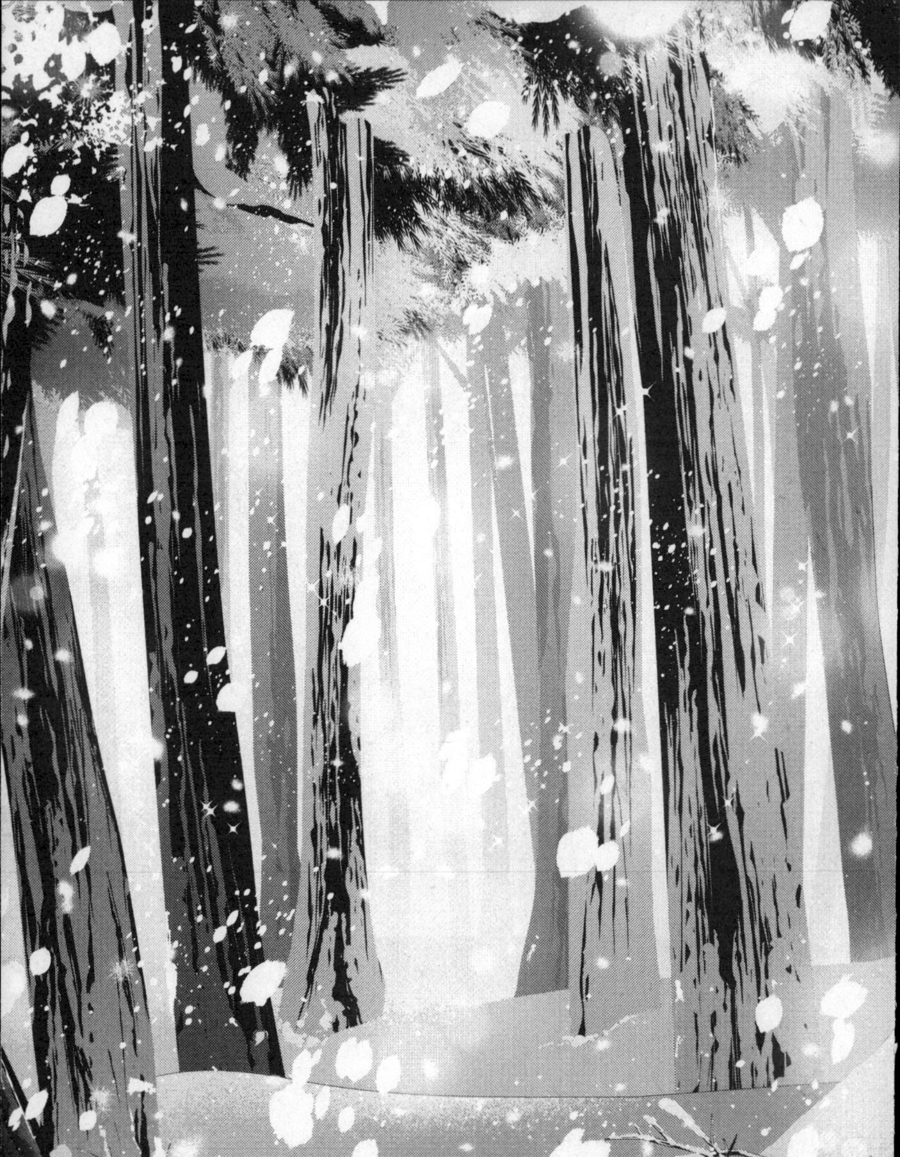

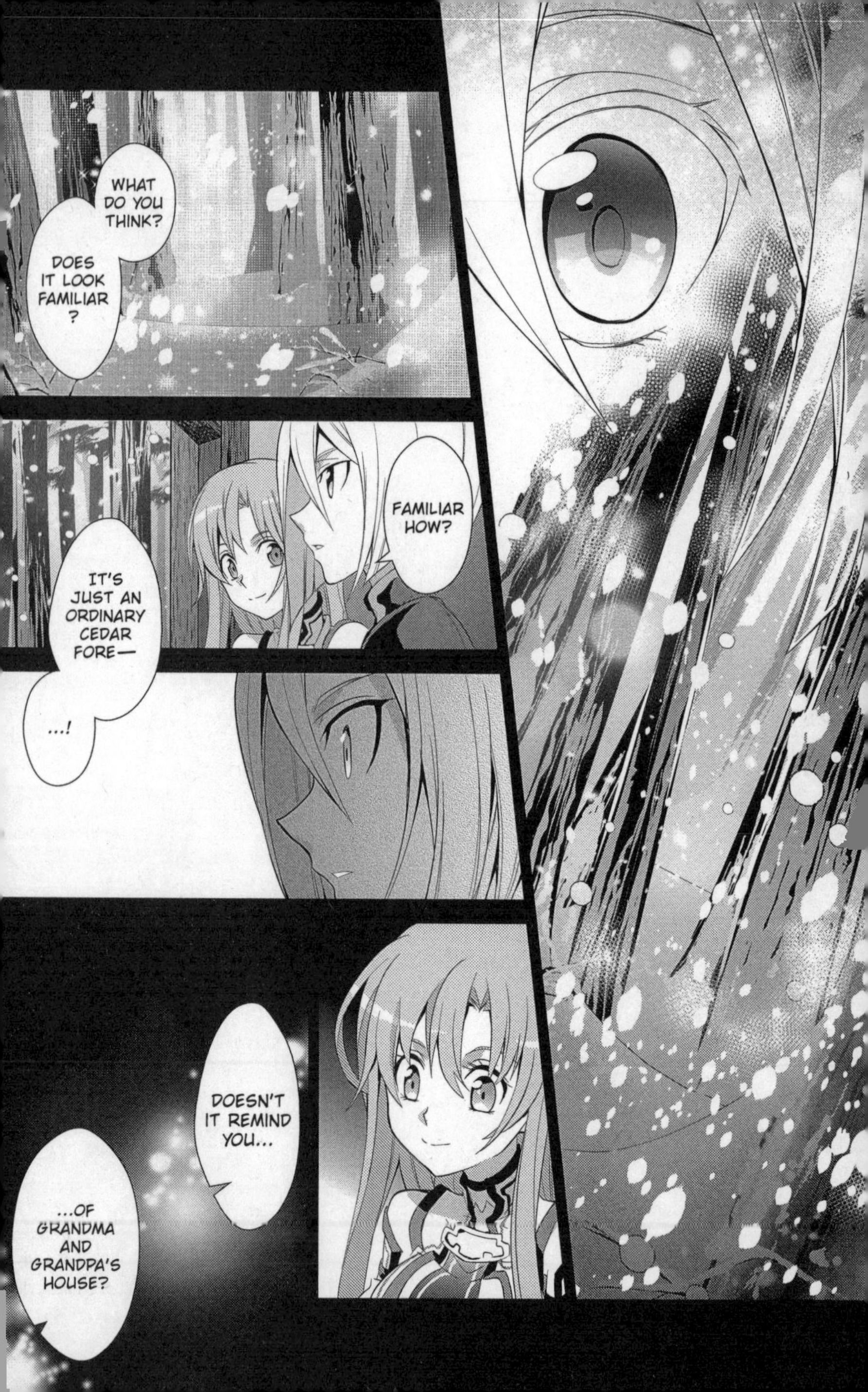
WHAT DO YOU THINK?
DOES IT LOOK FAMILIAR?
FAMILIAR HOW?
IT'S JUST AN ORDINARY CEDAR FORE—
...!
DOESN'T IT REMIND YOU...
...OF GRANDMA AND GRANDPA'S HOUSE?

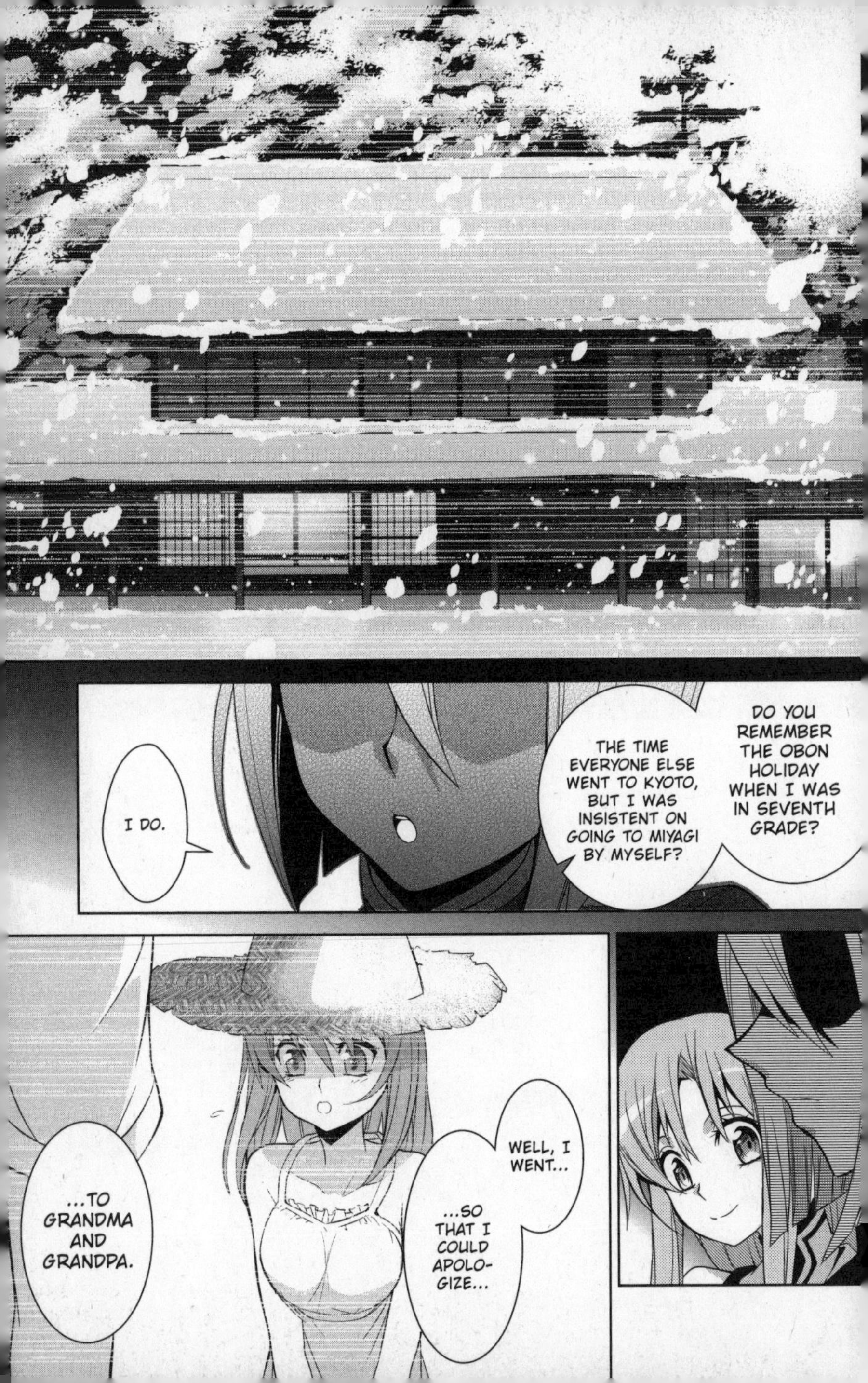
DO YOU REMEMBER THE OBON HOLIDAY WHEN I WAS IN SEVENTH GRADE?
THE TIME EVERYONE ELSE WENT TO KYOTO, BUT I WAS INSISTENT ON GOING TO MIYAGI BY MYSELF?
I DO.
WELL, I WENT...
...SO THAT I COULD APOLO-GIZE...
...TO GRANDMA AND GRANDPA.

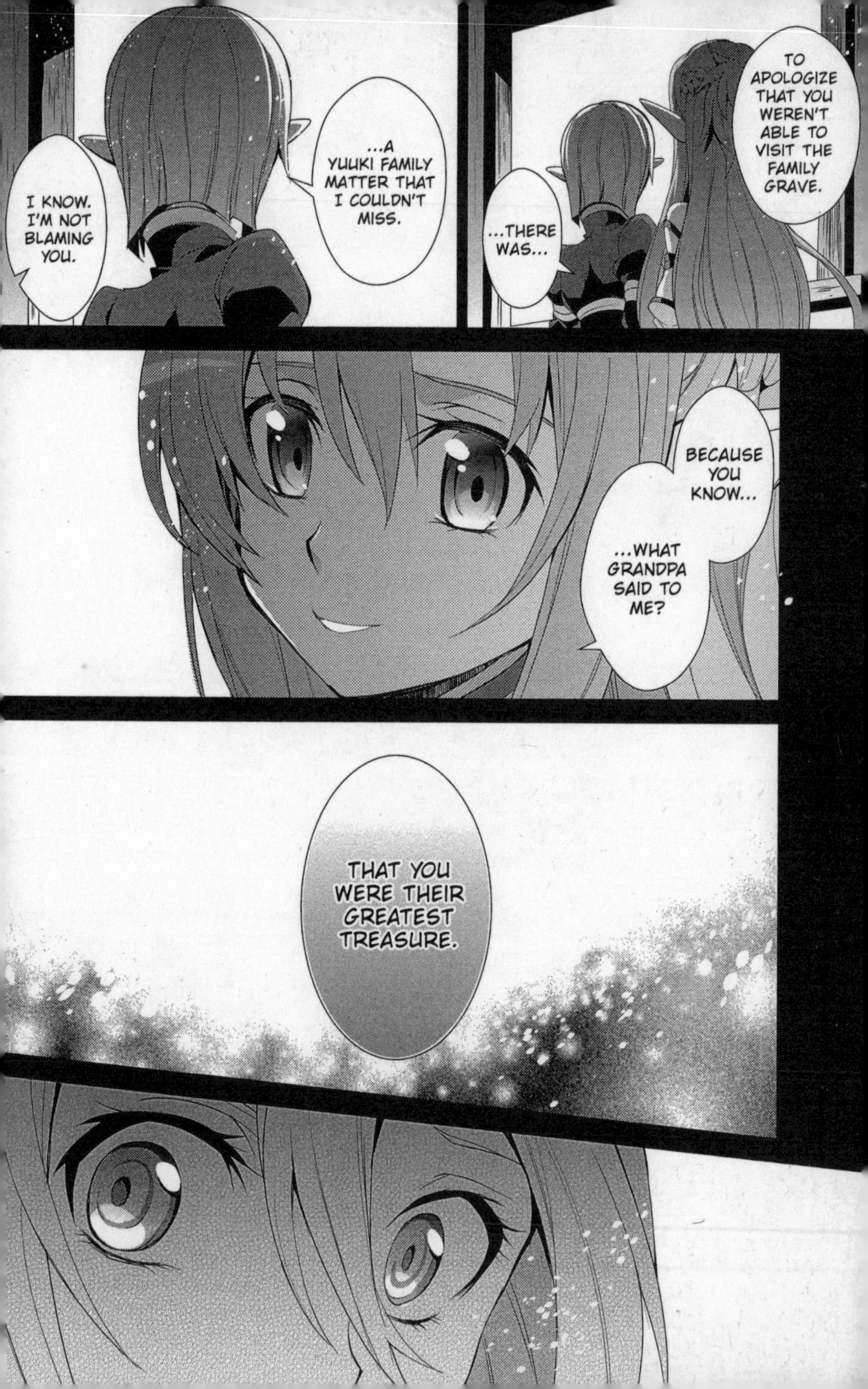
TO APOLOGIZE THAT YOU WEREN'T ABLE TO VISIT THE FAMILY GRAVE.
...THERE WAS...
...A YUUKI FAMILY MATTER THAT I COULDN'T MISS.
I KNOW. I'M NOT BLAMING YOU.
BECAUSE YOU KNOW...
...WHAT GRANDPA SAID TO ME?
THAT YOU WERE THEIR GREATEST TREASURE.

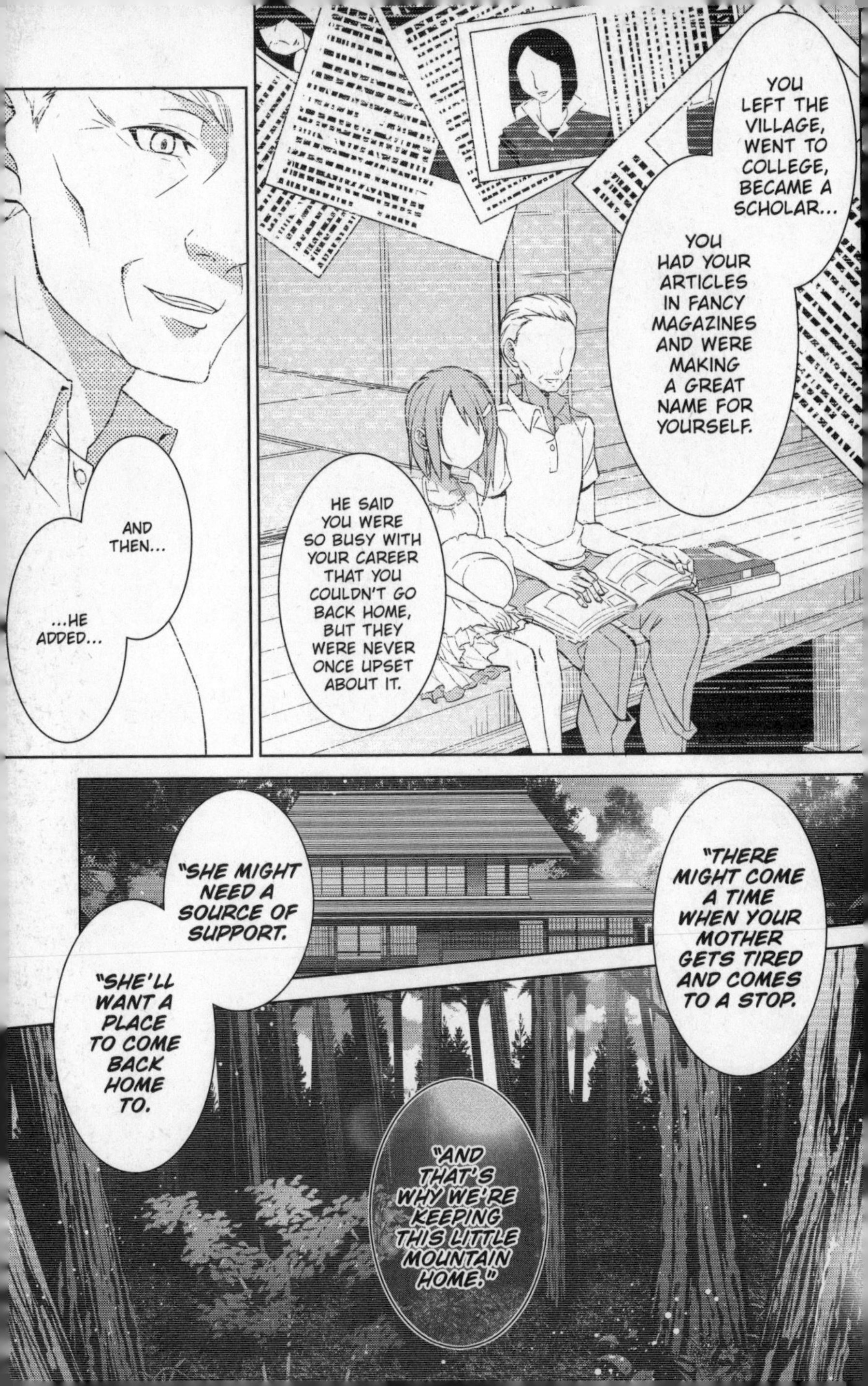
YOU LEFT THE VILLAGE, WENT TO COLLEGE, BECAME A SCHOLAR...
YOU HAD YOUR ARTICLES IN FANCY MAGAZINES AND WERE MAKING A GREAT NAME FOR YOURSELF.
HE SAID YOU WERE SO BUSY WITH YOUR CAREER THAT YOU COULDN'T GO BACK HOME, BUT THEY WERE NEVER ONCE UPSET ABOUT IT.
AND THEN...
...HE ADDED...
"THERE MIGHT COME A TIME WHEN YOUR MOTHER GETS TIRED AND COMES TO A STOP.
"SHE MIGHT NEED A SOURCE OF SUPPORT.
"SHE'LL WANT A PLACE TO COME BACK HOME TO.
"AND THAT'S WHY WE'RE KEEPING THIS LITTLE MOUNTAIN HOME."

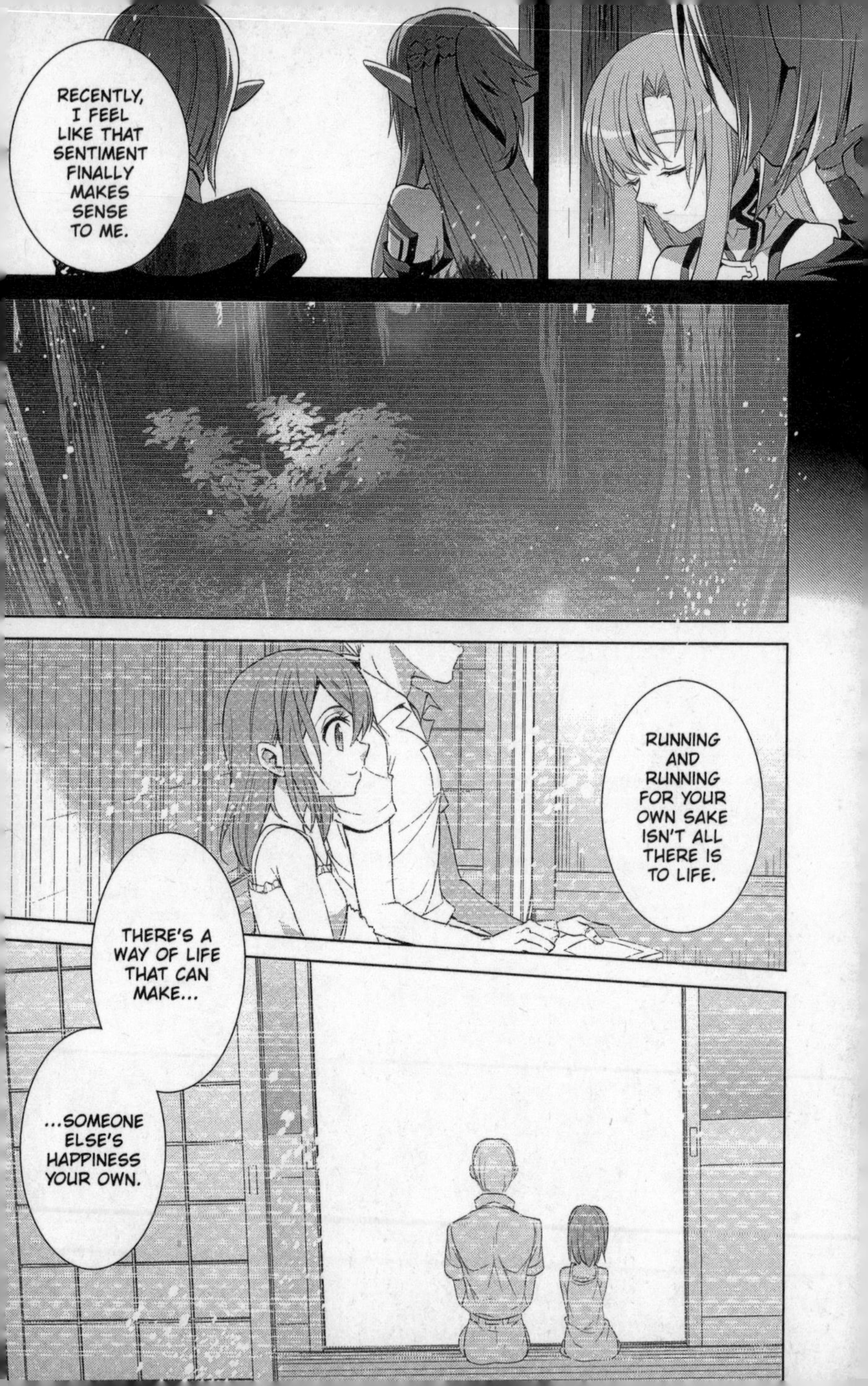
RECENTLY, I FEEL LIKE THAT SENTIMENT FINALLY MAKES SENSE TO ME.
RUNNING AND RUNNING FOR YOUR OWN SAKE ISN'T ALL THERE IS TO LIFE.
THERE'S A WAY OF LIFE THAT CAN MAKE...
...SOMEONE ELSE'S HAPPINESS YOUR OWN.

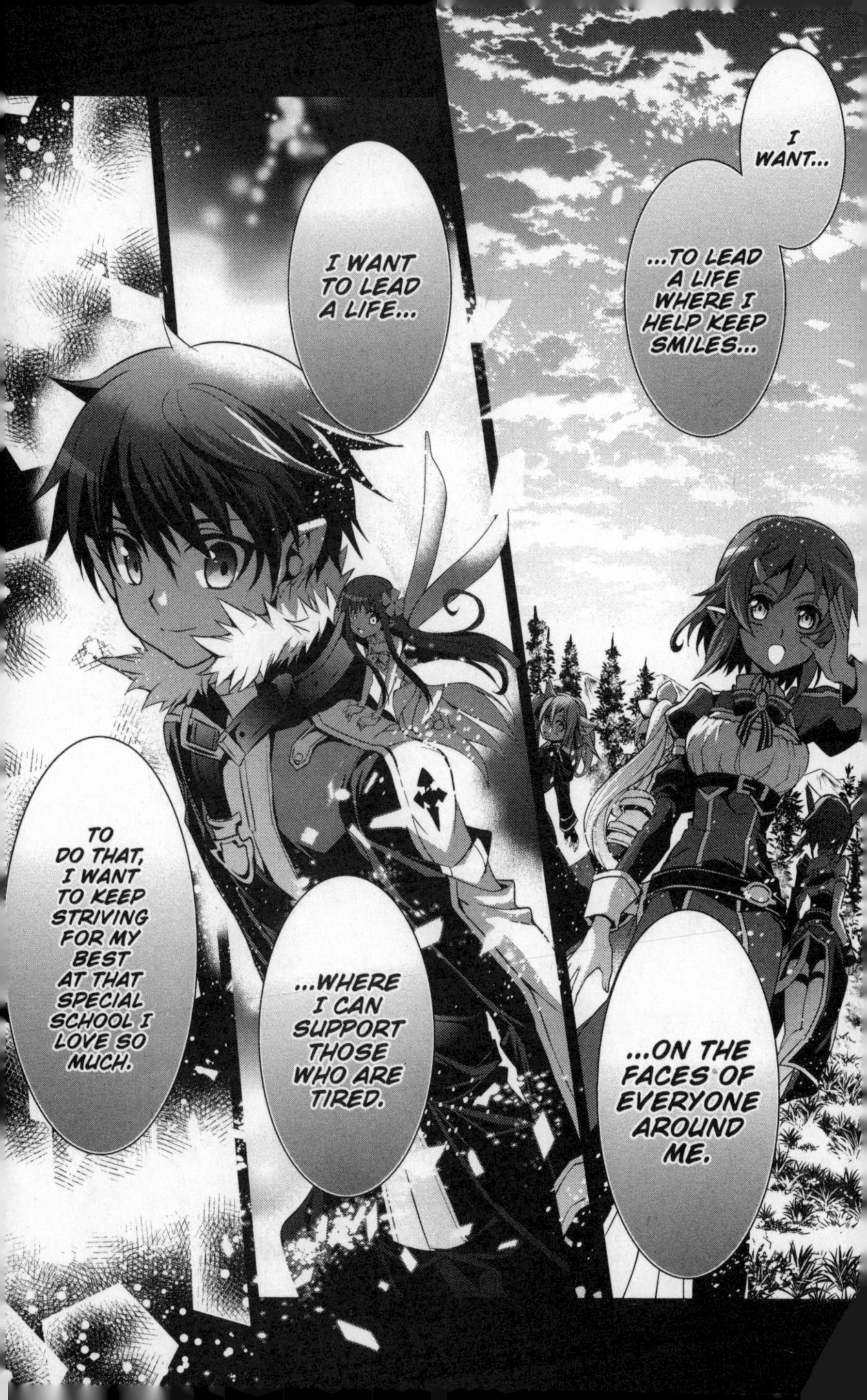
I WANT...
...TO LEAD A LIFE WHERE I HELP KEEP SMILES...
...ON THE FACES OF EVERYONE AROUND ME.
I WANT TO LEAD A LIFE...
...WHERE I CAN SUPPORT THOSE WHO ARE TIRED.
TO DO THAT, I WANT TO KEEP STRIVING FOR MY BEST AT THAT SPECIAL SCHOOL I LOVE SO MUCH.

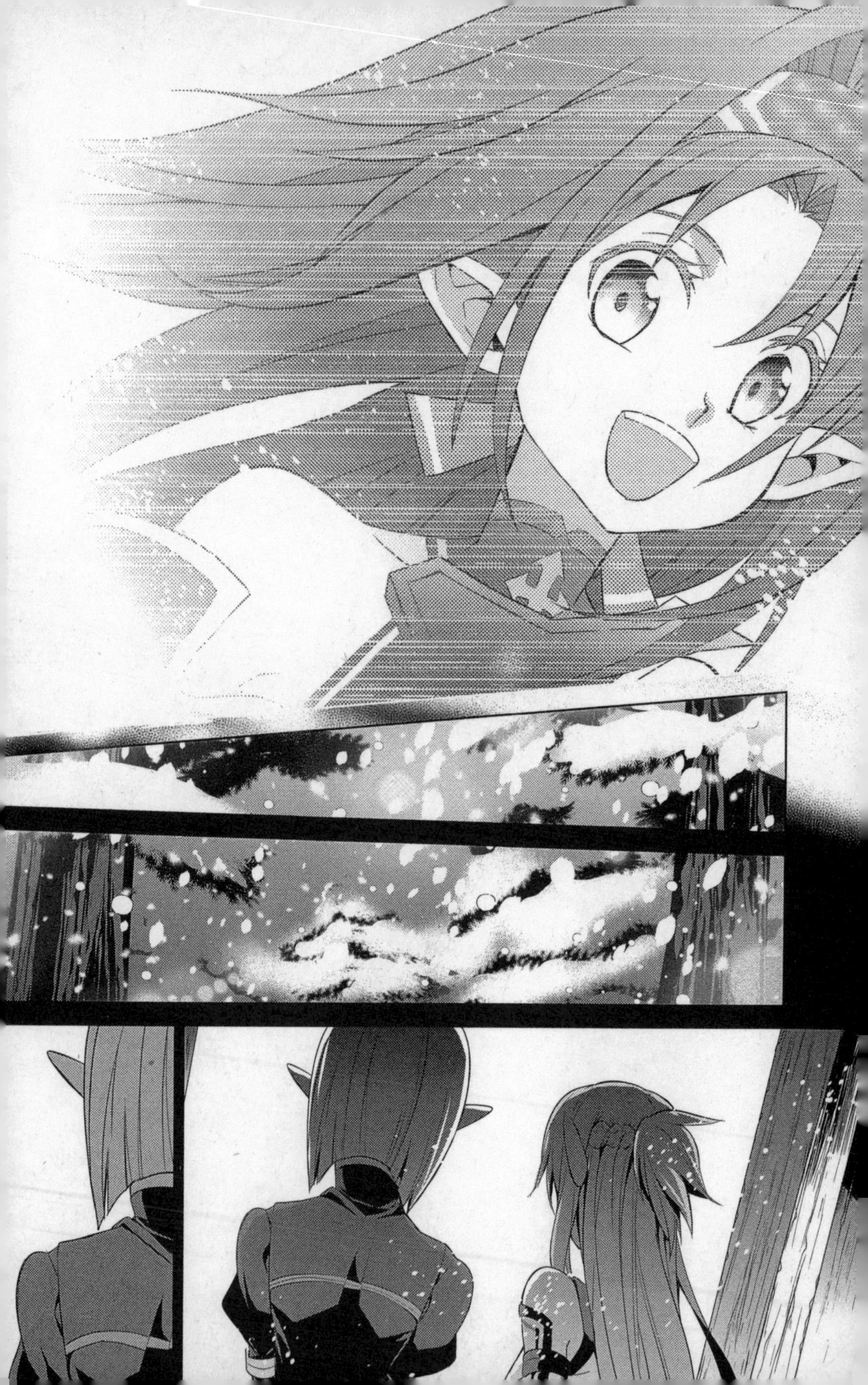

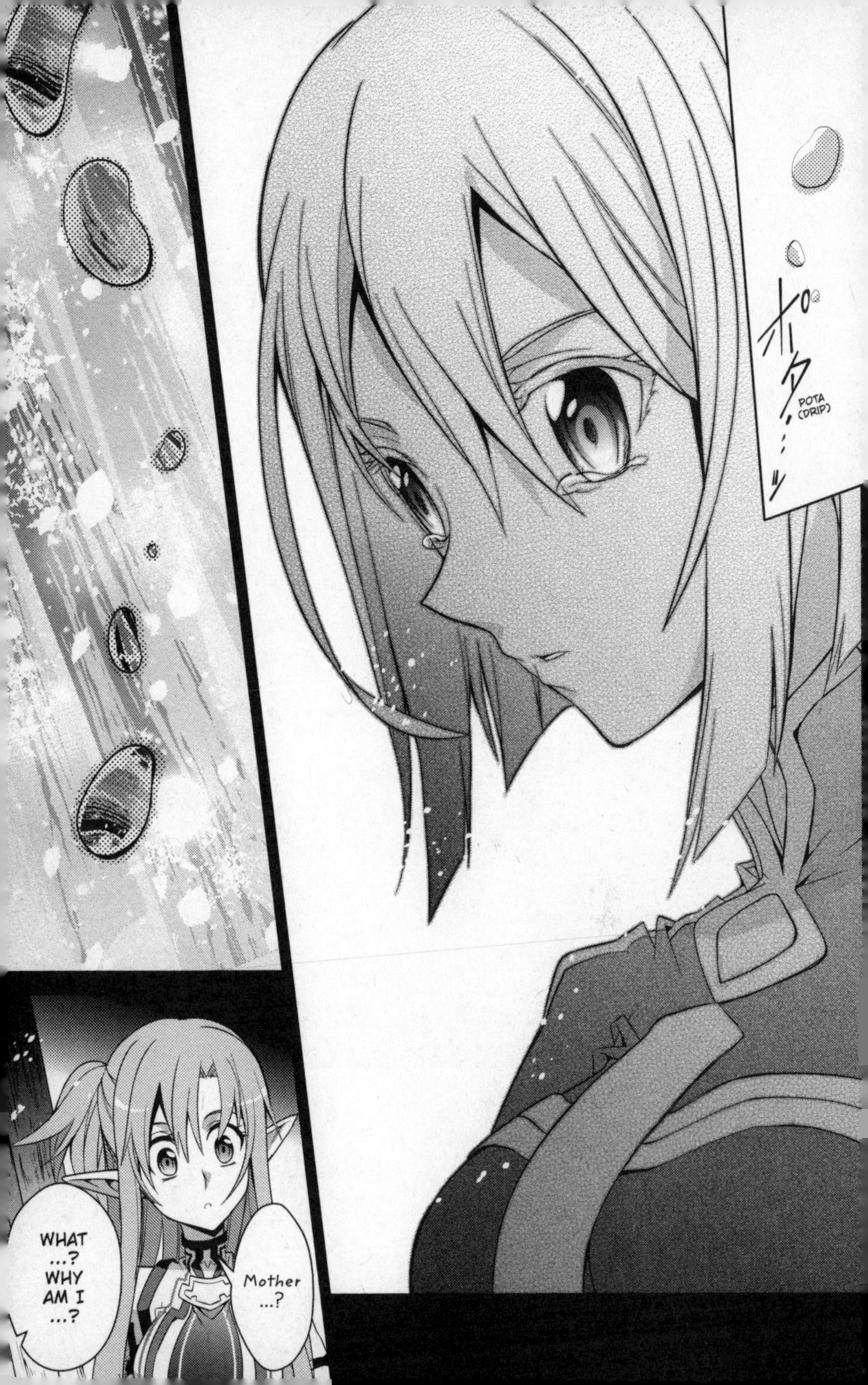
ポタ
POTA (DRIP)
Mother ...?
WHAT ...? WHY AM I ...?

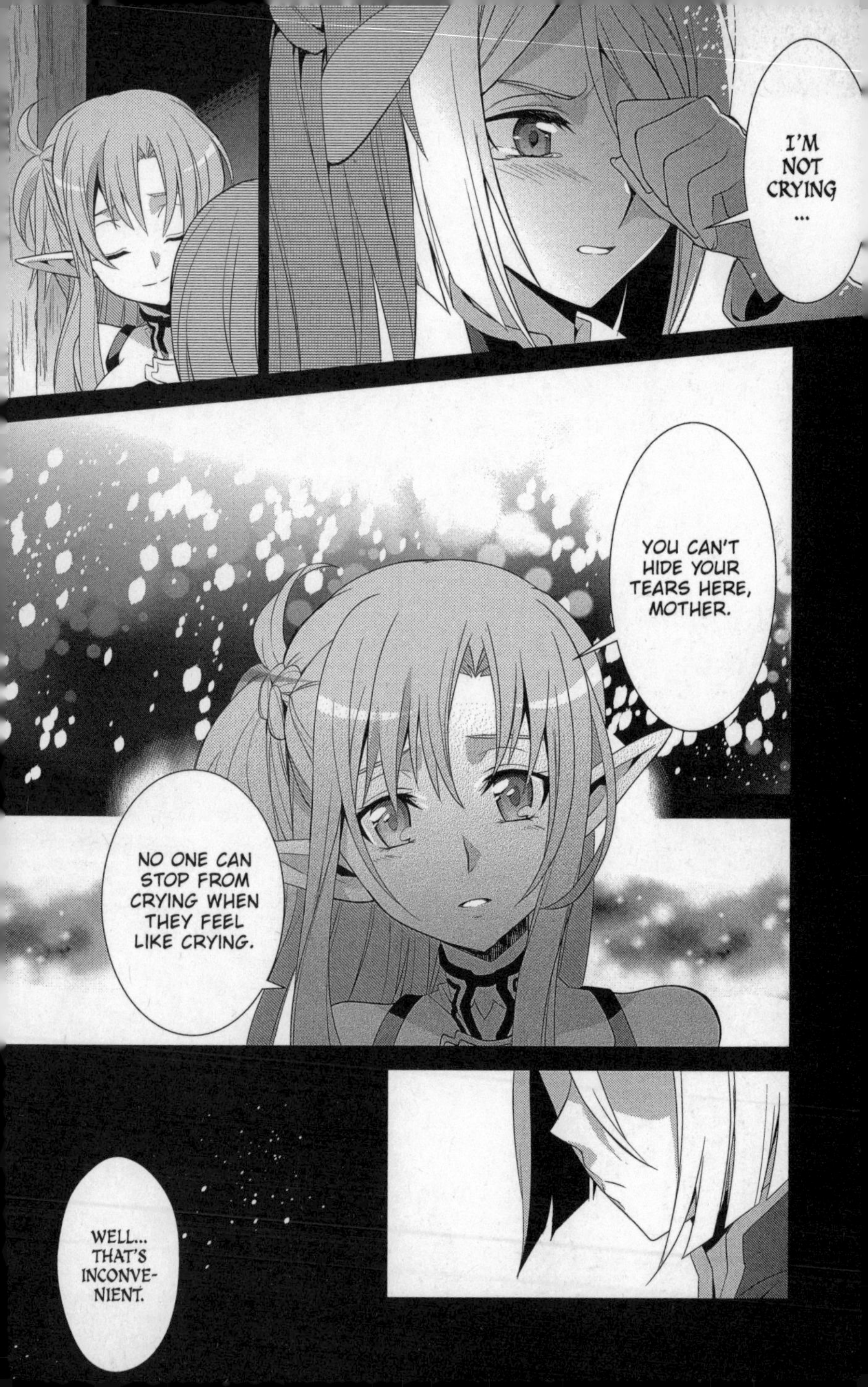
I'M NOT CRYING ...
YOU CAN'T HIDE YOUR TEARS HERE, MOTHER.
NO ONE CAN STOP FROM CRYING WHEN THEY FEEL LIKE CRYING.
WELL... THAT'S INCONVE-NIENT.

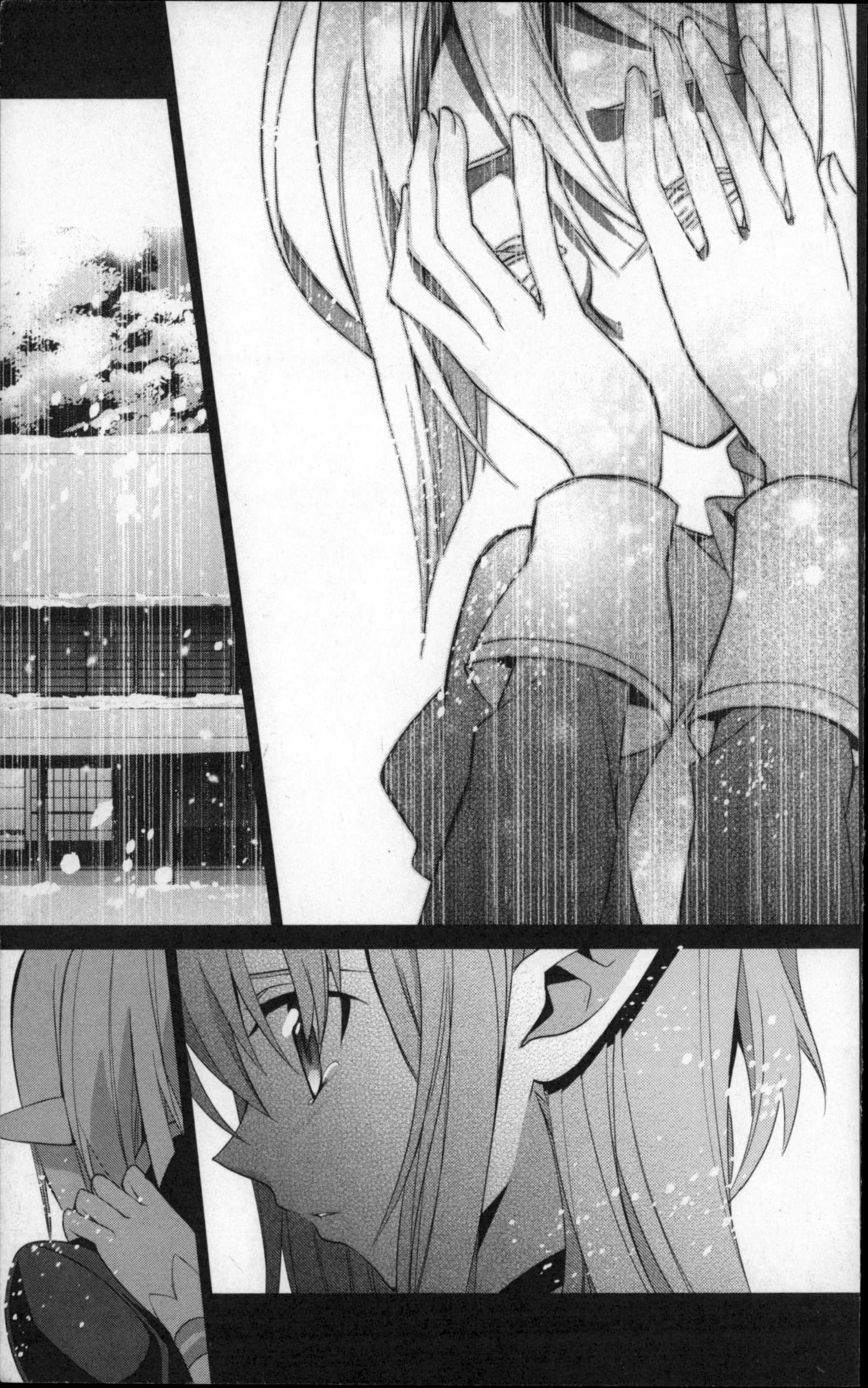

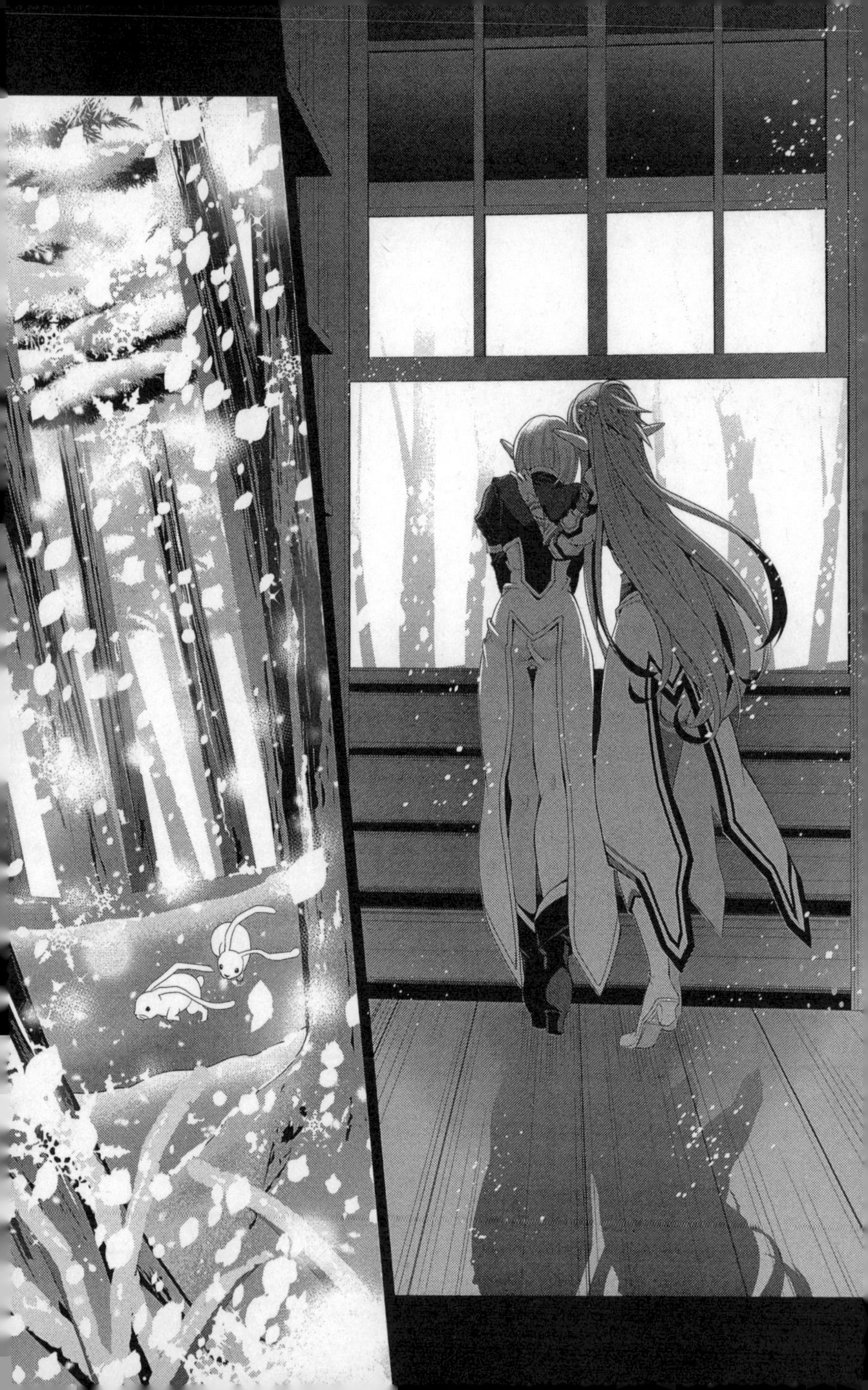

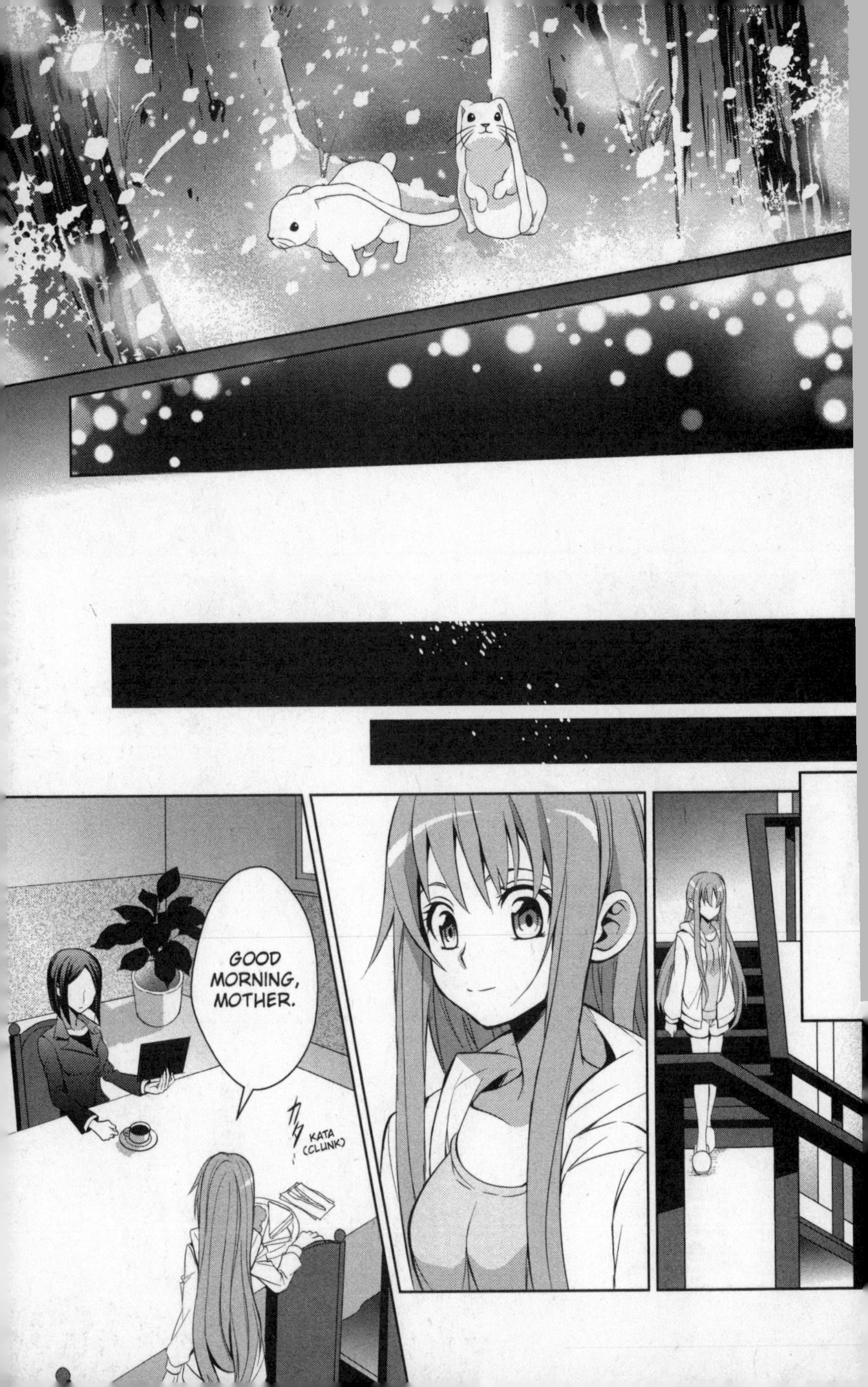
GOOD MORNING, MOTHER.
KATA (CLUNK)

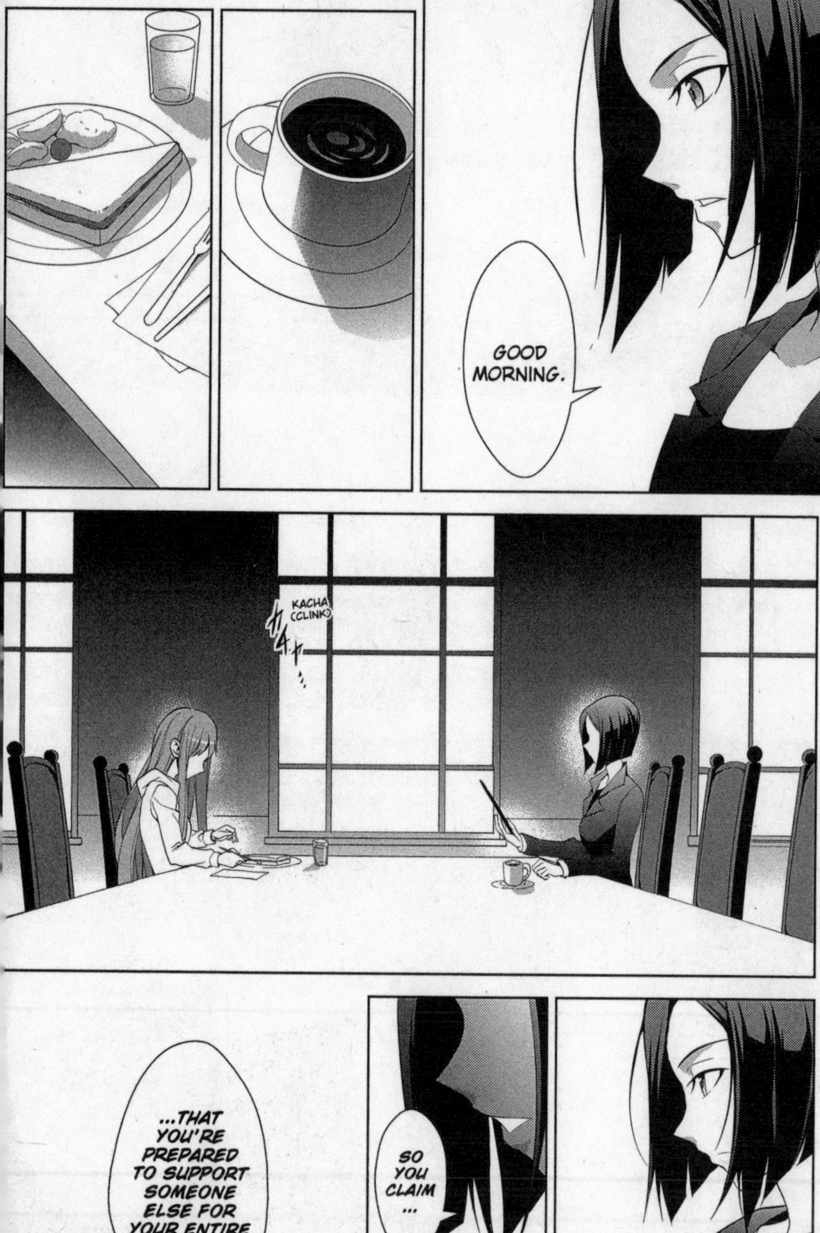
GOOD MORNING.
KACHA (CLINK)
SO YOU CLAIM ...
...THAT YOU'RE PREPARED TO SUPPORT SOMEONE ELSE FOR YOUR ENTIRE LIFE.

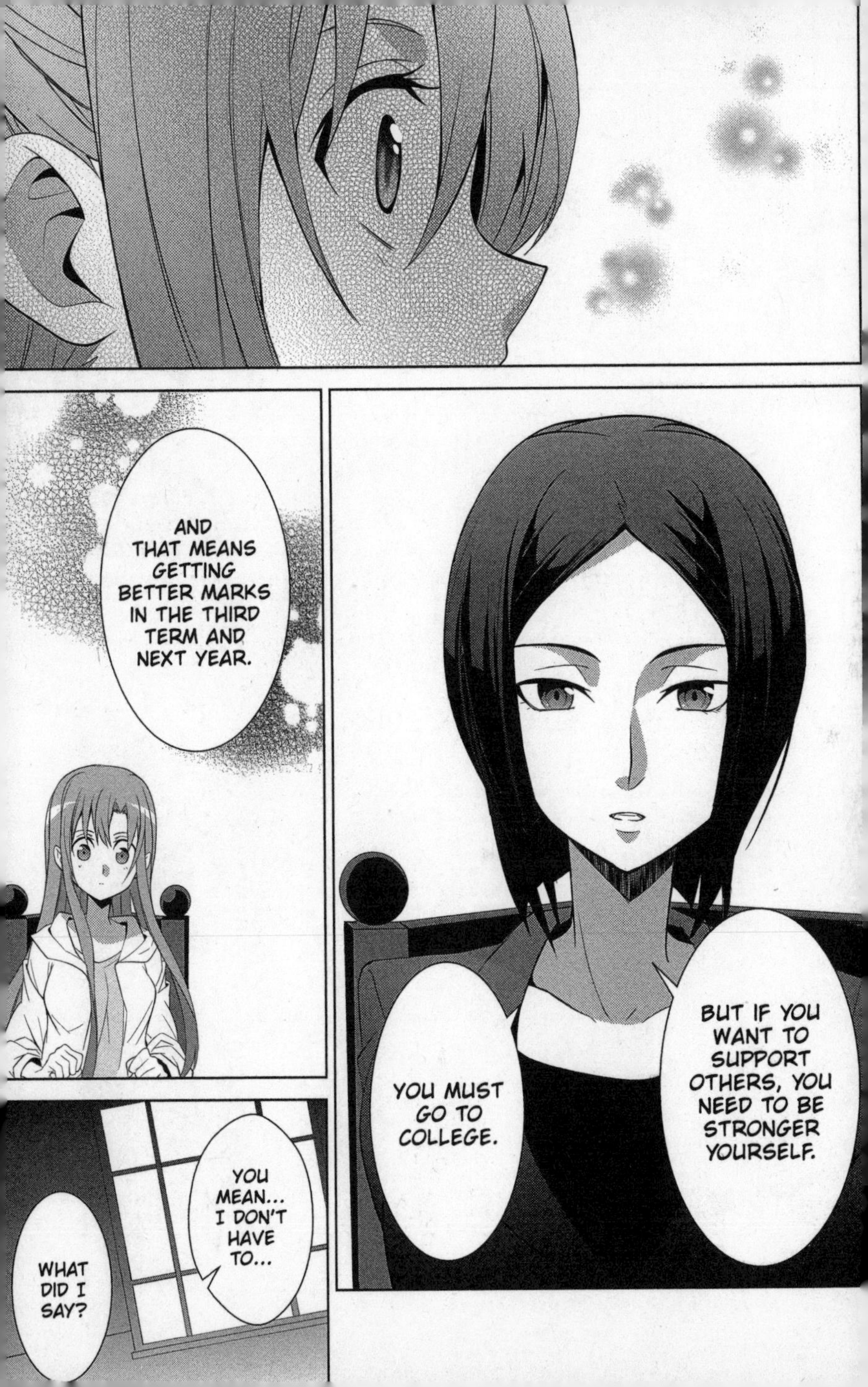
BUT IF YOU WANT TO SUPPORT OTHERS, YOU NEED TO BE STRONGER YOURSELF.
YOU MUST GO TO COLLEGE.
AND THAT MEANS GETTING BETTER MARKS IN THE THIRD TERM AND NEXT YEAR.
YOU MEAN... I DON'T HAVE TO...
WHAT DID I SAY?

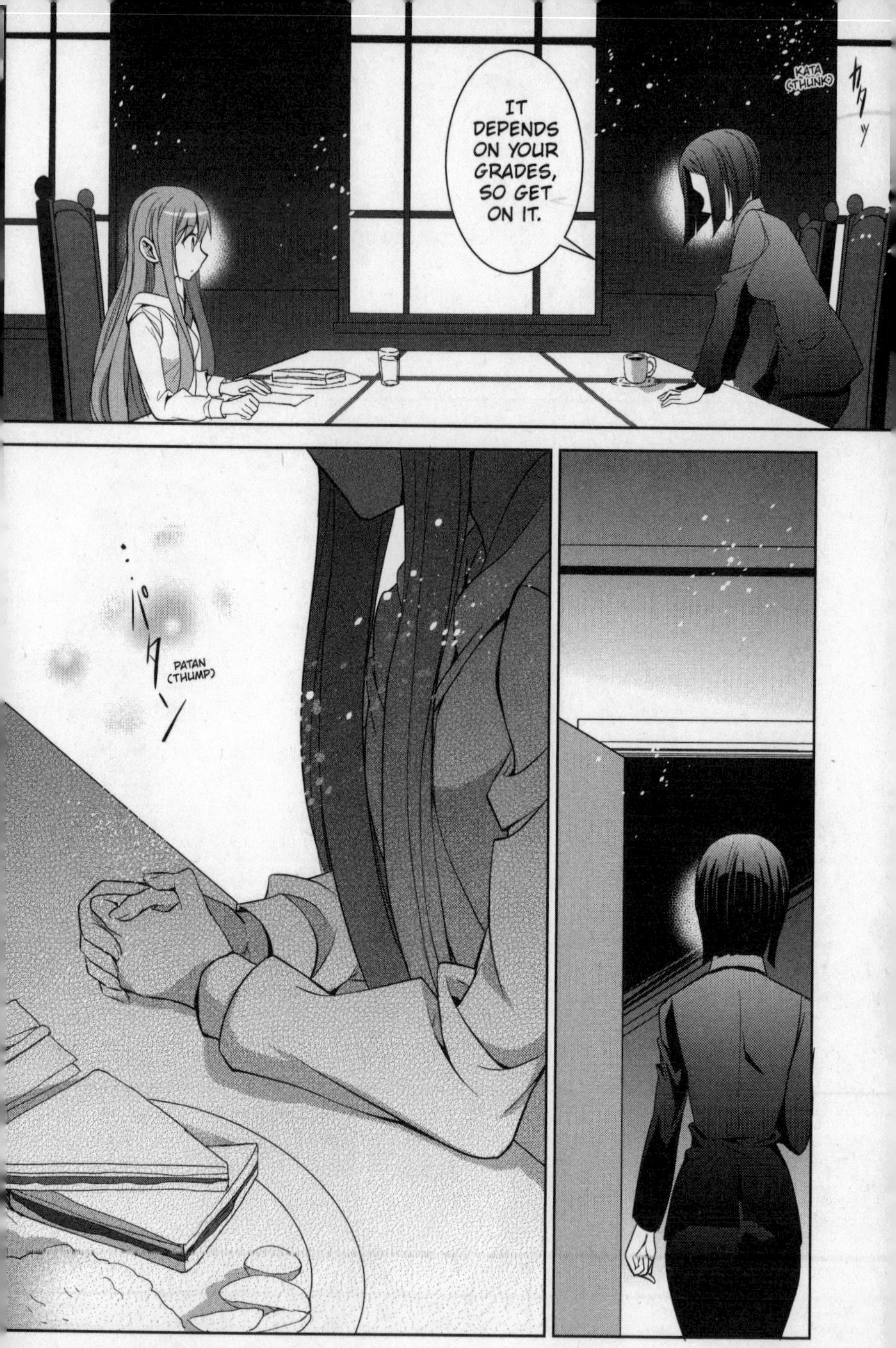
KATA (THUNK)
IT DEPENDS ON YOUR GRADES, SO GET ON IT.
PATAN (THUMP)

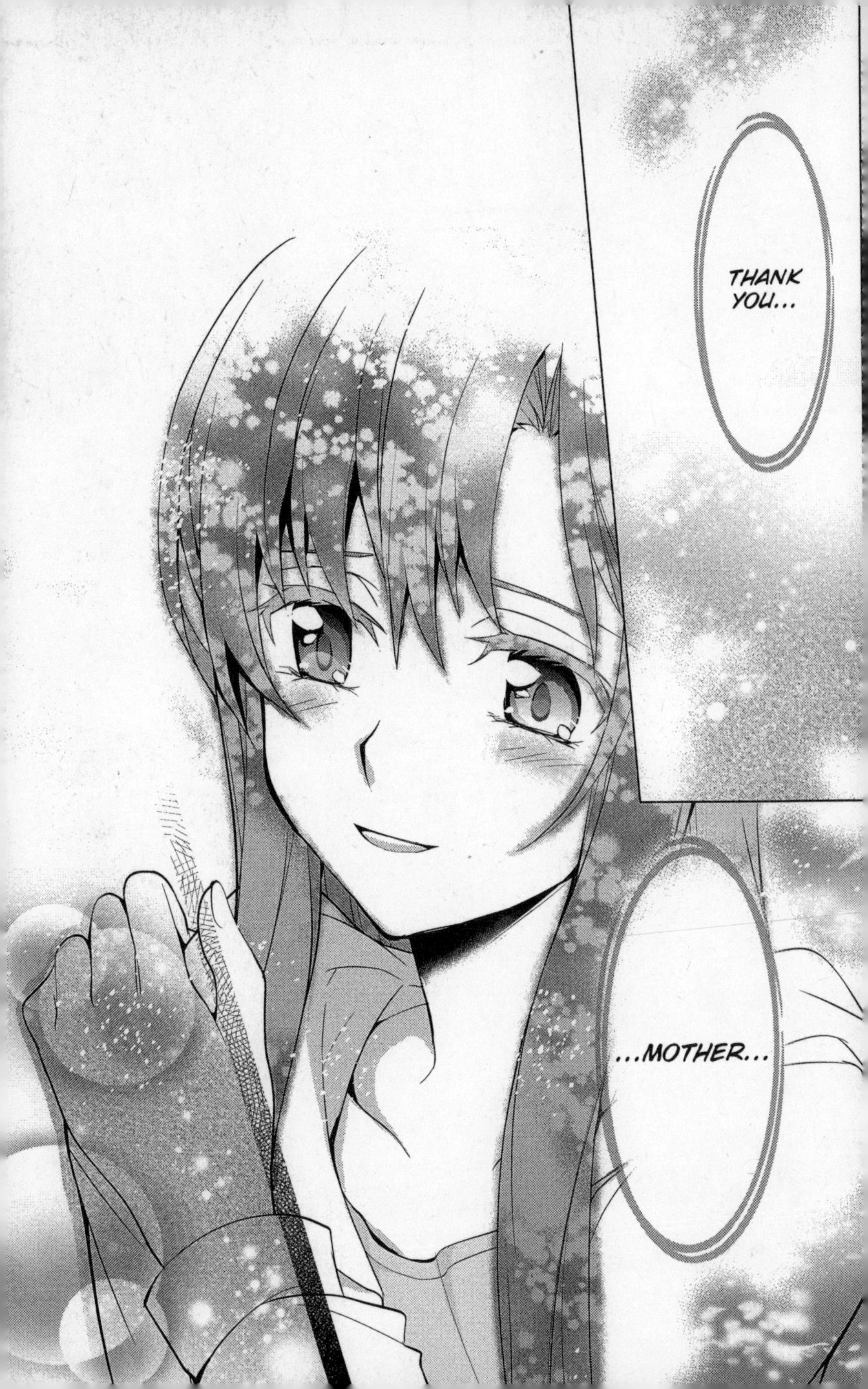
THANK YOU...
...MOTHER...

...YUUKI.

THANK YOU...

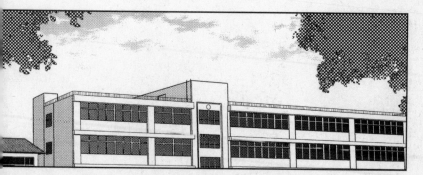

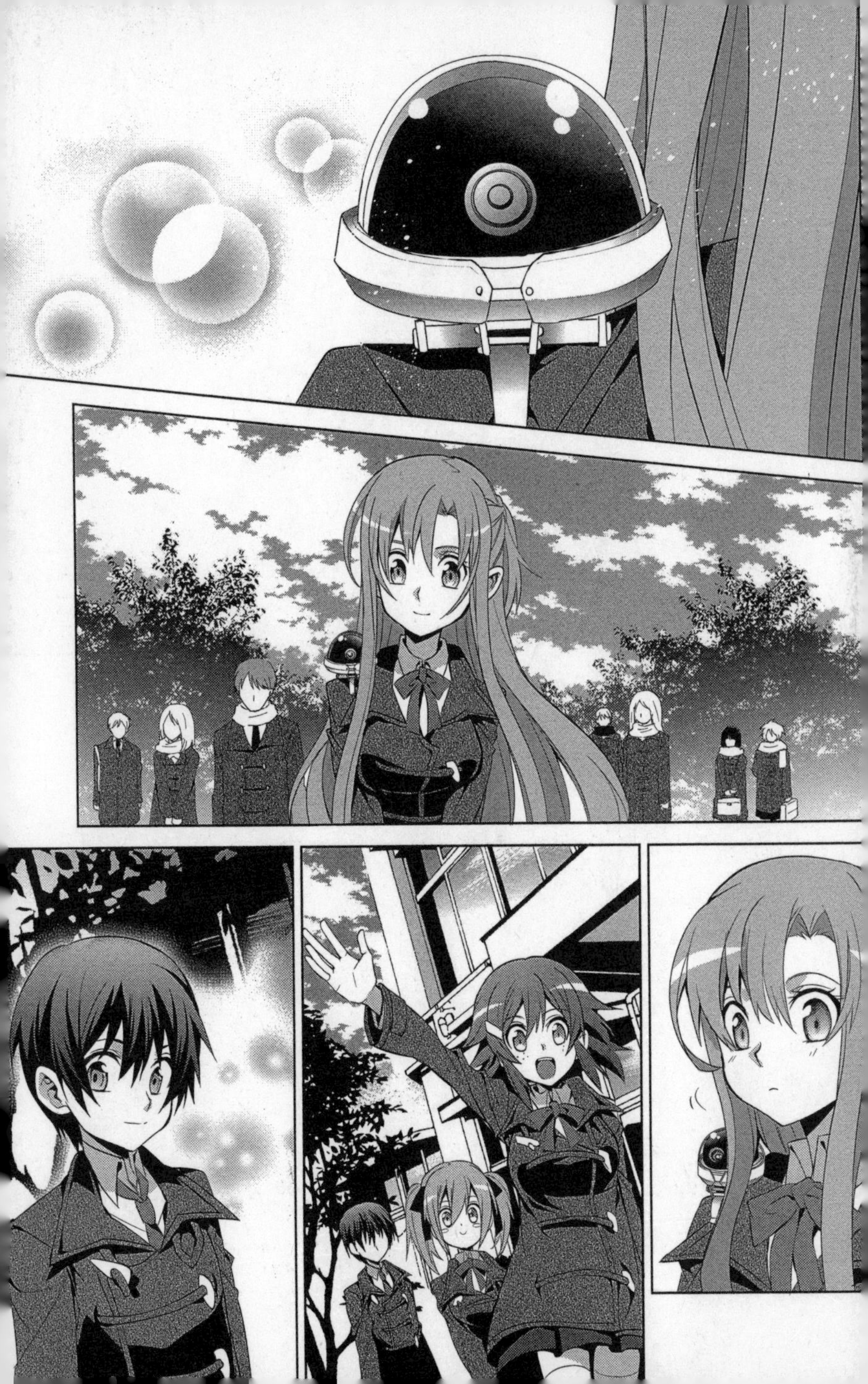

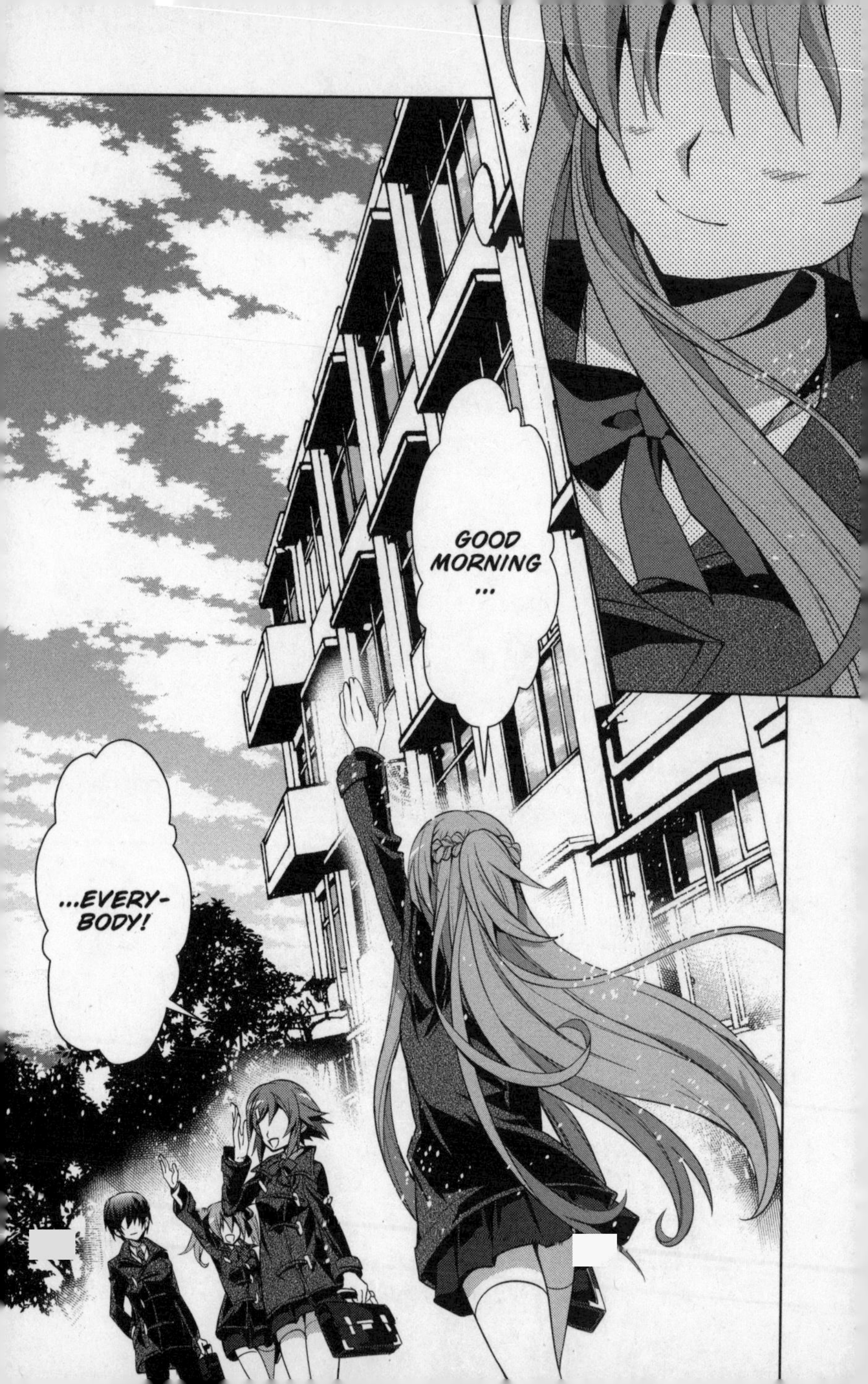
GOOD MORNING ...
...EVERY-BODY!

SWORD ART ONLINE
mother's rosary

SWORD ART ONLINE mother's rosary **03**
BACKGROUND GUIDE

ERIKA

ASUNA'S ALTERNATE CHARACTER, WHICH SHE ALLOWED HER MOTHER, KYOUKO, TO USE. ERIKA IS A SYLPH WHO SPECIALIZES IN DAGGERS AND CLOSE-QUARTERS COMBAT.

IN THE ORIGINAL NOVEL, ASUNA'S REASON FOR HAVING THE ALT WAS SO SHE COULD USE A DIFFERENT FACE EVERY NOW AND THEN. THIS MAKES SENSE, AS ONE OF THE GREAT BENEFITS OF ONLINE GAMES IS THE OPPORTUNITY TO PLAY AS A DIFFERENT PERSON. IN FACT, WE TAKE IT FOR GRANTED BECAUSE WE WOULD FIND IT STRANGE TO HAVE TO WEAR OUR OWN FACES IN A GAME. AFTER TWO YEARS IN SAO, THE SURVIVORS HAVE SPECIAL REASON TO WANT TO WEAR DIFFERENT FACES.

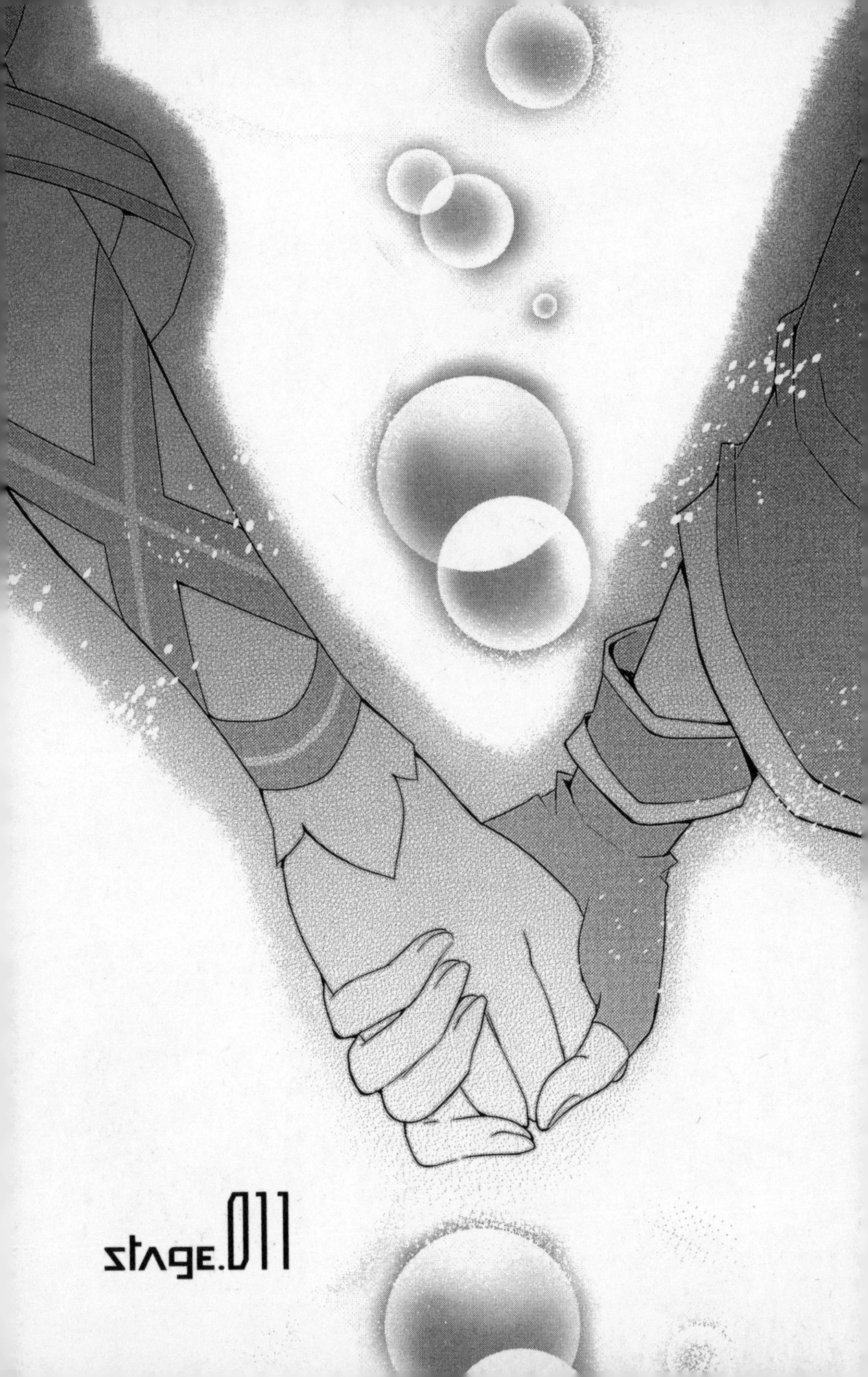
stage.011

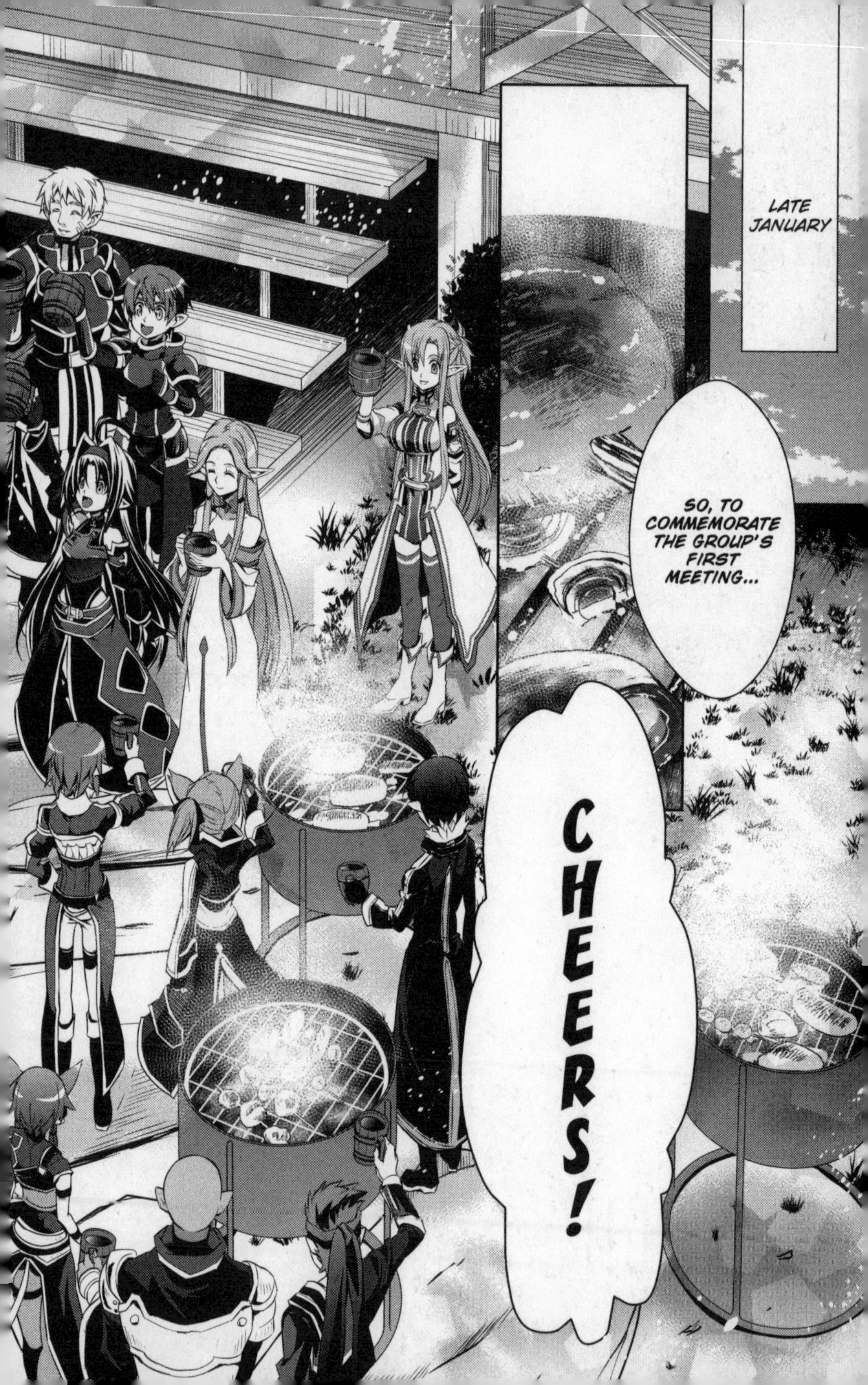
LATE JANUARY
SO, TO COMMEMORATE THE GROUP'S FIRST MEETING...
CHEERS!

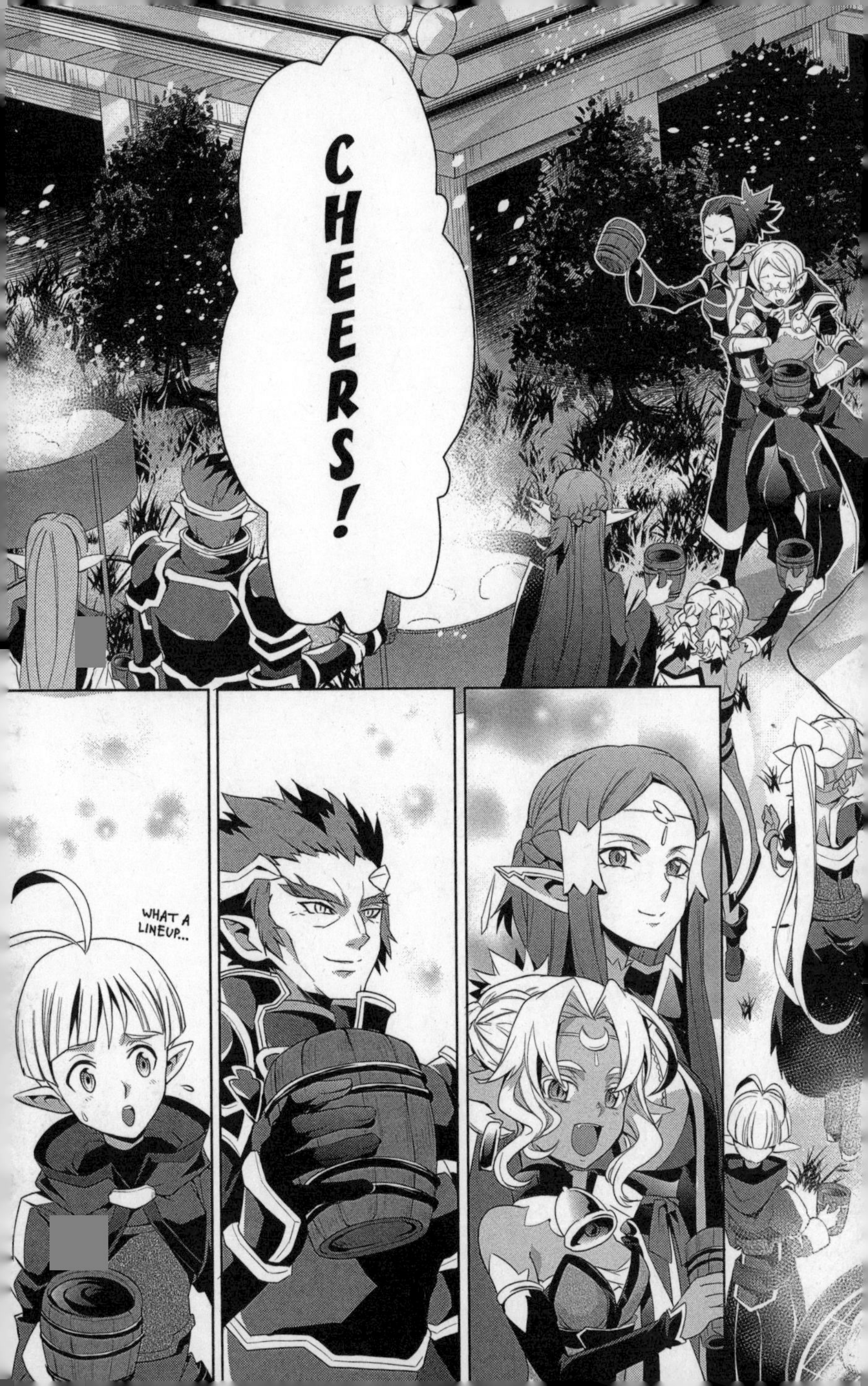
CHEERS!
WHAT A LINEUP...

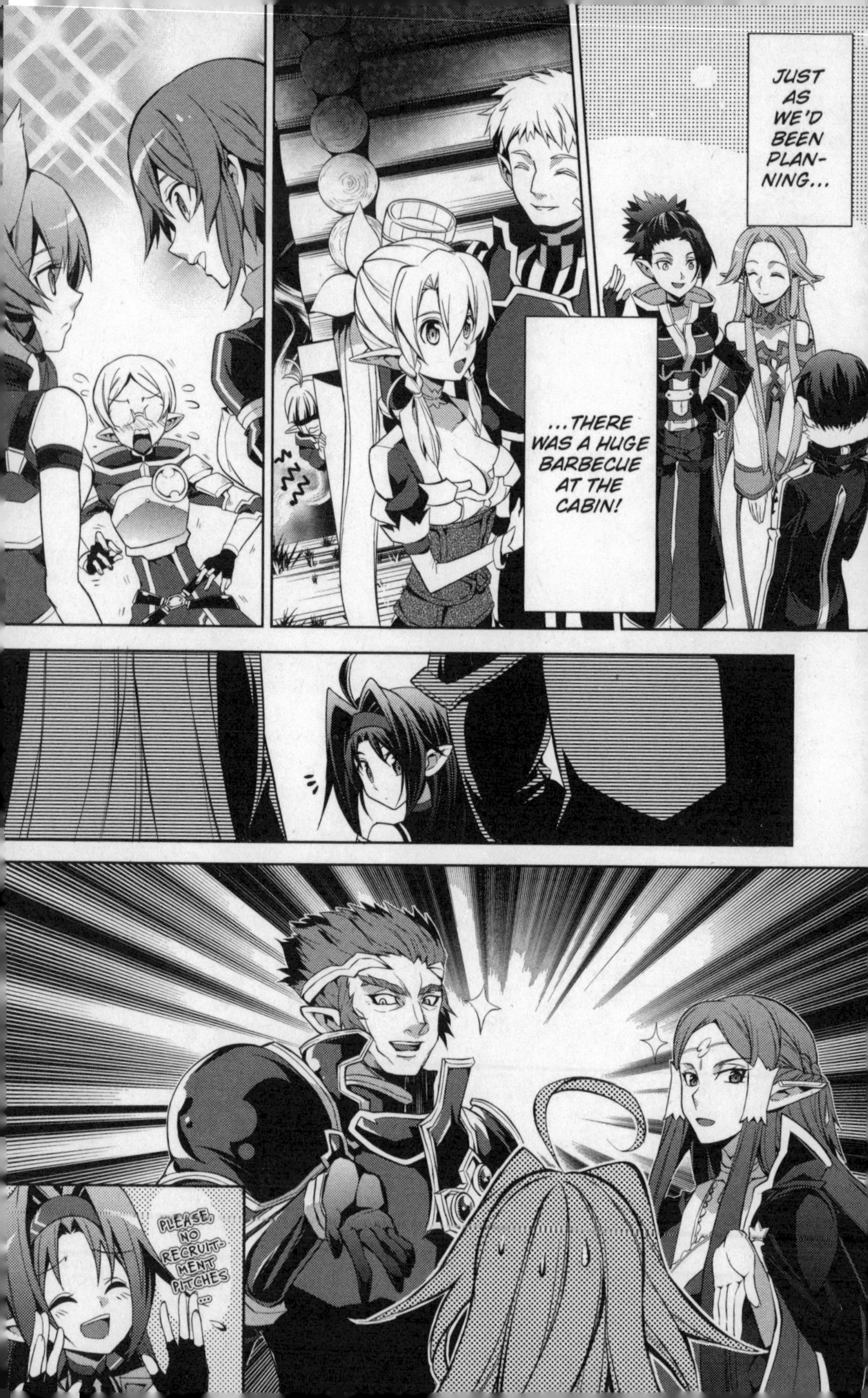
JUST AS WE'D BEEN PLAN-NING...
...THERE WAS A HUGE BARBECUE AT THE CABIN!
PLEASE, NO RECRUIT-MENT PITCHES...

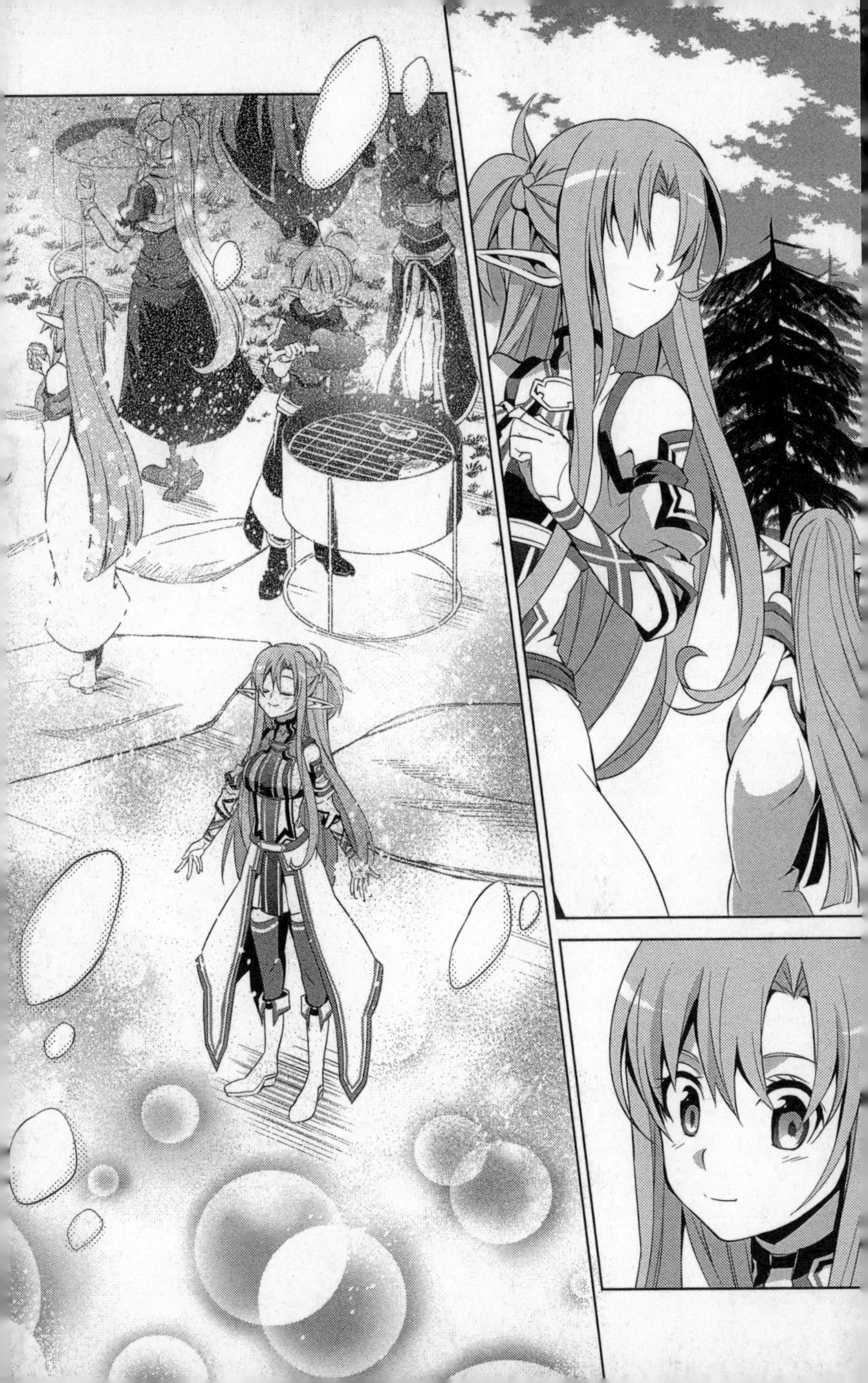

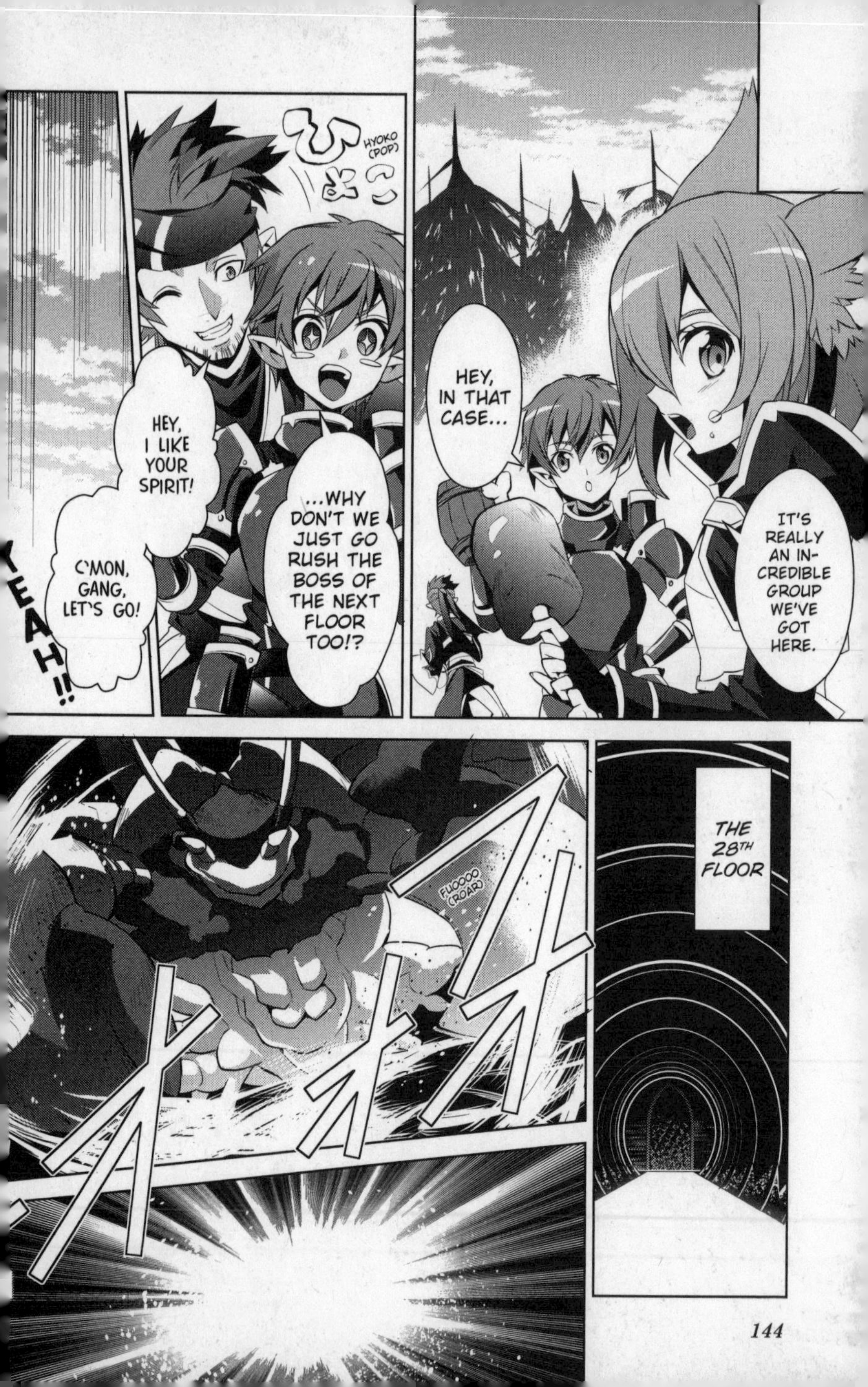
IT'S REALLY AN INCREDIBLE GROUP WE'VE GOT HERE.
HEY, IN THAT CASE...
ひょこ
HYOKO (POP)
...WHY DON'T WE JUST GO RUSH THE BOSS OF THE NEXT FLOOR TOO!?
HEY, I LIKE YOUR SPIRIT!
C'MON, GANG, LET'S GO!
YEAH!!
THE 28TH FLOOR
FUOOOO (ROAR)

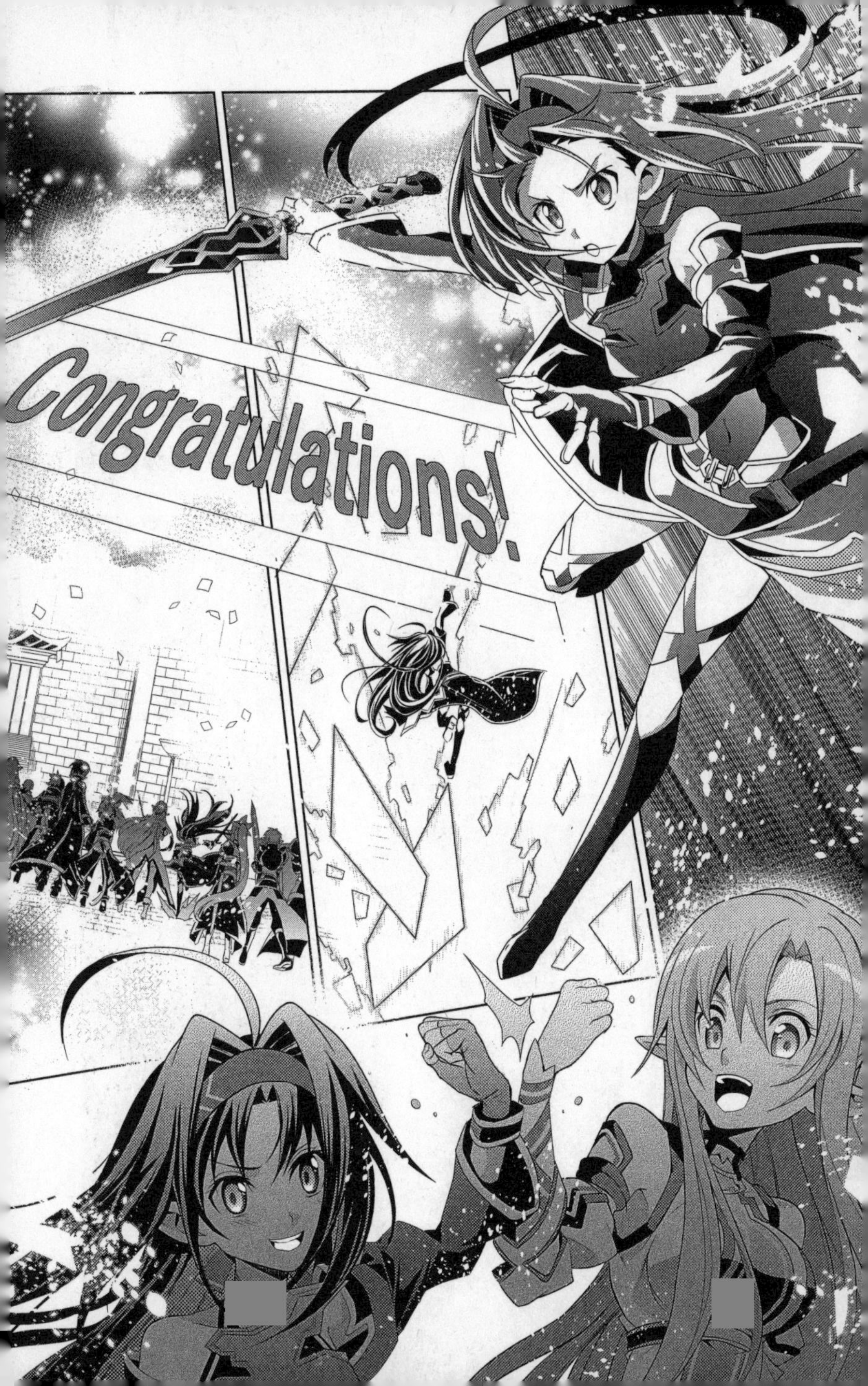
Congratulations!

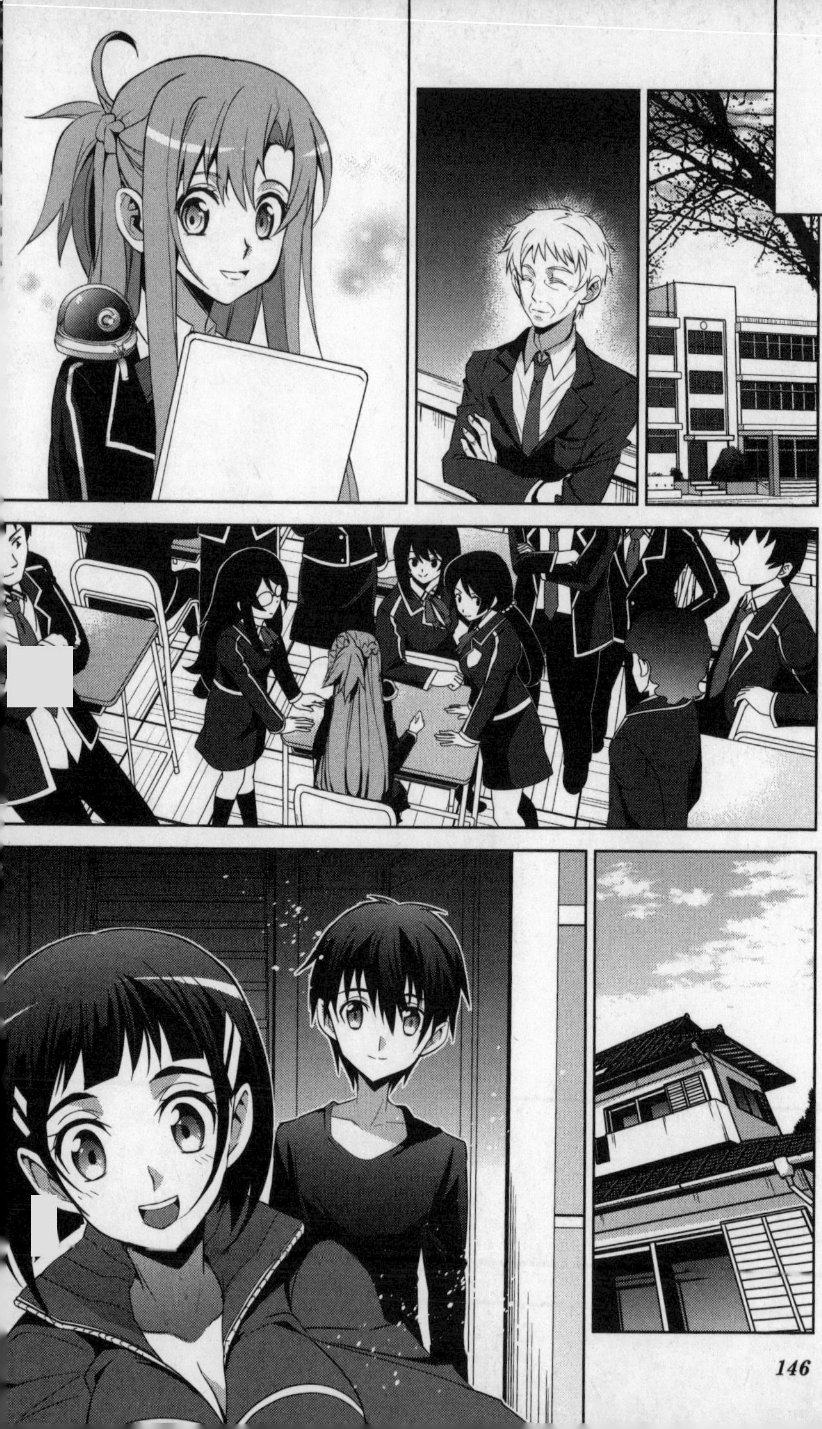

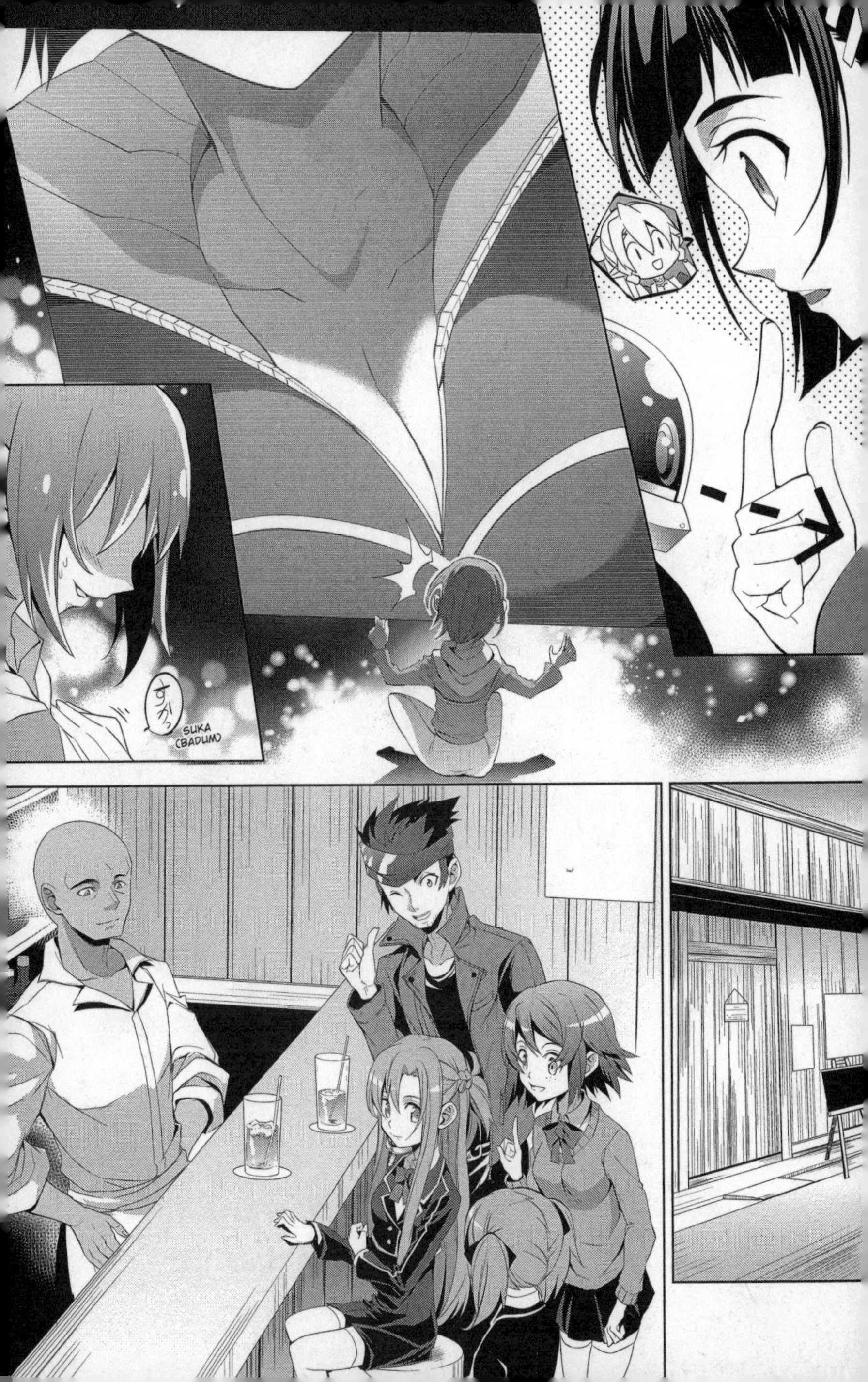

すかっ
SUKA
(BADUM)

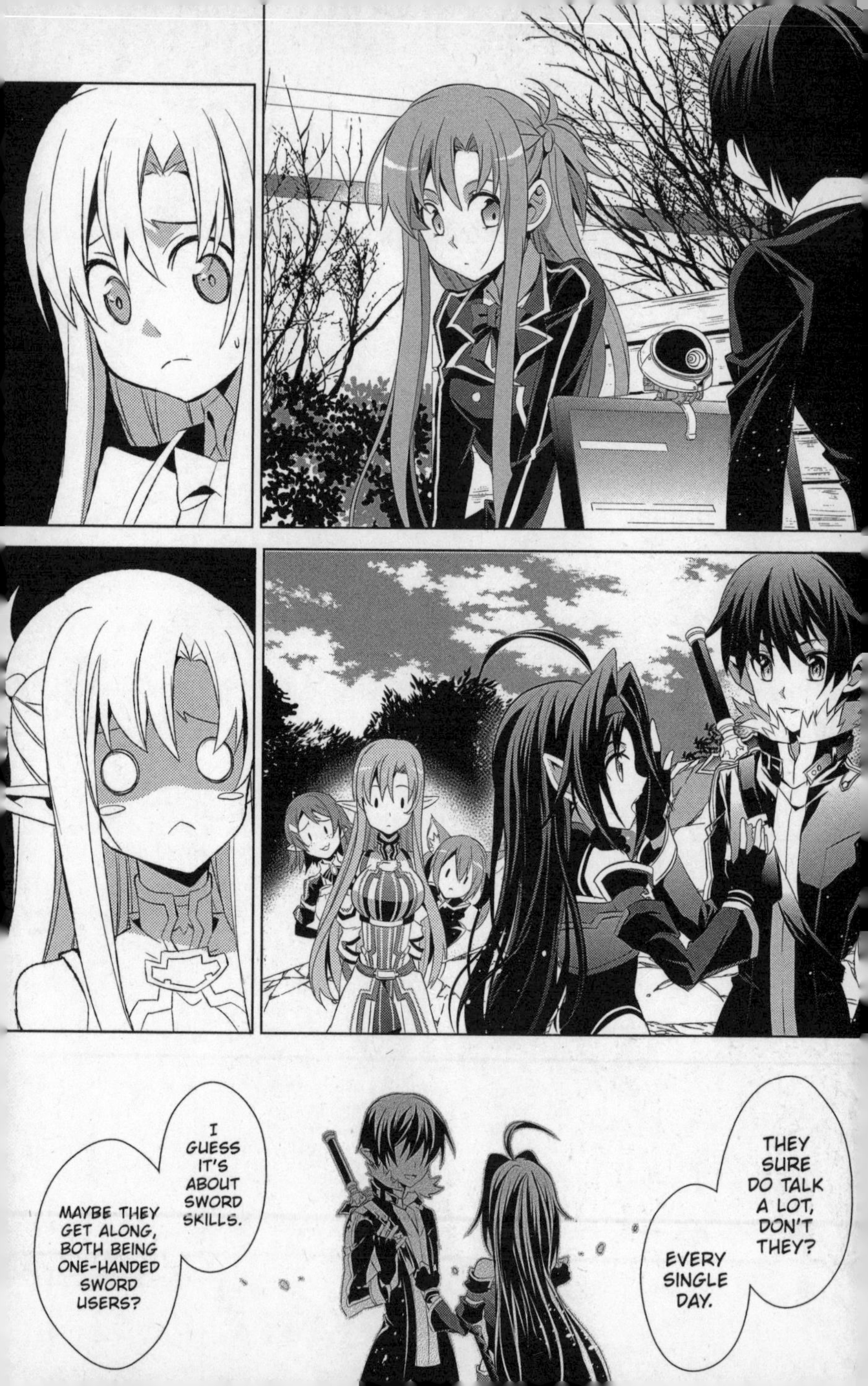
THEY SURE DO TALK A LOT, DON'T THEY?
EVERY SINGLE DAY.
I GUESS IT'S ABOUT SWORD SKILLS.
MAYBE THEY GET ALONG, BOTH BEING ONE-HANDED SWORD USERS?

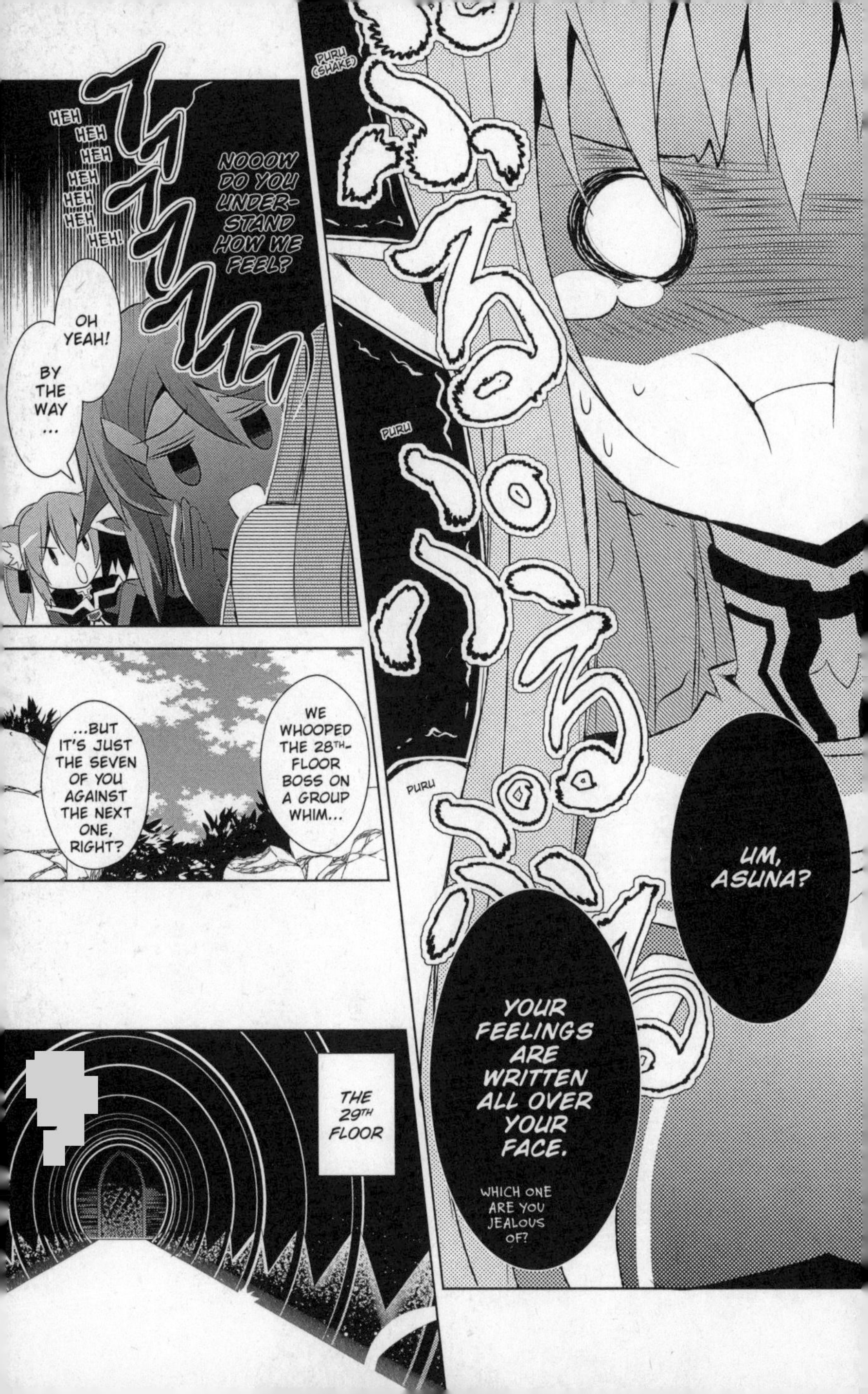
UM, ASUNA?
YOUR FEELINGS ARE WRITTEN ALL OVER YOUR FACE.
WHICH ONE ARE YOU JEALOUS OF?
PURU (SHAKE)
PURU
PURU
NOOOW DO YOU UNDER-STAND HOW WE FEEL?
HEH HEH HEH HEH HEH HEH HEH!
OH YEAH!
BY THE WAY...
WE WHOOPED THE 28TH-FLOOR BOSS ON A GROUP WHIM...
...BUT IT'S JUST THE SEVEN OF YOU AGAINST THE NEXT ONE, RIGHT?
THE 29TH FLOOR

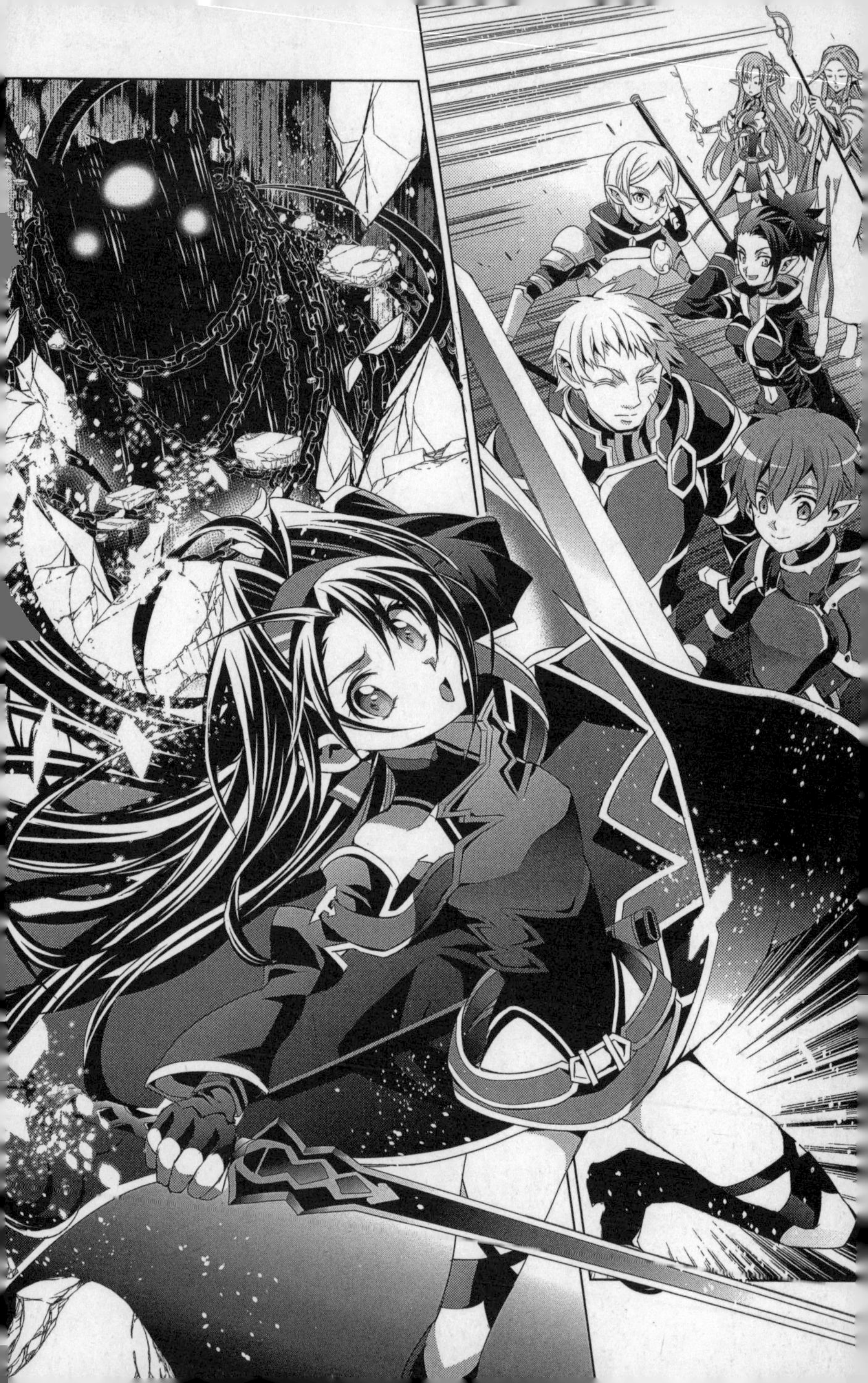

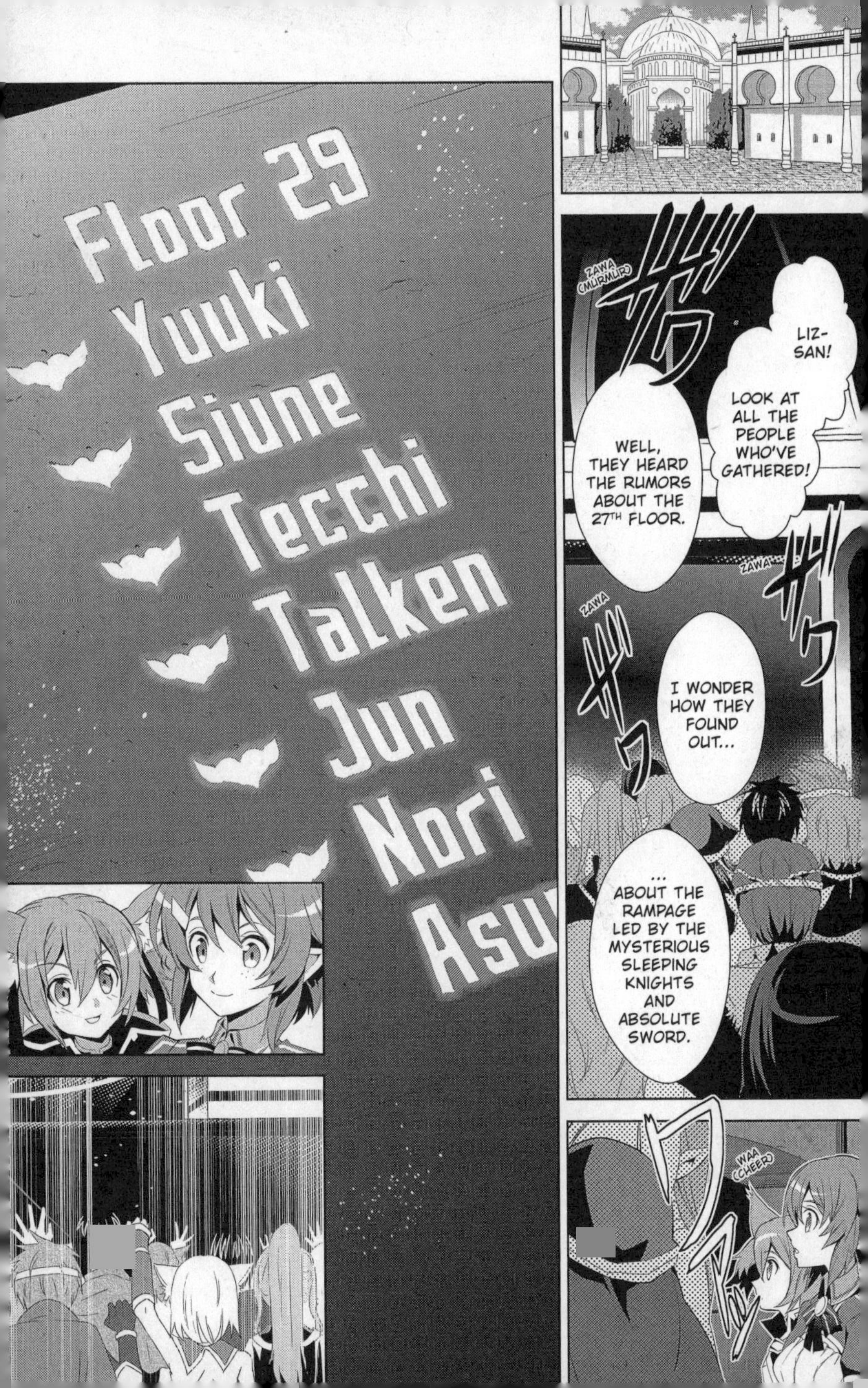
ZAWA (MURMUR)
LIZ-SAN!
LOOK AT ALL THE PEOPLE WHO'VE GATHERED!
WELL, THEY HEARD THE RUMORS ABOUT THE 27TH FLOOR.
ZAWA
ZAWA
I WONDER HOW THEY FOUND OUT...
...ABOUT THE RAMPAGE LED BY THE MYSTERIOUS SLEEPING KNIGHTS AND ABSOLUTE SWORD.
WAA (CHEER)
Floor 29
Yuuki
Siune
Tecchi
Talken
Jun
Nori
Asu

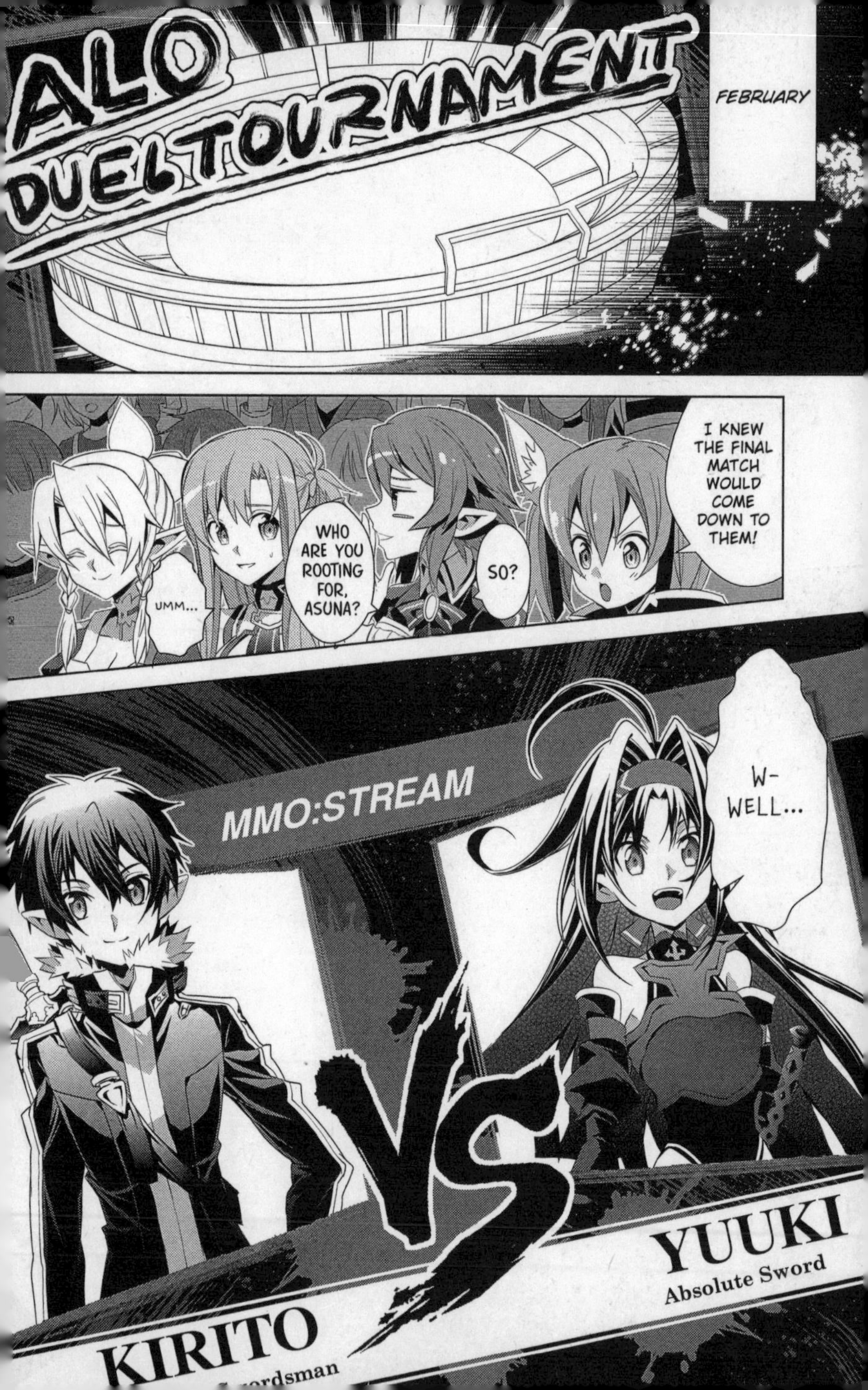
FEBRUARY
ALO DUEL TOURNAMENT
I KNEW THE FINAL MATCH WOULD COME DOWN TO THEM!
SO?
WHO ARE YOU ROOTING FOR, ASUNA?
UMM...
W-WELL...
MMO:STREAM
YUUKI
Absolute Sword
VS
KIRITO

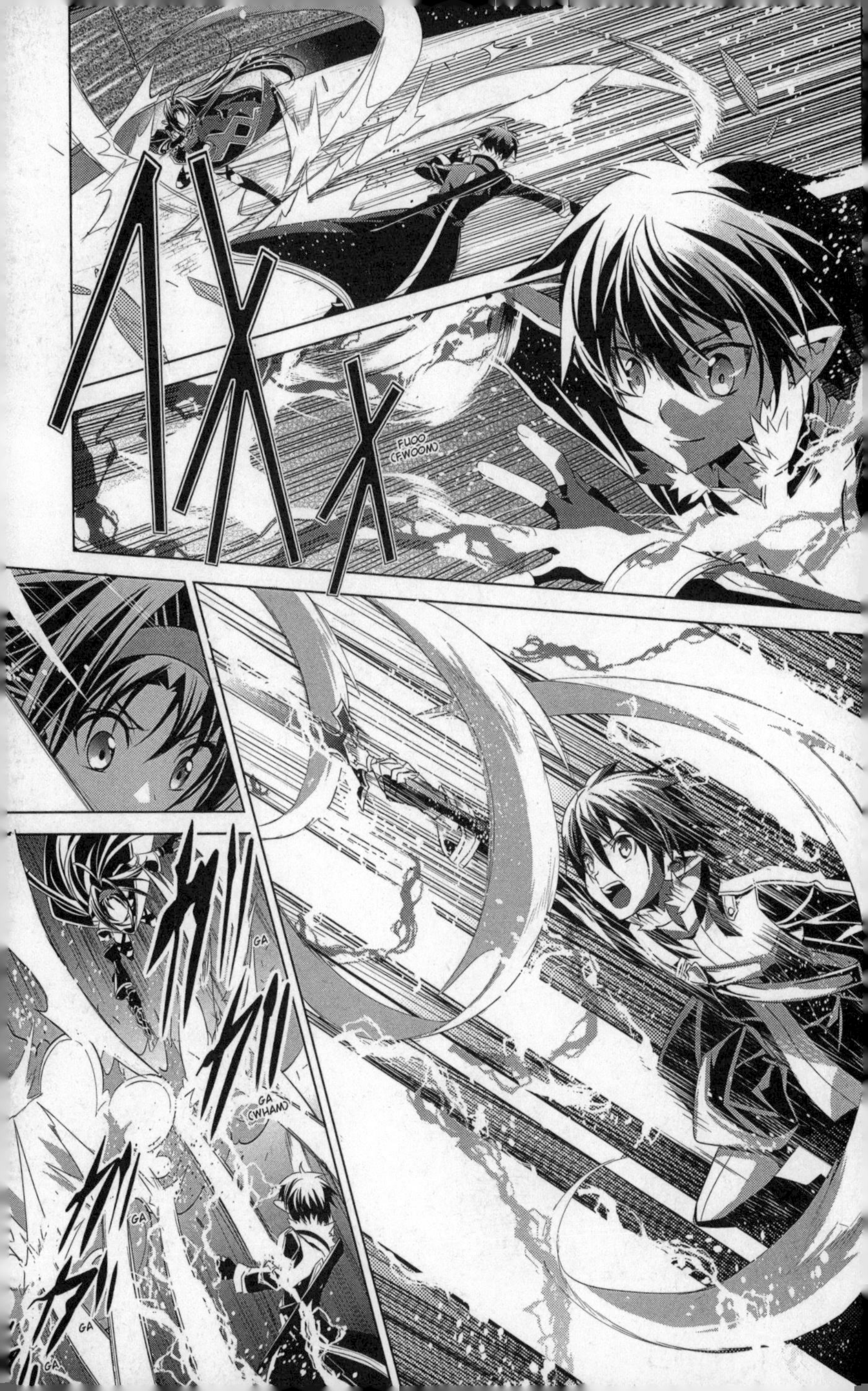

FUOO (FWOOM)
GA
GA (WHAM)
GA
GA
GA

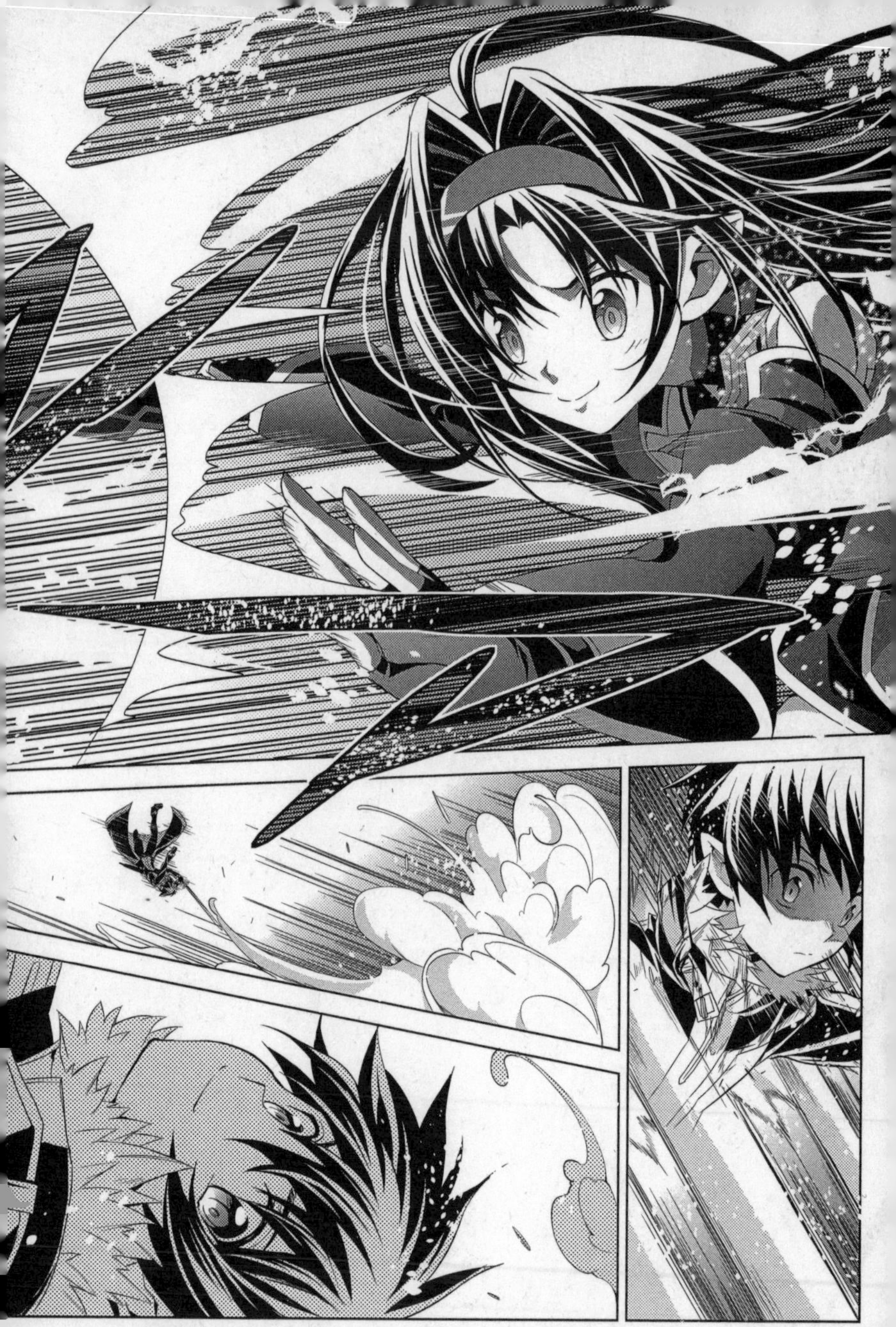

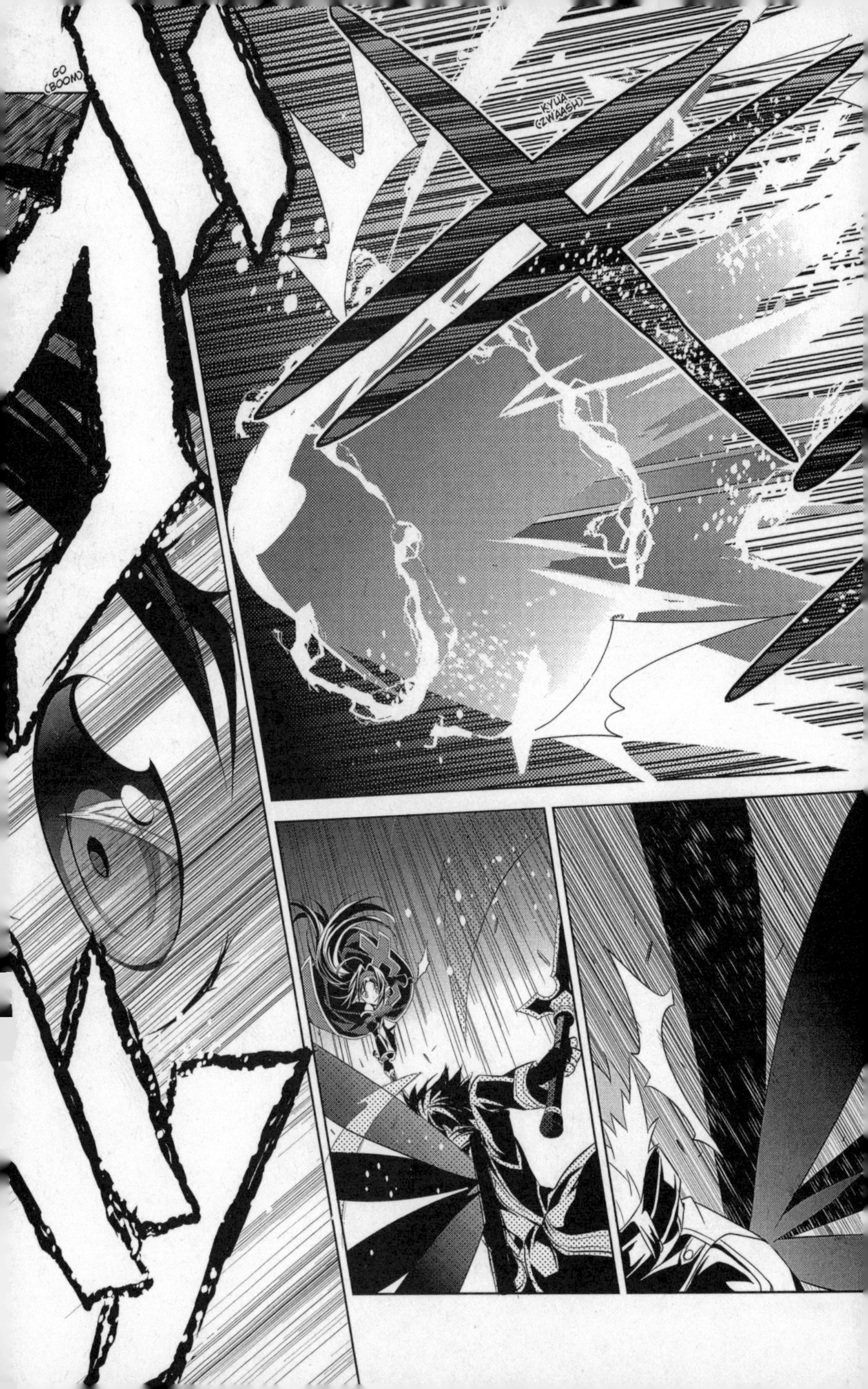
KYUA (ZWAASH)
GO (BOOM)

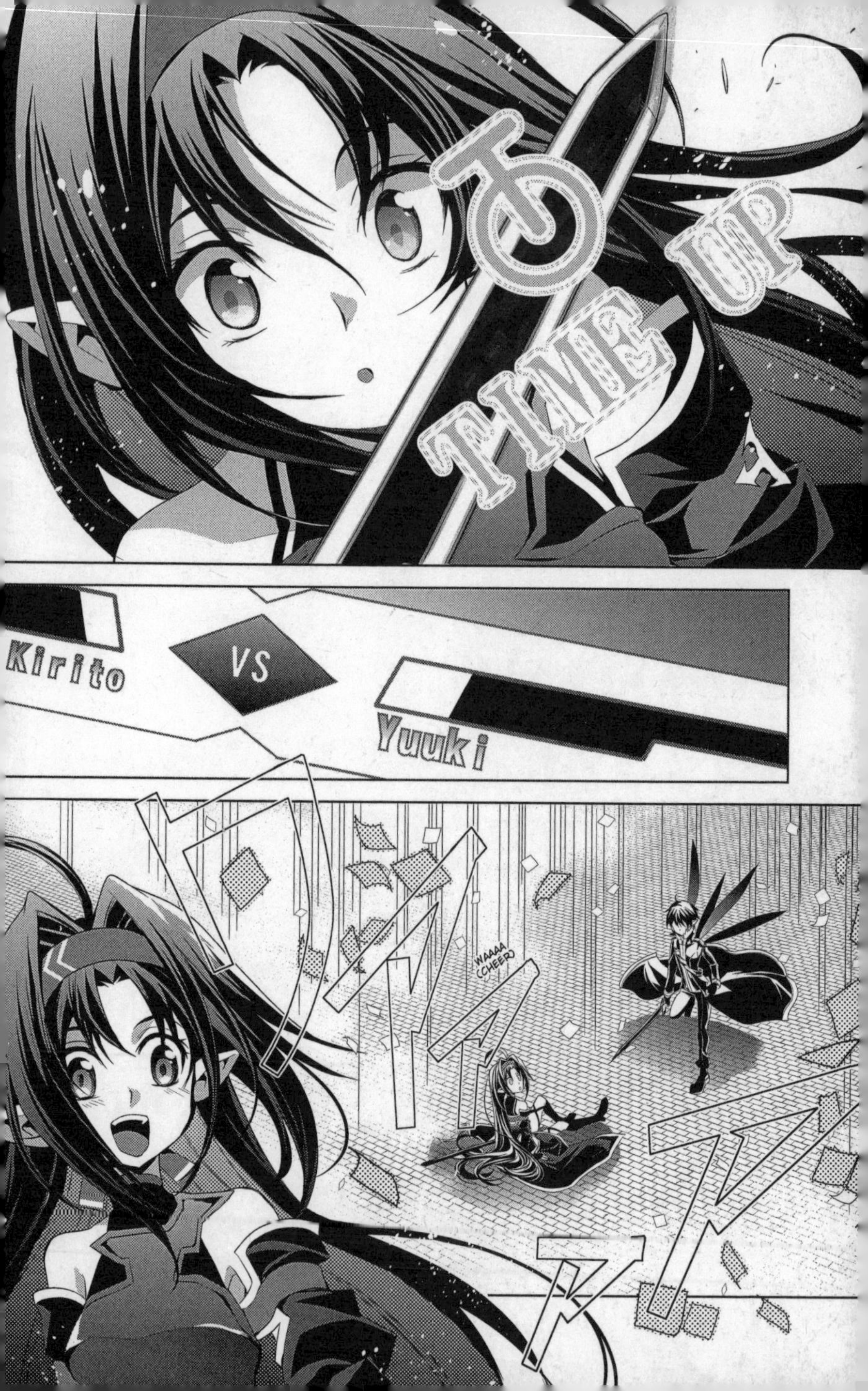
TIME UP
Kirito
VS
Yuuki
WAAAA (CHEER)

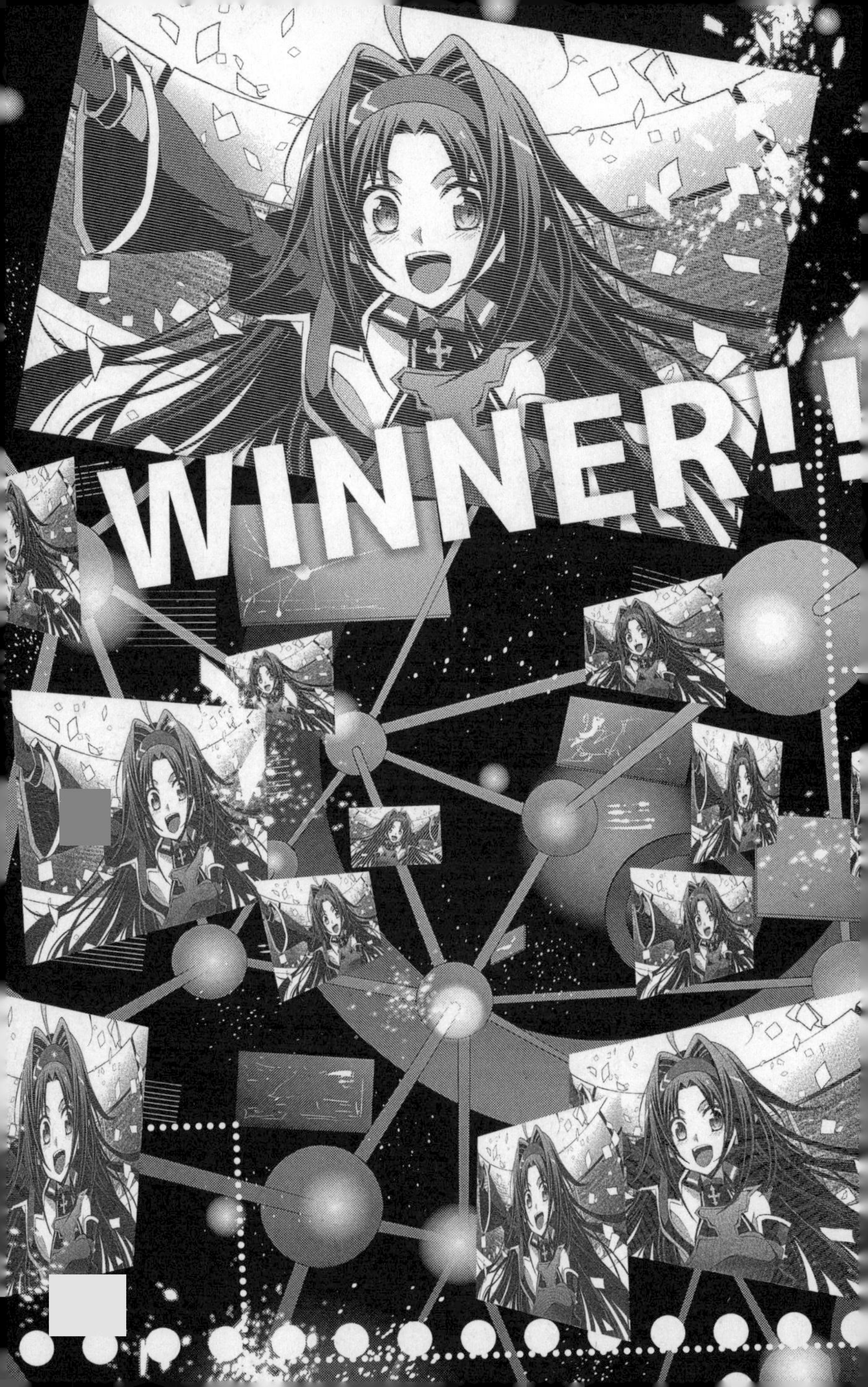
WINNER!!

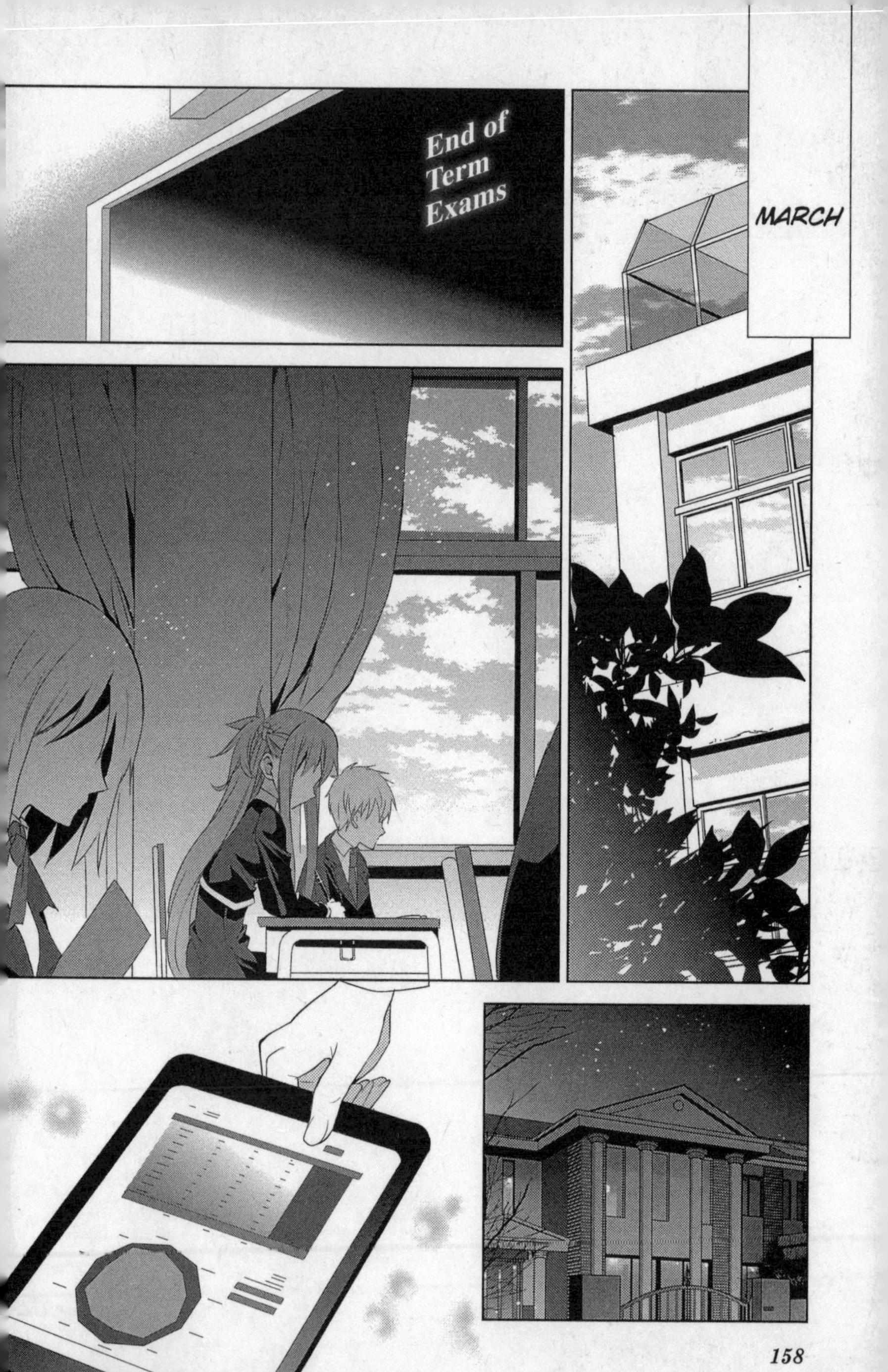
MARCH
End of Term Exams

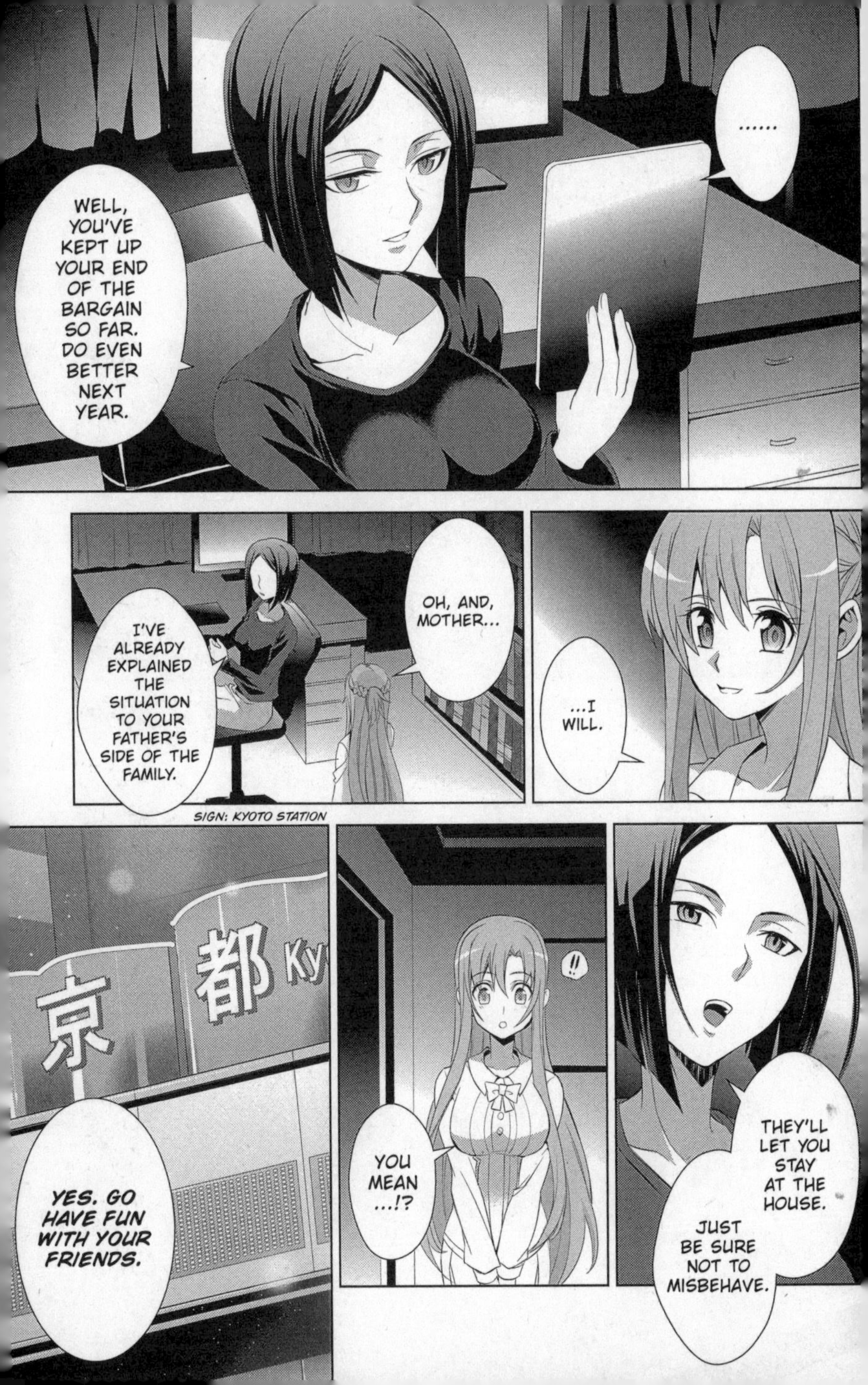
......
WELL, YOU'VE KEPT UP YOUR END OF THE BARGAIN SO FAR. DO EVEN BETTER NEXT YEAR.
...I WILL.
OH, AND, MOTHER...
I'VE ALREADY EXPLAINED THE SITUATION TO YOUR FATHER'S SIDE OF THE FAMILY.
SIGN: KYOTO STATION
THEY'LL LET YOU STAY AT THE HOUSE.
JUST BE SURE NOT TO MISBEHAVE.
!!
YOU MEAN ...!?
京都 Ky
YES. GO HAVE FUN WITH YOUR FRIENDS.

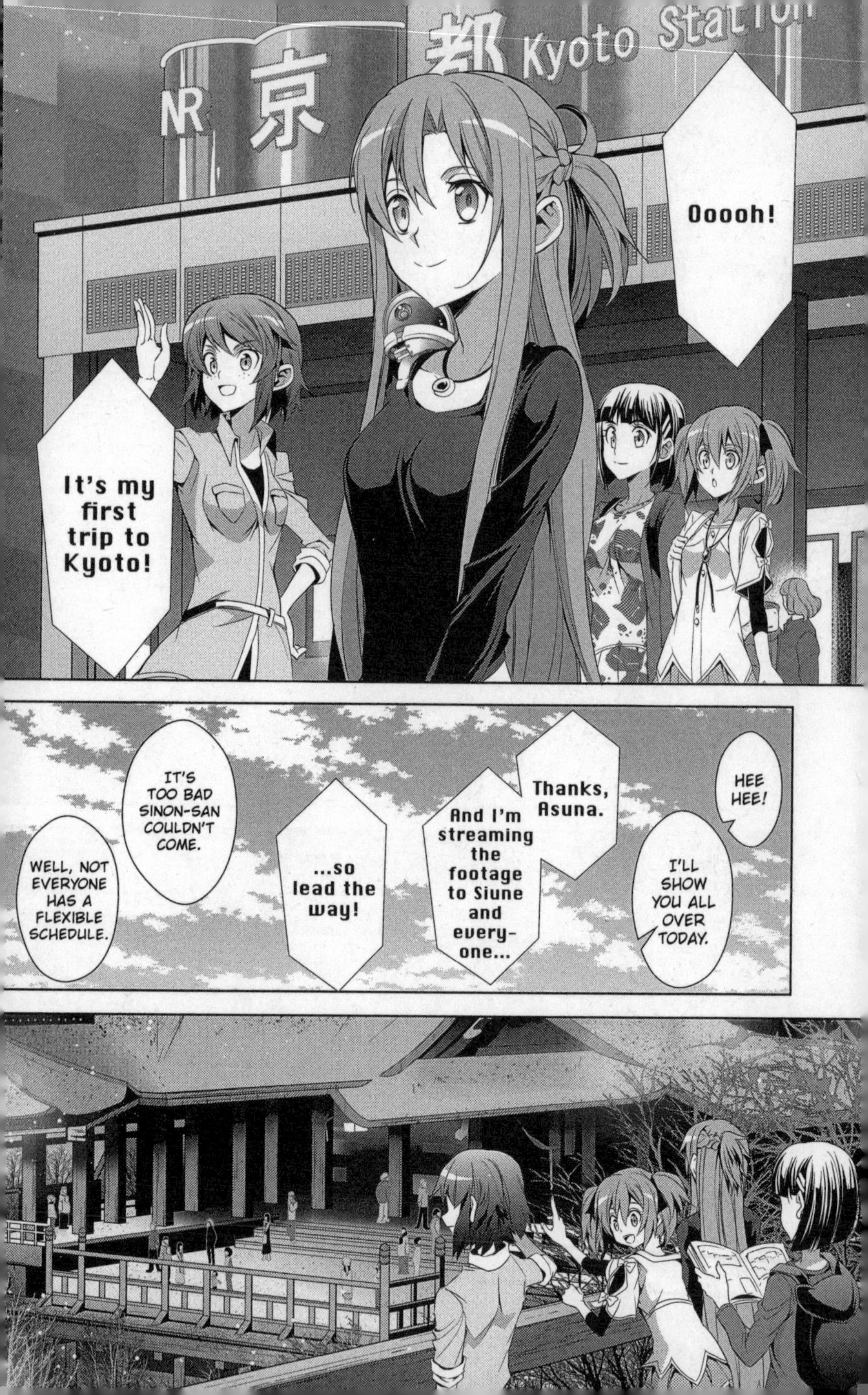
NR 京 都 Kyoto Station
Ooooh!
It's my first trip to Kyoto!
HEE HEE!
I'LL SHOW YOU ALL OVER TODAY.
Thanks, Asuna.
And I'm streaming the footage to Siune and every-one...
...so lead the way!
IT'S TOO BAD SINON-SAN COULDN'T COME.
WELL, NOT EVERYONE HAS A FLEXIBLE SCHEDULE.

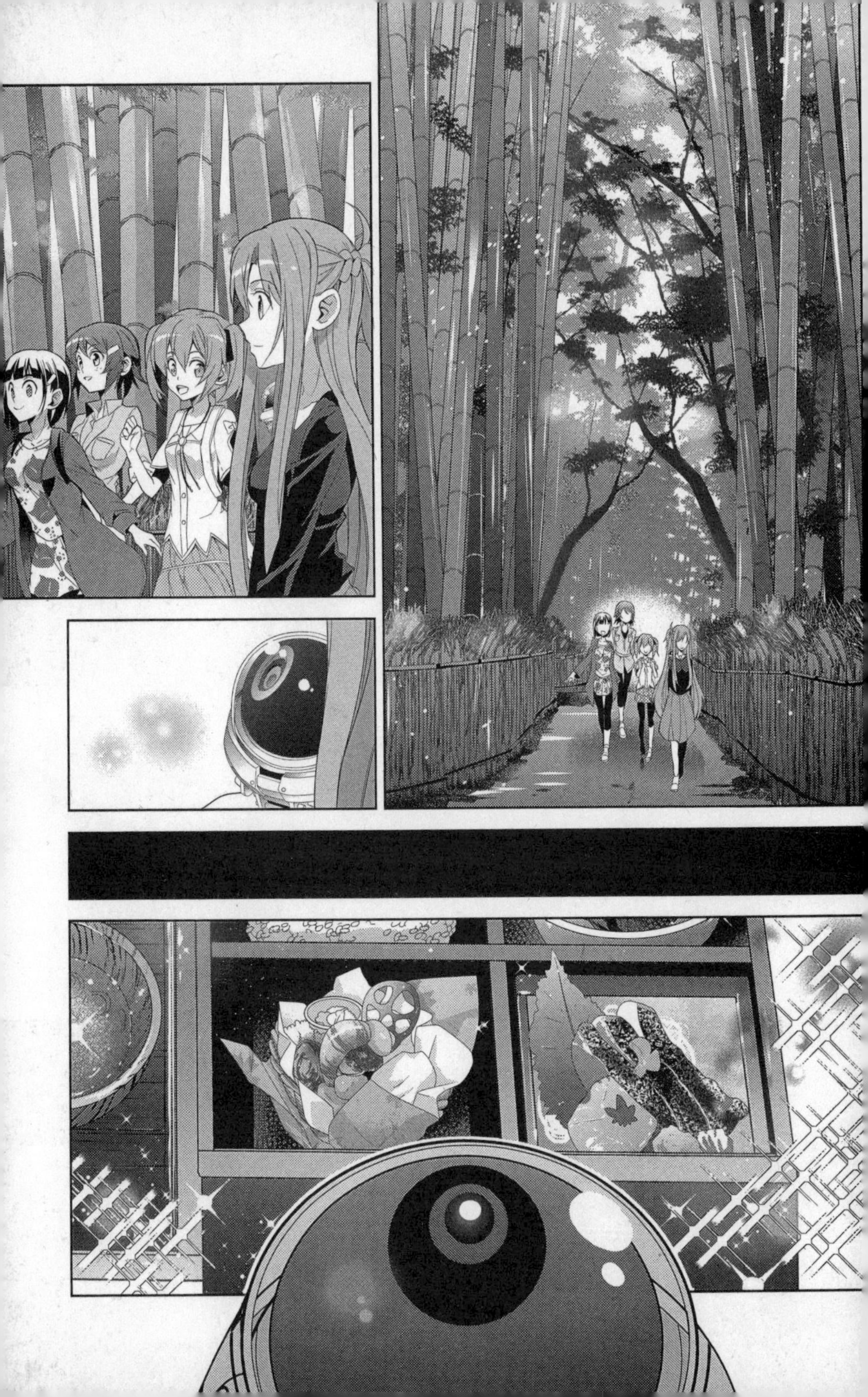

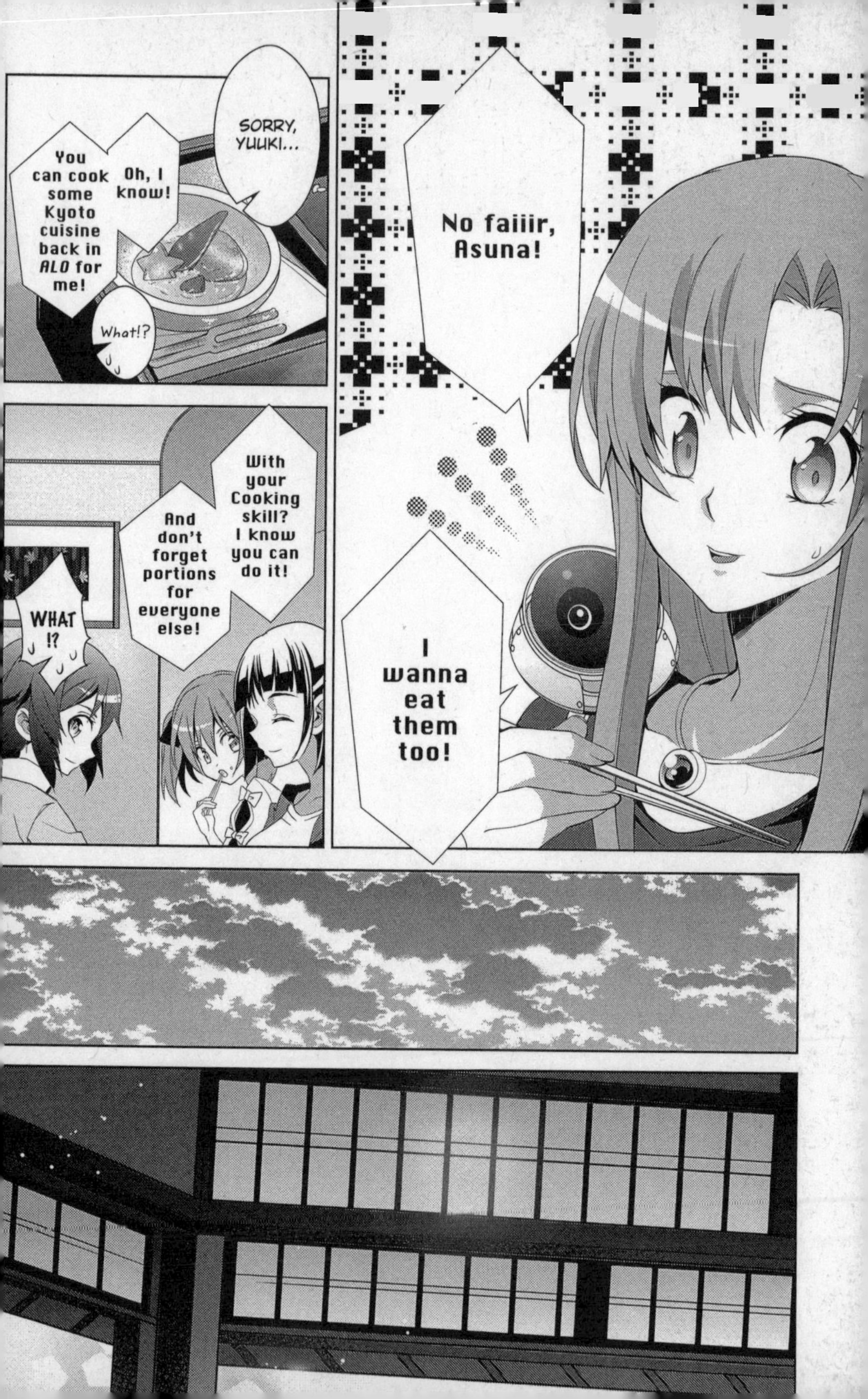
No faiiir, Asuna!
I wanna eat them too!
SORRY, YUUKI...
Oh, I know!
You can cook some Kyoto cuisine back in ALO for me!
What!?
With your Cooking skill? I know you can do it!
And don't forget portions for everyone else!
WHAT!?

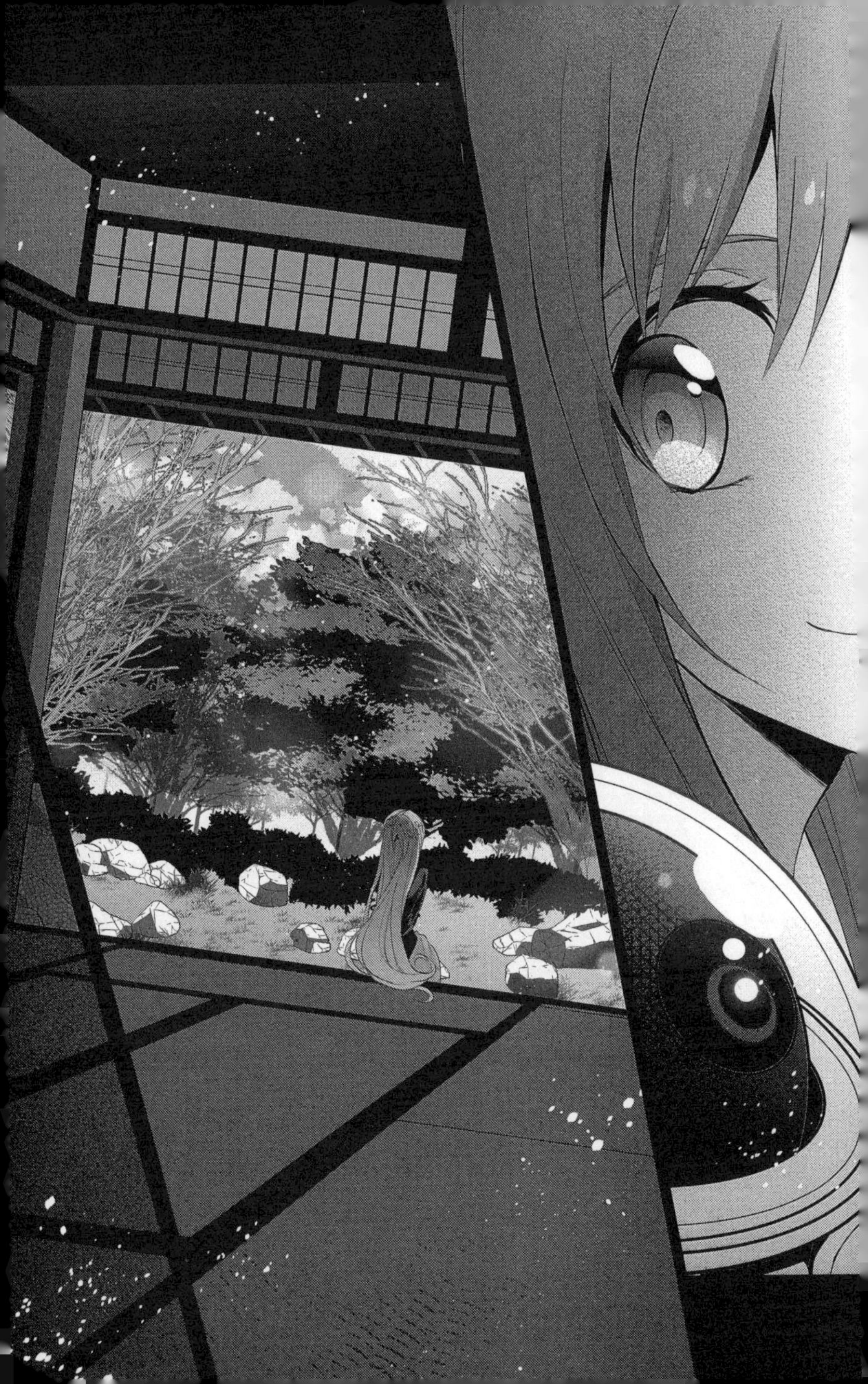

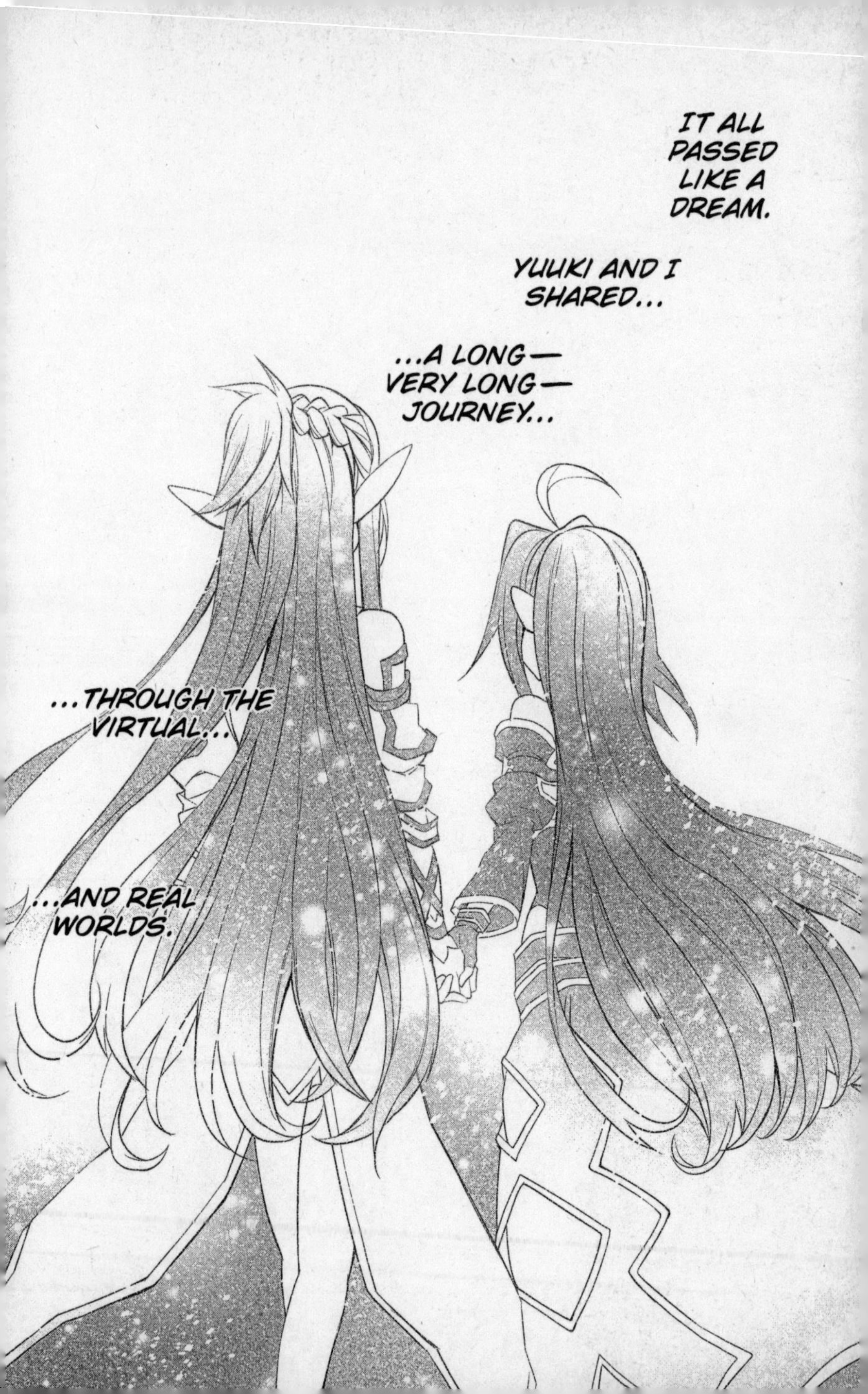
IT ALL PASSED LIKE A DREAM.
YUUKI AND I SHARED...
...A LONG— VERY LONG— JOURNEY...
...THROUGH THE VIRTUAL...
...AND REAL WORLDS.

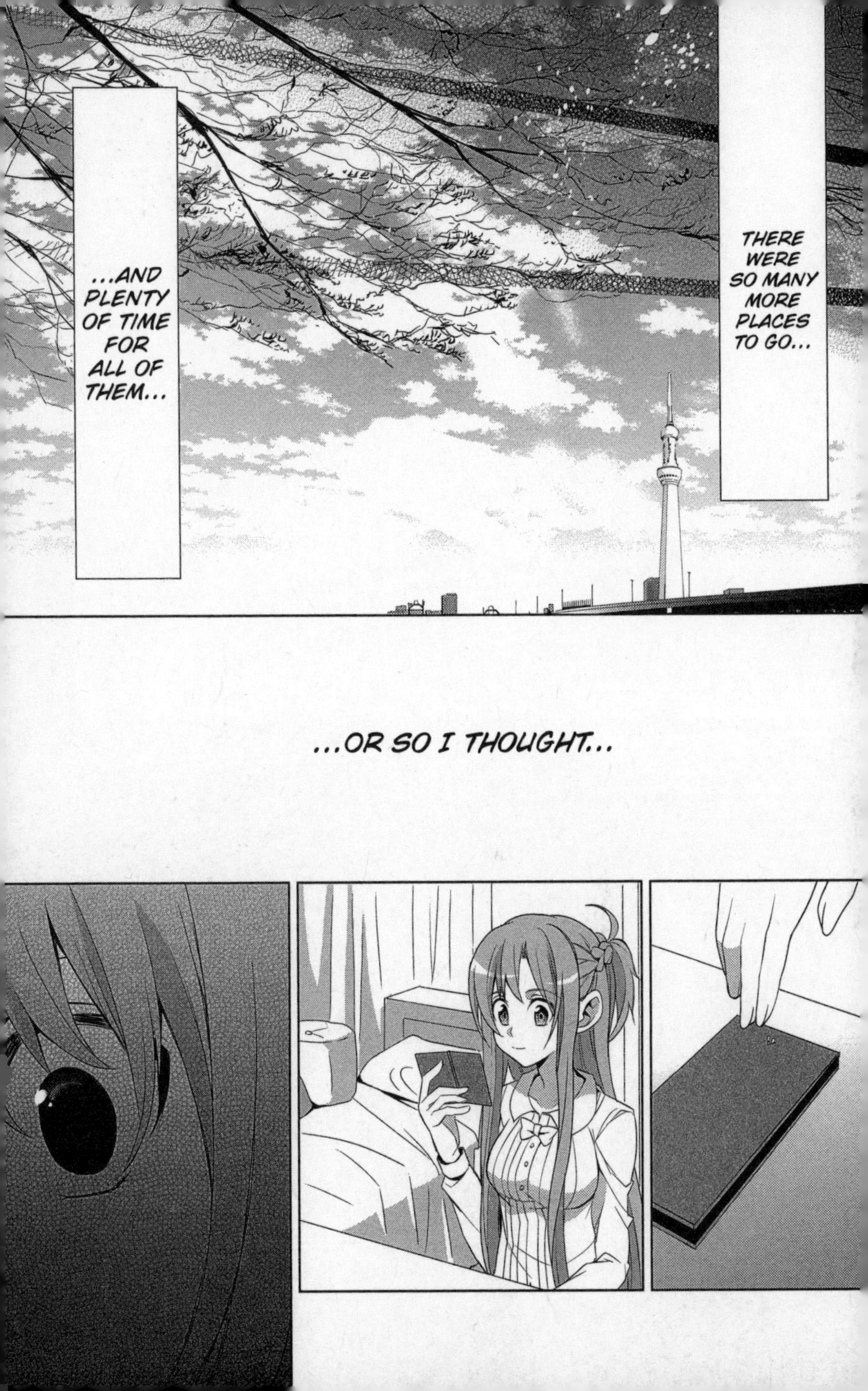
THERE WERE SO MANY MORE PLACES TO GO...
...AND PLENTY OF TIME FOR ALL OF THEM...
...OR SO I THOUGHT...

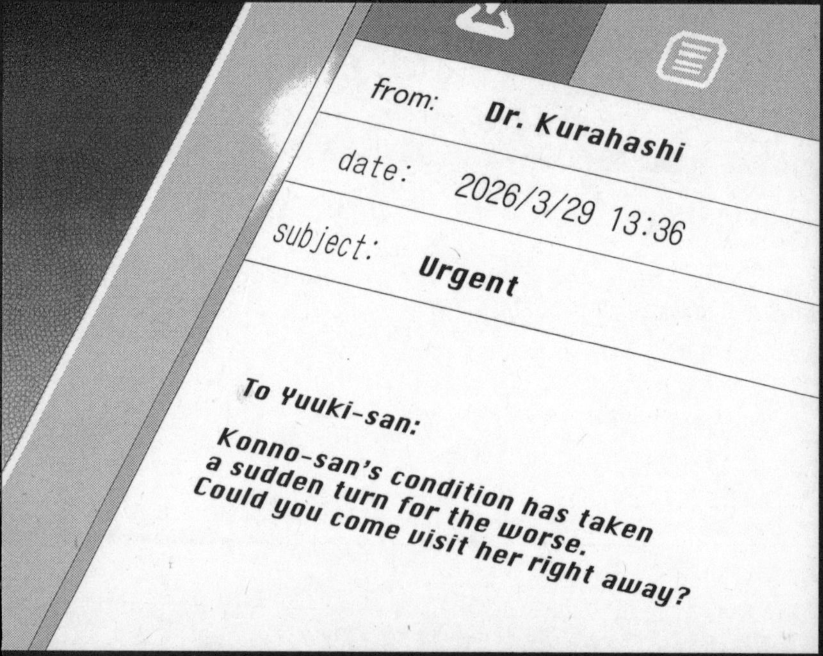
from: Dr. Kurahashi
date: 2026/3/29 13:36
subject: Urgent
To Yuuki-san:
Konno-san's condition has taken a sudden turn for the worse. Could you come visit her right away?

SWORD ART ONLINE
mother's ROSARY

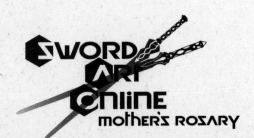

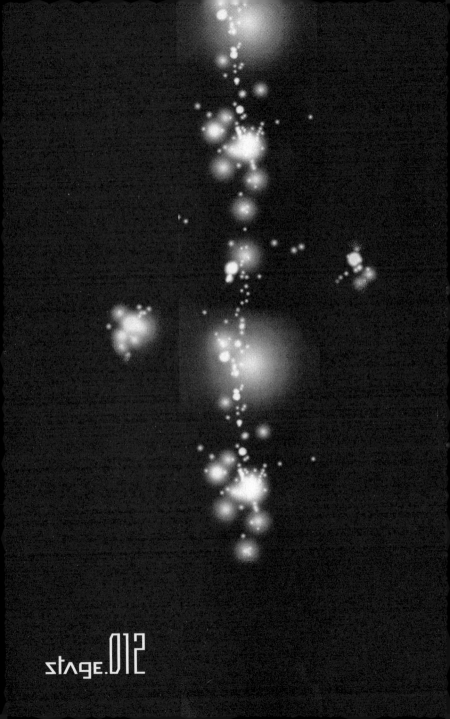

stage.012

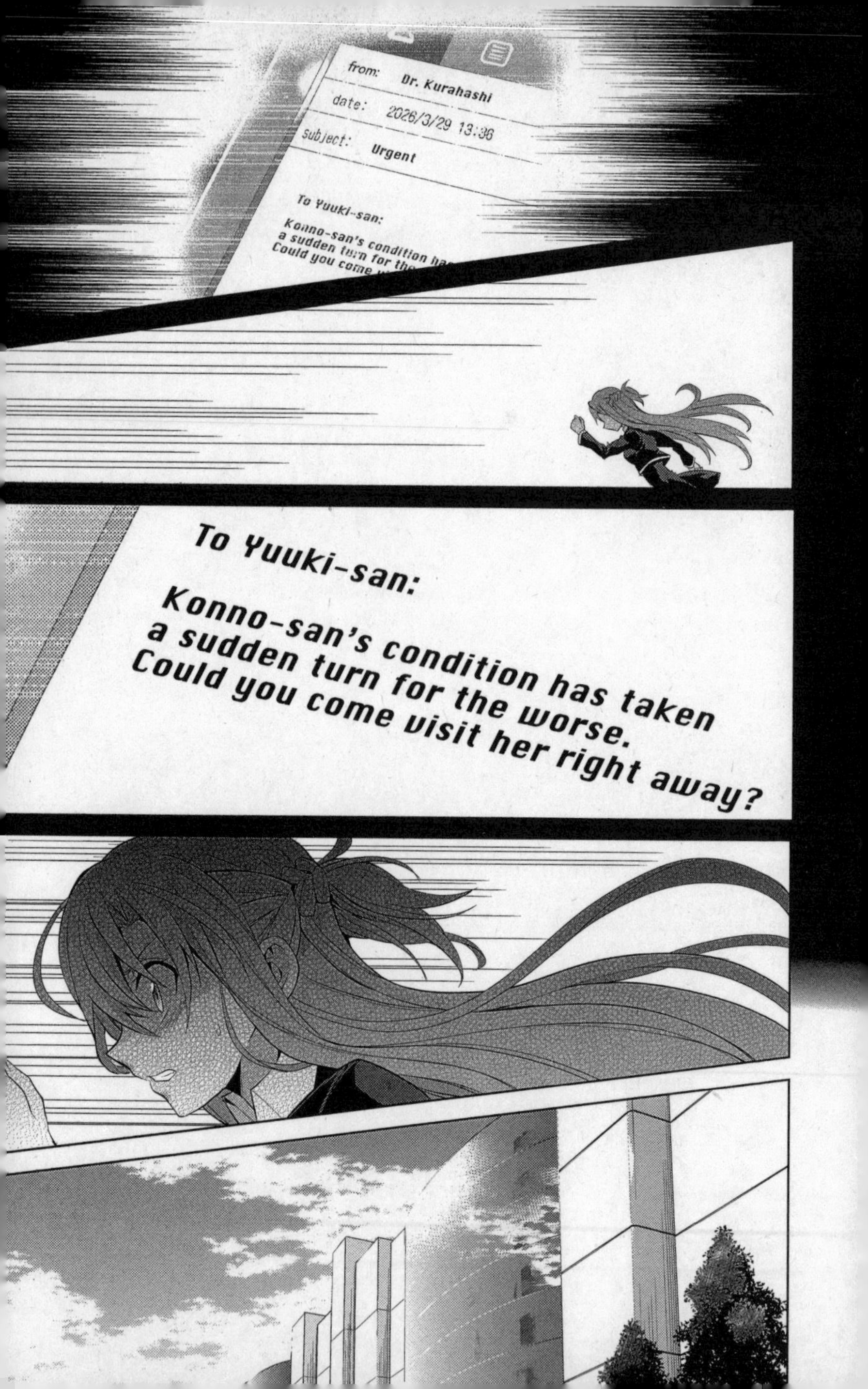
from: Dr. Kurahashi
date: 2026/3/29 13:36
subject: Urgent
To Yuuki-san:
Konno-san's condition
a sudden turn for
Could you come
To Yuuki-san:
Konno-san's condition has taken a sudden turn for the worse. Could you come visit her right away?

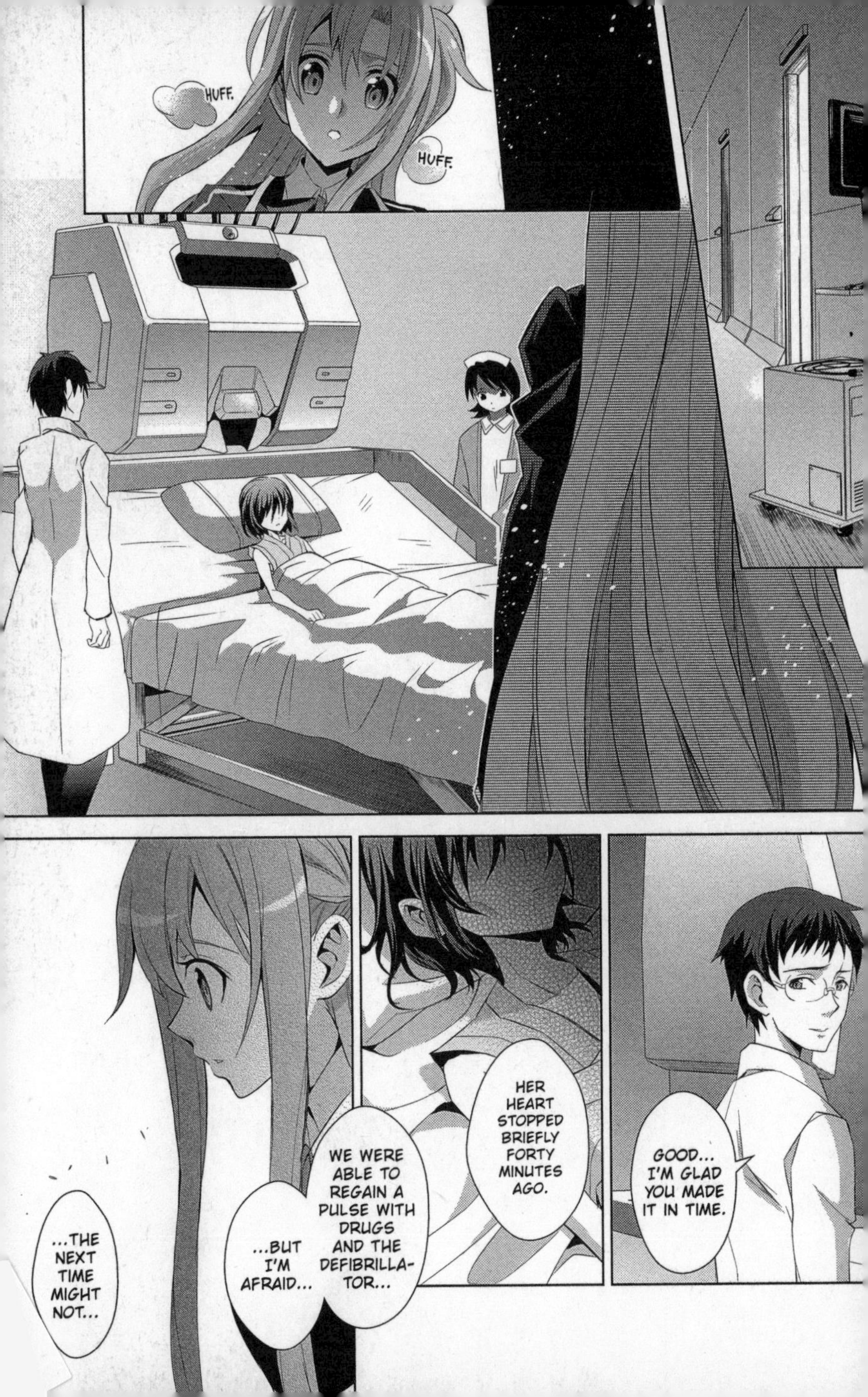
HUFF.
HUFF.
GOOD... I'M GLAD YOU MADE IT IN TIME.
HER HEART STOPPED BRIEFLY FORTY MINUTES AGO.
WE WERE ABLE TO REGAIN A PULSE WITH DRUGS AND THE DEFIBRILLA-TOR...
...BUT I'M AFRAID...
...THE NEXT TIME MIGHT NOT...

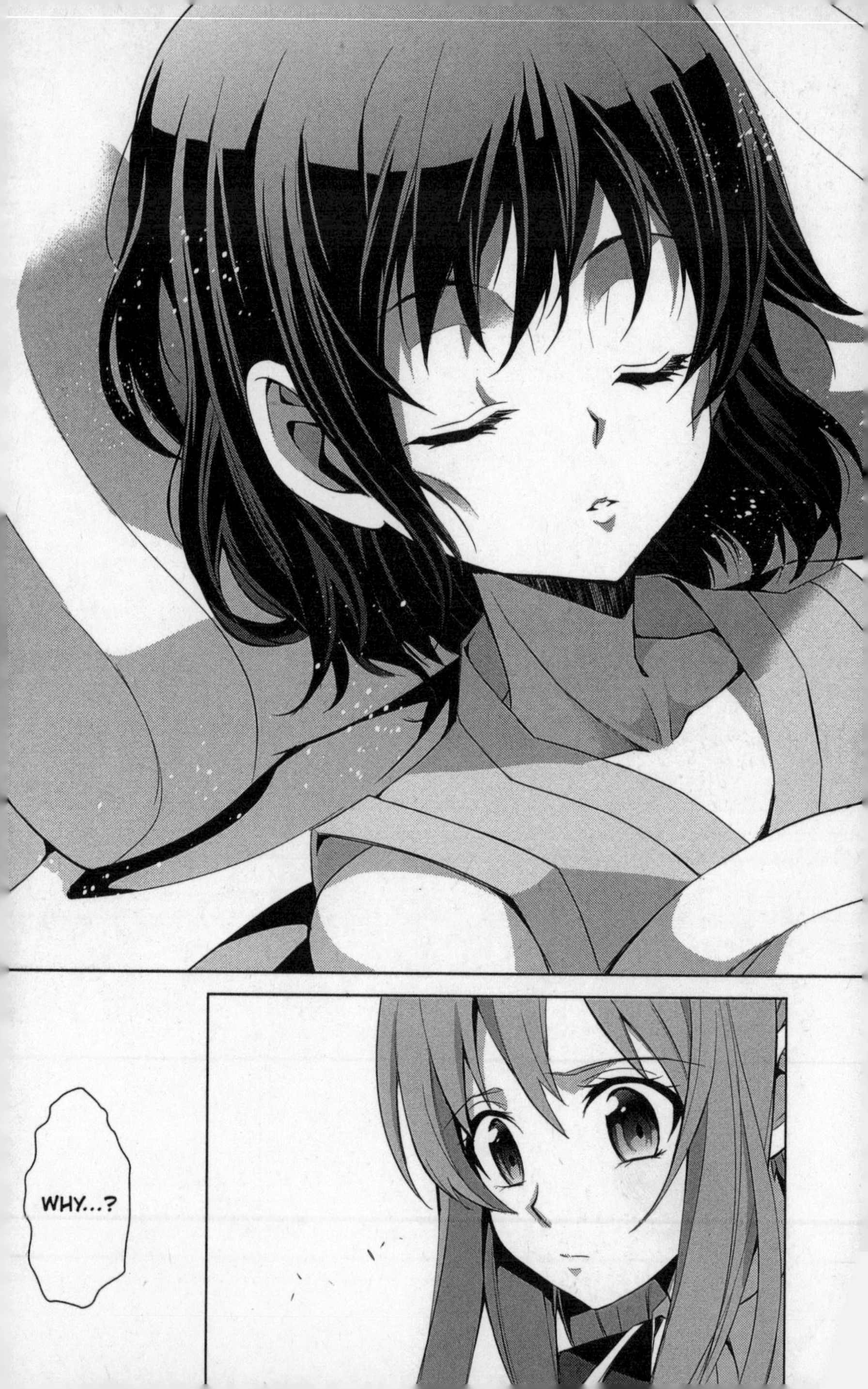
WHY...?

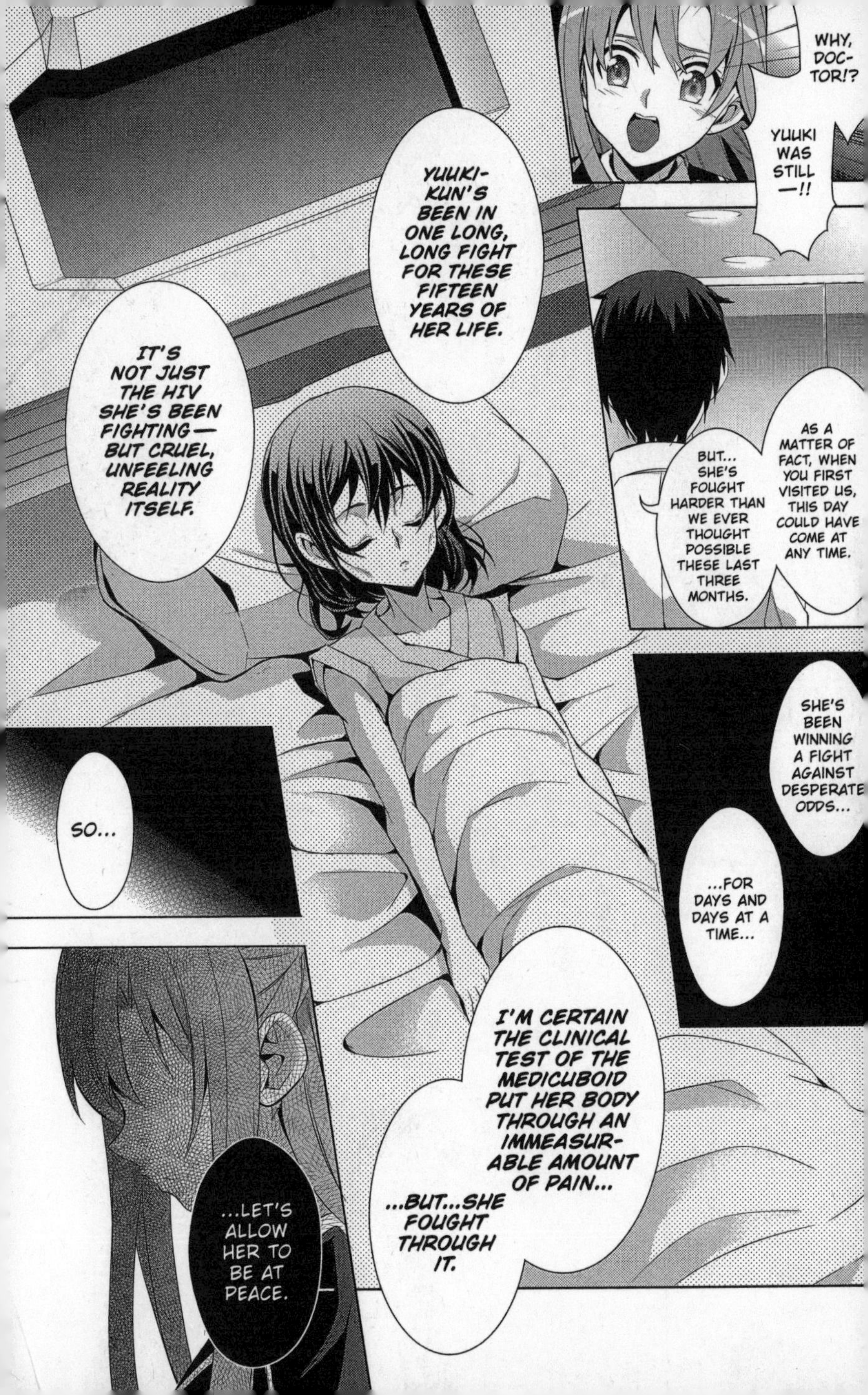
WHY, DOC-TOR!?
YUUKI WAS STILL—!!
AS A MATTER OF FACT, WHEN YOU FIRST VISITED US, THIS DAY COULD HAVE COME AT ANY TIME.
BUT... SHE'S FOUGHT HARDER THAN WE EVER THOUGHT POSSIBLE THESE LAST THREE MONTHS.
YUUKI-KUN'S BEEN IN ONE LONG, LONG FIGHT FOR THESE FIFTEEN YEARS OF HER LIFE.
IT'S NOT JUST THE HIV SHE'S BEEN FIGHTING—BUT CRUEL, UNFEELING REALITY ITSELF.
SHE'S BEEN WINNING A FIGHT AGAINST DESPERATE ODDS...
...FOR DAYS AND DAYS AT A TIME...
I'M CERTAIN THE CLINICAL TEST OF THE MEDICUBOID PUT HER BODY THROUGH AN IMMEASUR-ABLE AMOUNT OF PAIN...
...BUT...SHE FOUGHT THROUGH IT.
SO...
...LET'S ALLOW HER TO BE AT PEACE.

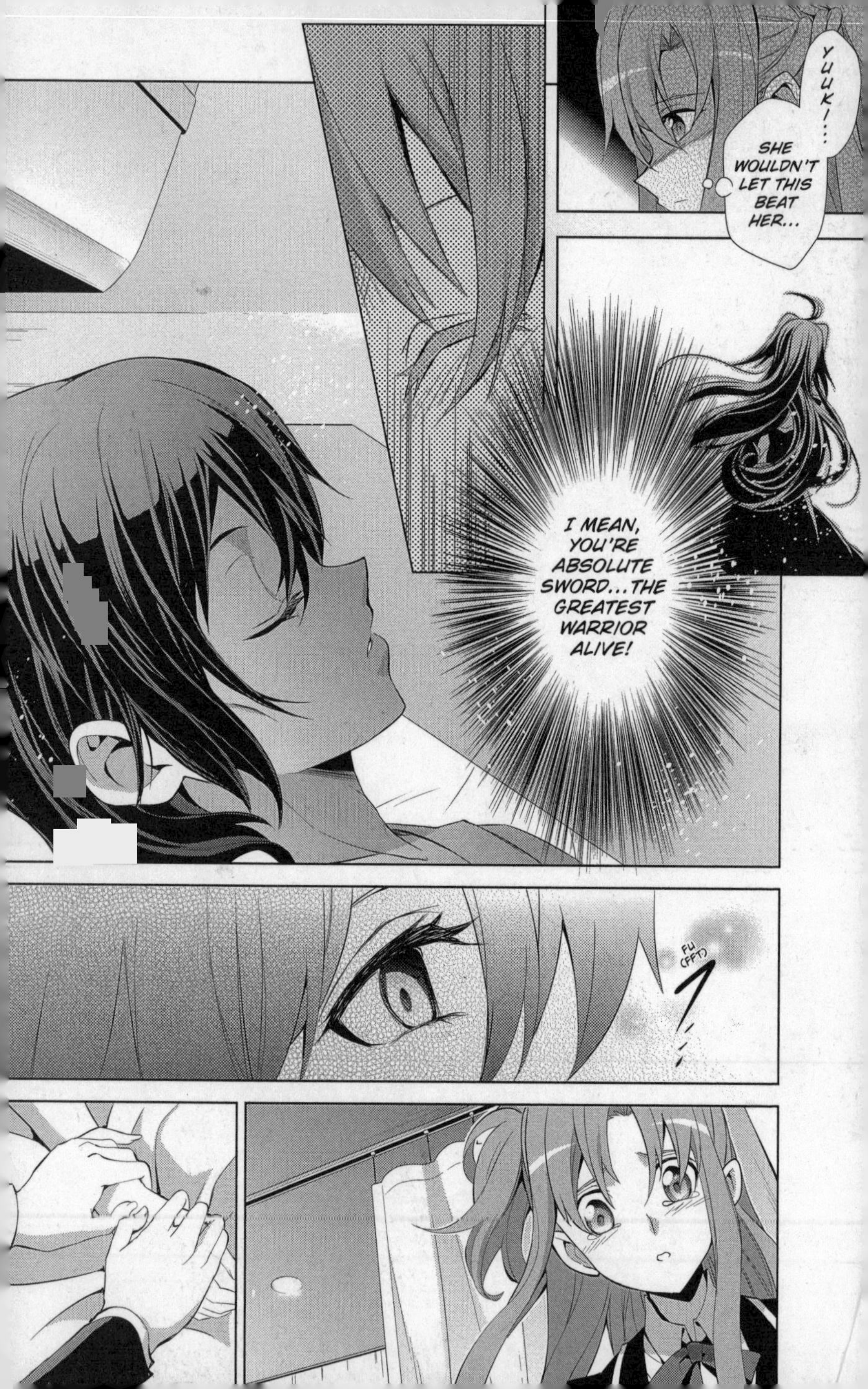
YUUKI...
SHE WOULDN'T LET THIS BEAT HER...
I MEAN, YOU'RE ABSOLUTE SWORD...THE GREATEST WARRIOR ALIVE!
FU (FFT)

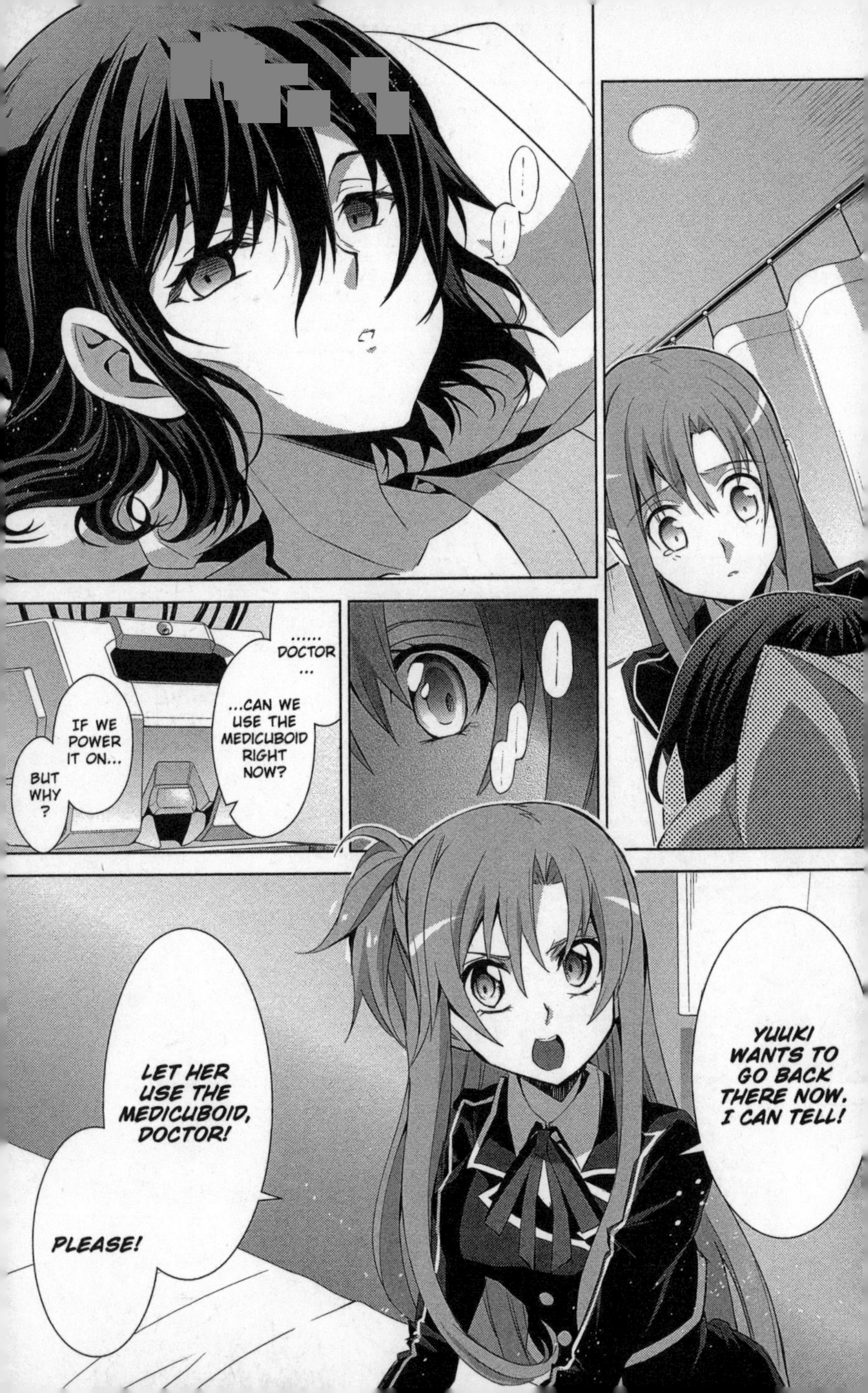
!!
!
......DOCTOR ... ...CAN WE USE THE MEDICUBOID RIGHT NOW?
IF WE POWER IT ON...
BUT WHY ?
YUUKI WANTS TO GO BACK THERE NOW. I CAN TELL!
LET HER USE THE MEDICUBOID, DOCTOR!
PLEASE!

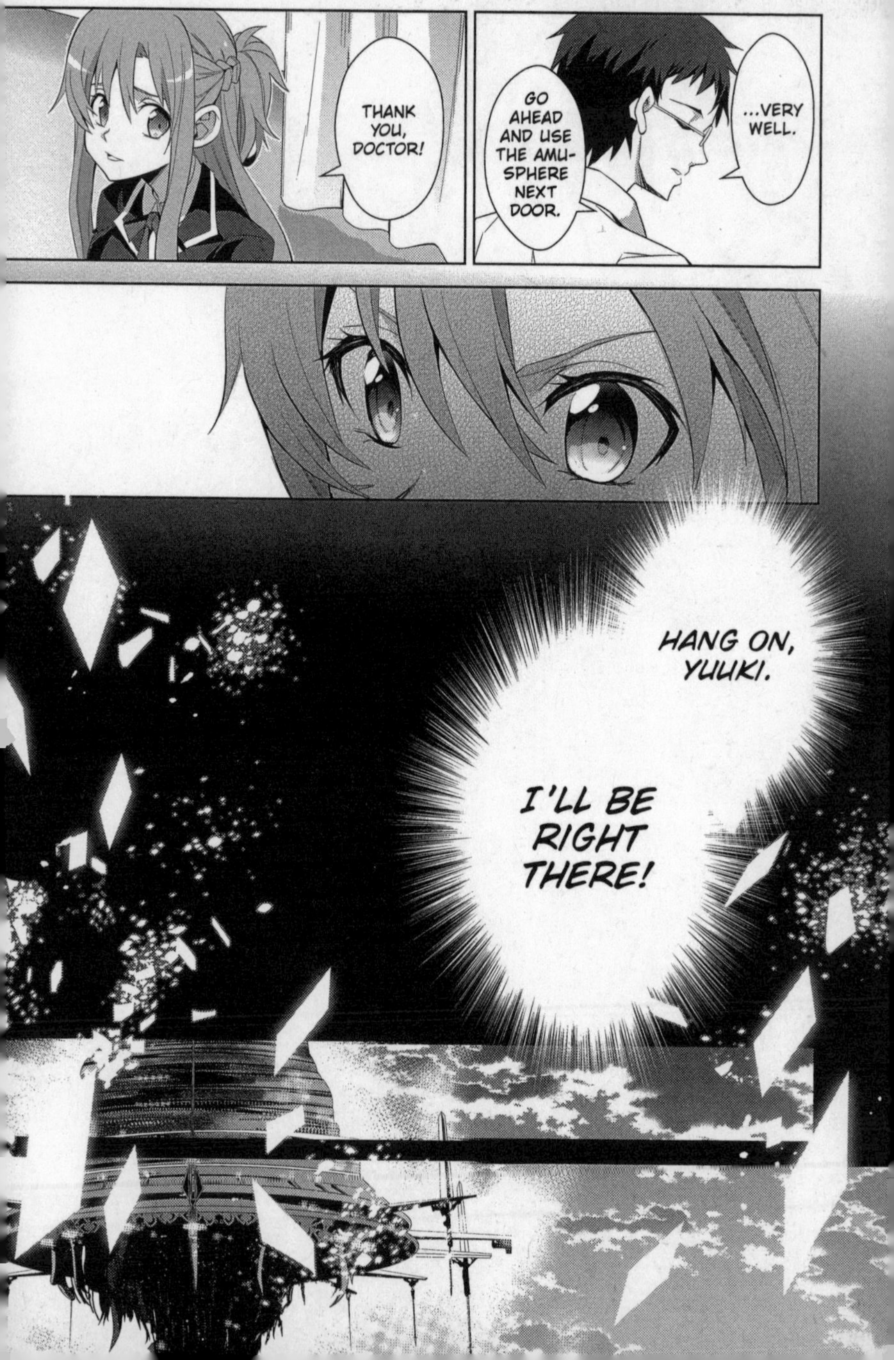
...VERY WELL.
GO AHEAD AND USE THE AMU-SPHERE NEXT DOOR.
THANK YOU, DOCTOR!
HANG ON, YUUKI.
I'LL BE RIGHT THERE!

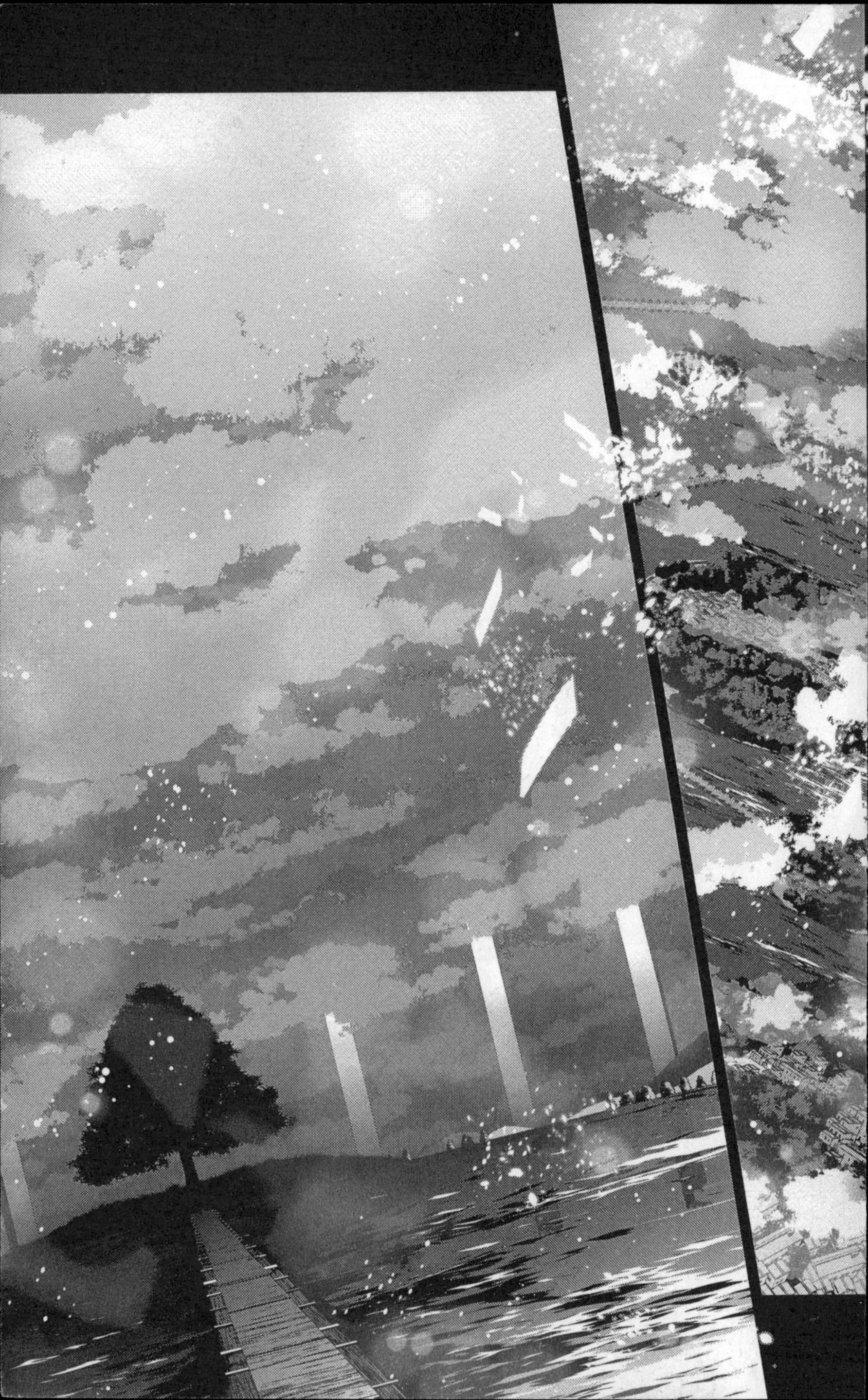

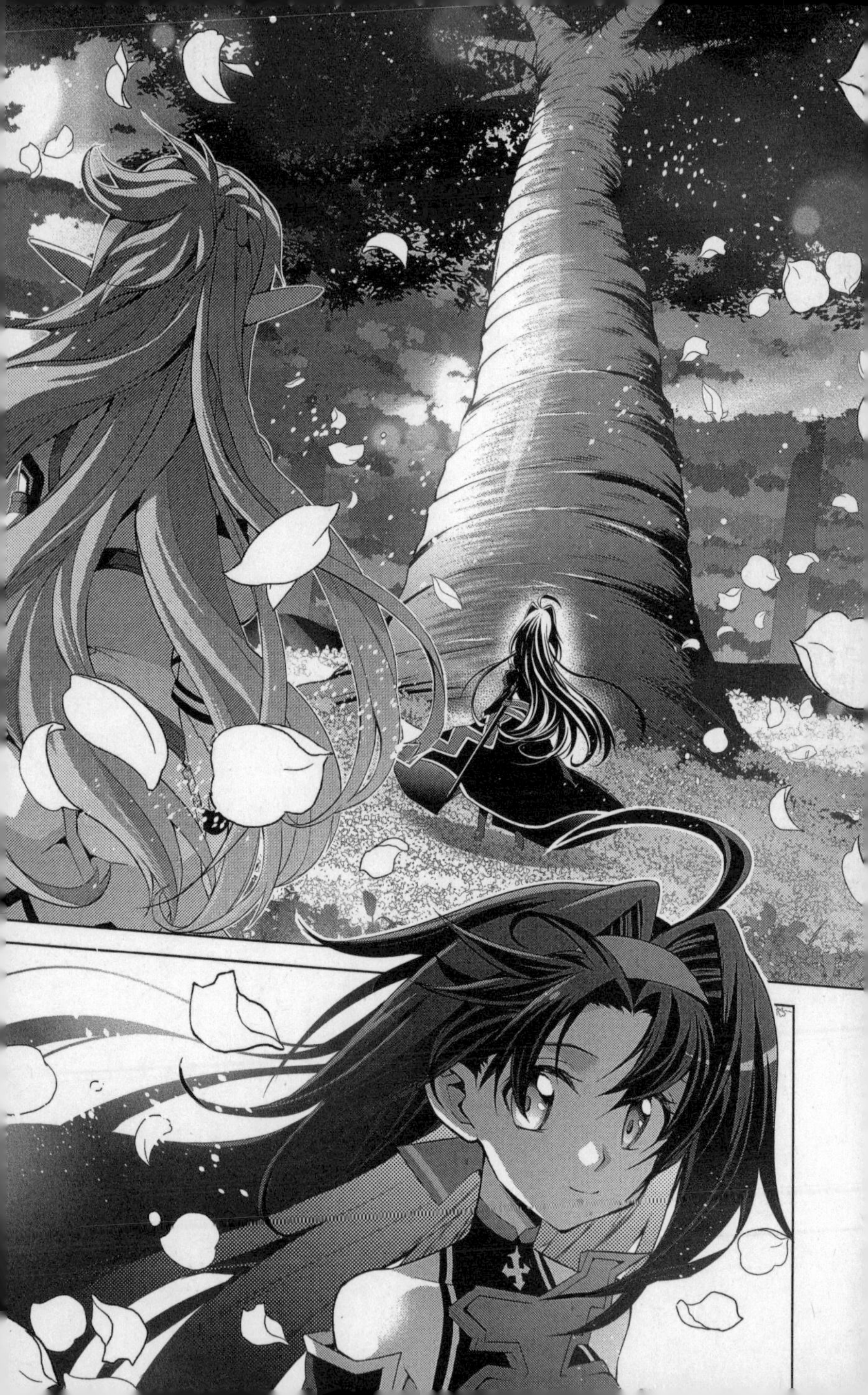

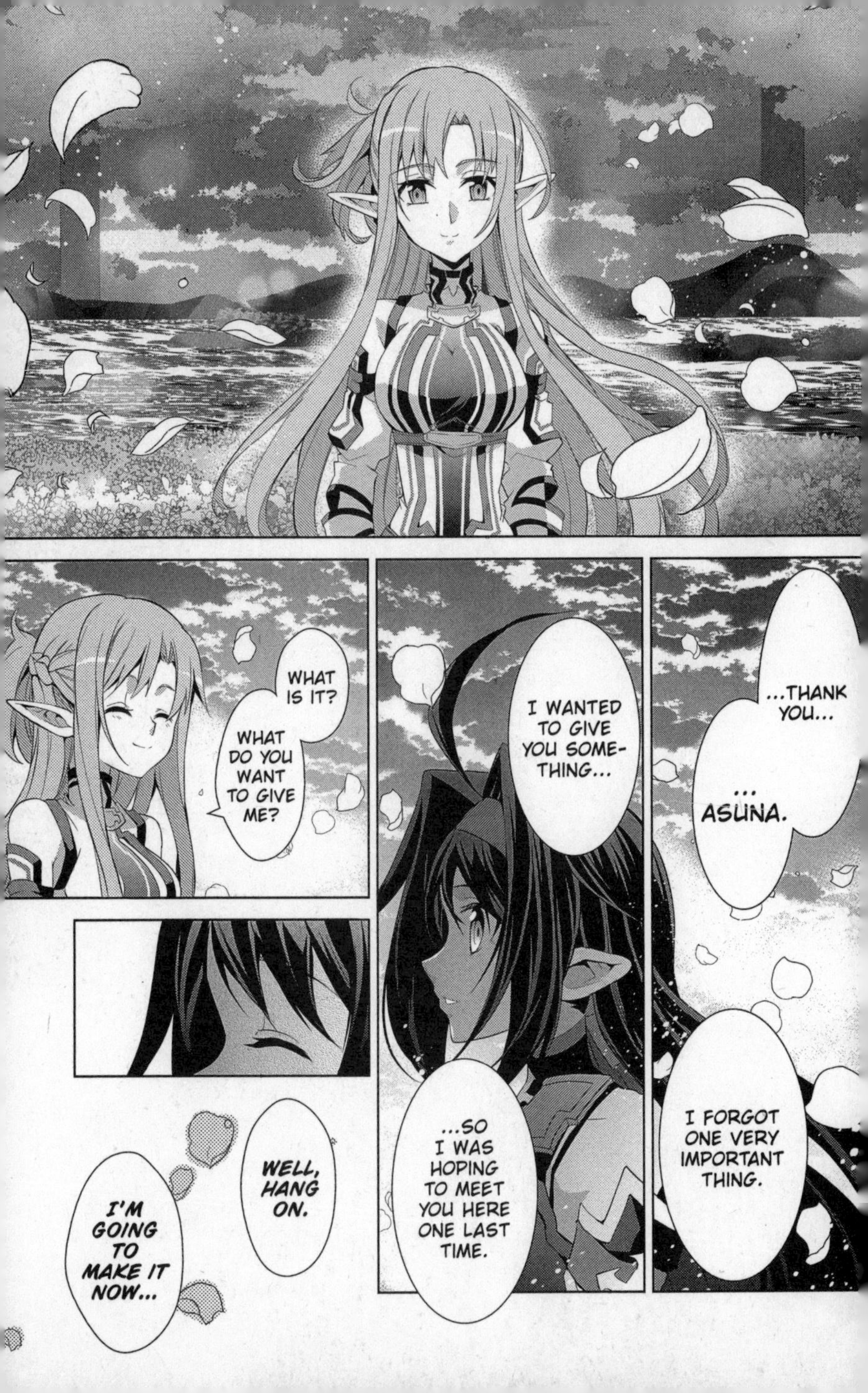
...THANK YOU...
... ASUNA.
I FORGOT ONE VERY IMPORTANT THING.
I WANTED TO GIVE YOU SOME-THING...
...SO I WAS HOPING TO MEET YOU HERE ONE LAST TIME.
WHAT IS IT?
WHAT DO YOU WANT TO GIVE ME?
WELL, HANG ON.
I'M GOING TO MAKE IT NOW...

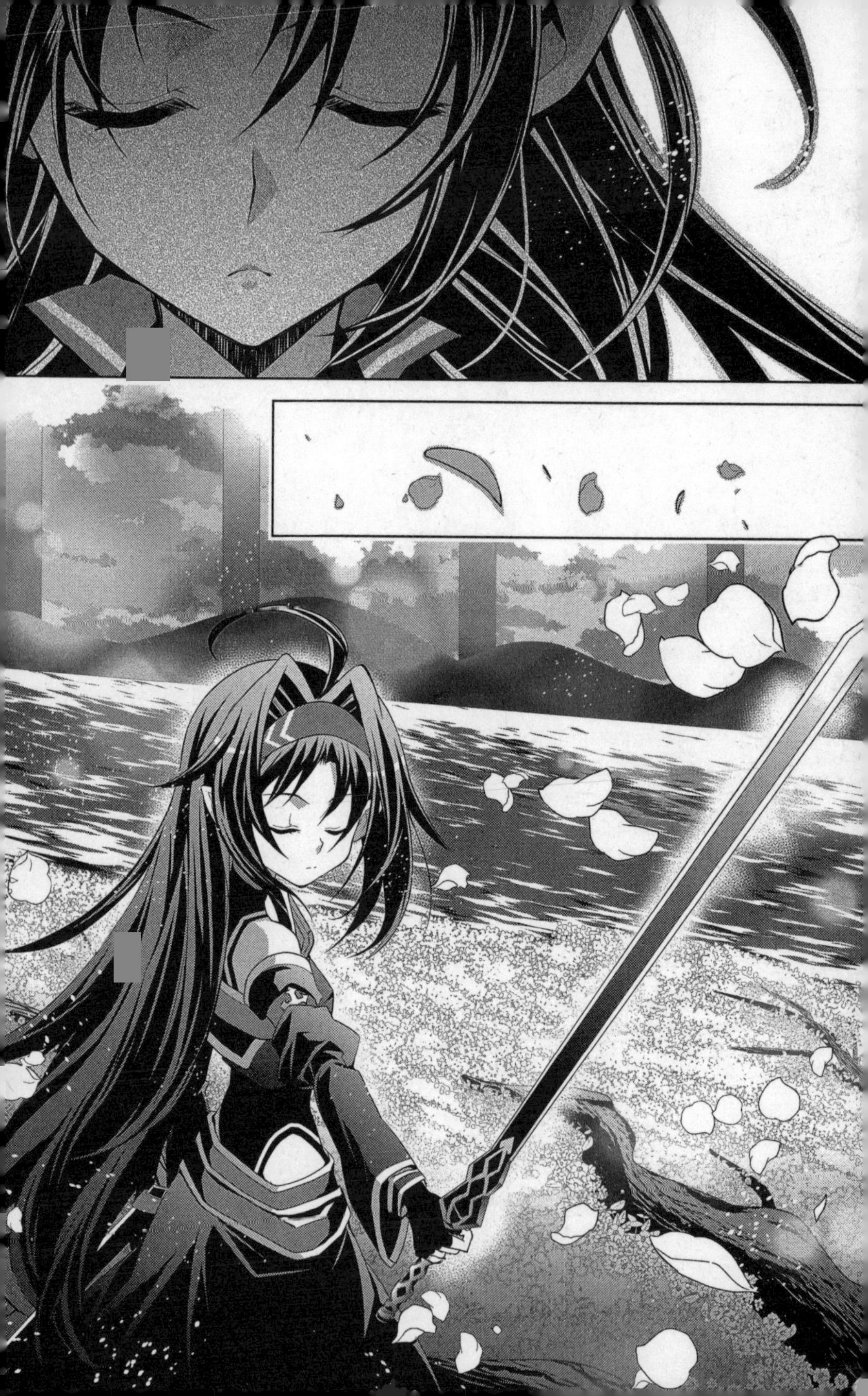

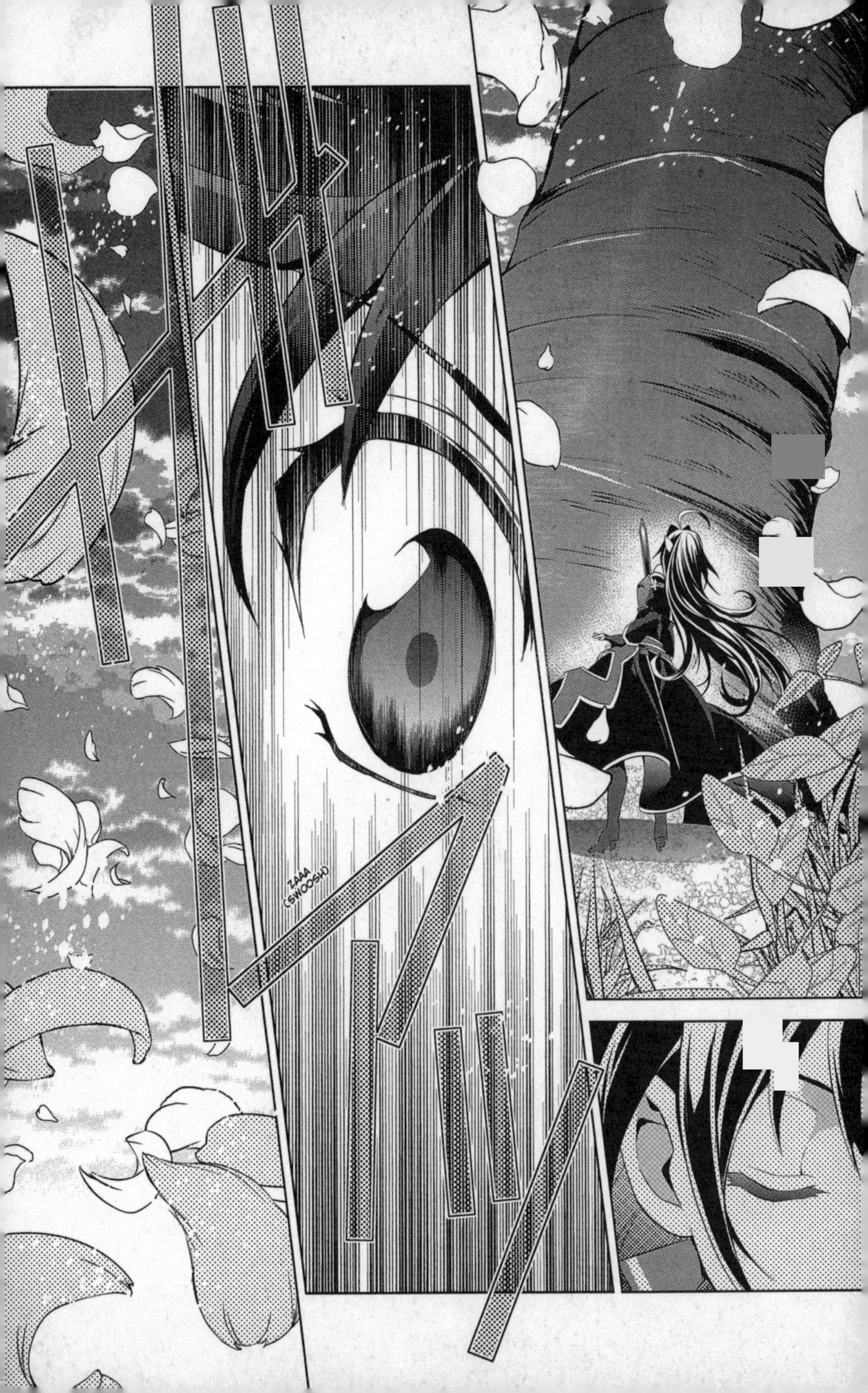
ZAAA
(SWOOSH)

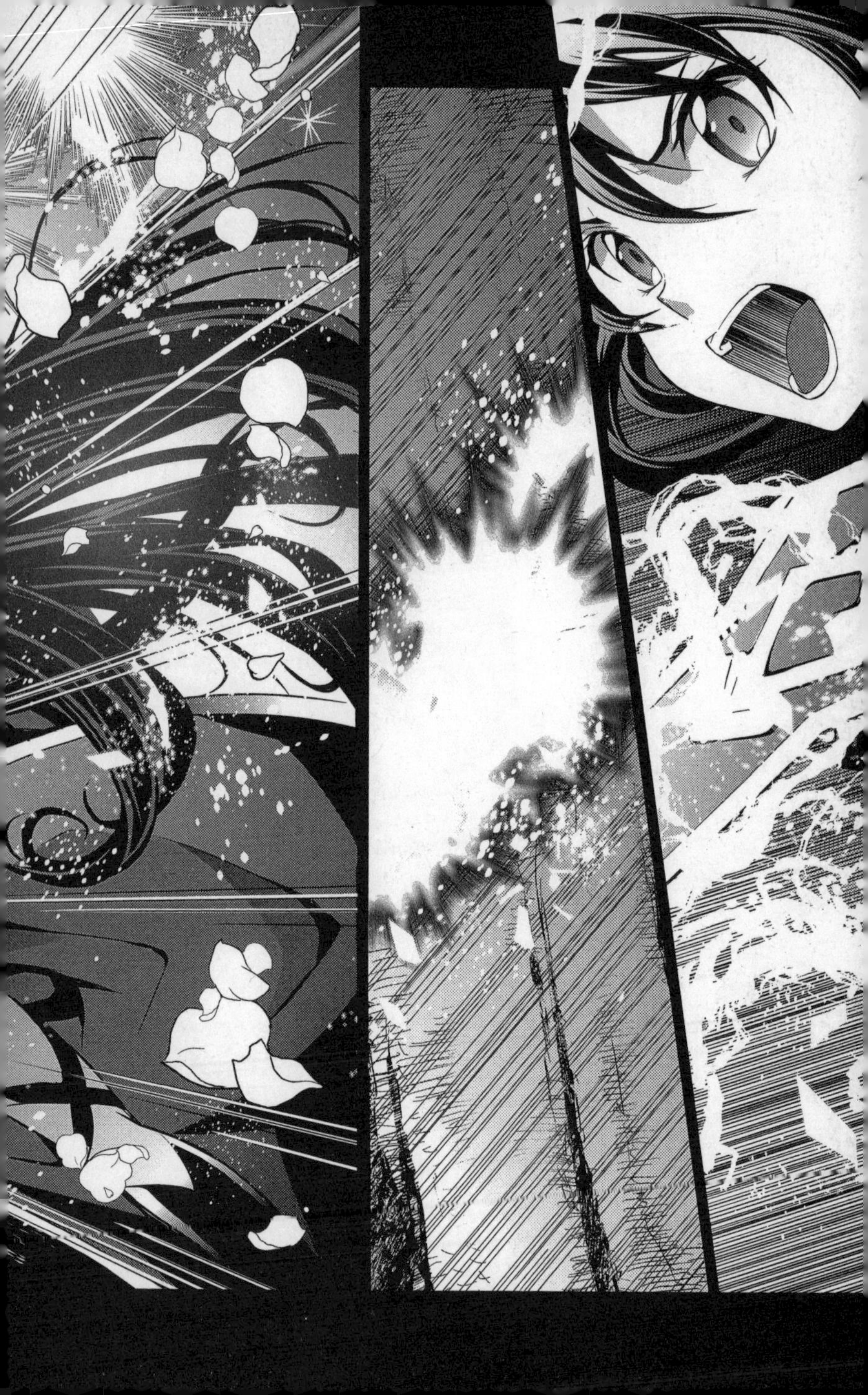

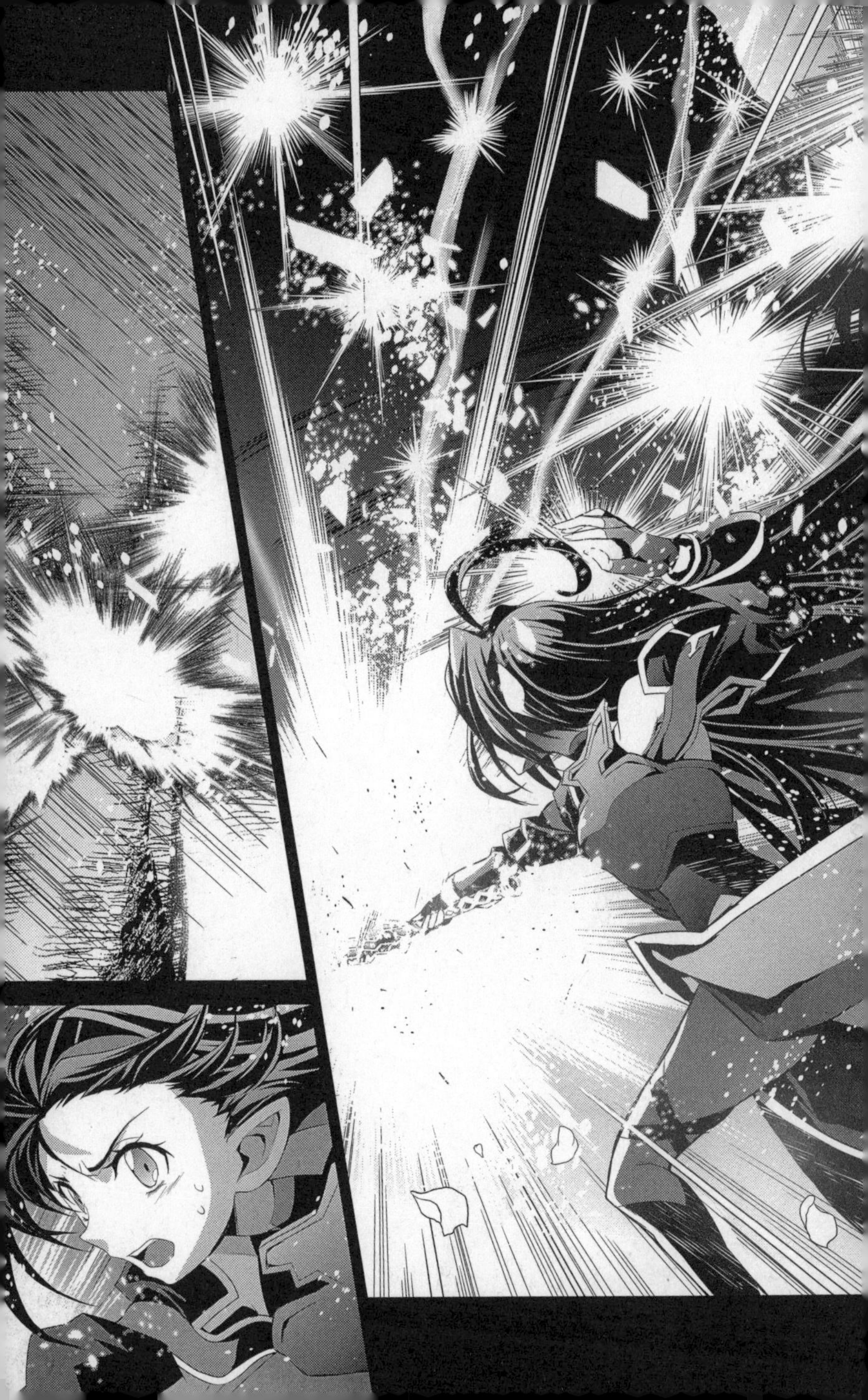

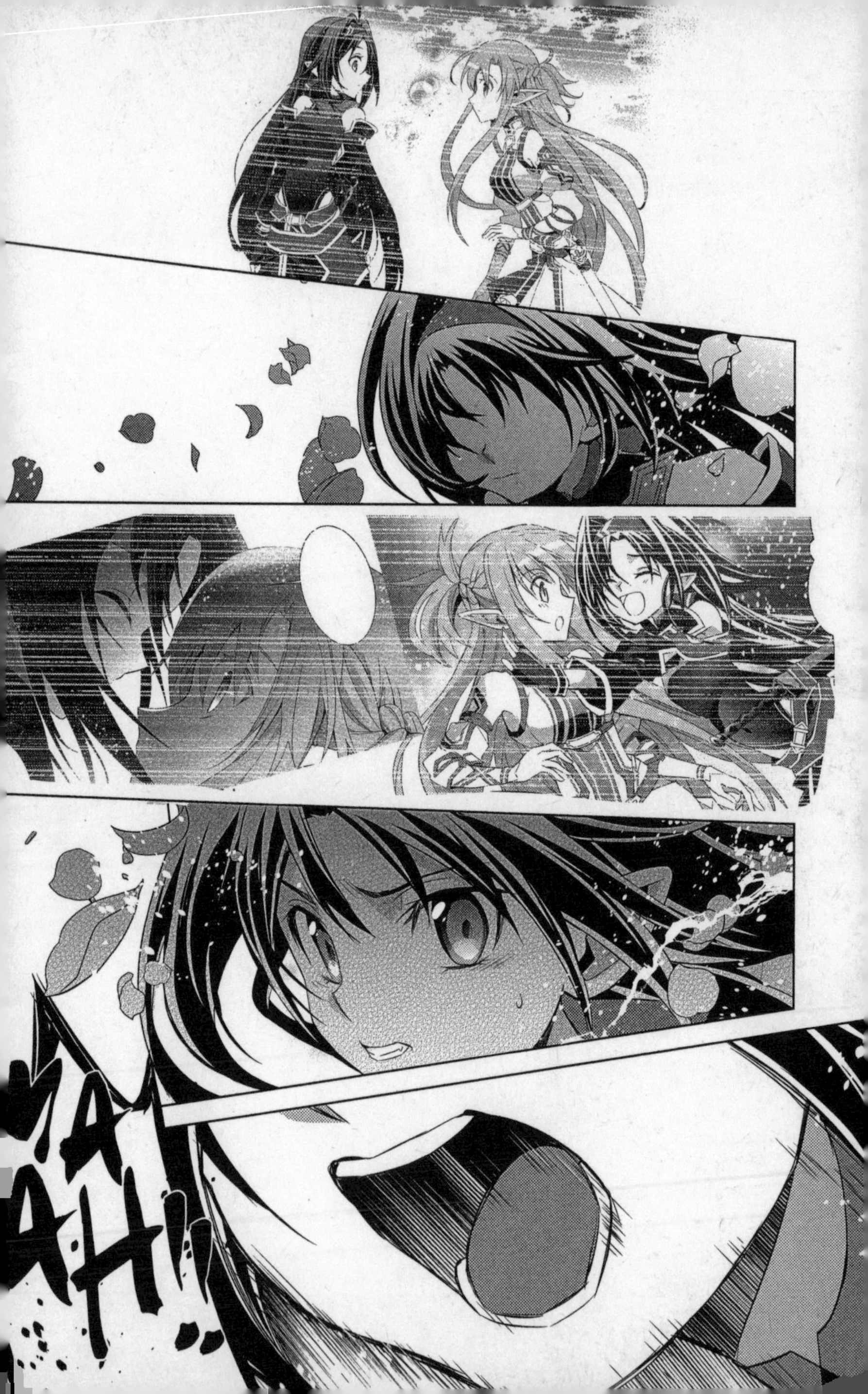
AA
AH!!

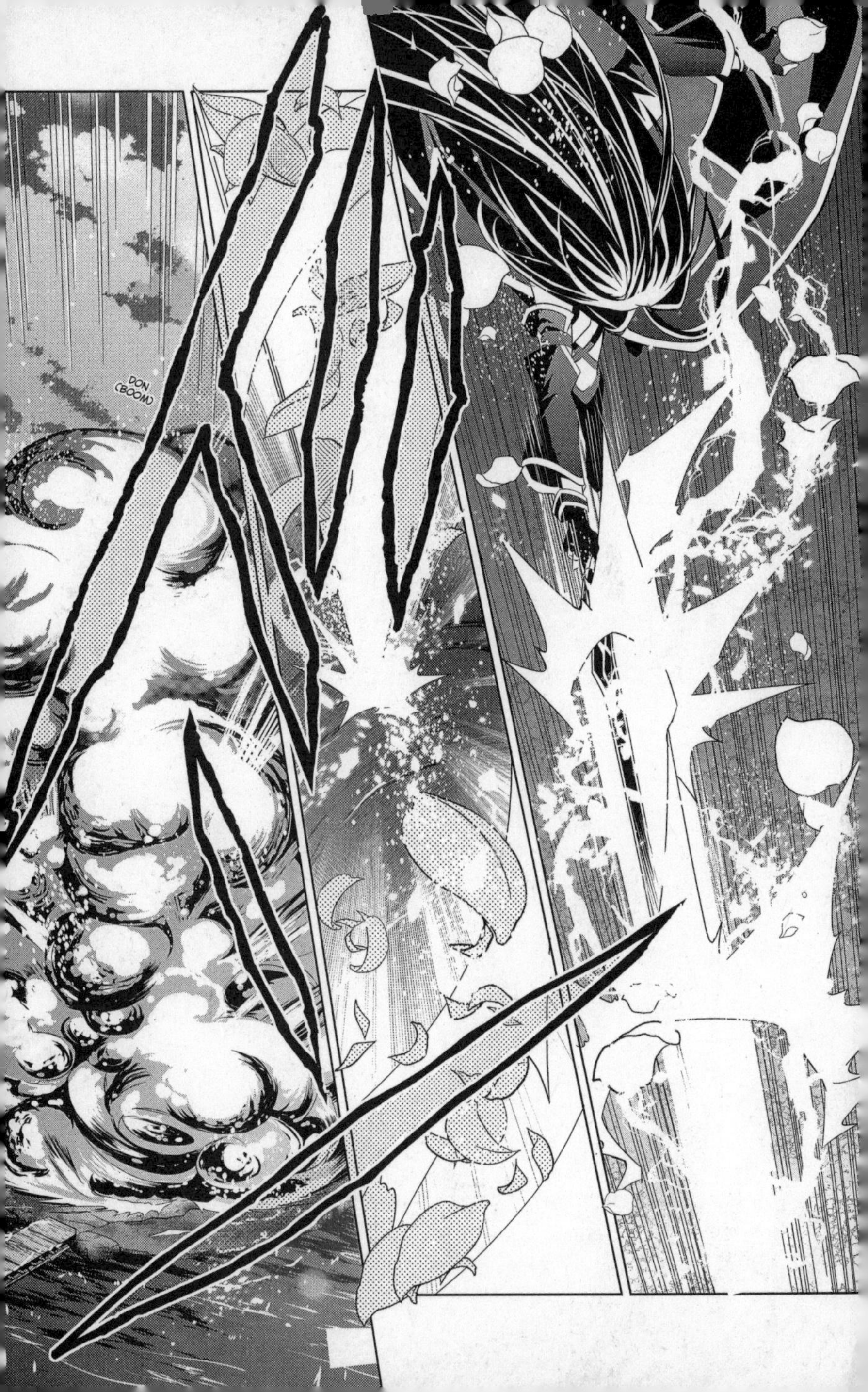
DON
(BOOM)

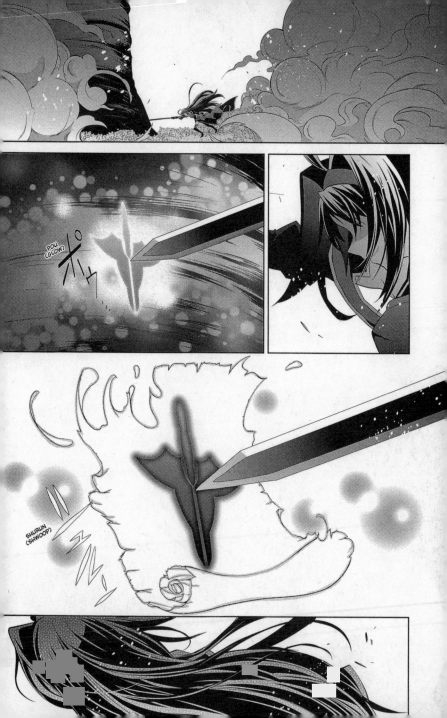

POU
(GLOW)

SHURIN
(SHWOOP)

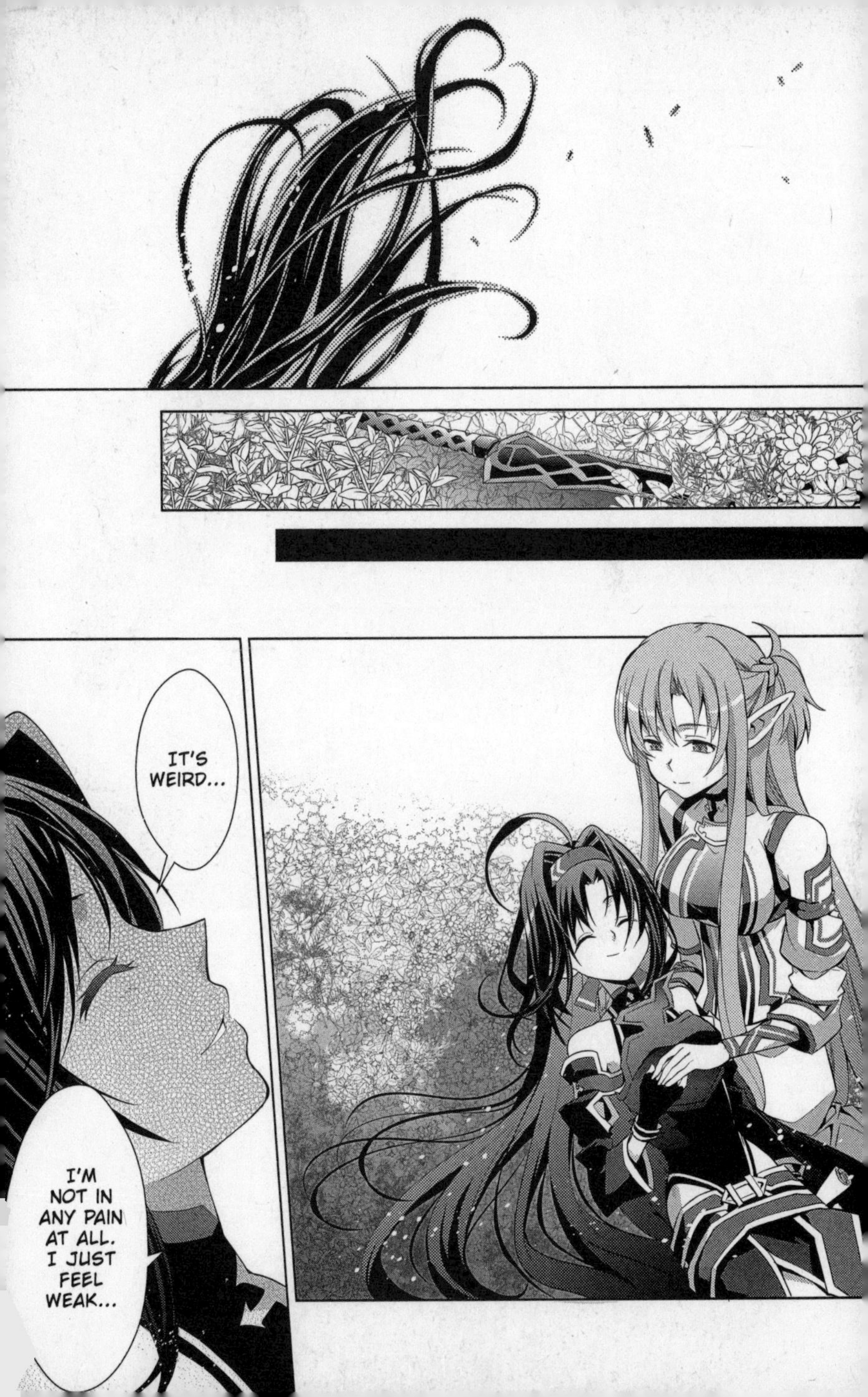
IT'S WEIRD...
I'M NOT IN ANY PAIN AT ALL. I JUST FEEL WEAK...

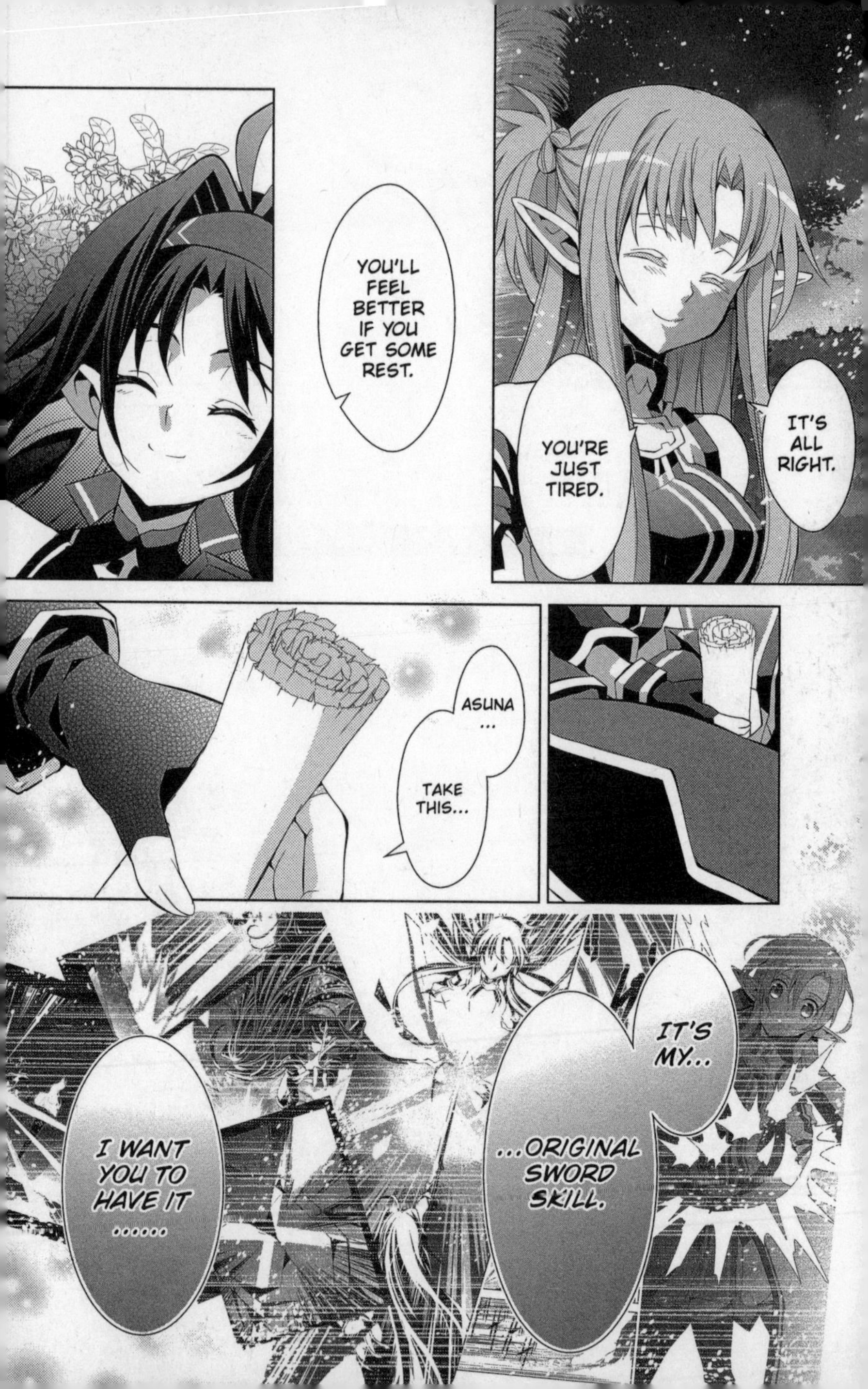
IT'S ALL RIGHT.
YOU'RE JUST TIRED.
YOU'LL FEEL BETTER IF YOU GET SOME REST.
ASUNA...
TAKE THIS...
IT'S MY...
...ORIGINAL SWORD SKILL.
I WANT YOU TO HAVE IT ....

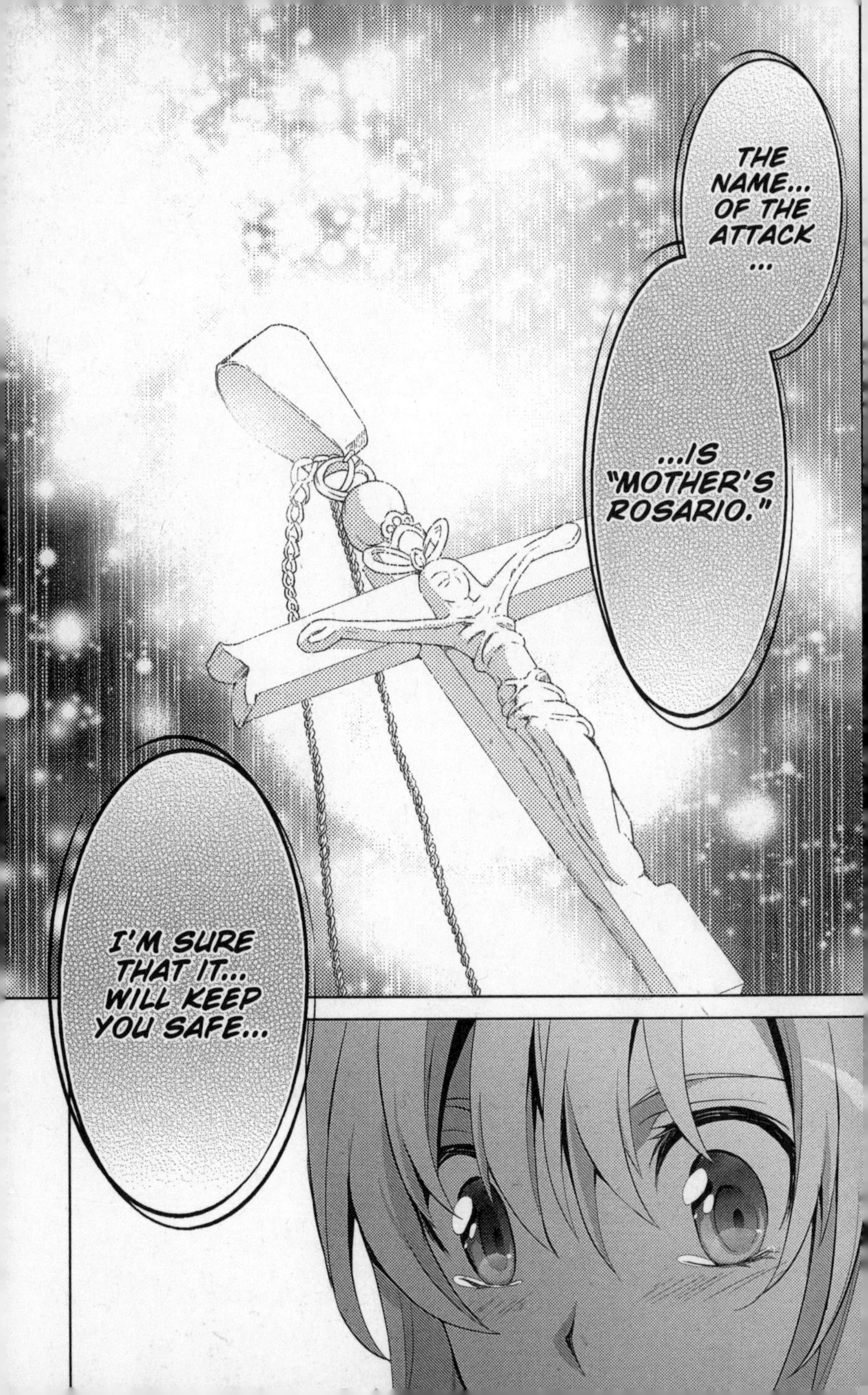
THE NAME... OF THE ATTACK ...
...IS "MOTHER'S ROSARIO."
I'M SURE THAT IT... WILL KEEP YOU SAFE...

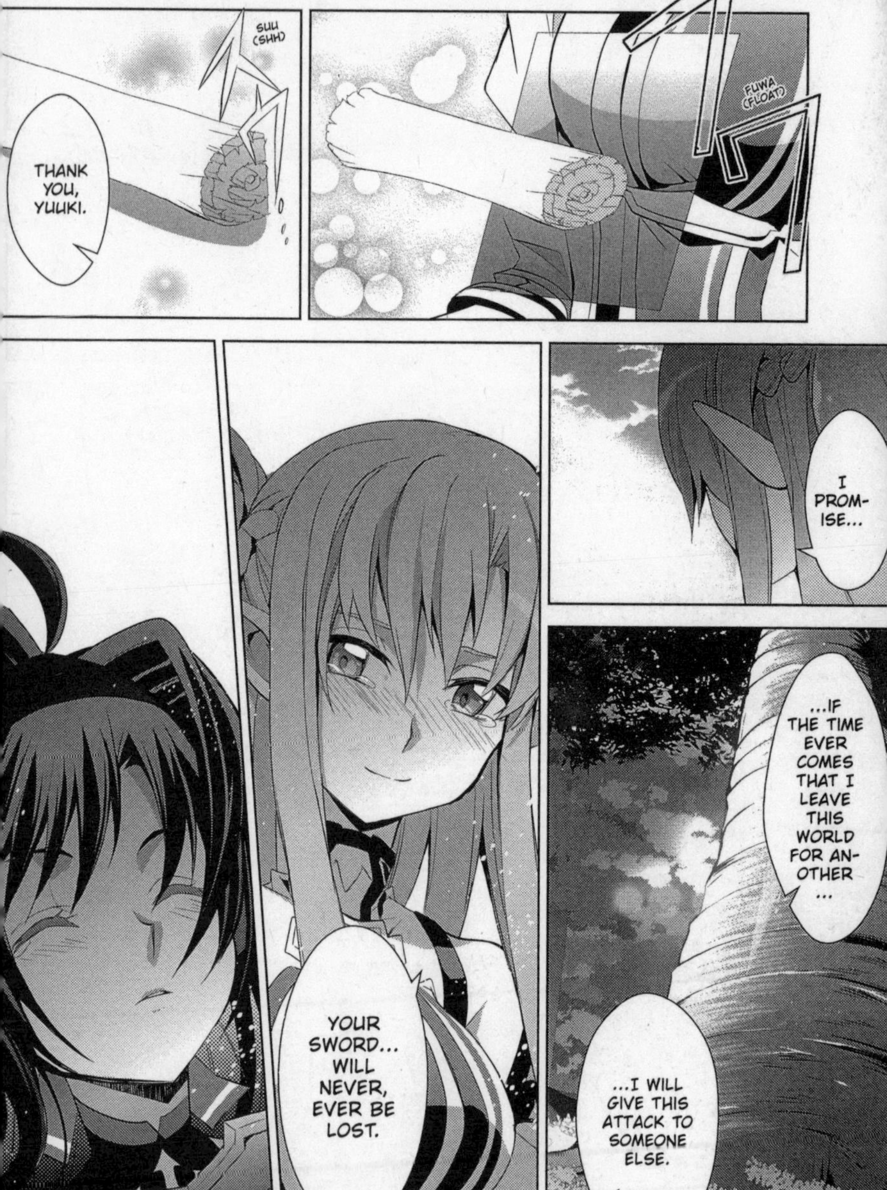
FUWA (FLOAT)
SUU (SHH)
THANK YOU, YUUKI.
I PROM-ISE...
...IF THE TIME EVER COMES THAT I LEAVE THIS WORLD FOR AN-OTHER...
...I WILL GIVE THIS ATTACK TO SOMEONE ELSE.
YOUR SWORD... WILL NEVER, EVER BE LOST.

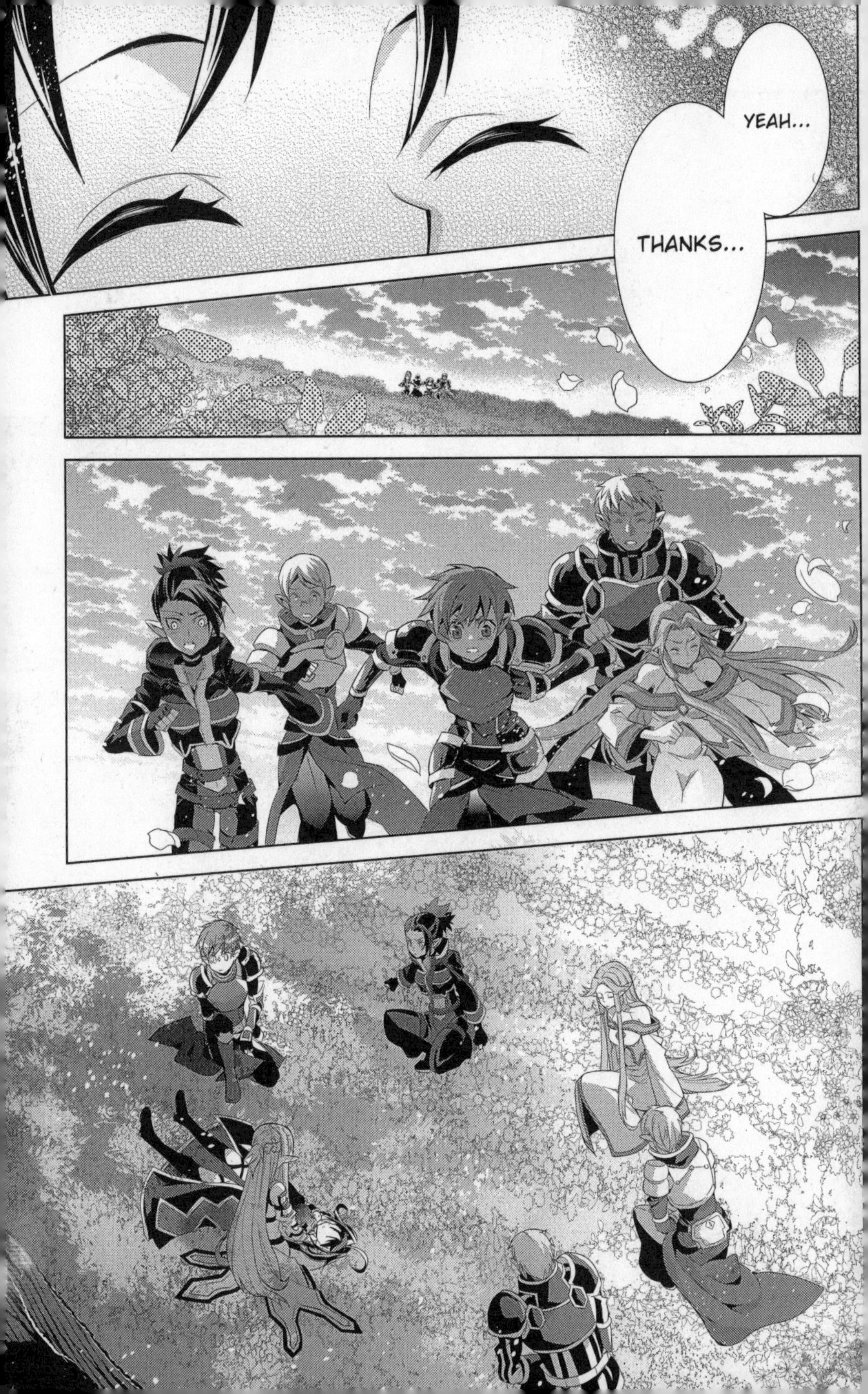
YEAH...
THANKS...

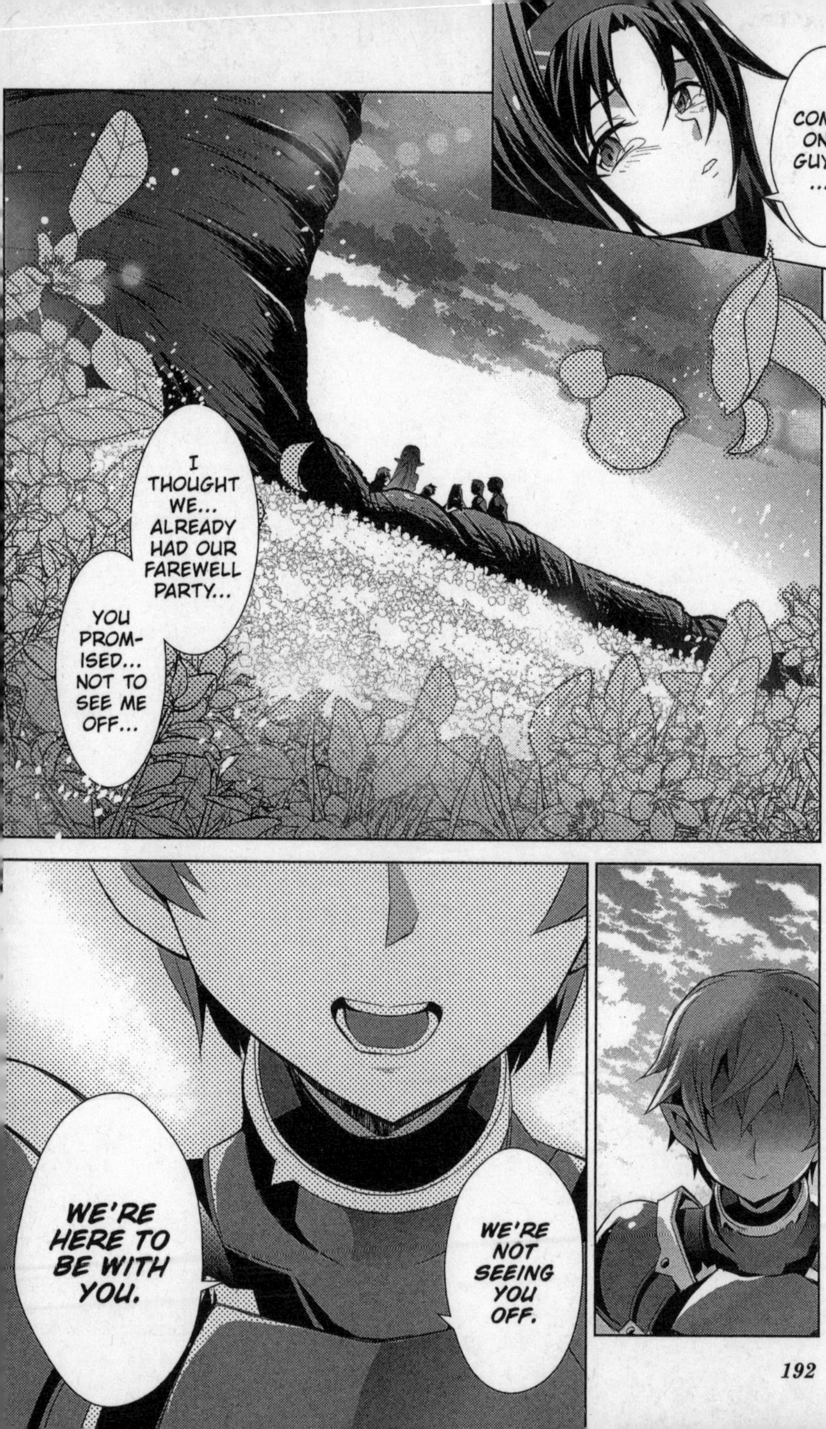
COME ON, GUYS...
I THOUGHT WE... ALREADY HAD OUR FAREWELL PARTY...
YOU PROMISED... NOT TO SEE ME OFF...
WE'RE NOT SEEING YOU OFF.
WE'RE HERE TO BE WITH YOU.

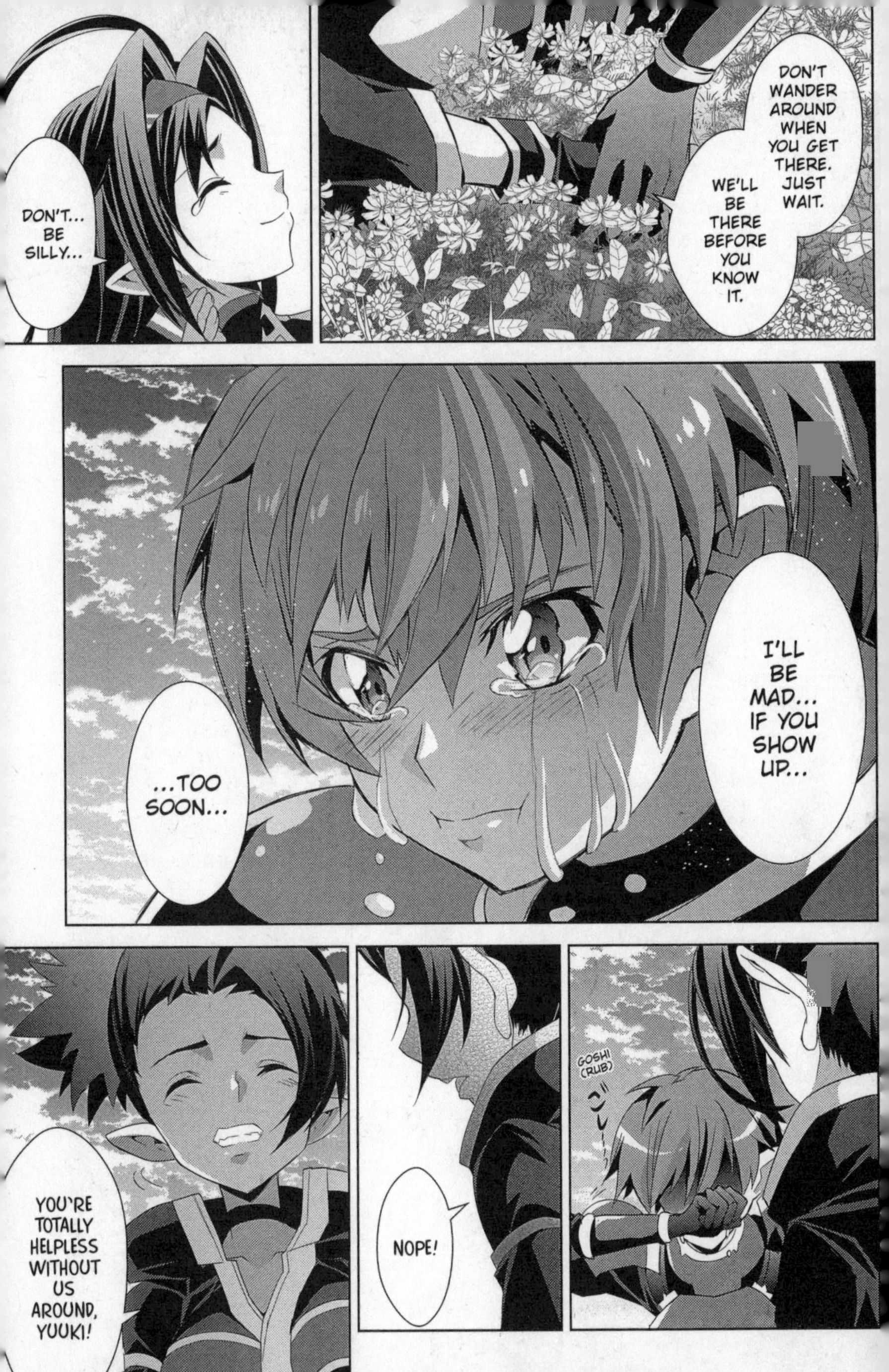

DON'T WANDER AROUND WHEN YOU GET THERE. JUST WAIT.
WE'LL BE THERE BEFORE YOU KNOW IT.
DON'T... BE SILLY...
I'LL BE MAD... IF YOU SHOW UP...
...TOO SOON...
GOSHI (RUB)
NOPE!
YOU'RE TOTALLY HELPLESS WITHOUT US AROUND, YUUKI!

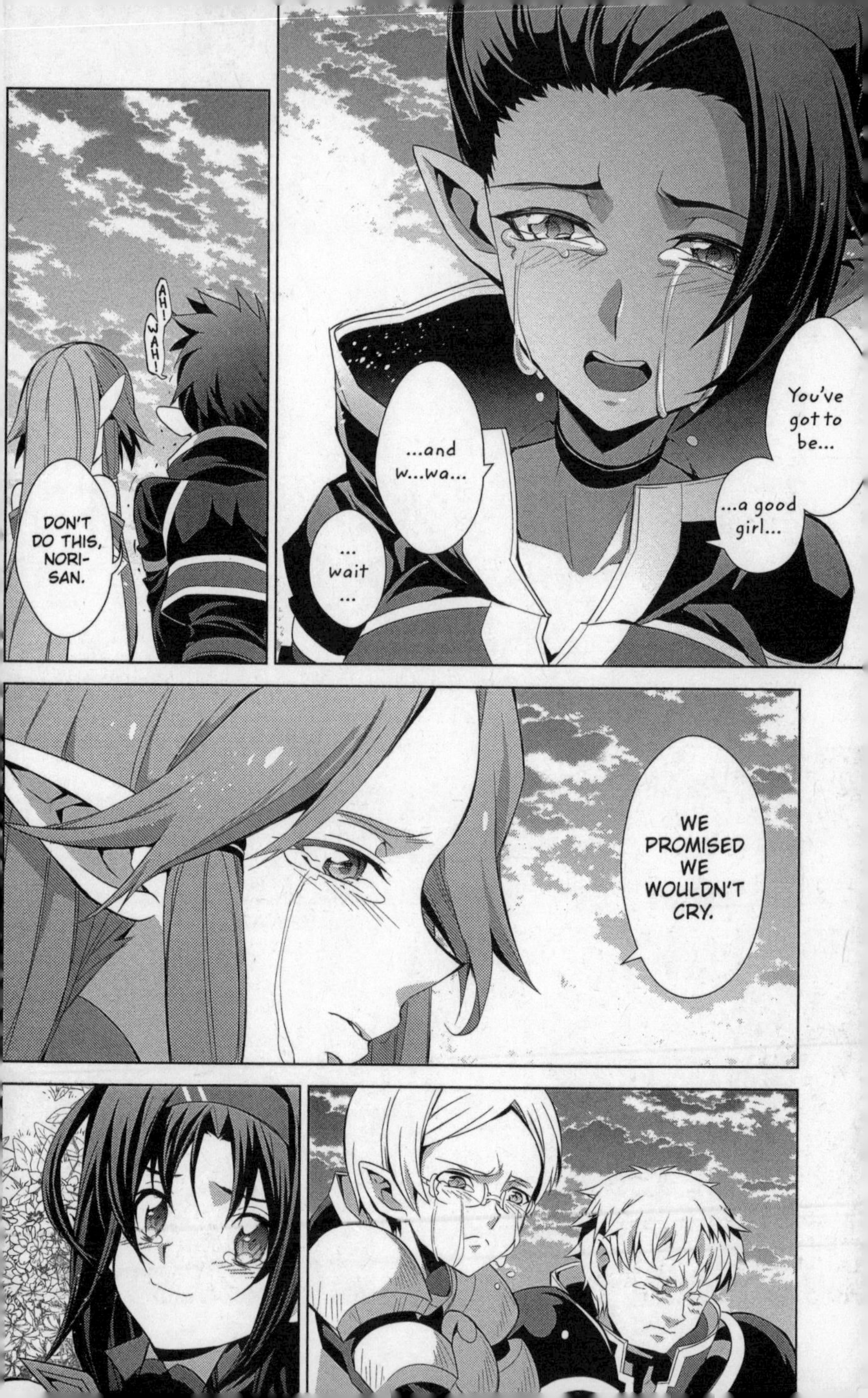
You've got to be...
...a good girl...
...and w...wa...
... wait ...
AH! WAH!
DON'T DO THIS, NORI-SAN.
WE PROMISED WE WOULDN'T CRY.

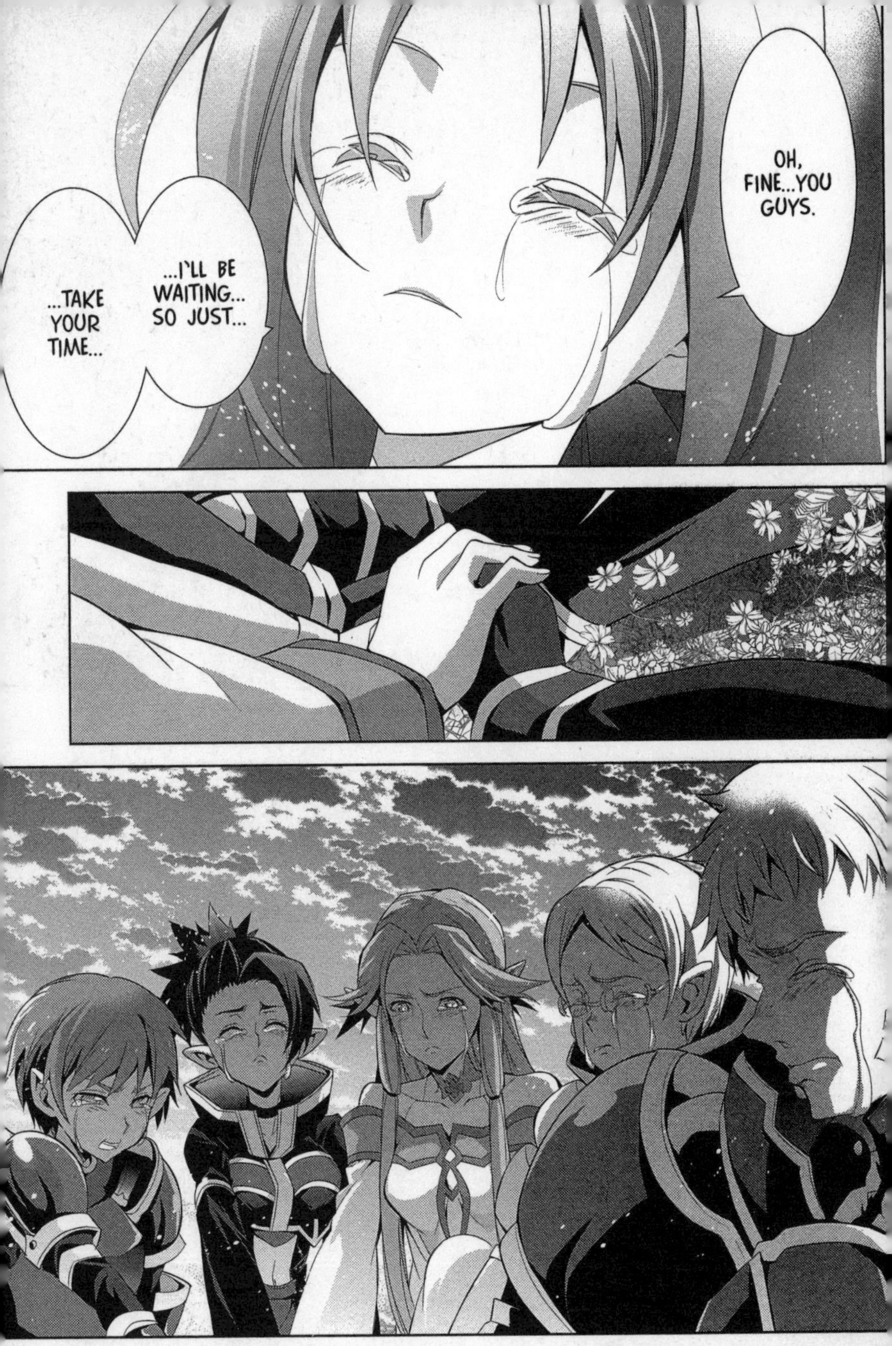
OH, FINE...YOU GUYS.
...I'LL BE WAITING...
SO JUST...
...TAKE YOUR TIME...

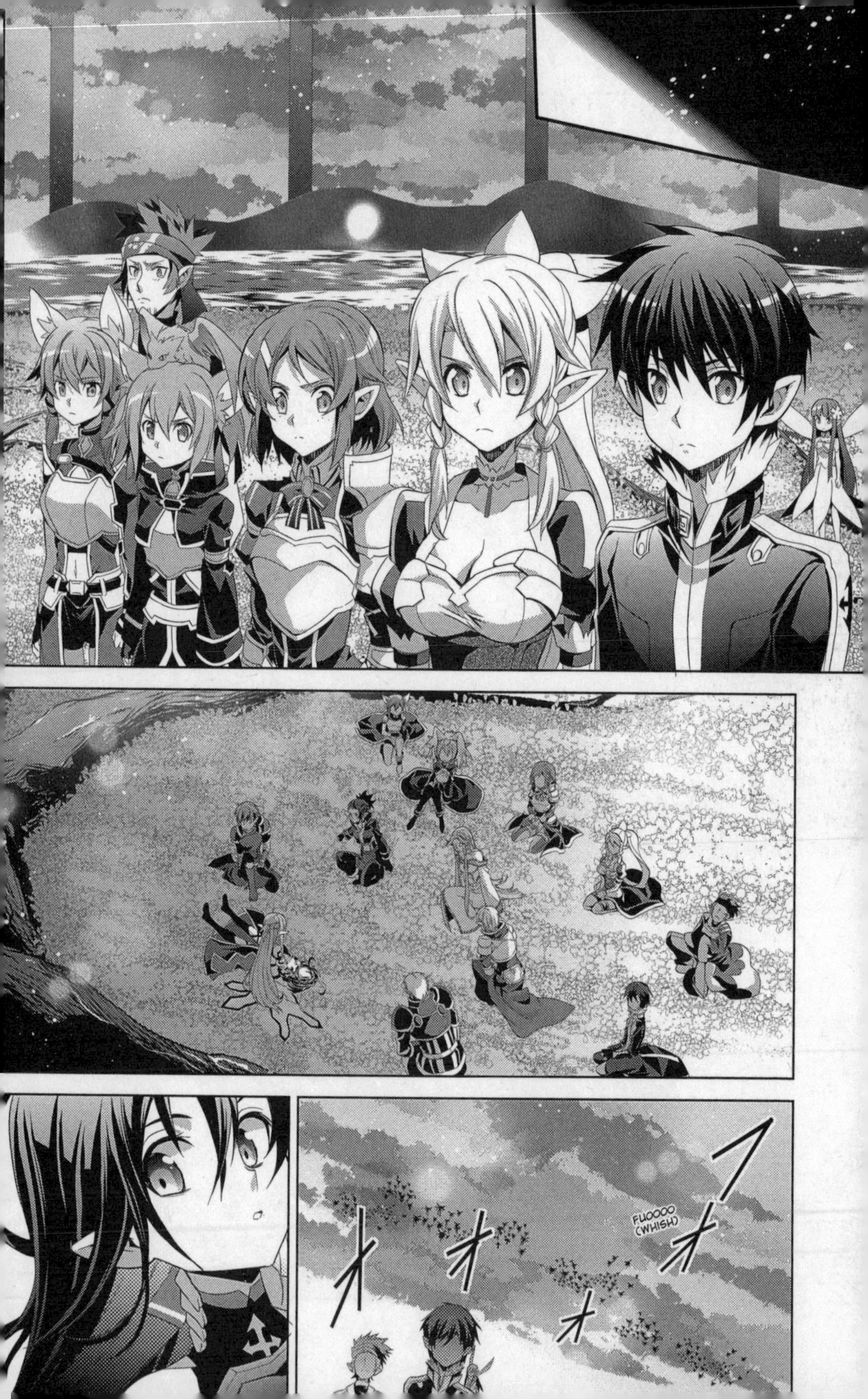
FUOOOO
(WHISH)

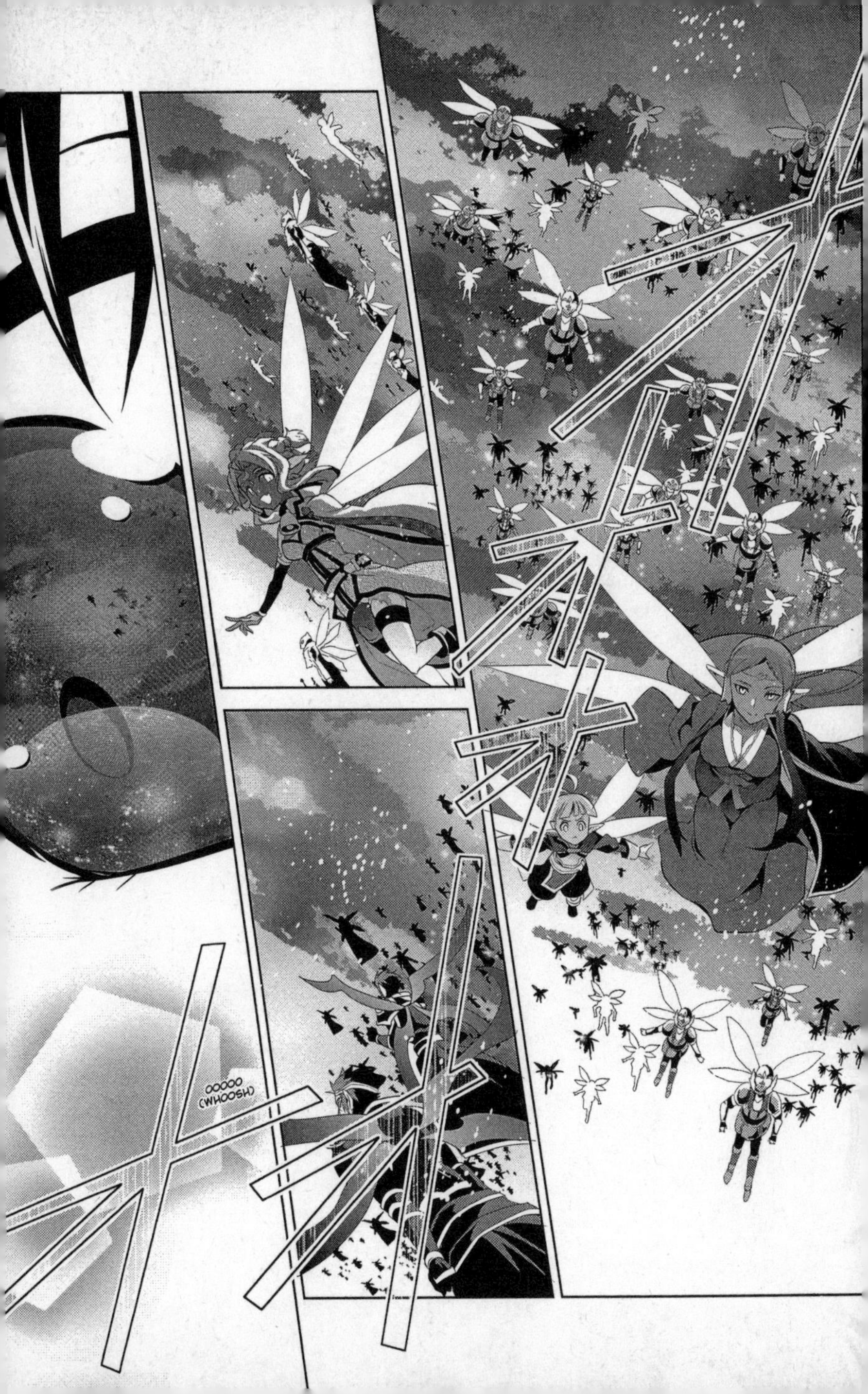
OOOOO (WHOOSH)

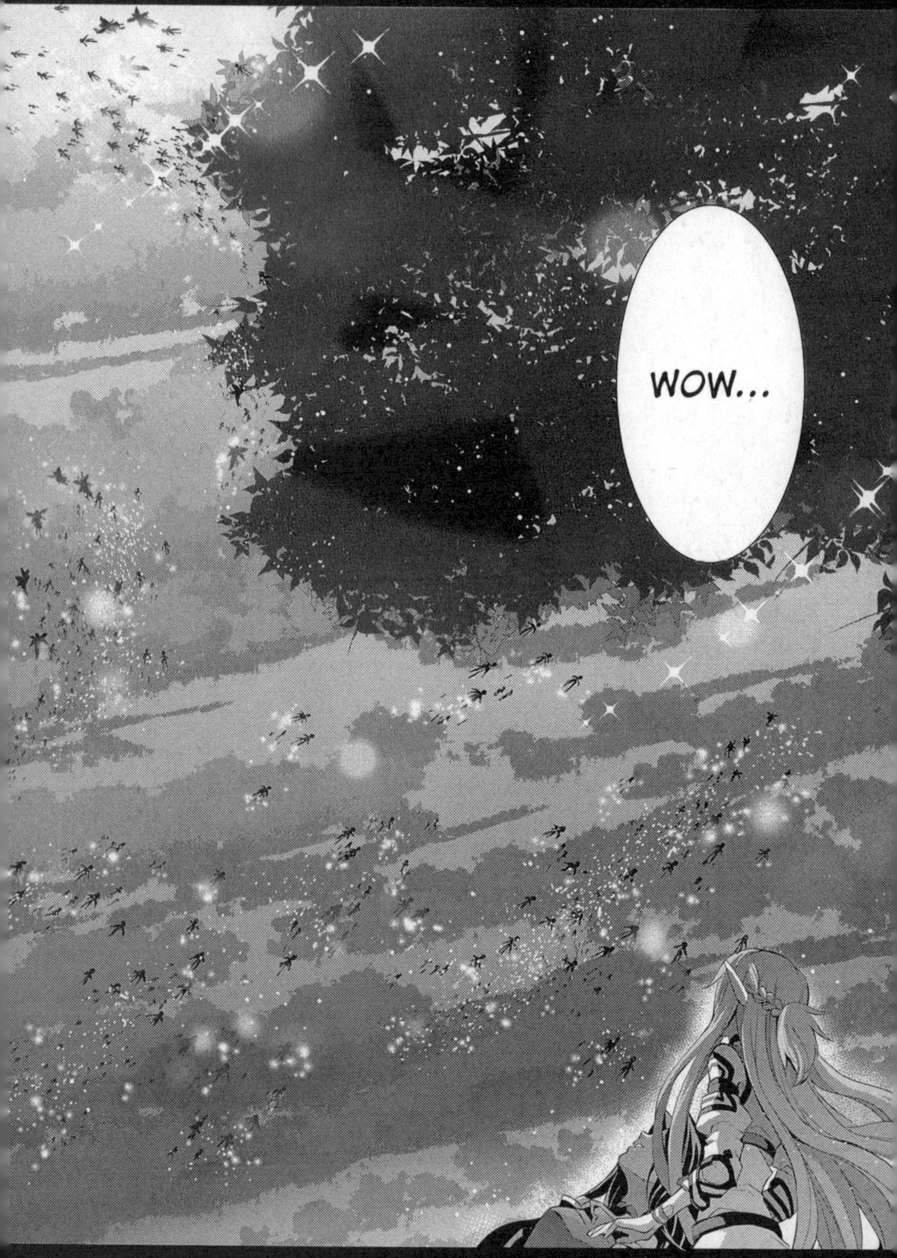
WOW...

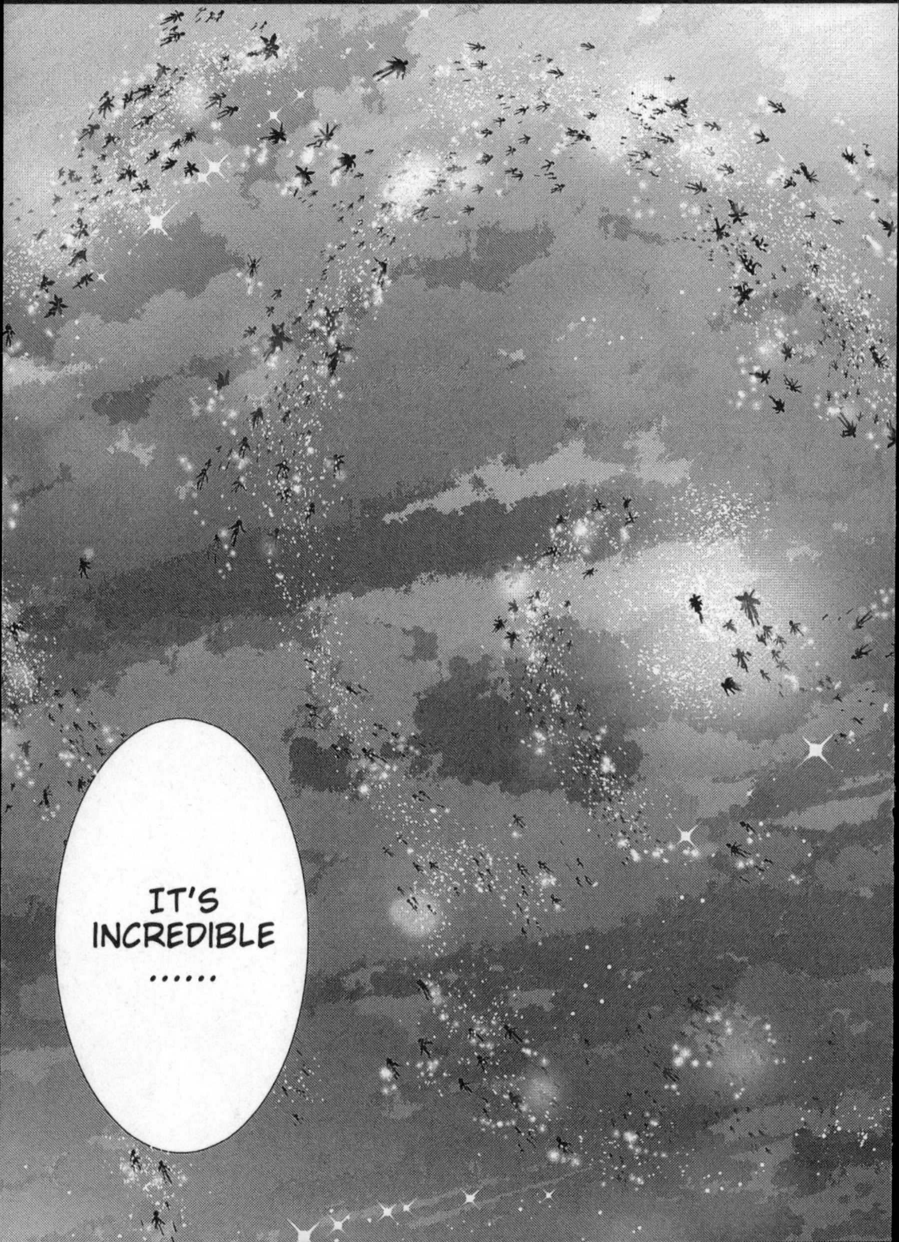
IT'S INCREDIBLE ......

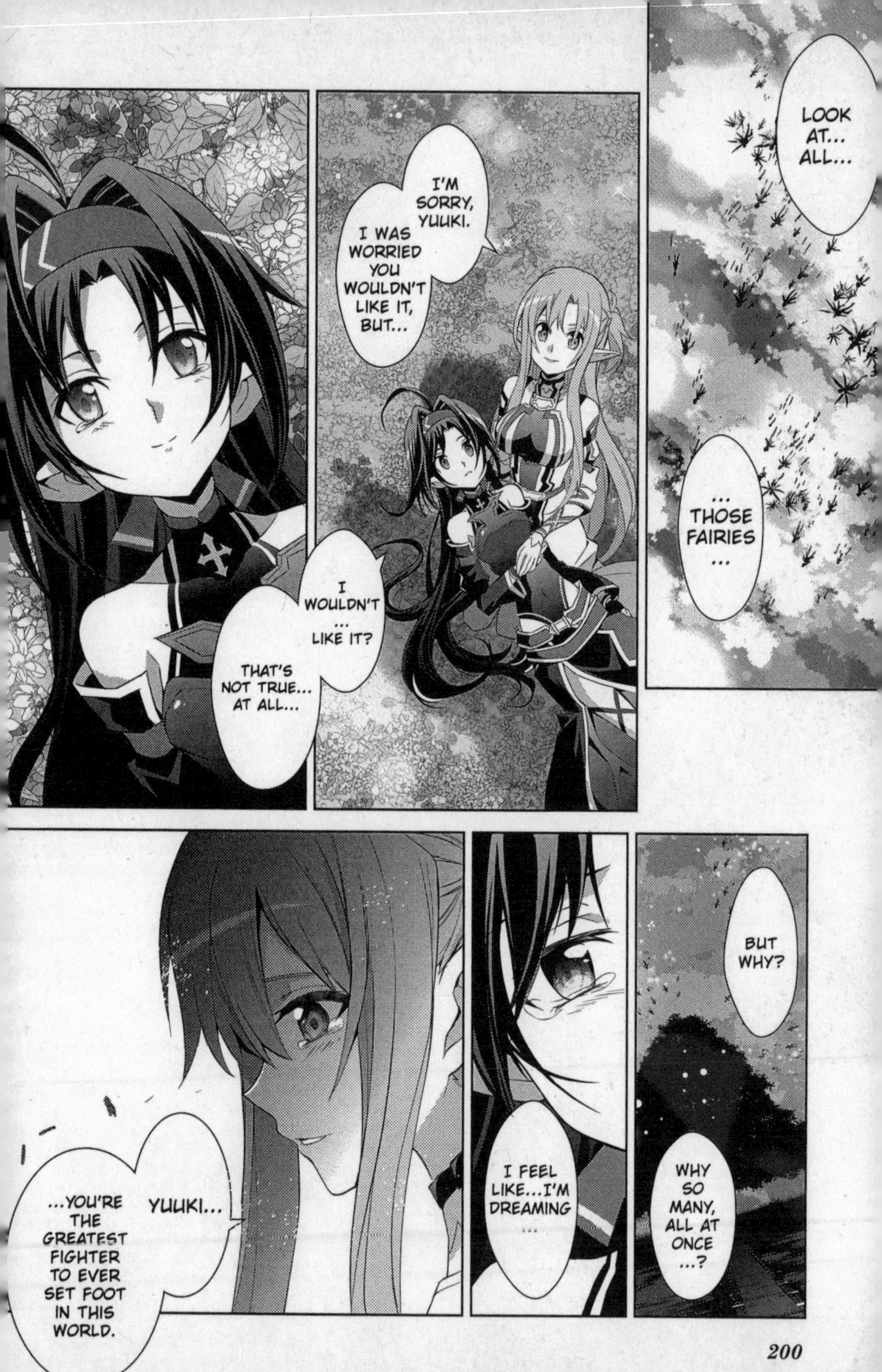
LOOK AT... ALL...
... THOSE FAIRIES ...
I'M SORRY, YUUKI.
I WAS WORRIED YOU WOULDN'T LIKE IT, BUT...
I WOULDN'T ... LIKE IT?
THAT'S NOT TRUE... AT ALL...
BUT WHY?
WHY SO MANY, ALL AT ONCE ...?
I FEEL LIKE...I'M DREAMING ...
YUUKI...
...YOU'RE THE GREATEST FIGHTER TO EVER SET FOOT IN THIS WORLD.

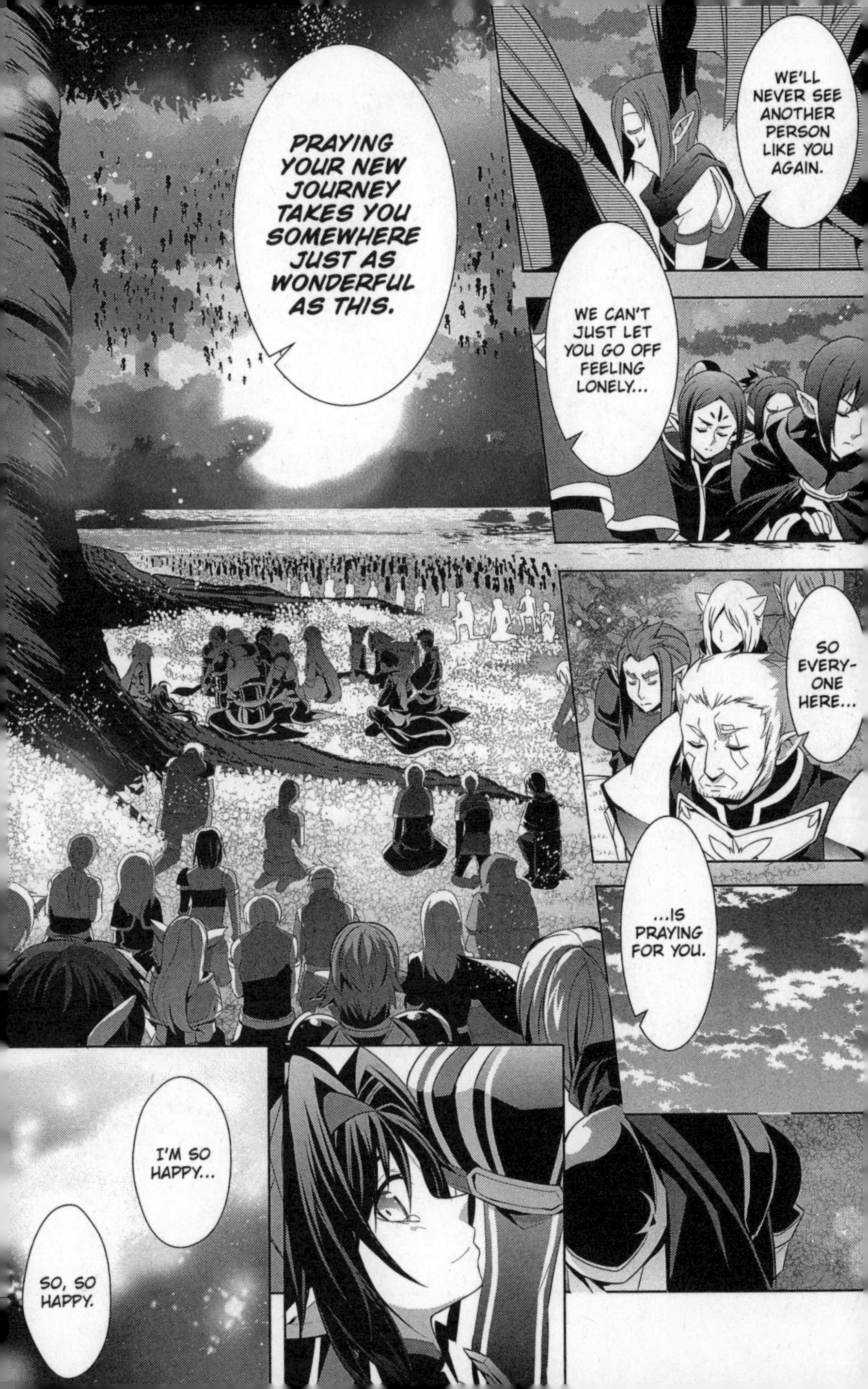
WE'LL NEVER SEE ANOTHER PERSON LIKE YOU AGAIN.
WE CAN'T JUST LET YOU GO OFF FEELING LONELY...
SO EVERY-ONE HERE...
...IS PRAYING FOR YOU.
PRAYING YOUR NEW JOURNEY TAKES YOU SOMEWHERE JUST AS WONDERFUL AS THIS.
I'M SO HAPPY...
SO, SO HAPPY.

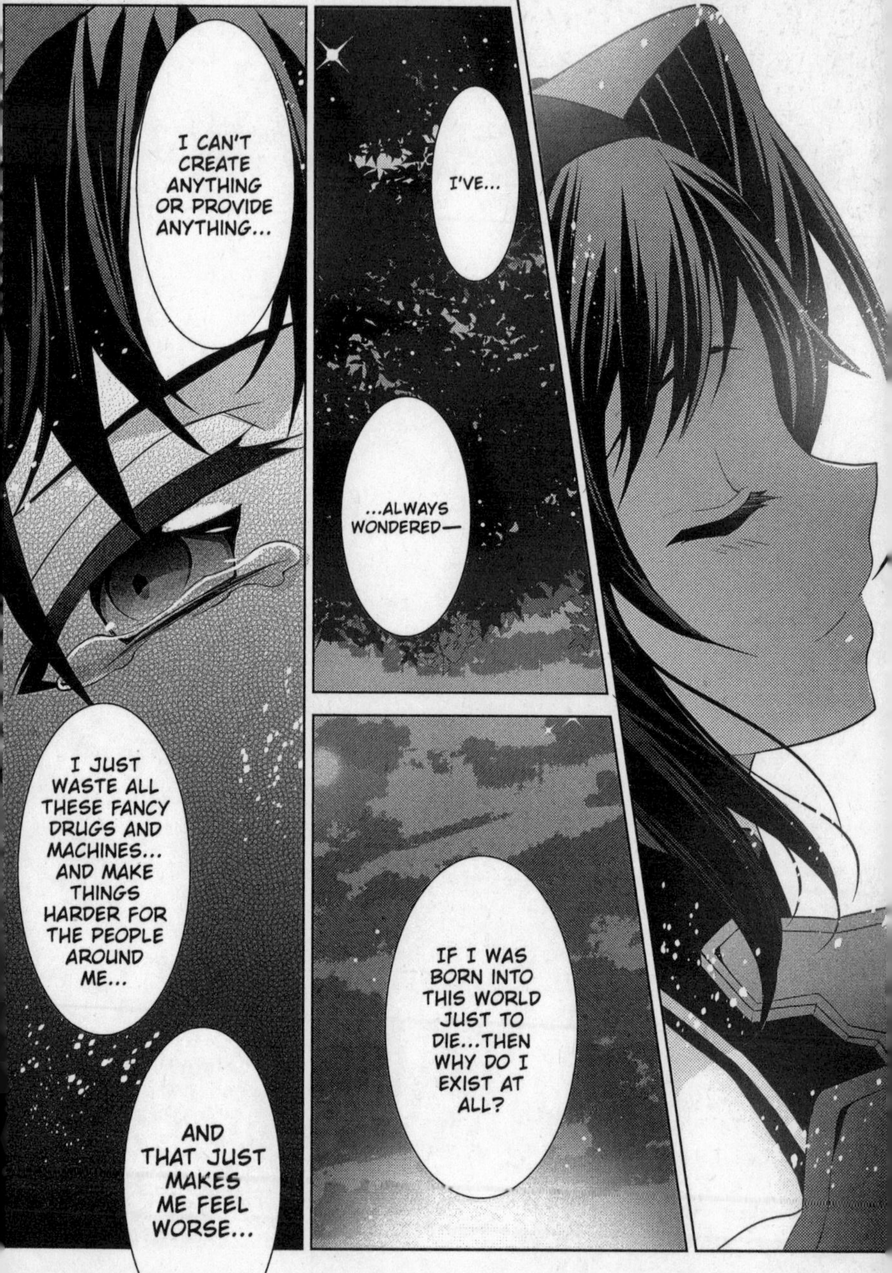
I'VE...
...ALWAYS WONDERED—
IF I WAS BORN INTO THIS WORLD JUST TO DIE...THEN WHY DO I EXIST AT ALL?
I CAN'T CREATE ANYTHING OR PROVIDE ANYTHING...
I JUST WASTE ALL THESE FANCY DRUGS AND MACHINES... AND MAKE THINGS HARDER FOR THE PEOPLE AROUND ME...
AND THAT JUST MAKES ME FEEL WORSE...

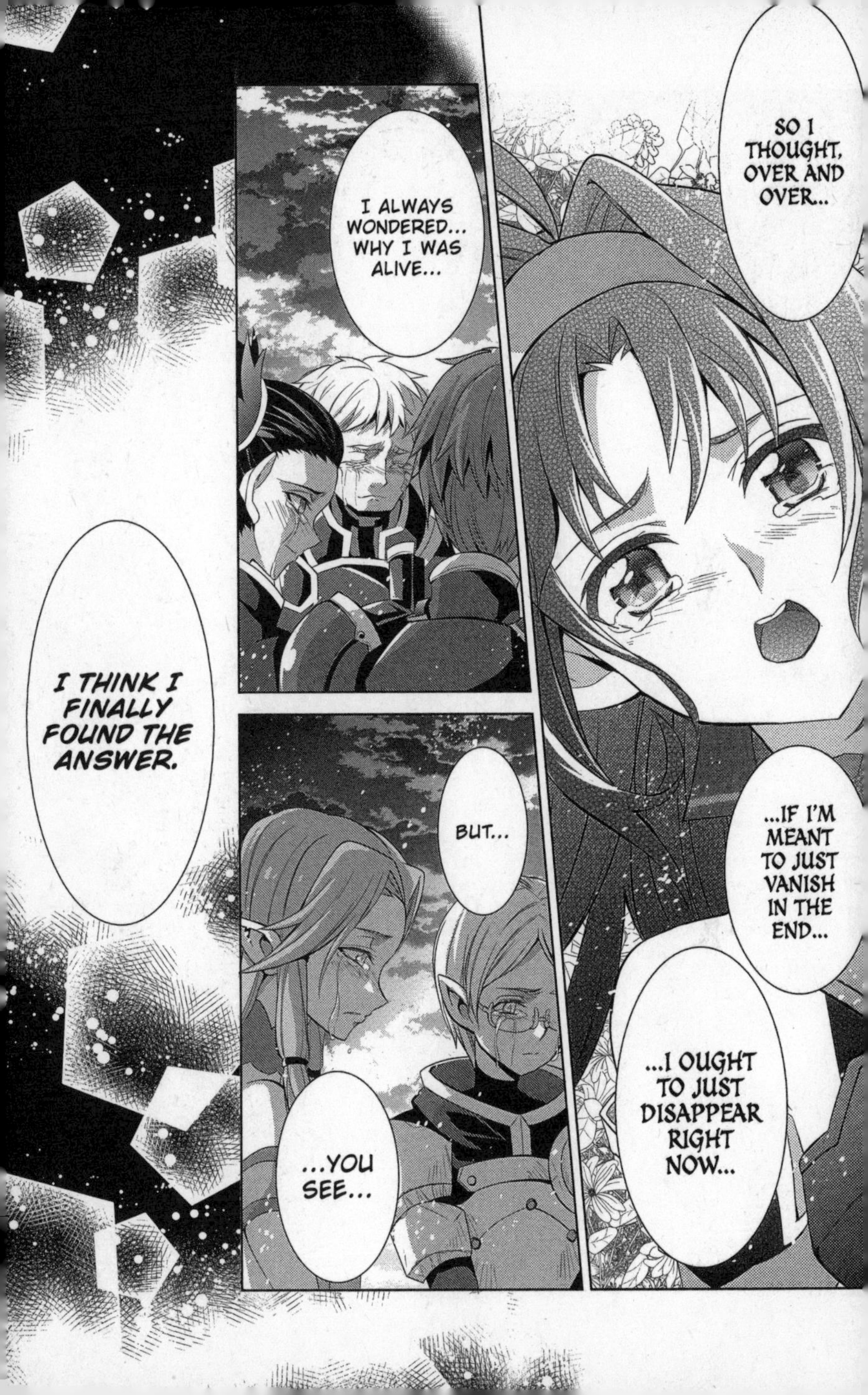
SO I THOUGHT, OVER AND OVER...
...IF I'M MEANT TO JUST VANISH IN THE END...
...I OUGHT TO JUST DISAPPEAR RIGHT NOW...
I ALWAYS WONDERED... WHY I WAS ALIVE...
BUT...
...YOU SEE...
I THINK I FINALLY FOUND THE ANSWER.

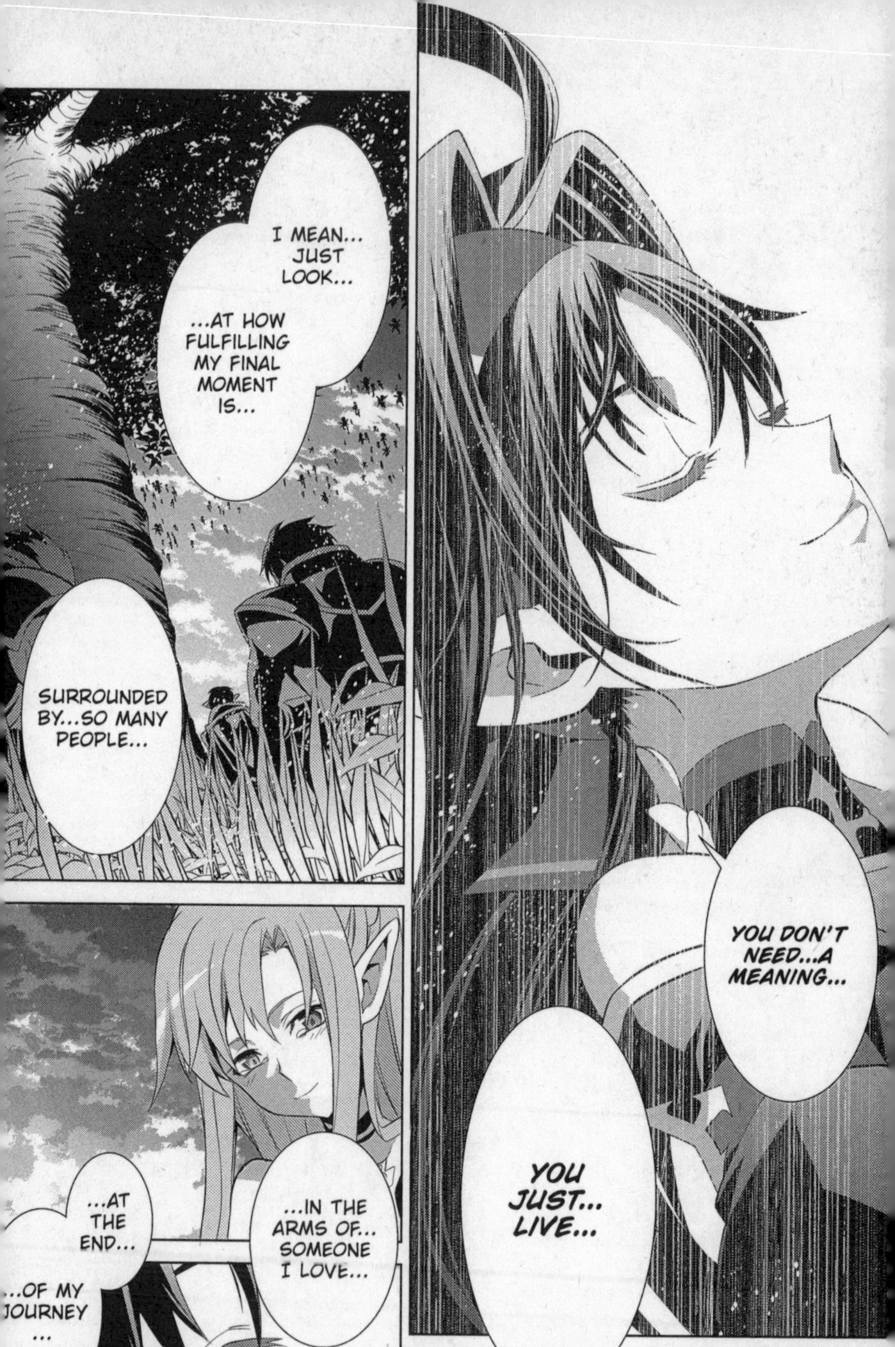
YOU DON'T NEED...A MEANING...
YOU JUST... LIVE...
I MEAN... JUST LOOK...
...AT HOW FULFILLING MY FINAL MOMENT IS...
SURROUNDED BY...SO MANY PEOPLE...
...IN THE ARMS OF... SOMEONE I LOVE...
...AT THE END...
...OF MY JOURNEY ...

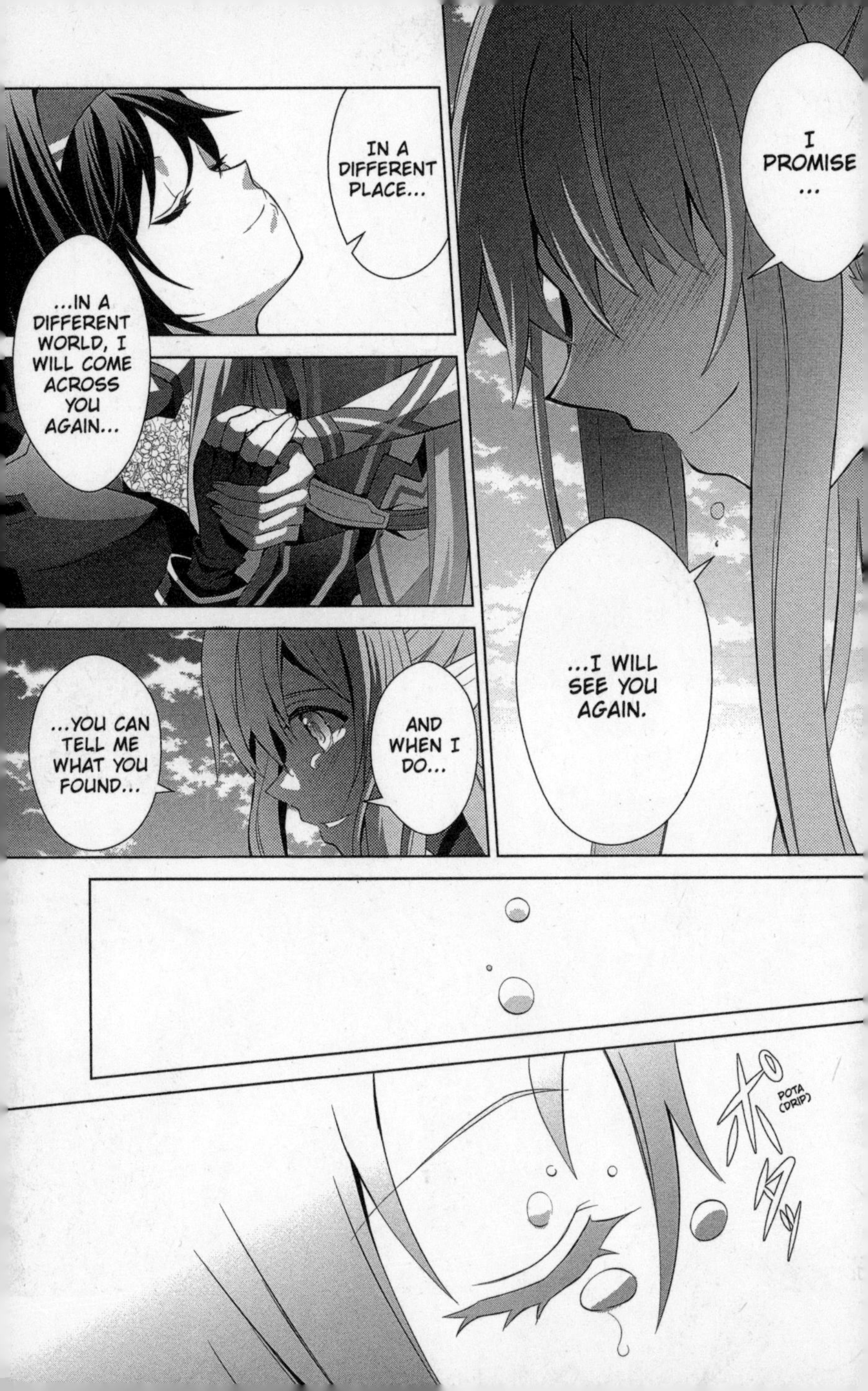
I PROMISE ...
...I WILL SEE YOU AGAIN.
IN A DIFFERENT PLACE...
...IN A DIFFERENT WORLD, I WILL COME ACROSS YOU AGAIN...
AND WHEN I DO...
...YOU CAN TELL ME WHAT YOU FOUND...
POTA (DRIP)

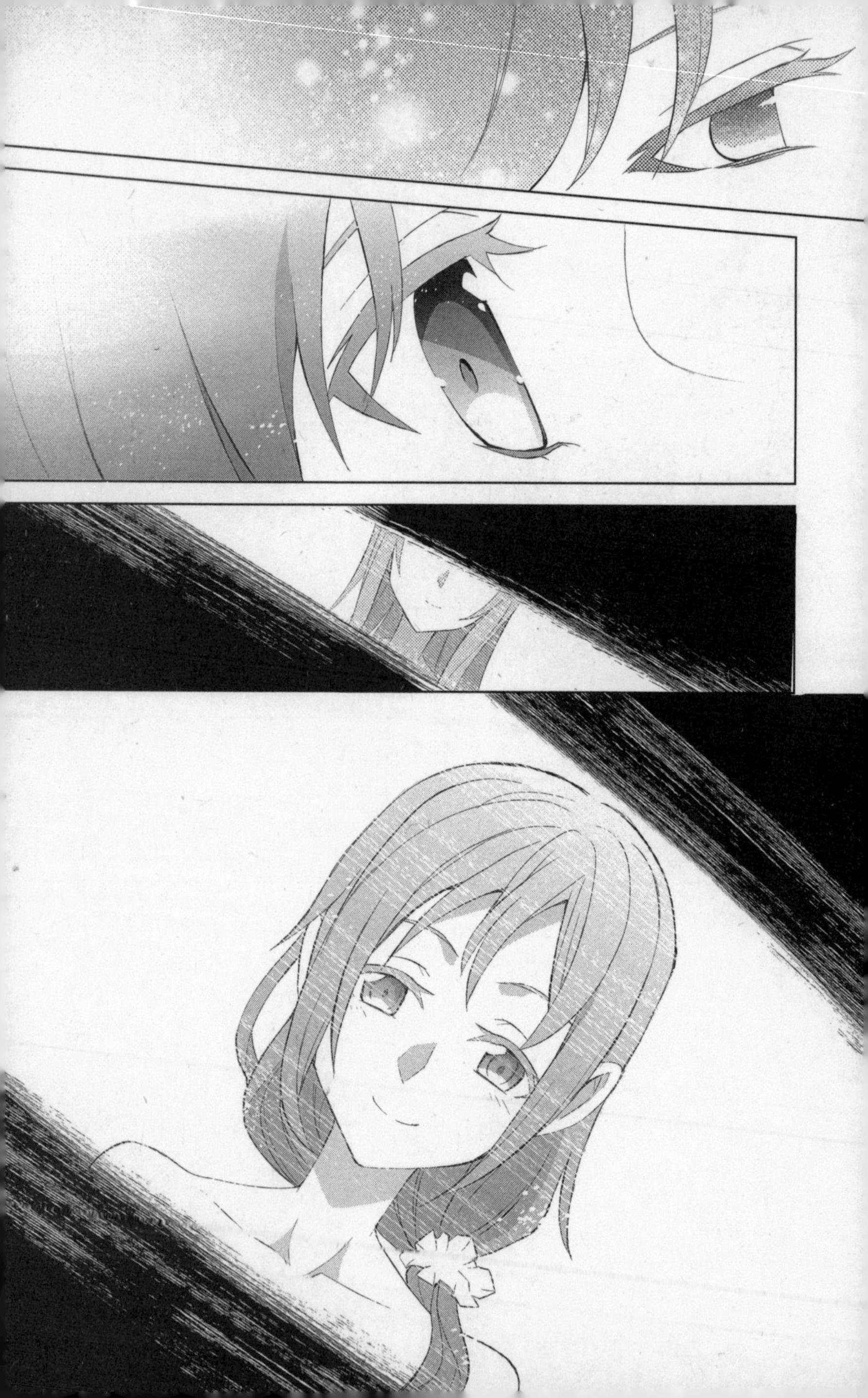

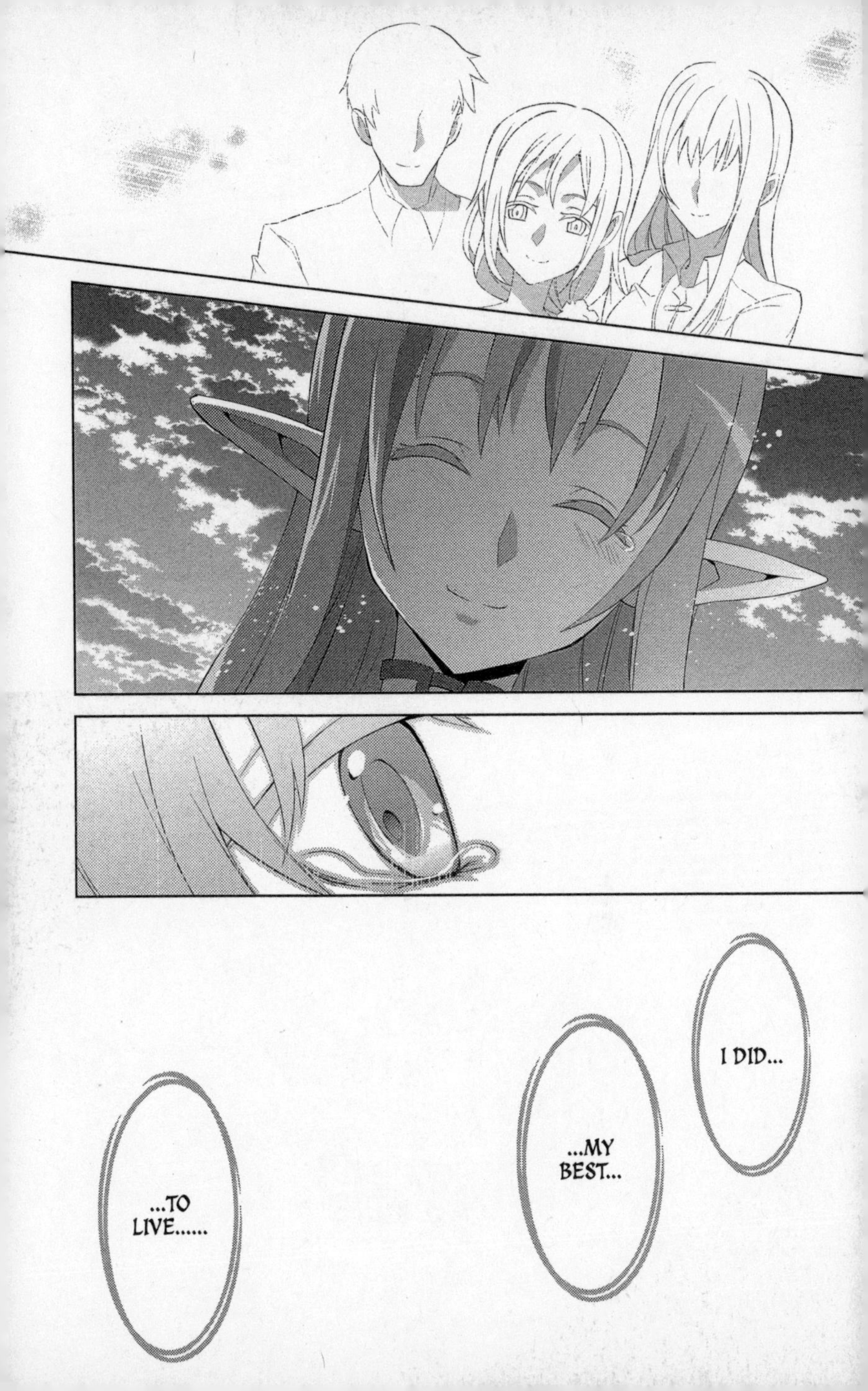
I DID...
...MY BEST...
...TO LIVE......

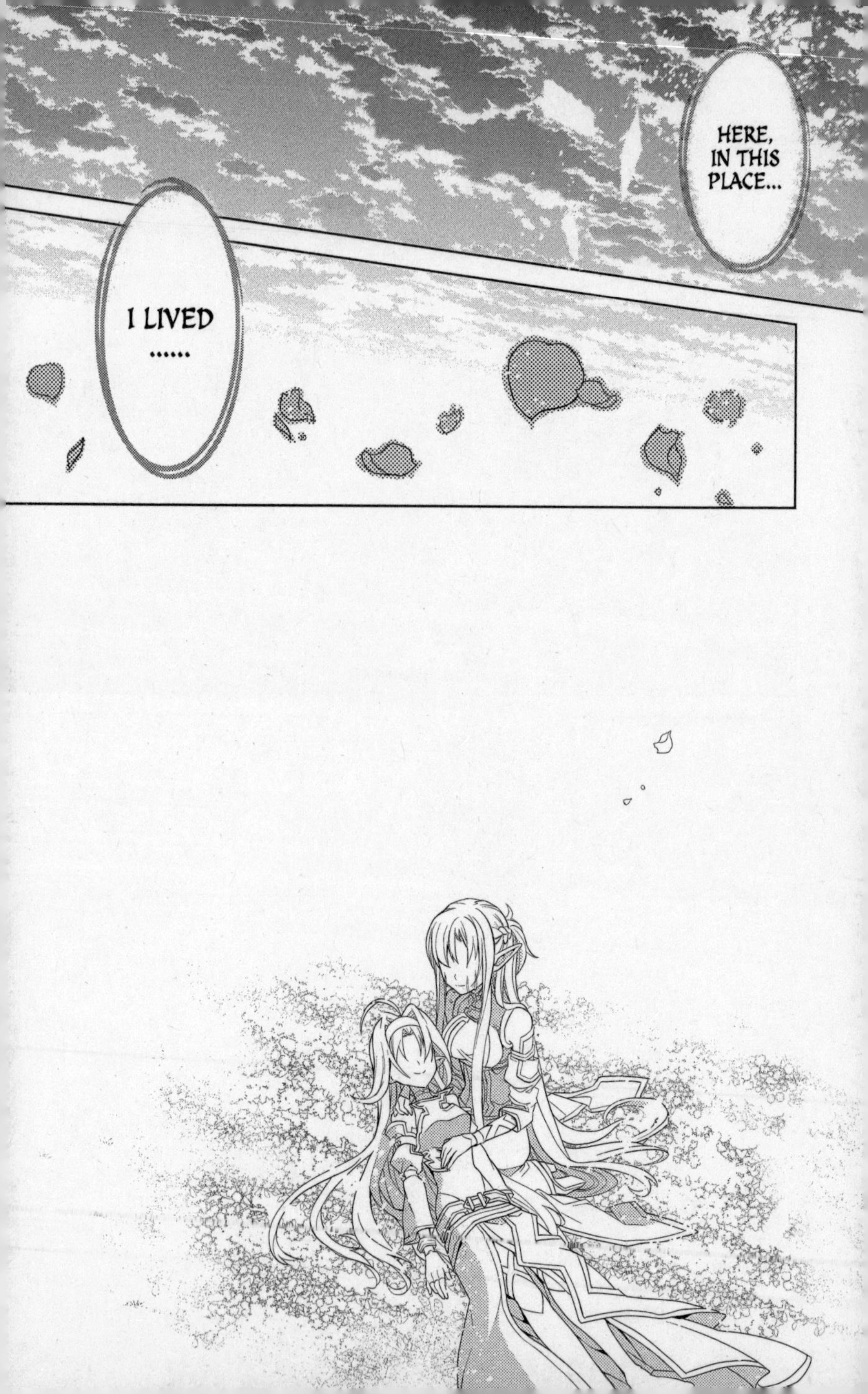
HERE, IN THIS PLACE...
I LIVED ......

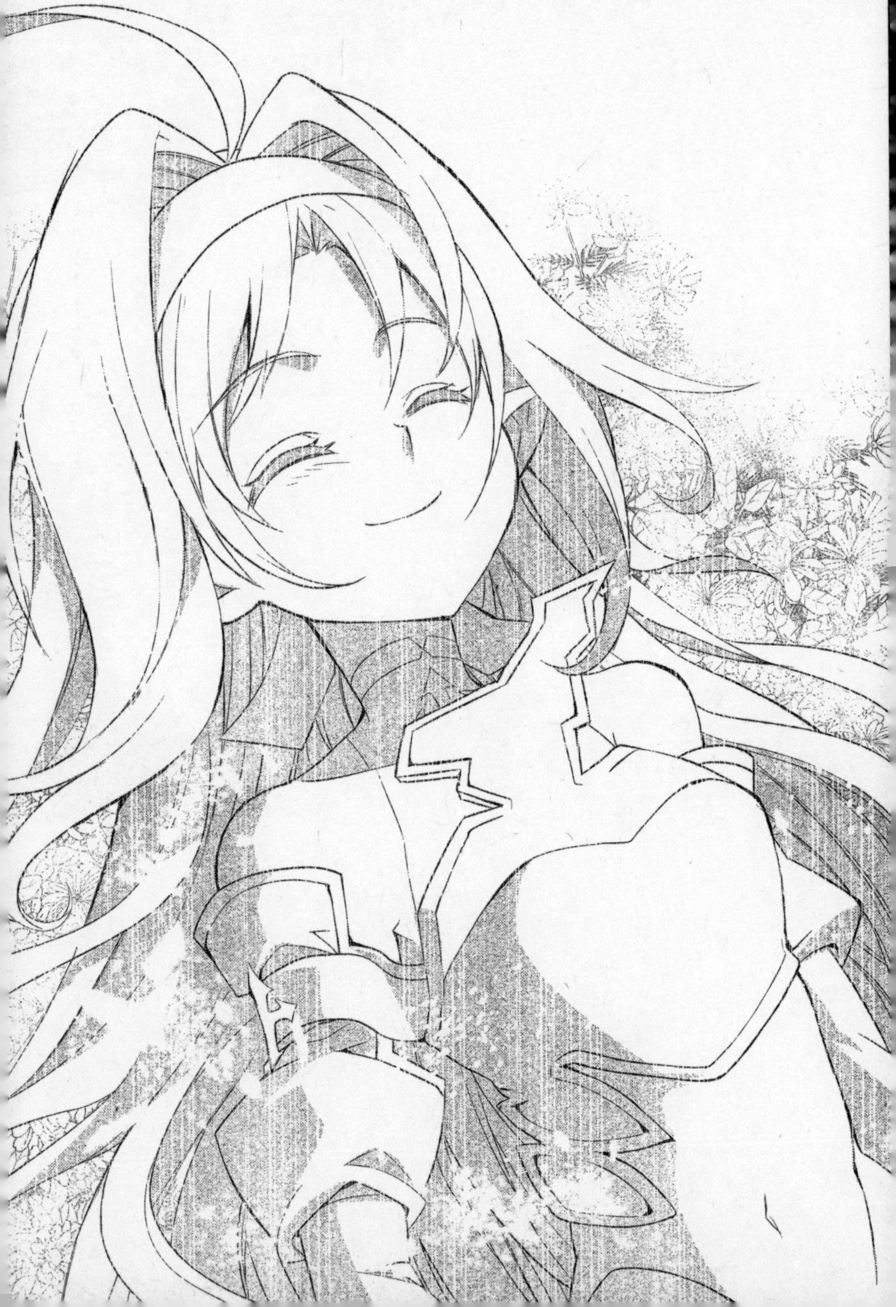

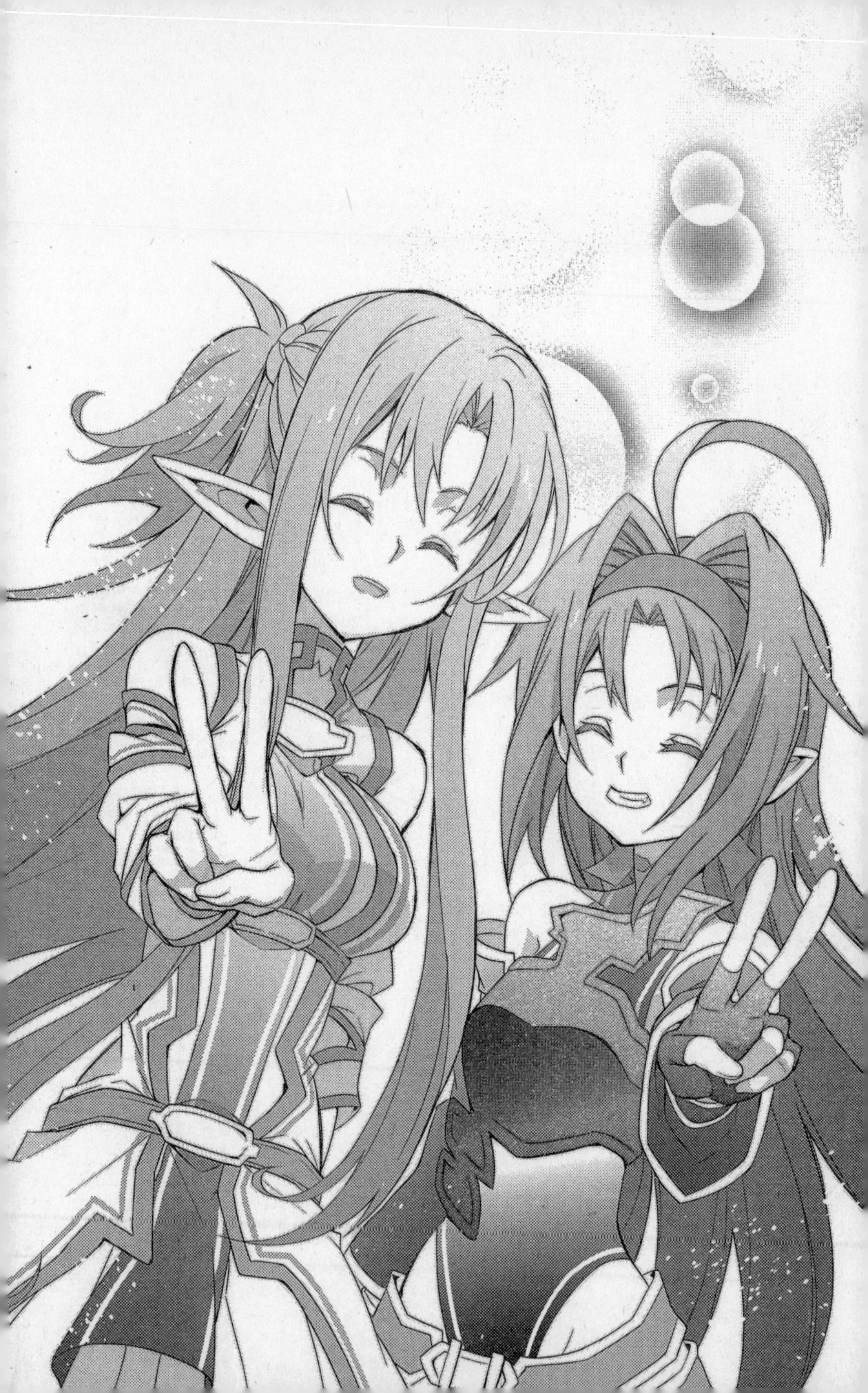

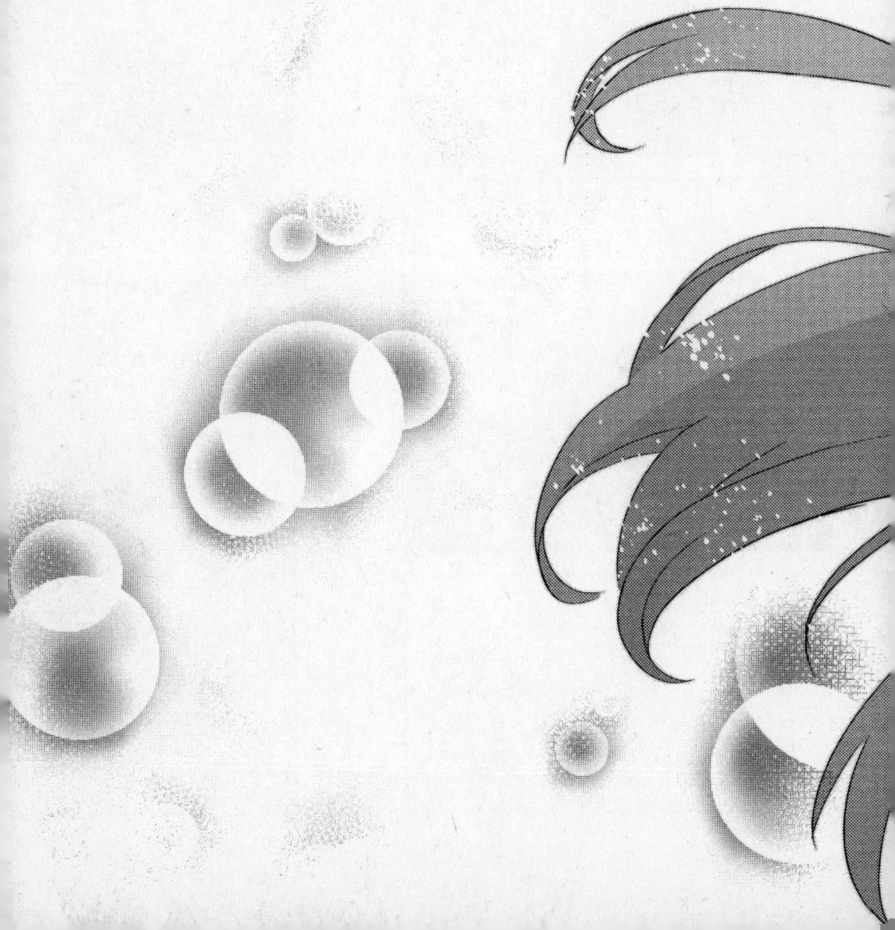

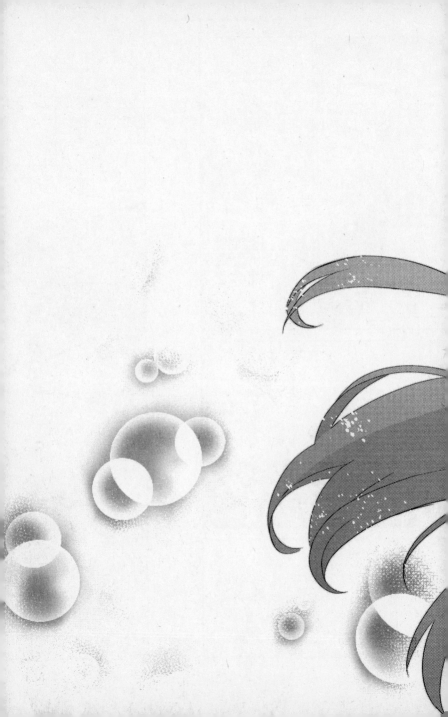

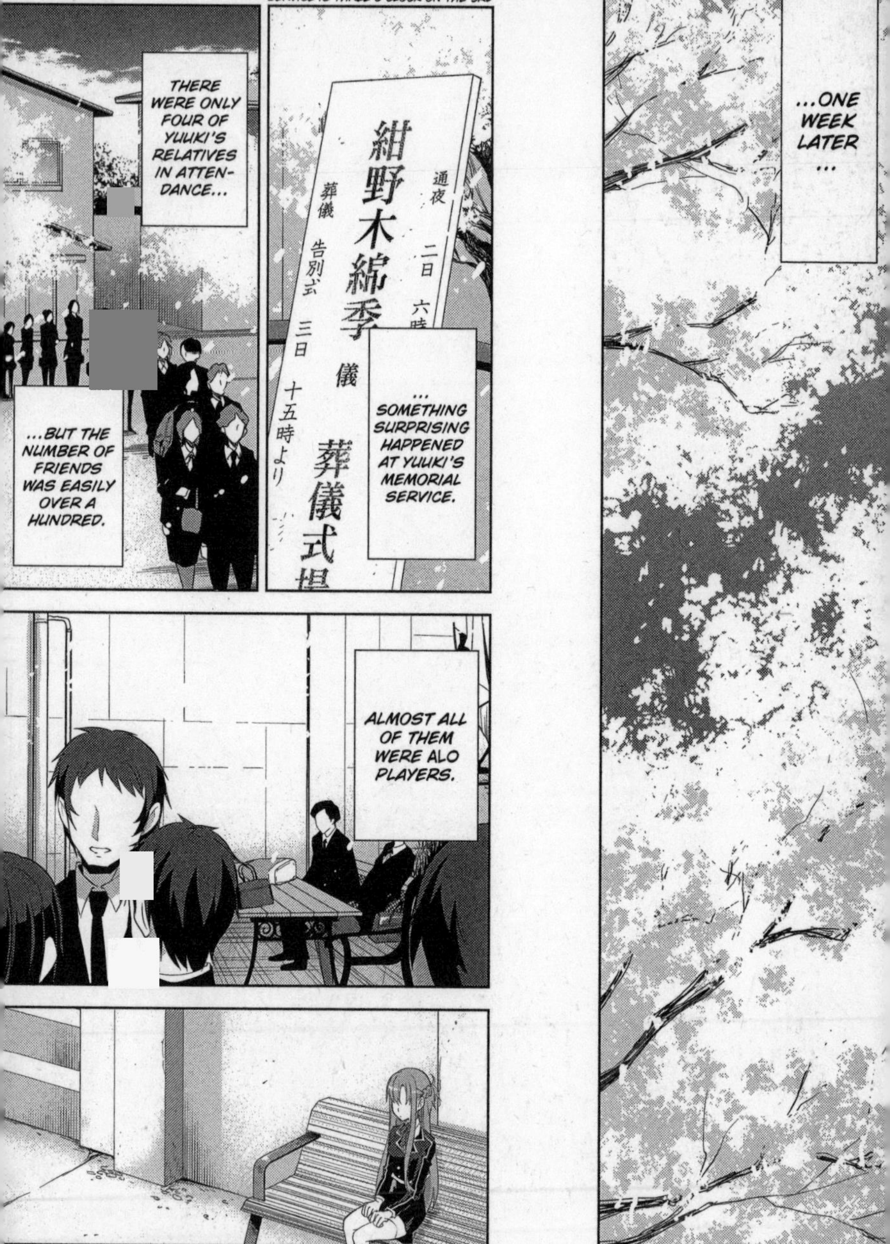
...ONE WEEK LATER...
SIGN: FUNERAL SERVICE OF YUUKI KONNO / WAKE IS SIX O'CLOCK ON THE 2ND / SERVICE IS THREE O'CLOCK ON THE 3RD
紺野木綿季 儀
通夜 二日 六時
葬儀 告別式 三日 十五時より
葬儀式
...SOMETHING SURPRISING HAPPENED AT YUUKI'S MEMORIAL SERVICE.
THERE WERE ONLY FOUR OF YUUKI'S RELATIVES IN ATTEN-DANCE...
...BUT THE NUMBER OF FRIENDS WAS EASILY OVER A HUNDRED.
ALMOST ALL OF THEM WERE ALO PLAYERS.

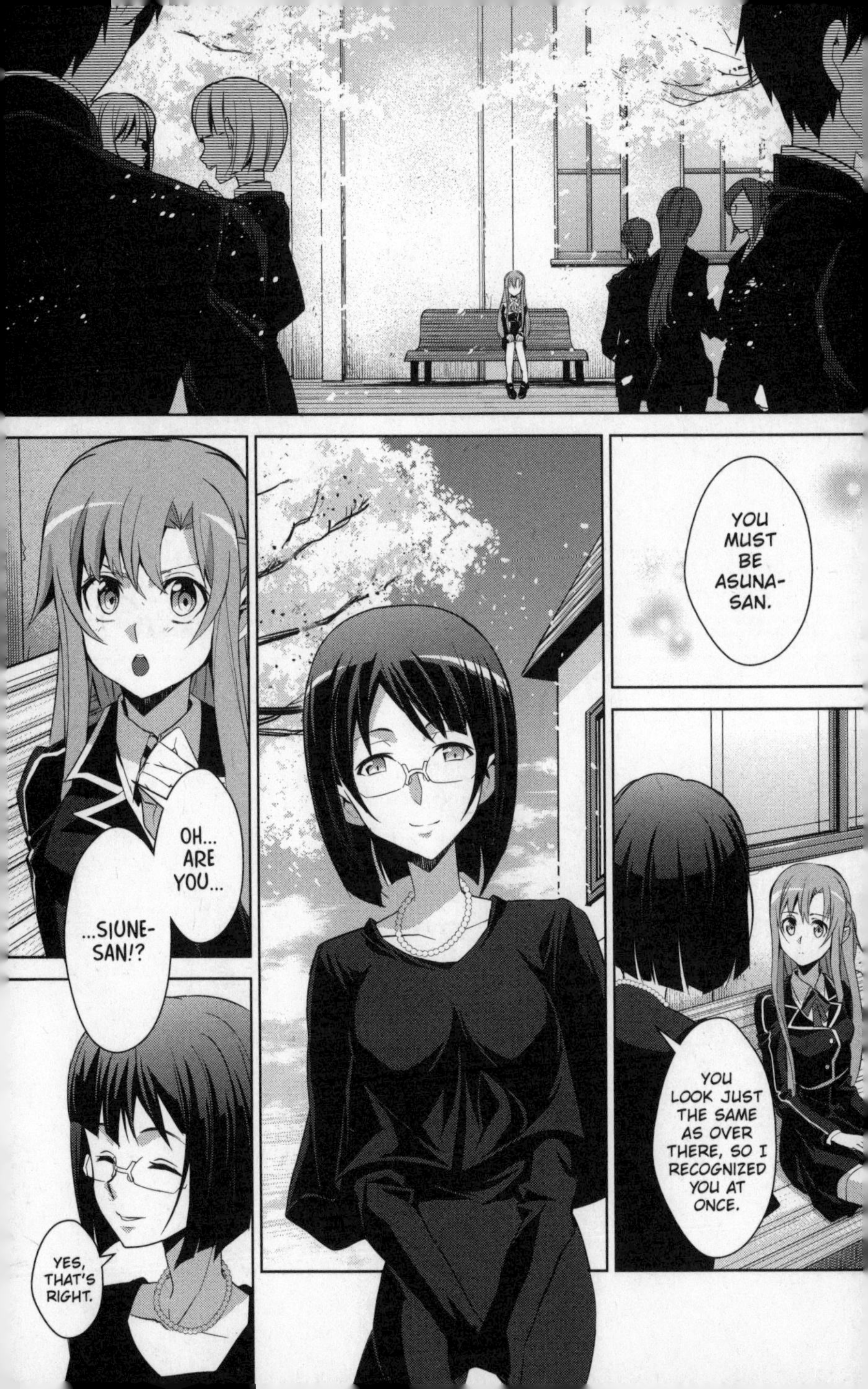
YOU MUST BE ASUNA-SAN.
YOU LOOK JUST THE SAME AS OVER THERE, SO I RECOGNIZED YOU AT ONCE.
OH... ARE YOU...
...SIUNE-SAN!?
YES, THAT'S RIGHT.

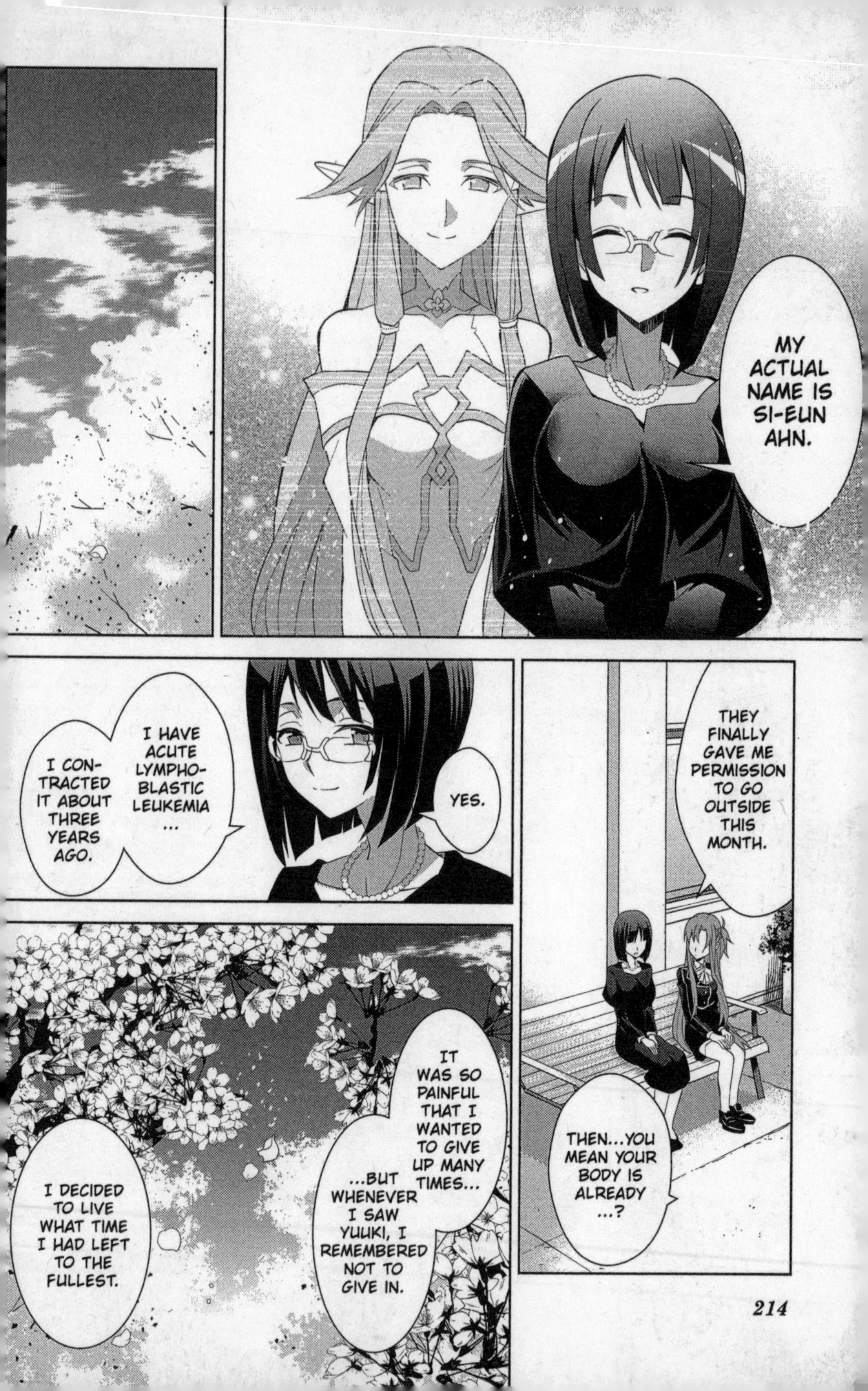
MY ACTUAL NAME IS SI-EUN AHN.
THEY FINALLY GAVE ME PERMISSION TO GO OUTSIDE THIS MONTH.
THEN...YOU MEAN YOUR BODY IS ALREADY ...?
YES.
I HAVE ACUTE LYMPHO-BLASTIC LEUKEMIA ...
I CON-TRACTED IT ABOUT THREE YEARS AGO.
IT WAS SO PAINFUL THAT I WANTED TO GIVE UP MANY TIMES...
...BUT WHENEVER I SAW YUUKI, I REMEMBERED NOT TO GIVE IN.
I DECIDED TO LIVE WHAT TIME I HAD LEFT TO THE FULLEST.

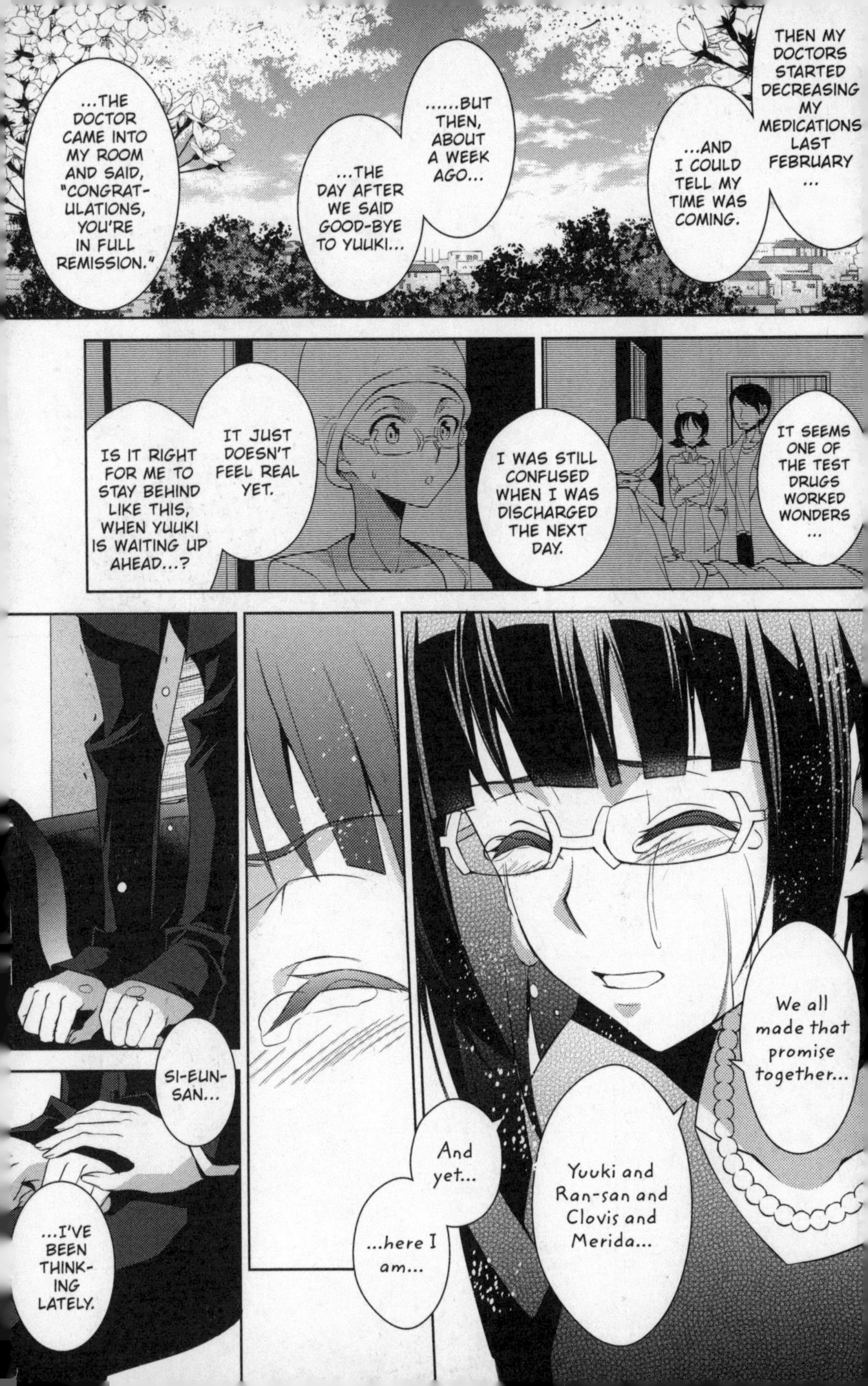

THEN MY DOCTORS STARTED DECREASING MY MEDICATIONS LAST FEBRUARY...
...AND I COULD TELL MY TIME WAS COMING.
......BUT THEN, ABOUT A WEEK AGO...
...THE DAY AFTER WE SAID GOOD-BYE TO YUUKI...
...THE DOCTOR CAME INTO MY ROOM AND SAID, "CONGRAT-ULATIONS, YOU'RE IN FULL REMISSION."
IT SEEMS ONE OF THE TEST DRUGS WORKED WONDERS...
I WAS STILL CONFUSED WHEN I WAS DISCHARGED THE NEXT DAY.
IT JUST DOESN'T FEEL REAL YET.
IS IT RIGHT FOR ME TO STAY BEHIND LIKE THIS, WHEN YUUKI IS WAITING UP AHEAD...?
We all made that promise together...
Yuuki and Ran-san and Clovis and Merida...
And yet...
...here I am...
SI-EUN-SAN...
...I'VE BEEN THINKING-ING LATELY.

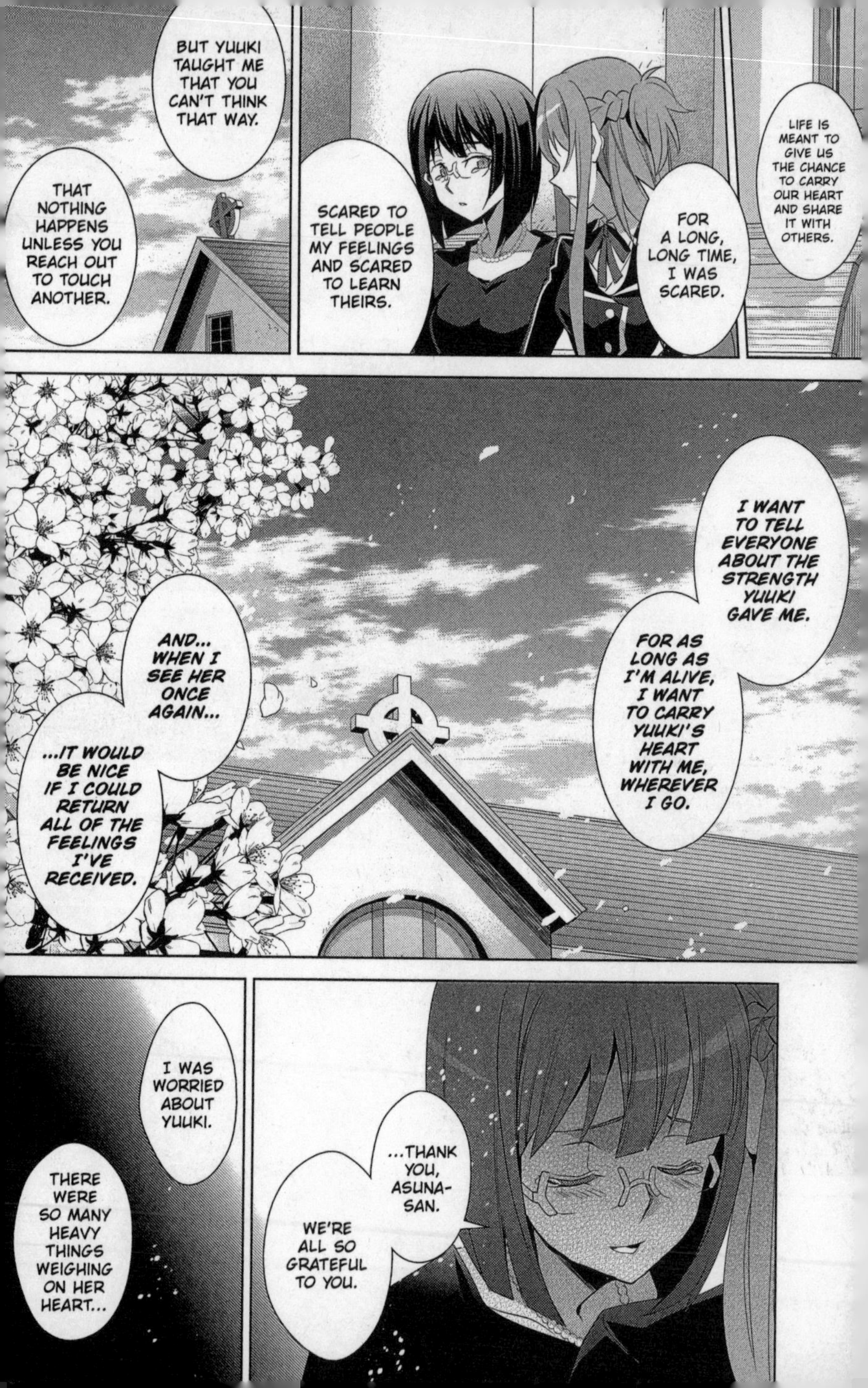
LIFE IS MEANT TO GIVE US THE CHANCE TO CARRY OUR HEART AND SHARE IT WITH OTHERS.
FOR A LONG, LONG TIME, I WAS SCARED.
SCARED TO TELL PEOPLE MY FEELINGS AND SCARED TO LEARN THEIRS.
BUT YUUKI TAUGHT ME THAT YOU CAN'T THINK THAT WAY.
THAT NOTHING HAPPENS UNLESS YOU REACH OUT TO TOUCH ANOTHER.
I WANT TO TELL EVERYONE ABOUT THE STRENGTH YUUKI GAVE ME.
FOR AS LONG AS I'M ALIVE, I WANT TO CARRY YUUKI'S HEART WITH ME, WHEREVER I GO.
AND... WHEN I SEE HER ONCE AGAIN...
...IT WOULD BE NICE IF I COULD RETURN ALL OF THE FEELINGS I'VE RECEIVED.
...THANK YOU, ASUNA-SAN.
WE'RE ALL SO GRATEFUL TO YOU.
I WAS WORRIED ABOUT YUUKI.
THERE WERE SO MANY HEAVY THINGS WEIGHING ON HER HEART...

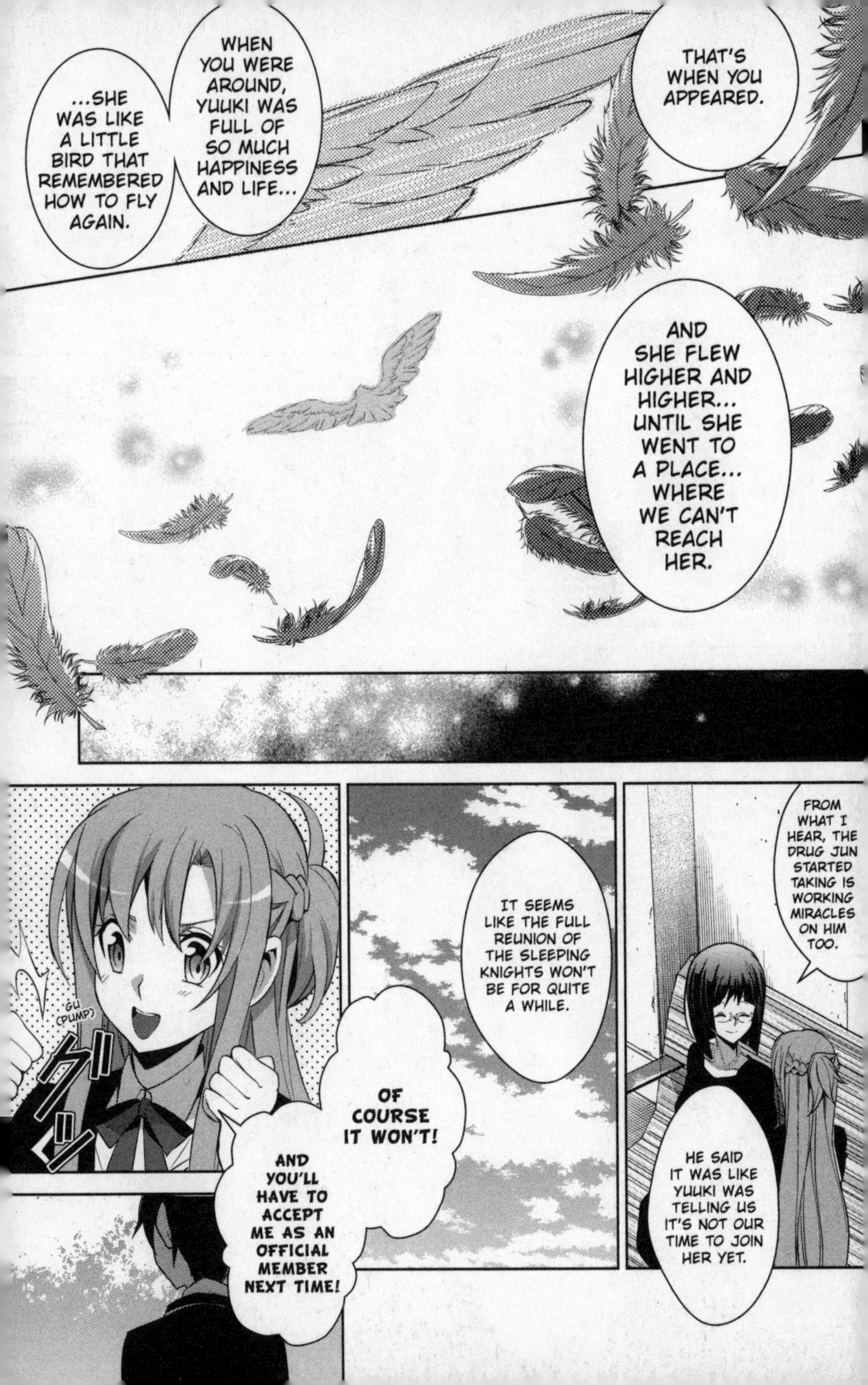
THAT'S WHEN YOU APPEARED.
WHEN YOU WERE AROUND, YUUKI WAS FULL OF SO MUCH HAPPINESS AND LIFE...
...SHE WAS LIKE A LITTLE BIRD THAT REMEMBERED HOW TO FLY AGAIN.
AND SHE FLEW HIGHER AND HIGHER... UNTIL SHE WENT TO A PLACE... WHERE WE CAN'T REACH HER.
FROM WHAT I HEAR, THE DRUG JUN STARTED TAKING IS WORKING MIRACLES ON HIM TOO.
HE SAID IT WAS LIKE YUUKI WAS TELLING US IT'S NOT OUR TIME TO JOIN HER YET.
IT SEEMS LIKE THE FULL REUNION OF THE SLEEPING KNIGHTS WON'T BE FOR QUITE A WHILE.
GU (PUMP)
OF COURSE IT WON'T!
AND YOU'LL HAVE TO ACCEPT ME AS AN OFFICIAL MEMBER NEXT TIME!

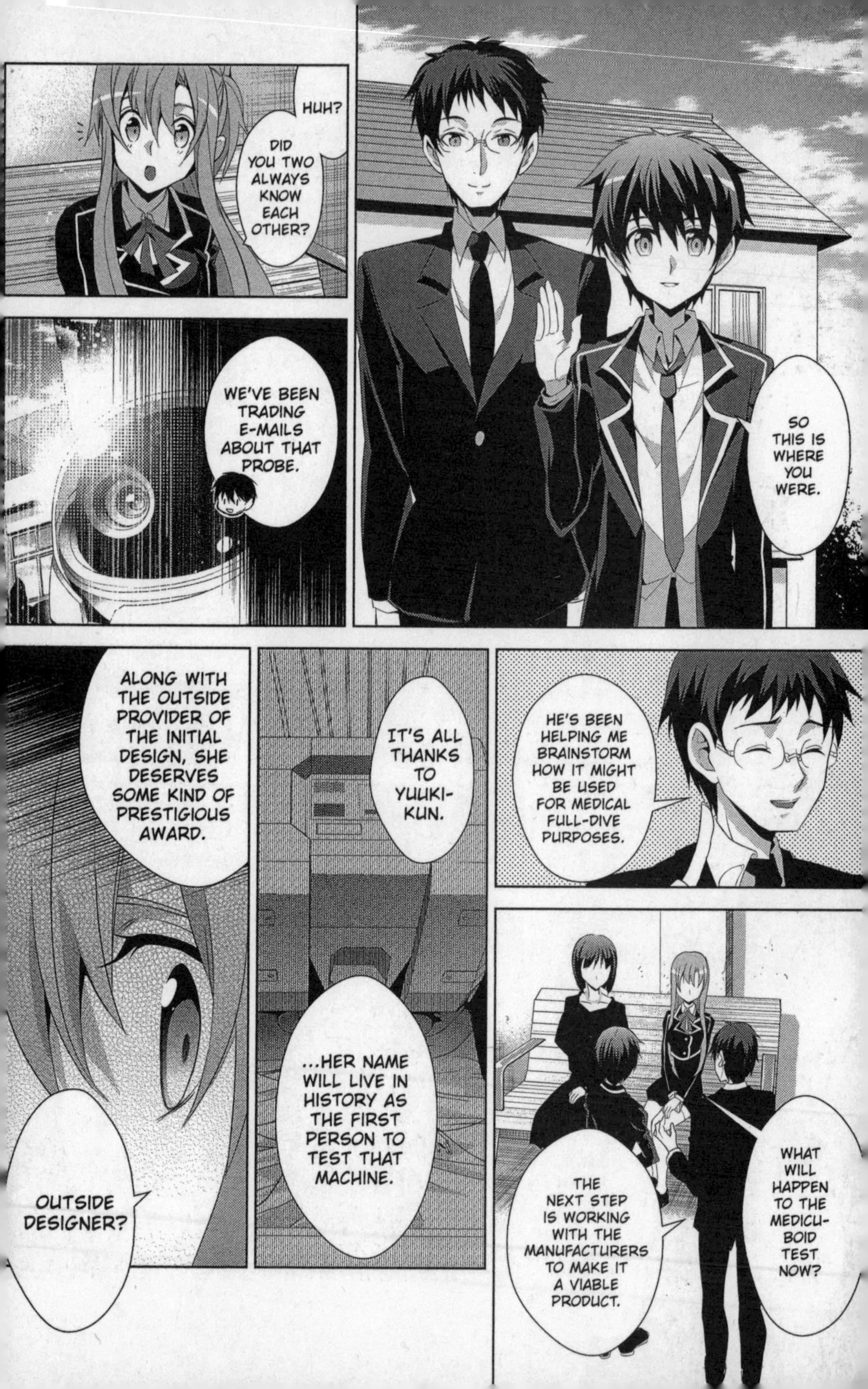
SO THIS IS WHERE YOU WERE.
HUH?
DID YOU TWO ALWAYS KNOW EACH OTHER?
WE'VE BEEN TRADING E-MAILS ABOUT THAT PROBE.
HE'S BEEN HELPING ME BRAINSTORM HOW IT MIGHT BE USED FOR MEDICAL FULL-DIVE PURPOSES.
WHAT WILL HAPPEN TO THE MEDICU-BOID TEST NOW?
THE NEXT STEP IS WORKING WITH THE MANUFACTURERS TO MAKE IT A VIABLE PRODUCT.
IT'S ALL THANKS TO YUUKI-KUN.
...HER NAME WILL LIVE IN HISTORY AS THE FIRST PERSON TO TEST THAT MACHINE.
ALONG WITH THE OUTSIDE PROVIDER OF THE INITIAL DESIGN, SHE DESERVES SOME KIND OF PRESTIGIOUS AWARD.
OUTSIDE DESIGNER?

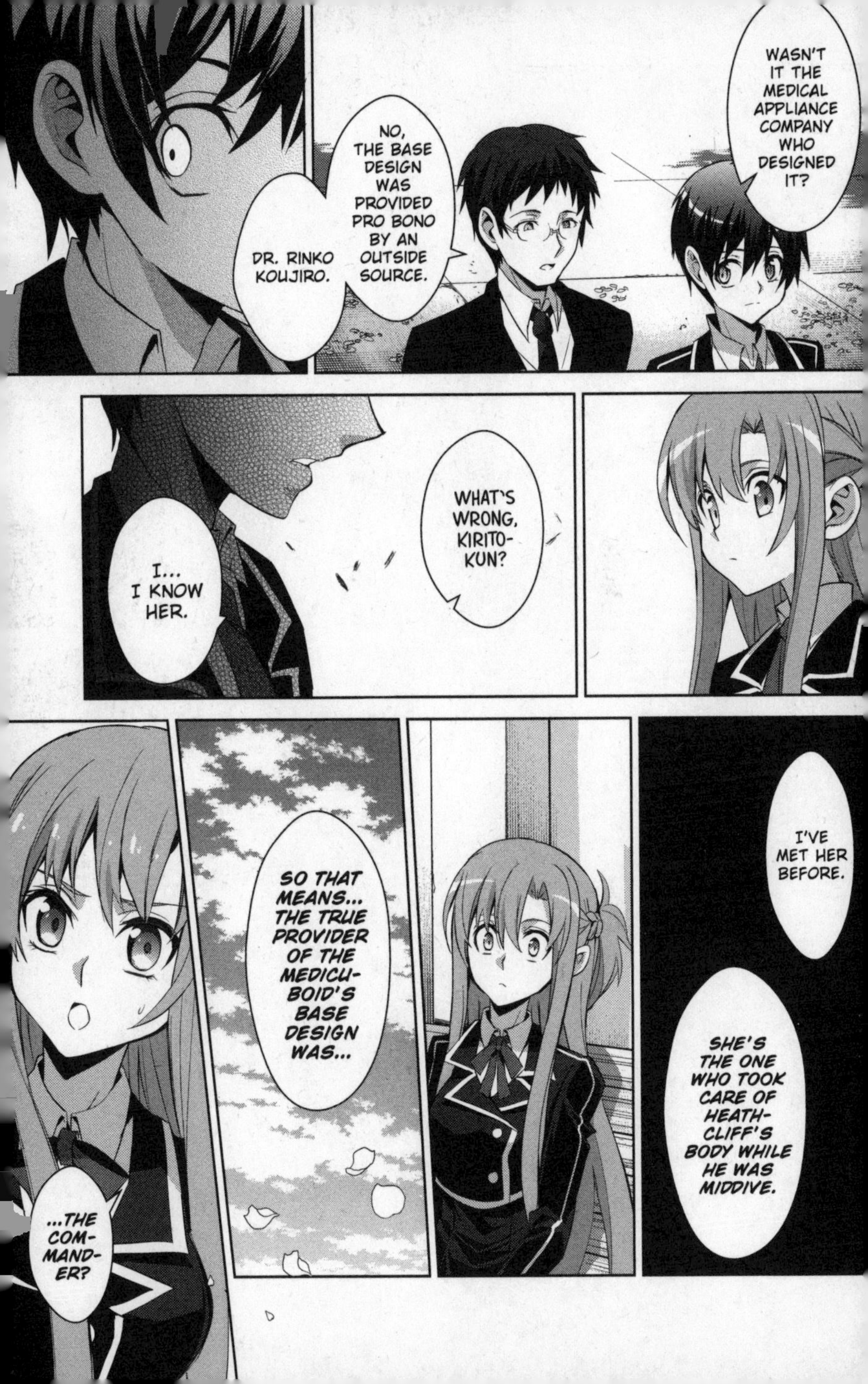
WASN'T IT THE MEDICAL APPLIANCE COMPANY WHO DESIGNED IT?
NO, THE BASE DESIGN WAS PROVIDED PRO BONO BY AN OUTSIDE SOURCE.
DR. RINKO KOUJIRO.
WHAT'S WRONG, KIRITO-KUN?
I... I KNOW HER.
I'VE MET HER BEFORE.
SHE'S THE ONE WHO TOOK CARE OF HEATH-CLIFF'S BODY WHILE HE WAS MIDDIVE.
SO THAT MEANS... THE TRUE PROVIDER OF THE MEDICU-BOID'S BASE DESIGN WAS...
...THE COM-MAND-ER?

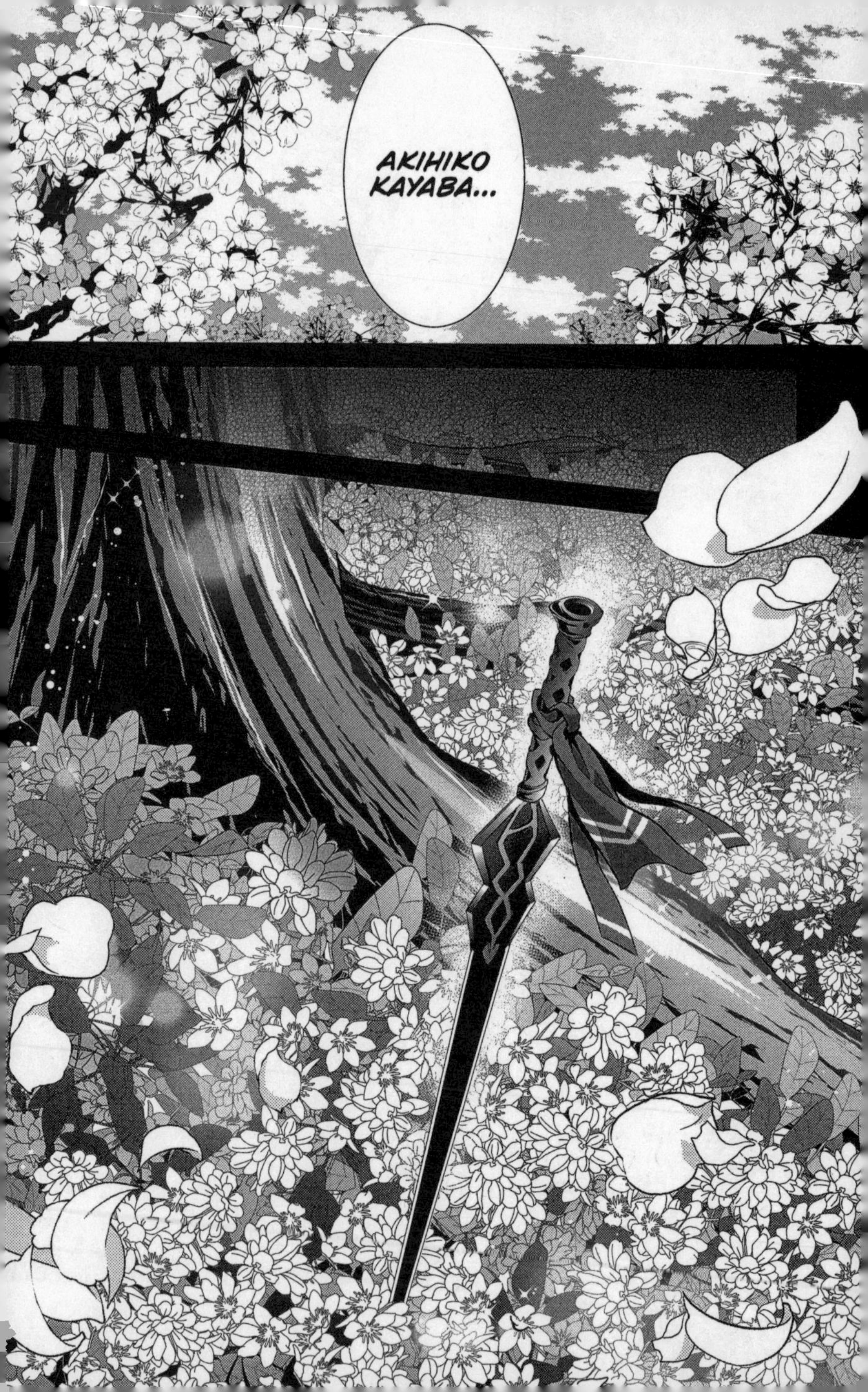
AKIHIKO KAYABA...

SWORD ART ONLINE
mother's rosary

Last Episode

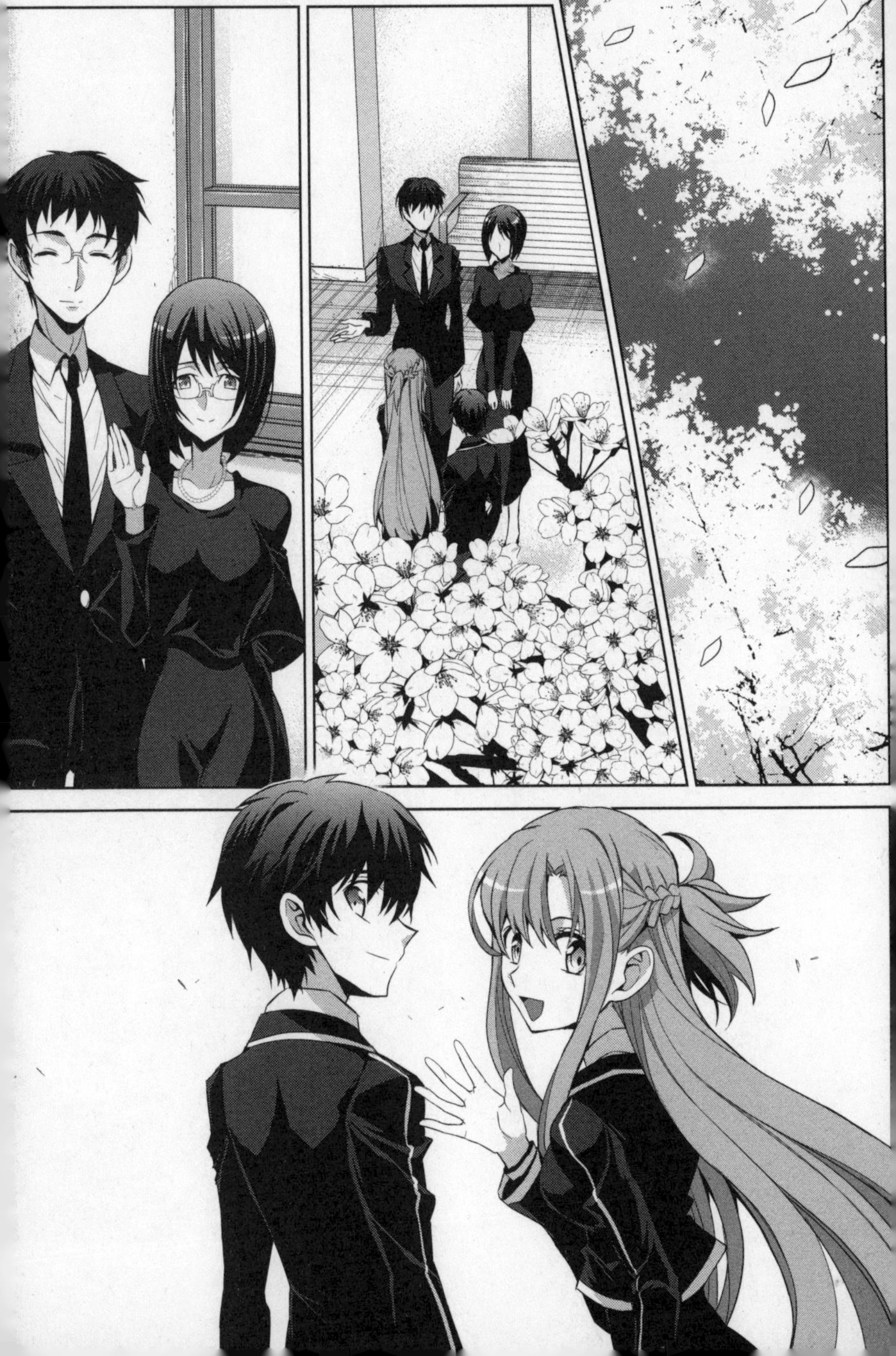

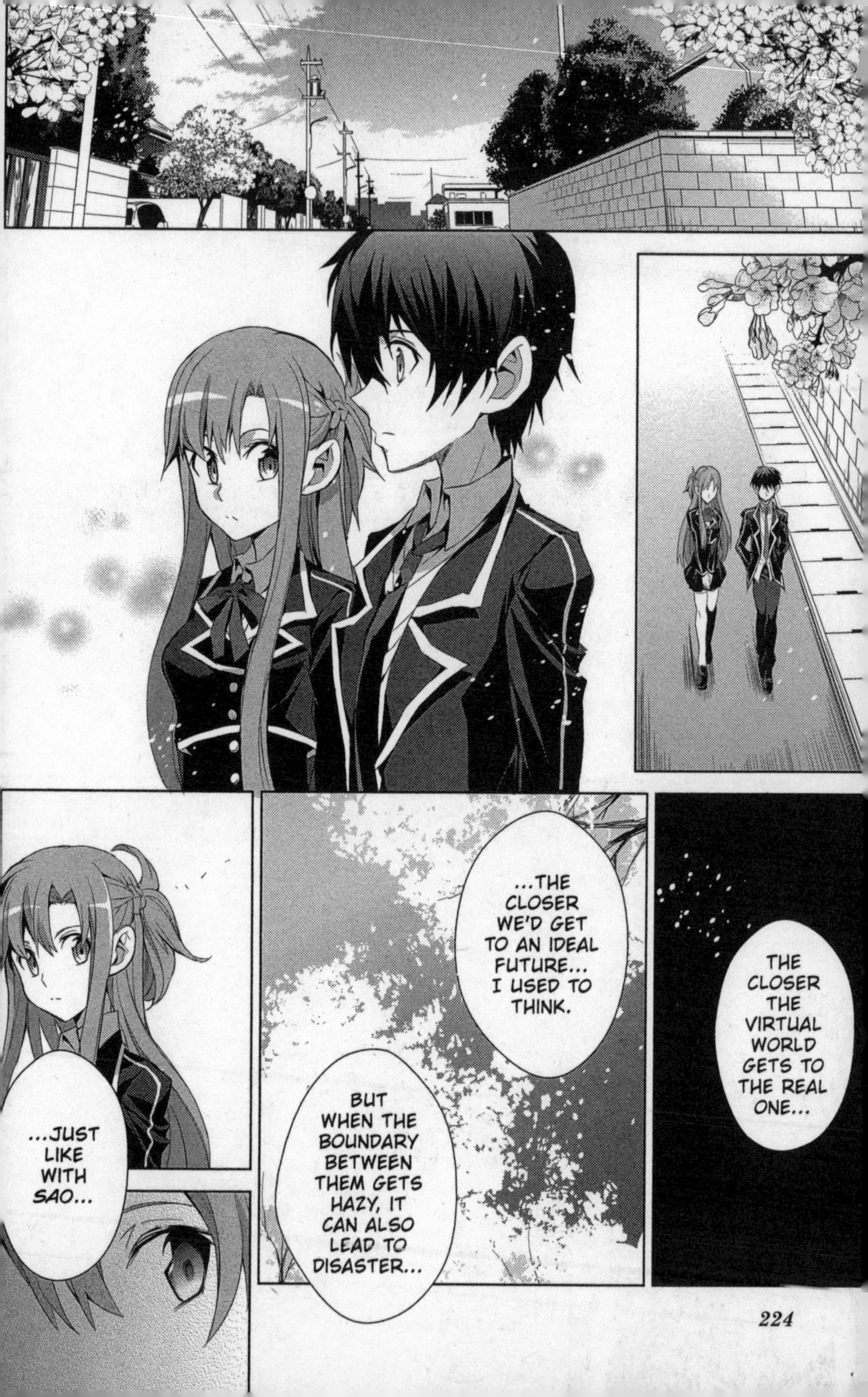
THE CLOSER THE VIRTUAL WORLD GETS TO THE REAL ONE...
...THE CLOSER WE'D GET TO AN IDEAL FUTURE... I USED TO THINK.
BUT WHEN THE BOUNDARY BETWEEN THEM GETS HAZY, IT CAN ALSO LEAD TO DISASTER...
...JUST LIKE WITH SAO...

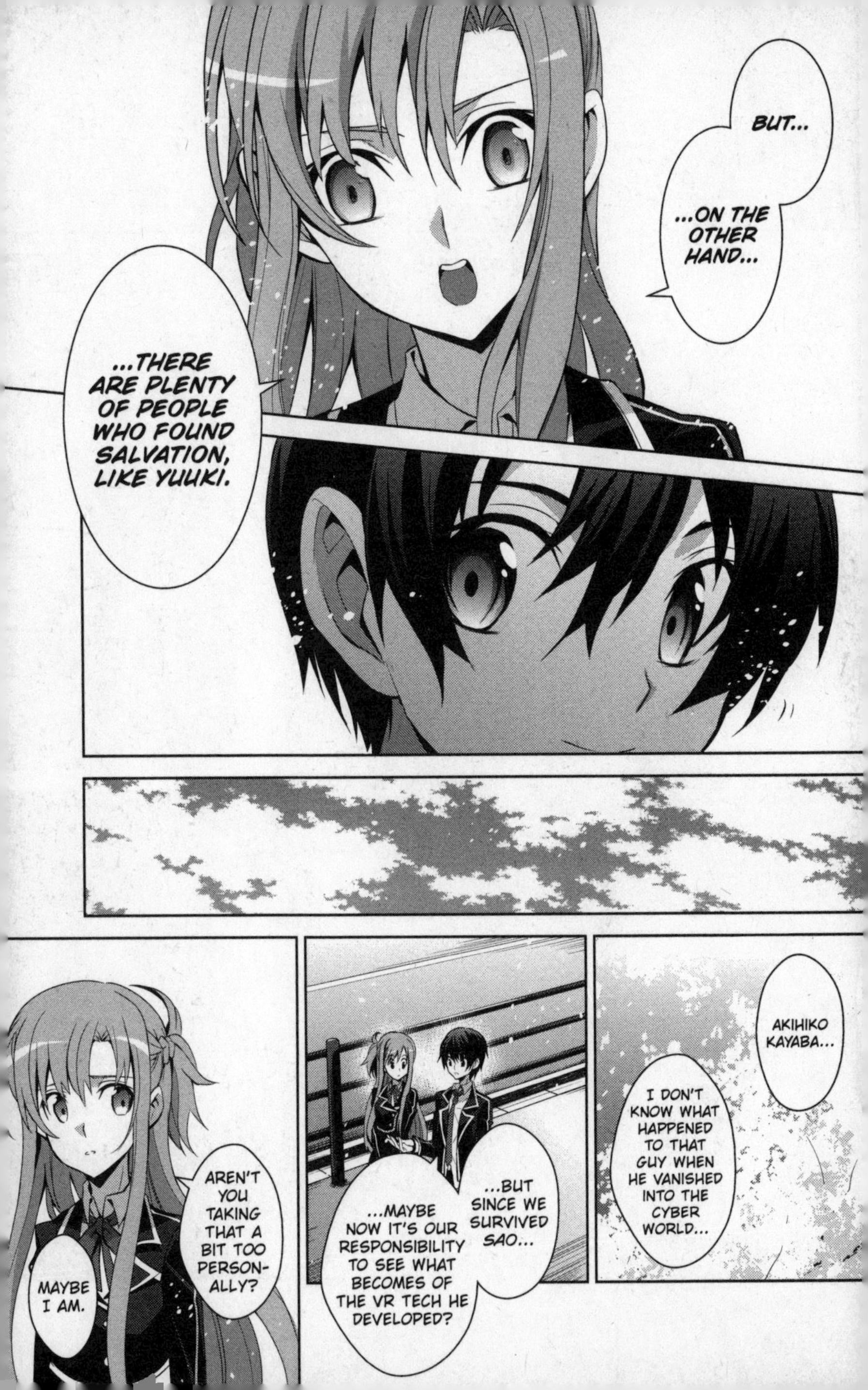
BUT...
...ON THE OTHER HAND...
...THERE ARE PLENTY OF PEOPLE WHO FOUND SALVATION, LIKE YUUKI.
AKIHIKO KAYABA...
I DON'T KNOW WHAT HAPPENED TO THAT GUY WHEN HE VANISHED INTO THE CYBER WORLD...
...BUT SINCE WE SURVIVED SAO...
...MAYBE NOW IT'S OUR RESPONSIBILITY TO SEE WHAT BECOMES OF THE VR TECH HE DEVELOPED?
AREN'T YOU TAKING THAT A BIT TOO PERSON-ALLY?
MAYBE I AM.

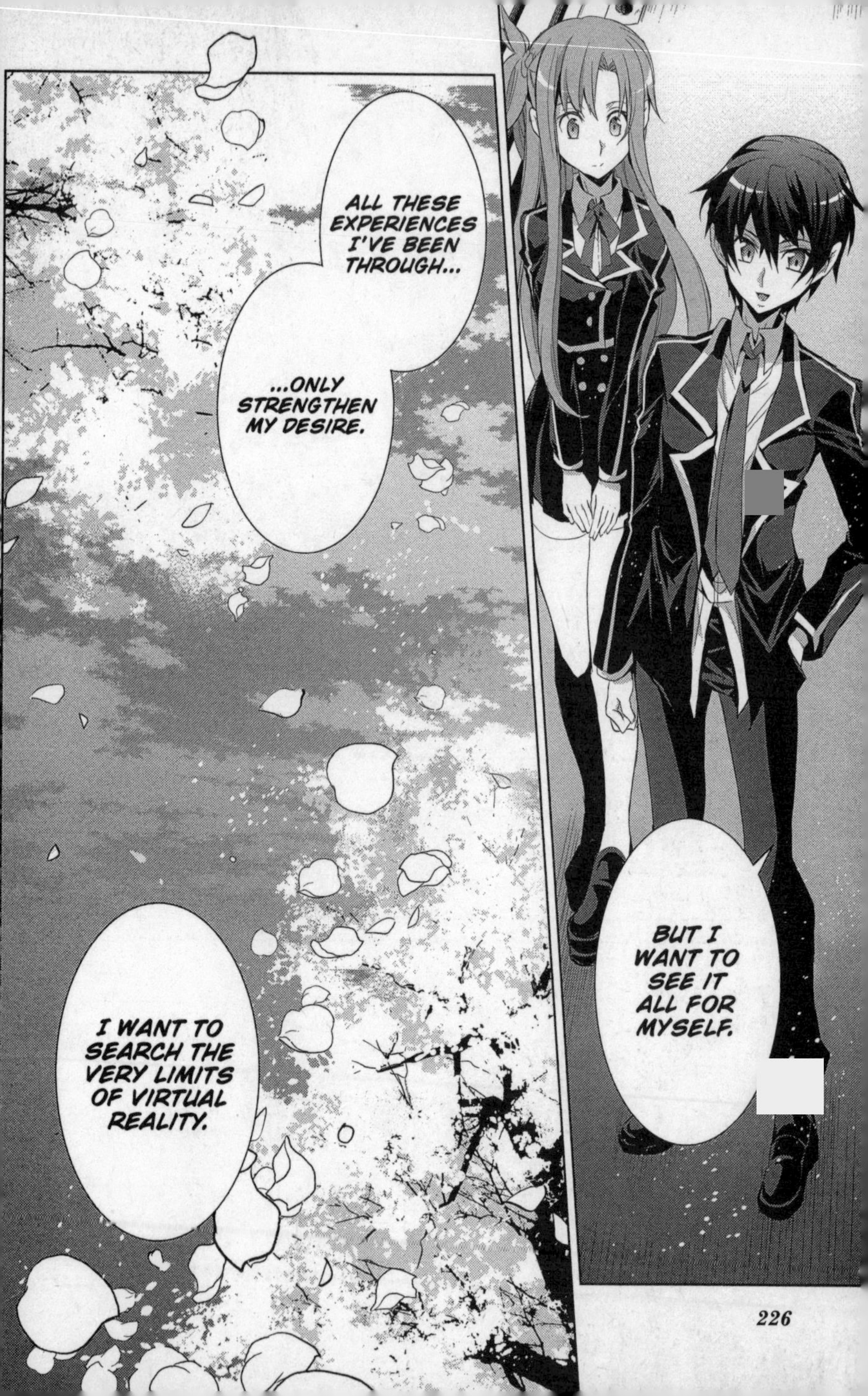
BUT I WANT TO SEE IT ALL FOR MYSELF.
ALL THESE EXPERIENCES I'VE BEEN THROUGH...
...ONLY STRENGTHEN MY DESIRE.
I WANT TO SEARCH THE VERY LIMITS OF VIRTUAL REALITY.

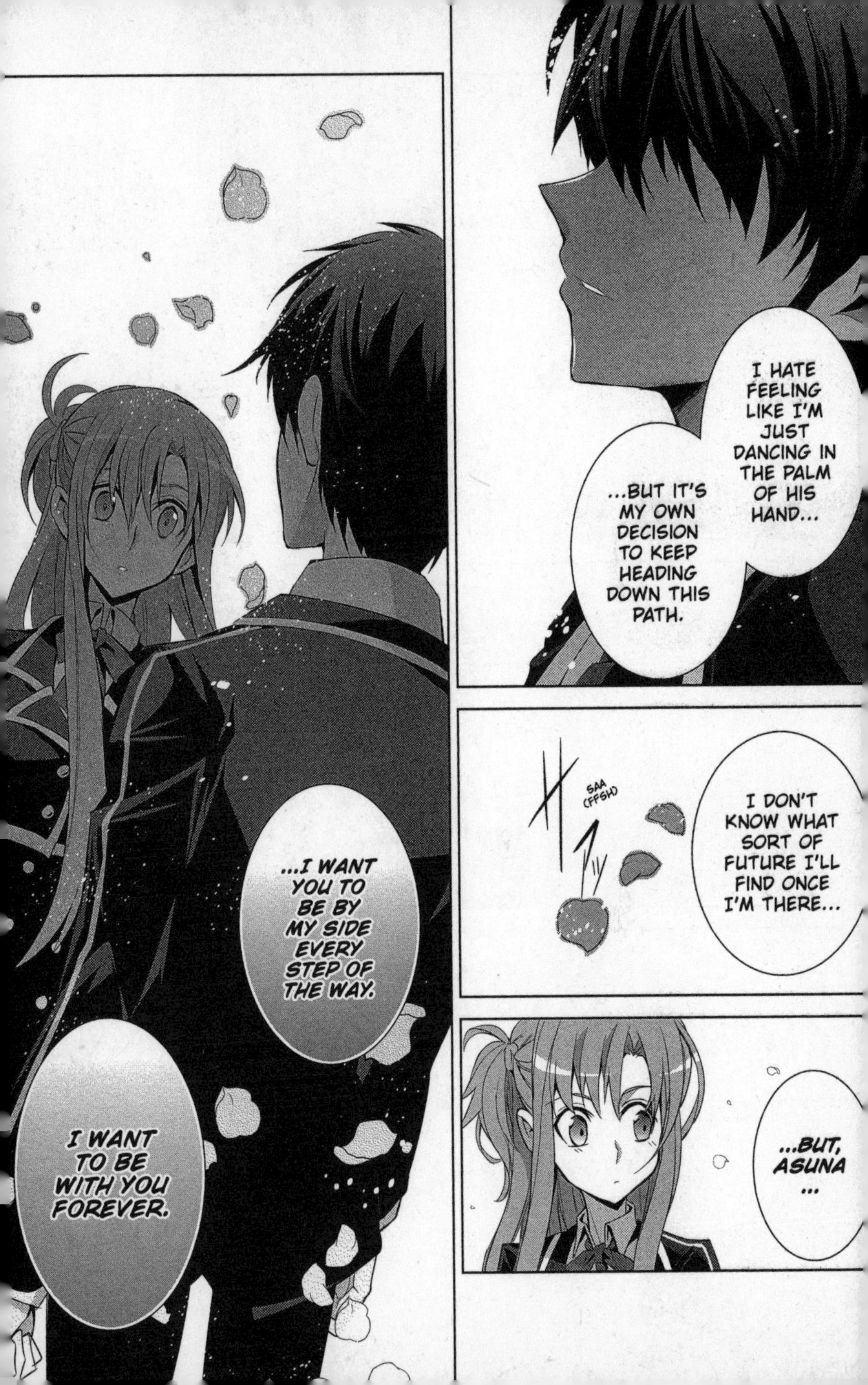
I HATE FEELING LIKE I'M JUST DANCING IN THE PALM OF HIS HAND...
...BUT IT'S MY OWN DECISION TO KEEP HEADING DOWN THIS PATH.
I DON'T KNOW WHAT SORT OF FUTURE I'LL FIND ONCE I'M THERE...
SAA (FFSH)
...BUT, ASUNA...
...I WANT YOU TO BE BY MY SIDE EVERY STEP OF THE WAY.
I WANT TO BE WITH YOU FOREVER.

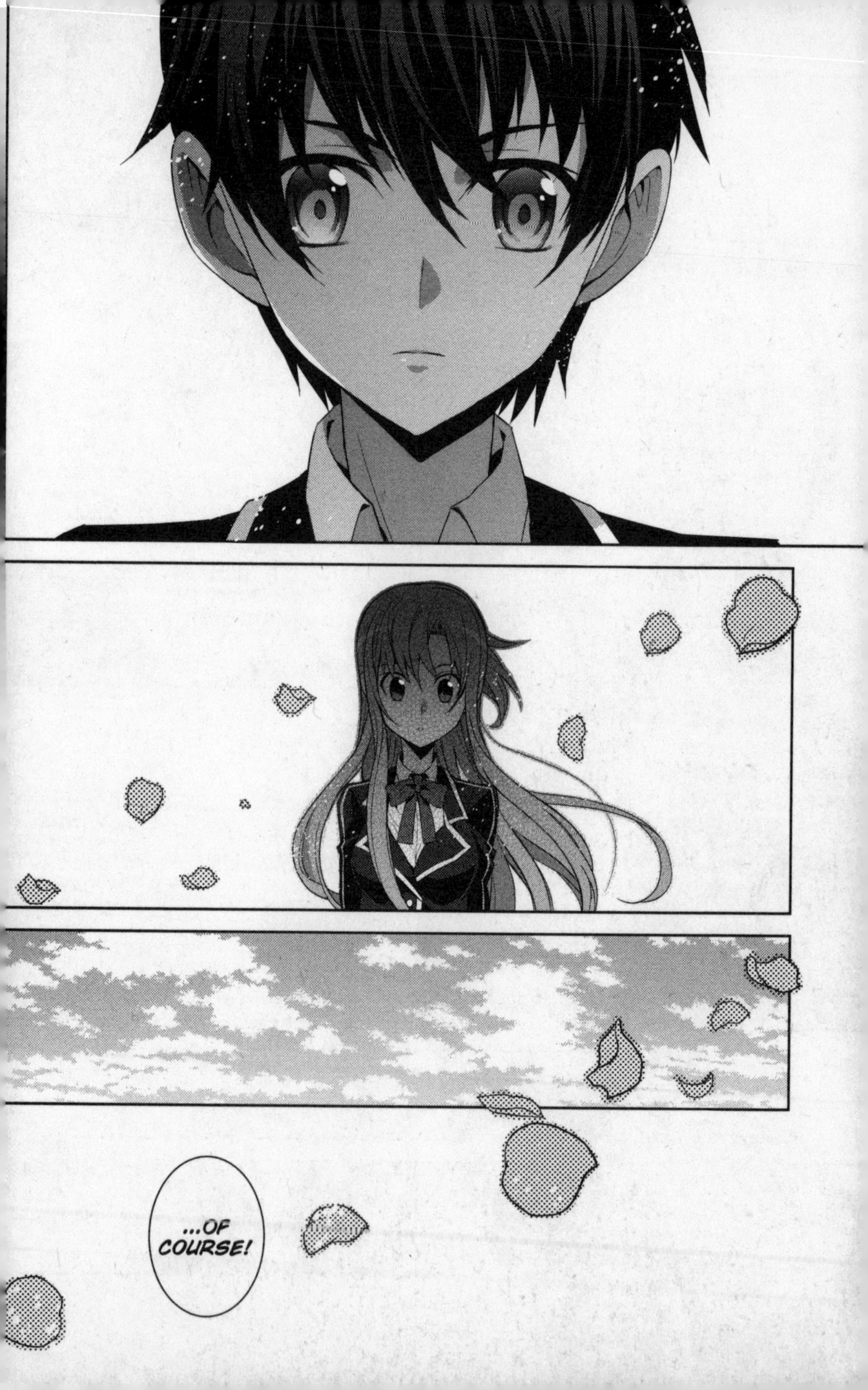
...OF COURSE!

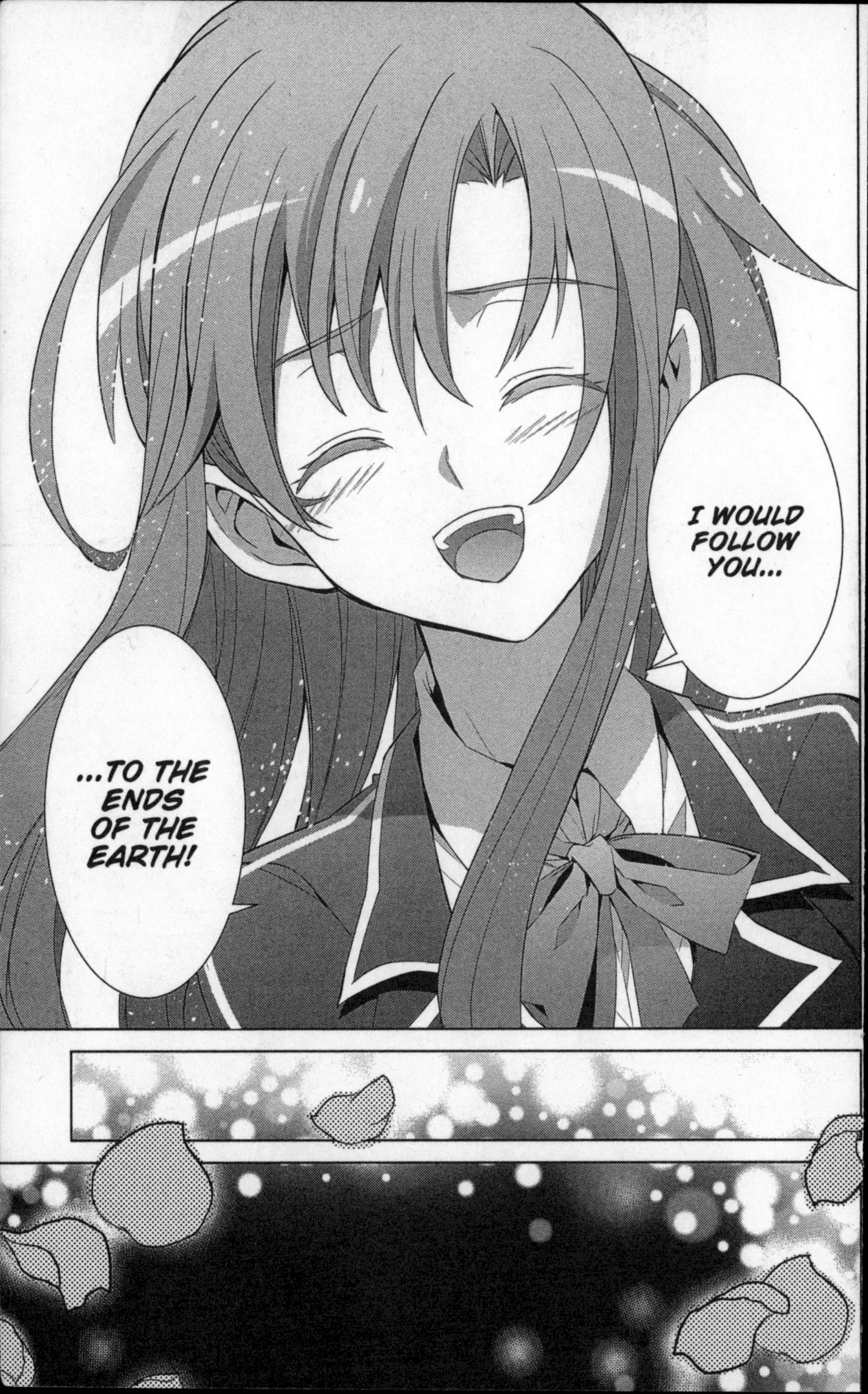
I WOULD FOLLOW YOU...
...TO THE ENDS OF THE EARTH!

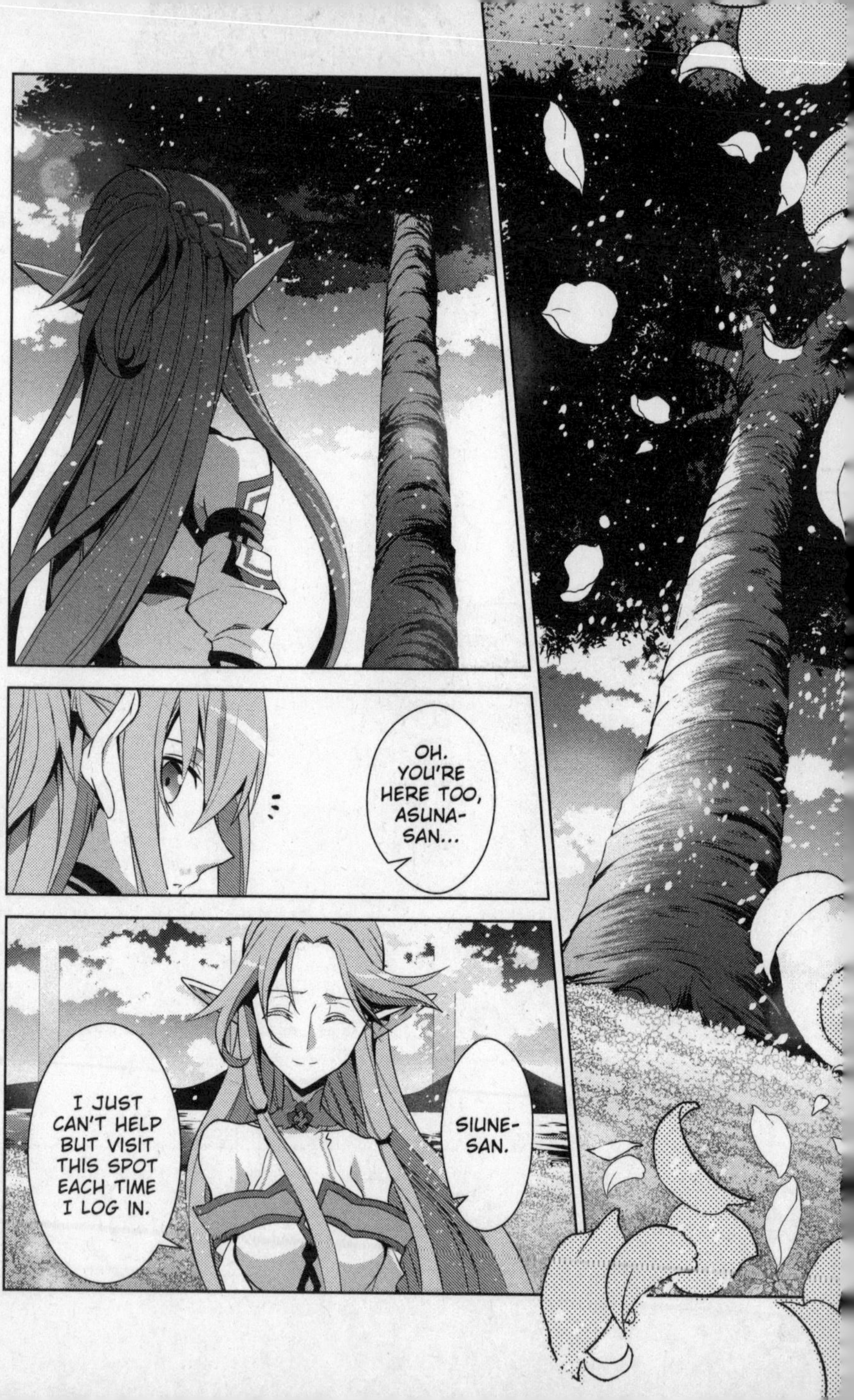
OH. YOU'RE HERE TOO, ASUNA-SAN...
SIUNE-SAN.
I JUST CAN'T HELP BUT VISIT THIS SPOT EACH TIME I LOG IN.

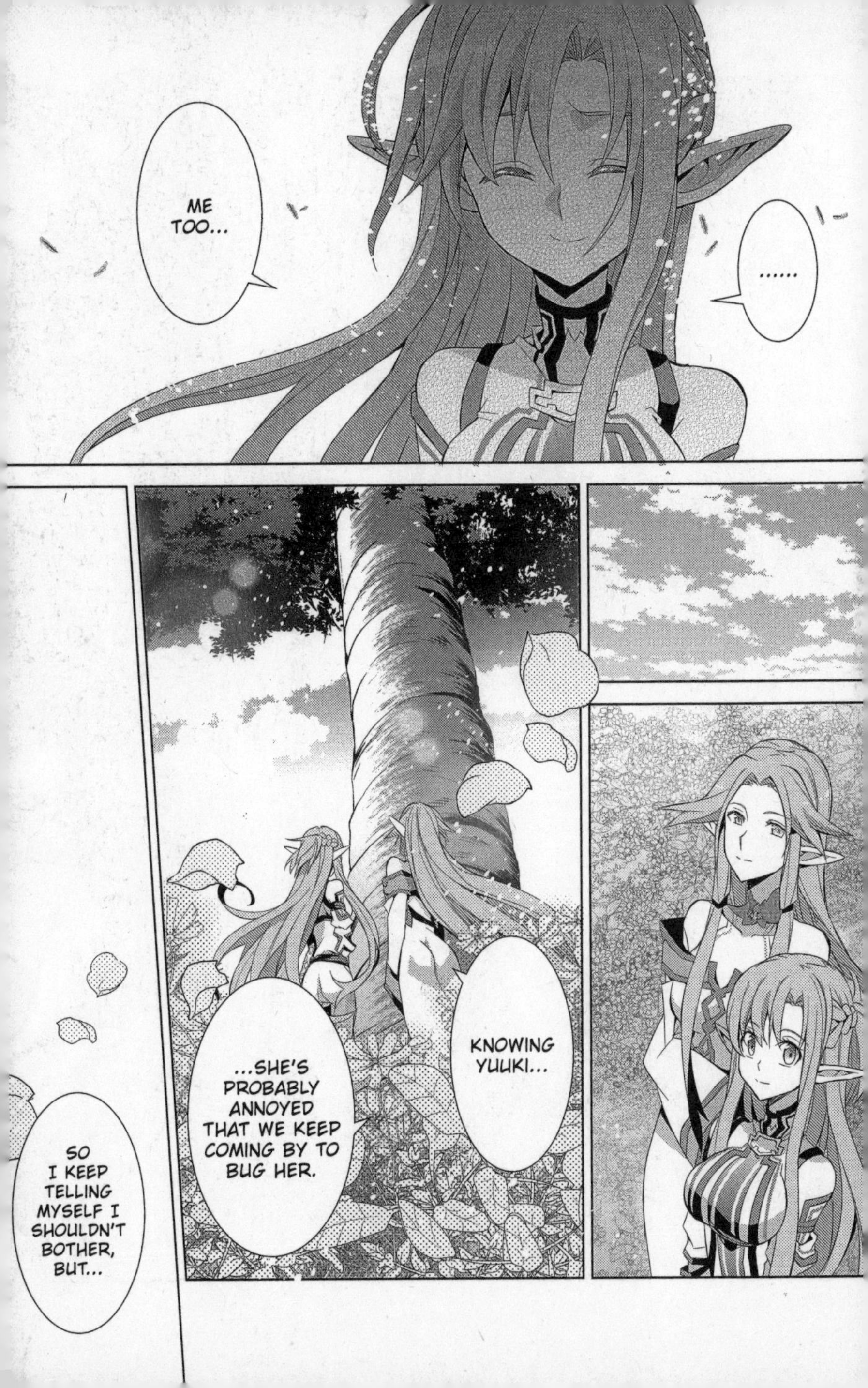
......
ME TOO...
KNOWING YUUKI...
...SHE'S PROBABLY ANNOYED THAT WE KEEP COMING BY TO BUG HER.
SO I KEEP TELLING MYSELF I SHOULDN'T BOTHER, BUT...

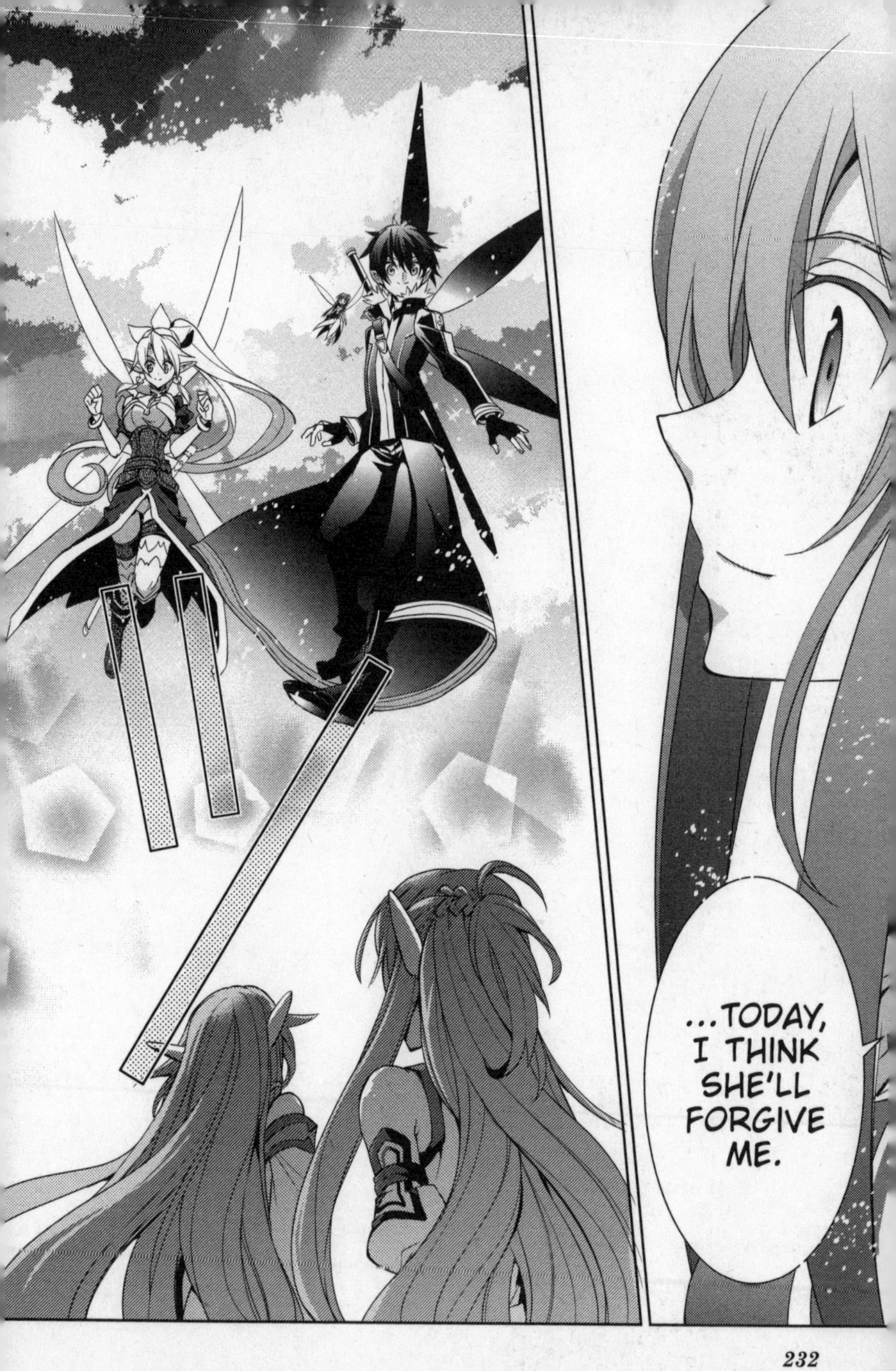
...TODAY, I THINK SHE'LL FORGIVE ME.

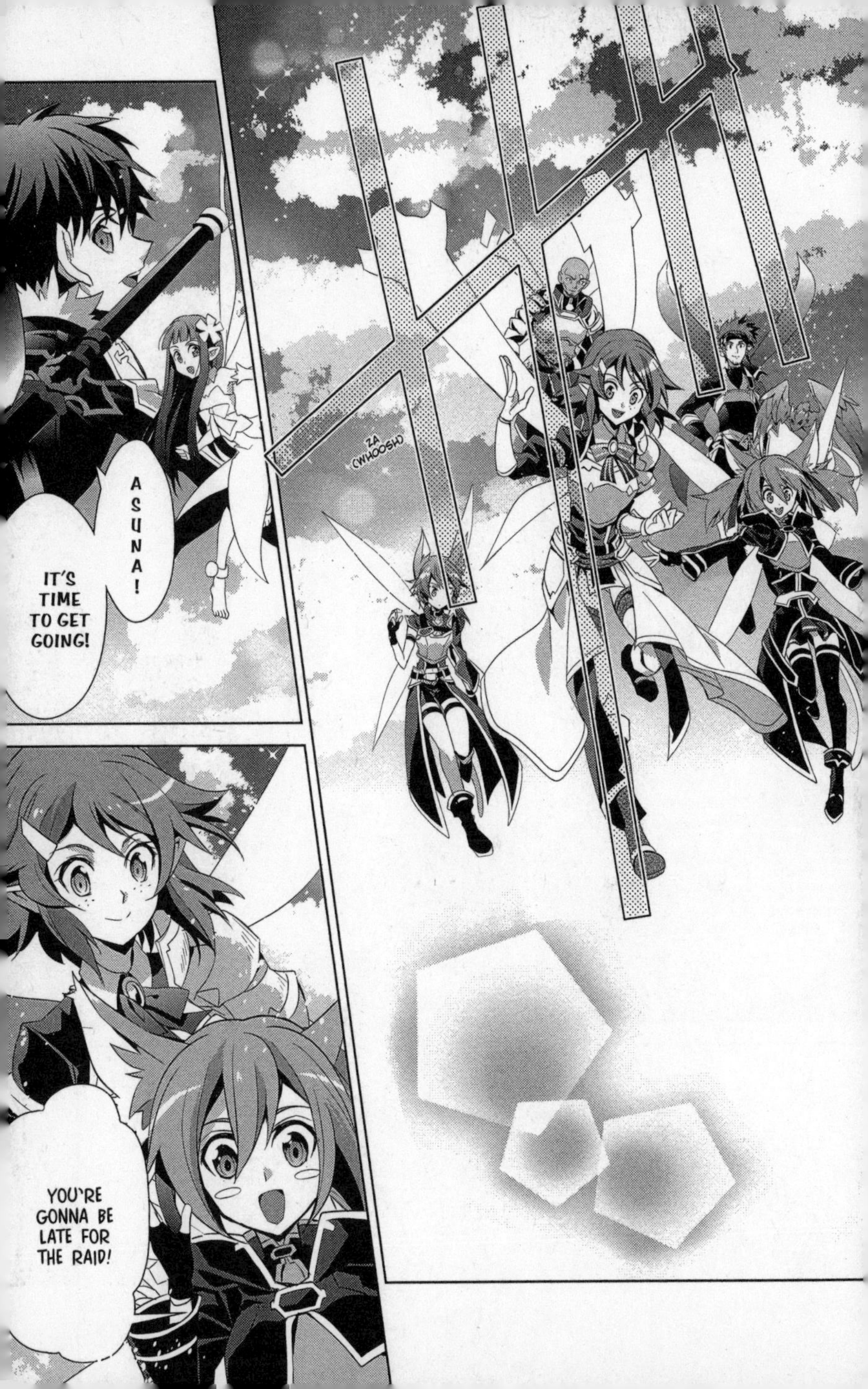
ZA (WHOOSH)
ASUNA!
IT'S TIME TO GET GOING!
YOU'RE GONNA BE LATE FOR THE RAID!

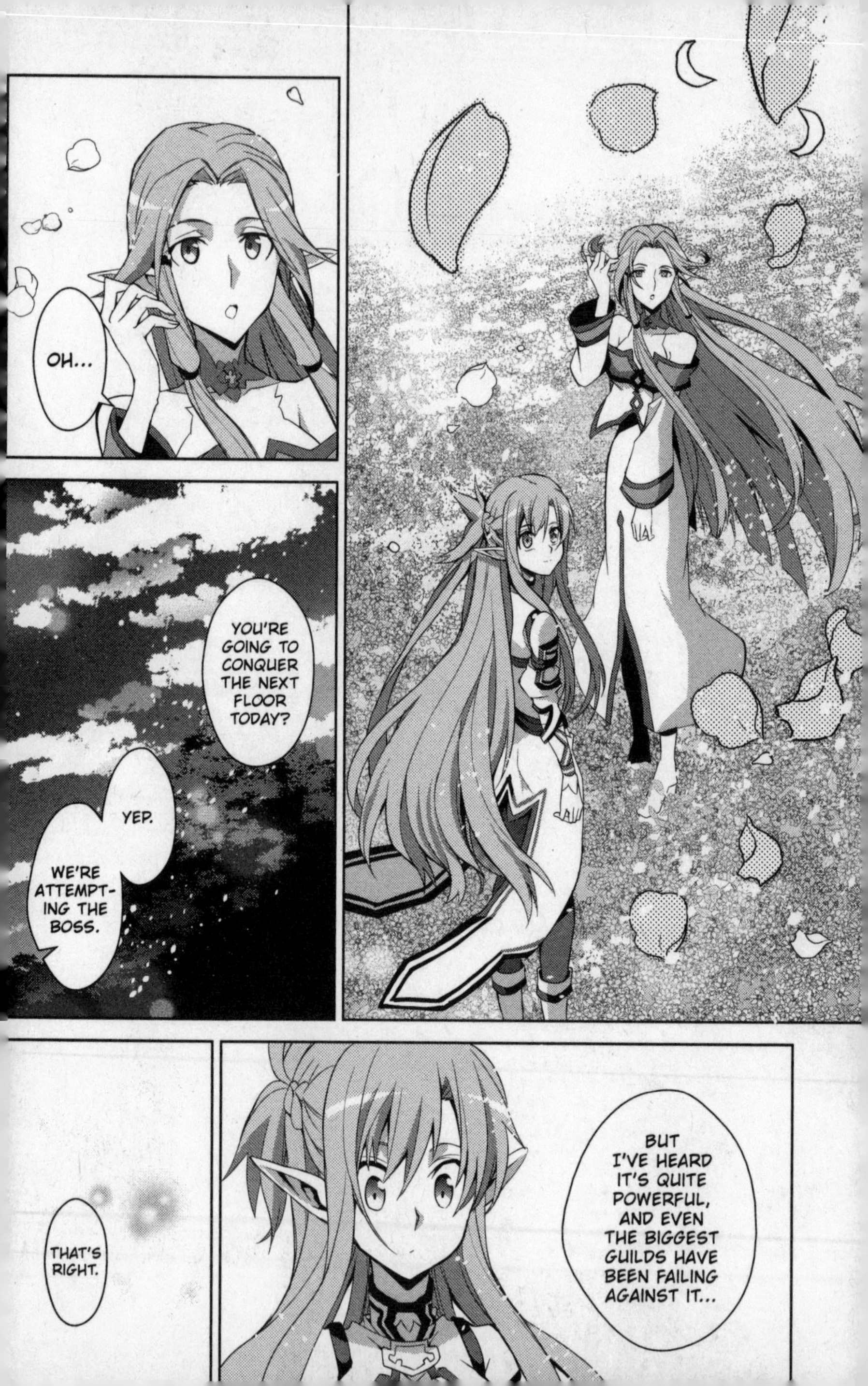
OH...
YOU'RE GOING TO CONQUER THE NEXT FLOOR TODAY?
YEP.
WE'RE ATTEMPT-ING THE BOSS.
BUT I'VE HEARD IT'S QUITE POWERFUL, AND EVEN THE BIGGEST GUILDS HAVE BEEN FAILING AGAINST IT...
THAT'S RIGHT.

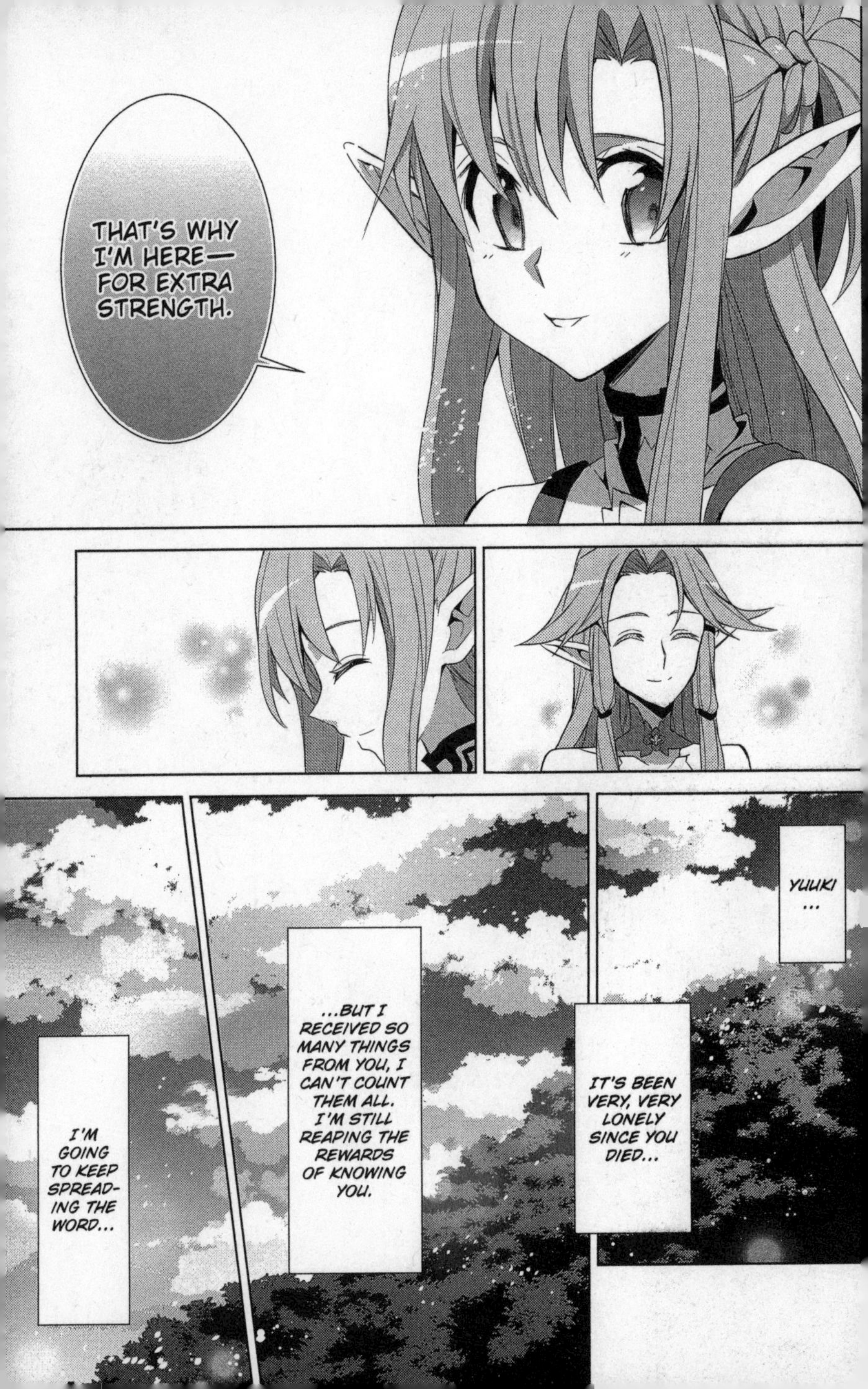
THAT'S WHY I'M HERE—FOR EXTRA STRENGTH.
YUUKI...
IT'S BEEN VERY, VERY LONELY SINCE YOU DIED...
...BUT I RECEIVED SO MANY THINGS FROM YOU, I CAN'T COUNT THEM ALL. I'M STILL REAPING THE REWARDS OF KNOWING YOU.
I'M GOING TO KEEP SPREAD-ING THE WORD...

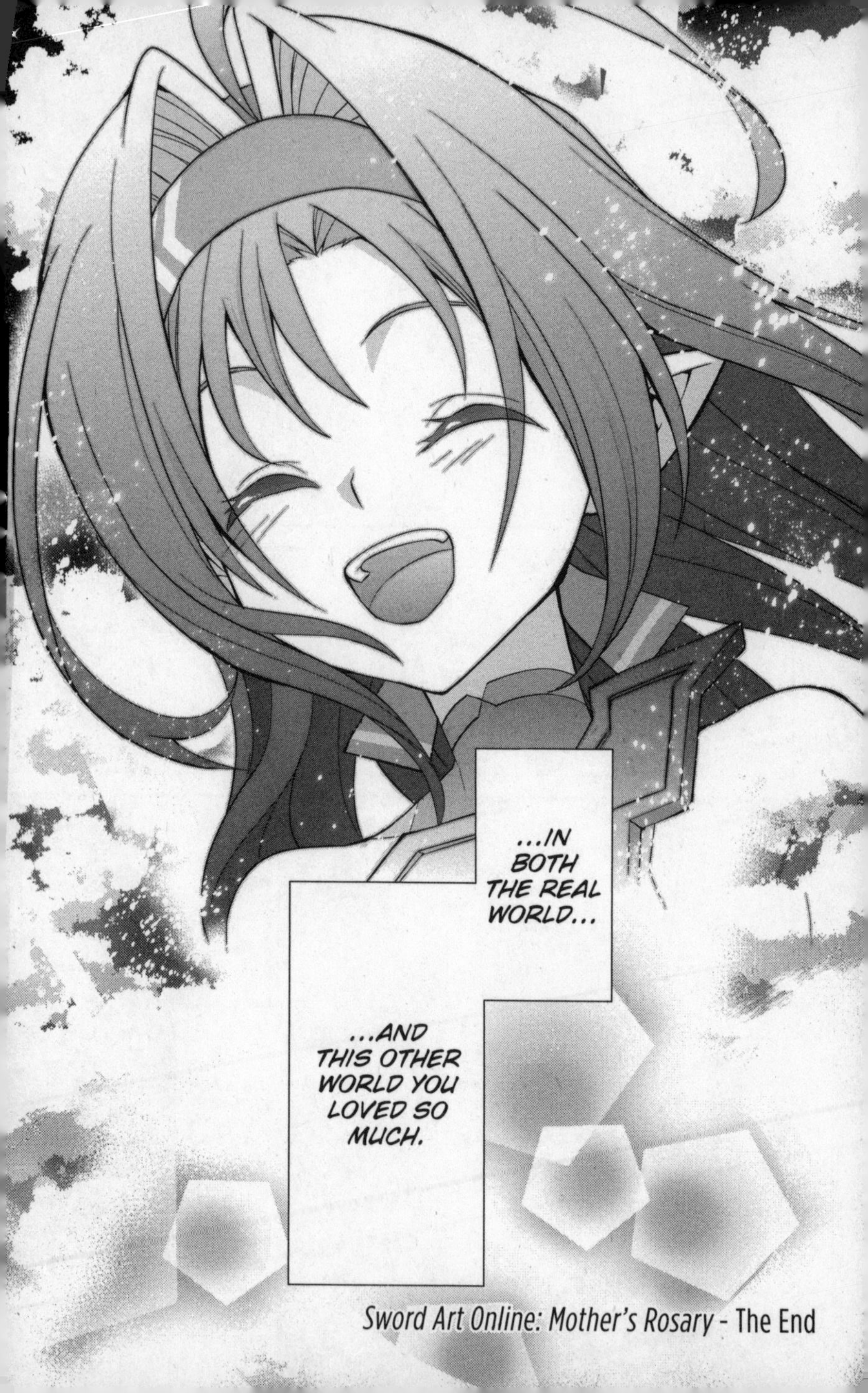
...IN BOTH THE REAL WORLD...
...AND THIS OTHER WORLD YOU LOVED SO MUCH.

Sword Art Online: Mother's Rosary - The End

AFTERWORD MANGA

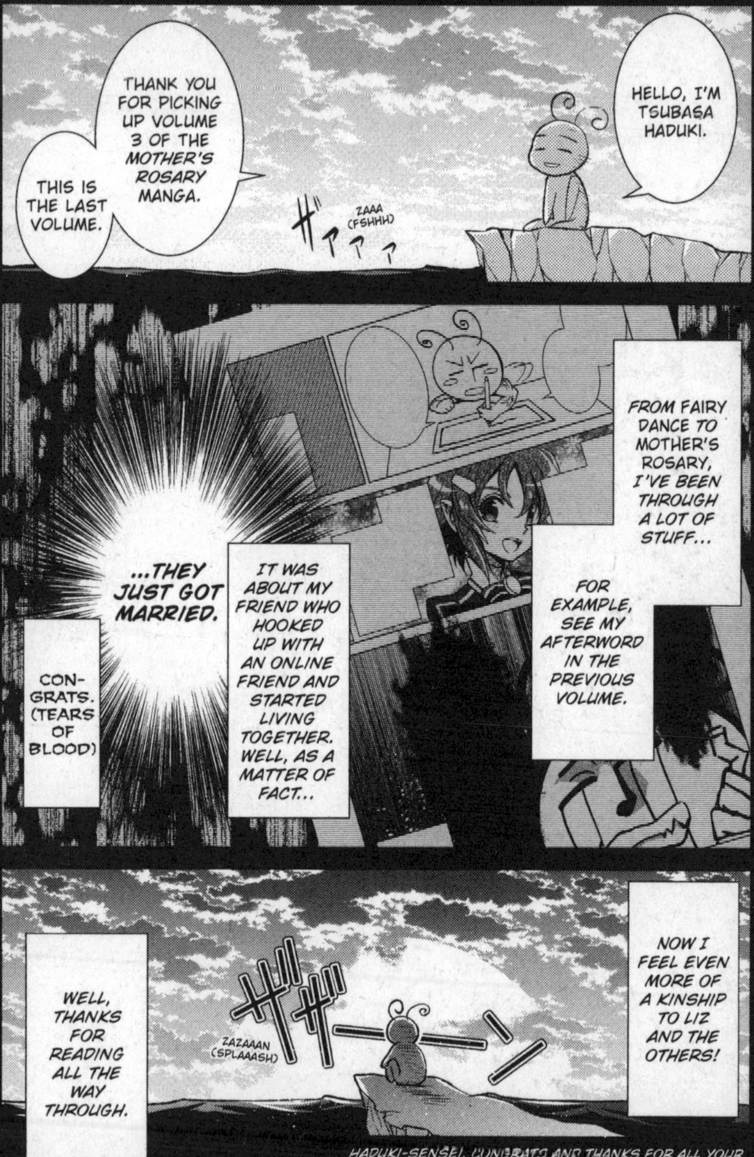
HELLO, I'M TSUBASA HADUKI.
THANK YOU FOR PICKING UP VOLUME 3 OF THE *MOTHER'S ROSARY* MANGA.
THIS IS THE LAST VOLUME.
ZAAA (FSHHH)
FROM FAIRY DANCE TO MOTHER'S ROSARY, I'VE BEEN THROUGH A LOT OF STUFF...
FOR EXAMPLE, SEE MY AFTERWORD IN THE PREVIOUS VOLUME.
IT WAS ABOUT MY FRIEND WHO HOOKED UP WITH AN ONLINE FRIEND AND STARTED LIVING TOGETHER. WELL, AS A MATTER OF FACT...
...THEY JUST GOT MARRIED.
CON-GRATS. (TEARS OF BLOOD)
NOW I FEEL EVEN MORE OF A KINSHIP TO LIZ AND THE OTHERS!
ZAZAAAN (SPLAAASH)
WELL, THANKS FOR READING ALL THE WAY THROUGH.

HADUKI-SENSEI, CONGRATS AND THANKS FOR ALL YOUR HARD WORK! WE'RE ALWAYS ACCEPTING YOUR LETTERS OF CONDOLENCE, DEAR READERS!
-EDITOR

SPECIAL THANKS

CORAL

MITSUHIRO ONODA
SAORI MIYAMOTO
TAKASHI SAKAI
EMIRI NIHEI
NICOE

REKI KAWAHARA
ABEC

KAZUMA MIKI
TOMOYUKI TSUCHIYA

THE STAFF OF THE SWORD ART ONLINE *ANIME* SERIES

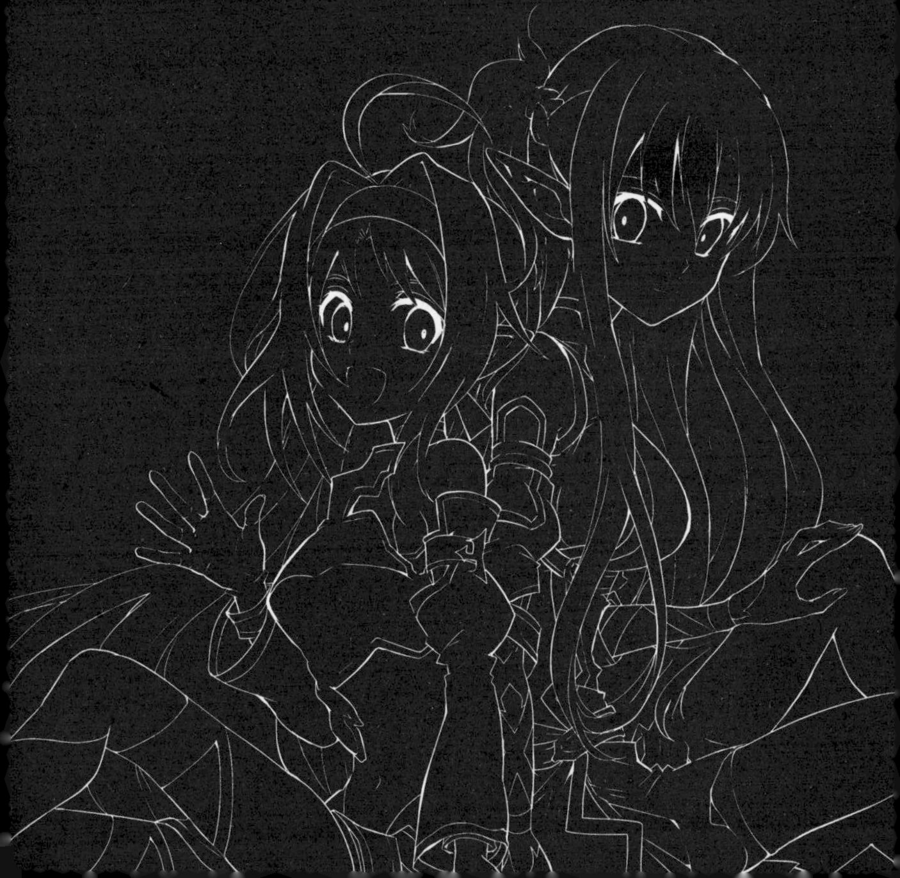

special comment

original story: reki kawahara

OF ALL THE MANY STORIES I'VE TOLD IN *SWORD ART ONLINE*, THE MOTHER'S ROSARY ARC IS ONE OF THE MOST MEMORABLE AND IMPORTANT, BUT IT'S ALSO A STORY WITH SOME PERSONAL REGRETS. I FEEL THAT I SHOULD HAVE DONE MUCH MORE RESEARCH ON THE MEDICAL BACKGROUND I WANTED TO DEPICT. I DIDN'T DO A GOOD ENOUGH JOB OF SHOWING ASUNA'S FEELINGS. MOST IMPORTANTLY, I QUESTIONED MY OWN JUDGMENT MANY TIMES: DID YUUKI REALLY HAVE TO DIE? I'VE BEEN GRAPPLING WITH THE REGRET FROM FEELING LIKE SHE DESERVED A HAPPY ENDING MORE THAN ANY OTHER CHARACTER IN *SAO*.

BUT READING THIS COMIC EDITION OF THE MOTHER'S ROSARY ARC AND COMING FACE-TO-FACE WITH HADUKI-SENSEI'S YUUKI, WHO WAS SO BURSTING WITH ENERGY, GOOD CHEER, AND THE INNER STRENGTH TO OVERCOME ANY HARDSHIP, I REALIZED THAT SHE TRULY LED A HAPPY LIFE. THANK YOU SO MUCH, AND CONGRATULATIONS ON FINISHING THE SERIES!

003

SWORD ART ONLINE mother's rosary

art: tsubasa haduki
original story: reki kawahara
character design: abec

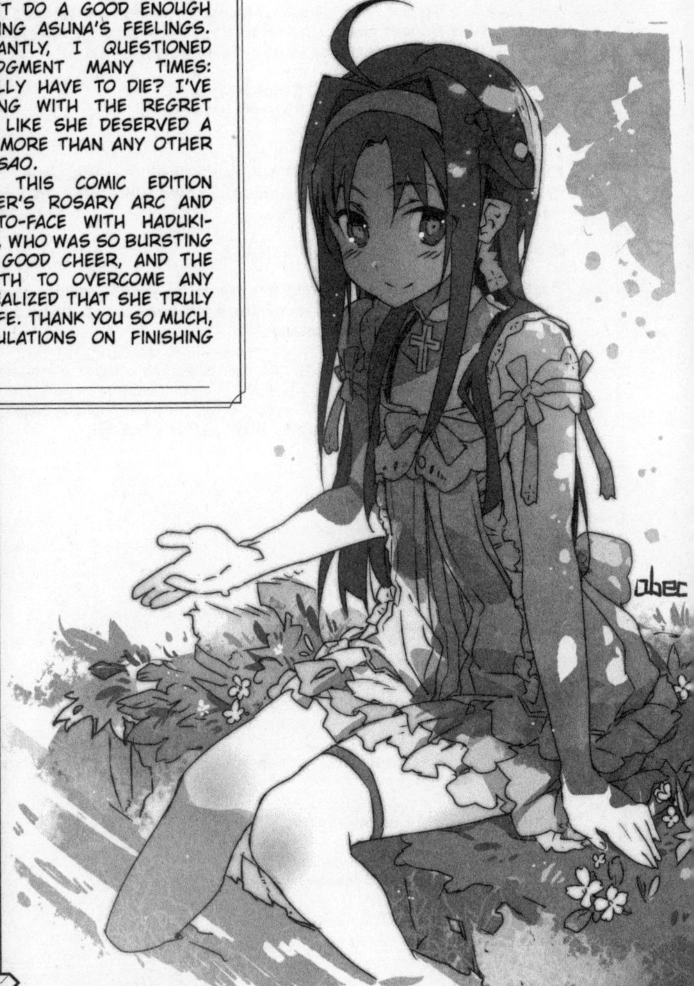

abec

SWORD ART ONLINE: MOTHER'S ROSARY 3

ART: TSUBASA HADUKI
ORIGINAL STORY: REKI KAWAHARA
CHARACTER DESIGN: abec

Translation: Stephen Paul
Lettering: Brndn Blakeslee

SWORD ART ONLINE: MOTHER'S ROSARY, Vol. 3
© REKI KAWAHARA/TSUBASA HADUKI 2016
All rights reserved.
Edited by ASCII MEDIA WORKS
First published in Japan in 2016 by KADOKAWA CORPORATION, Tokyo.
English translation rights arranged with KADOKAWA CORPORATION, Tokyo,
through Tuttle-Mori Agency, Inc., Tokyo.

English translation © 2017 by Yen Press, LLC

Yen Press
1290 Avenue of the Americas
New York, NY 10104

Visit us at yenpress.com
facebook.com/yenpress
twitter.com/yenpress
yenpress.tumblr.com
instagram.com/yenpress

First Yen Press Edition: September 2017

Yen Press is an imprint of Yen Press, LLC.
The Yen Press name and logo are trademarks of Yen Press, LLC.

The publisher is not responsible for websites (or their content) that are not owned by the publisher.

Library of Congress Control Number: 2015956858

ISBNs: 978-0-316-43975-6 (paperback)
978-0-316-44194-0 (ebook)

10 9 8 7 6 5 4 3 2 1

BVG

Printed in the United States of America